THE PSYCHOLOGY OF SKILL

A Life-Span Approach

Phillip D. Tomporowski

Westport, Connecticut
London

Library of Congress Cataloging-in-Publication Data

Tomporowski, Phillip D., 1948–
    The psychology of skill : a life-span approach / Phillip D. Tomporowski.
       p. cm.
    Includes bibliographical references and index.
    ISBN 0-275-97593-2 (alk. paper)
    1. Learning, Psychology of. 2. Performance. 3. Ability. 4. Ability, Influence of
age on. I. Title.
BF318.T66 2003
153.1′5—dc21   2002025214

British Library Cataloguing in Publication Data is available.

Library of Congress Catalog Card Number: 2002025214

ISBN: 0-275-97593-2

First published in 2003

Praeger Publishers, 88 Post Road West, Westport, CT 06881
An imprint of Greenwood Publishing Group, Inc.
www.praeger.com

Printed in the United States of America

The paper used in this book complies with the
Permanent Paper Standard issued by the National
Information Standards Organization (Z39.48-1984).

10 9 8 7 6 5 4 3 2 1

THE PSYCHOLOGY
OF SKILL

To Regina, for her support and guidance, and to Ellis, for her inspiration

Contents

Illustrations

Figures

Tables

Chapter 1

Skill and Learning

The images that usually come to mind when you think about skilled performances are often those that involve elite sports or professional expertise. The way
Tiger Woods plays golf or Itzhak Perlman plays the violin represents the epit-
ome of skillful performance, for some people. The actions of skilled performers
are followed closely by millions of avid fans. Highly skilled individuals are
often paid tremendous amounts of money to demonstrate their proficiencies.
Skills, however, are not limited to just a few individuals; we all depend on skills
to function every day of our lives.

WHAT IS SKILL?

The term *skill* has been defined by researchers in a variety of ways over the
past few decades. A sample of definitions of skill is provided in box 1.1. For the
purposes of this book, *skill* is defined as *the ability to use one's knowledge effectively and readily in execution of performance*. Researchers who study skill
and skill development have made clear distinctions between different types of
skills, however. *Motor skills* require voluntary body and/or limb movement to
achieve a goal (Magill, 1998, p. 7). Activities such as playing a musical instrument, football, and swimming are motor skills. *Cognitive skills* do not involve
muscular movement or motion to achieve a goal (Colley, 1989; Ericsson and
Oliver, 1995; Magill, 1993, p. 7). Activities such as problem solving, memory,
and reading are considered cognitive skills. Of course, this dichotomy is arbitrary and there are no clear-cut dividing lines that separate the processes underlying motor skills and cognitive skills (Magill, 1993, p. 213).

BOX 1.1   Definitions of Skill

Skill has been defined in a variety of ways; here are some examples:

"We shall use it here to designate among motor activities a particular category of finely coordinated voluntary movements, generally engaging certain privileged parts of the musculature in the performance of various technical acts which have as common characteristics the delicacy of their adjustment, the economy of their execution and the accuracy of their achievement" (Paillard, 1960).

"By a skilled response I shall mean one in which receptor-effector feedback processes are highly organized, both spatially and temporally. Spatial-temporal patterning, the interplay of receptor-effector-feedback processes, and such characteristics as timing, anticipation, and the graded response are thus seen as identifying characteristics of skill" (Fitts, 1964).

"Skill is concerned with all the factors which go to make up a competent, expert, rapid and accurate performance. Skill in this sense thus attaches, to a greater or lesser extent, to any performance and is not limited to manual operations but covers a wide range of mental activities as well" (Welford, 1968).

"It is an organized sequence of movements. It requires spatial and temporal organization. It involves accuracy and uniformity of execution; and it is done to accomplish a purpose" (Sage, 1971).

"Skill is the consistent degree of success in achieving an objective with efficiency and effectiveness" (Singer, 1972).

A skill is "(a) an action or a task that has a goal and that requires voluntary body and/or limb movement to achieve the goal; (b) a qualitative expression of performance. Expressed in terms of: (1) productivity of performance (2) consistency of performance" (Magill, 1993).

"Skill is goal-directed, well-organized behavior that is acquired through practice and performed with economy of effort" (Proctor and Dutta, 1995).

Skills are "movements that are dependent on practice and experience for their execution, as opposed to being genetically defined" (Schmidt and Lee, 1999).

Skills are domain specific; clearly, the skills needed to play baseball differ from those needed to solve mathematical problems. Being skilled in one domain does not necessarily mean one will be skilled in other domains. Despite their task-dependent nature, however, all skills have much in common. Consider the following two scenarios, for instance. Playing basketball and playing chess are quite different activities; each requires different types of skills. Yet there are certain commonalities between them.

The Athlete

Consider the professional basketball player as he dribbles down the court toward the opposing team. As he approaches the end of the court, the defensive players select and guard offensive players. The basketball player is presented with an extremely complex task. He must control his dribble while simultaneously avoiding the movements of the man guarding him. At the same time, he must scan both the actions and positions of his teammates and opposing players. Bobbing and weaving, the player sets his team into motion; teammates move to their areas. Scoring in basketball revolves around individuals obtaining and retaining position. Bodies collide and a one-on-one competition for space and position commences. The speed of movement is incredible, as is the ability of the player to respond to openings in the defense and to select the particular shot with the greatest chance of success. Under these conditions, the successful basketball player is totally absorbed in his play. He could be playing in a stadium with thousands cheering and screaming, or he could be playing in an empty gymnasium—it simply would not matter. All that the player is aware of is the game.

Despite the high level of physical and mental arousal during the heat of such competition, players sometimes describe themselves as being in a psychological "zone." As in a slow-motion movie, time seems to become distorted and the athlete acts without thinking, allowing years of training and practice to take over. There is no feeling of pain or discomfort from the physical contact that is part of the game. There is only a feeling of exhilaration as a shot is made, or a drive toward the basket begins and the ball is released toward the basket.

Athletes are highly skilled in their particular sport. Whether their sport is baseball, track and field, dancing, or swimming, participants display sophisticated skills under challenging situations. Regardless of the sport, athletes provide similar descriptions of their state of consciousness when they are at the peak of their game. They describe the feeling as one of being unbeatable, invincible, and in total control.

The Chess Player

Chess is a game that pits two players against each other in a test of skill and planning. It is an ancient game that brings to bear elements common in warfare. Each player commands the movements of king, queen, knights, and foot soldiers. Chess is similar to other games that have evolved in various cultures around the world. Success in this type of game requires that a player excel in many areas of mental activity. To master chess, a player must understand all elements of the game; for example, the specific movements of each chess piece, the function of those pieces, and how all the pieces interrelate to one another. Beyond merely understanding the elements of the game, the player must employ strategies that take into consideration how successive movements of pieces will lead to a positive outcome. Further, the player must be able to anticipate the moves of his or her opponent and to counteract them. The rules of the game are specified; however, the number of possible outcomes generated by the movement of a single piece is incredibly high. Under some conditions, players compete under time constraints that place additional burdens on optimal performance.

The psychological state of master chess players can be described as one of total concentration. The player may sit virtually motionless for extended periods of time, apparently lost in the game. Although the player's overt physical activity is minimal, considerable covert mental and physical activity is occurring. The positions of the pieces on the board provide a wealth of information that must be processed, stored in memory, and later retrieved to assist in decision making. Prior to moving a chess piece, a player can bring to conscious awareness possible countermoves and their effect on the overall game strategy. There is a constant interplay between memory processes and problem-solving activities. The chess player's mental concentration is associated with high levels of physiological arousal, as well. During the game, heart rate and respiration are elevated, blood flows freely to the skin, and sweating increases. At critical points of the game, pupillary dilation may increase, and the player's mouth becomes dry. Sometimes the game continues for hours; this places constant pressure on the player's physiological and psychological reserves.

Some chess players report momentary shifts in their conscious awareness during these periods of prolonged concentration. It is as if their entire world has shrunk to the size of the chess board. Attention to the details of the playing pieces becomes acute, and the player experiences a transcendence feeling during which he or she feels in absolute control. Only thoughts directly related to the game are part of consciousness, and an overall state of calm is felt.

Commonalities between the Scenarios

Each scenario above describes highly skilled individuals who have years of training and experience at tasks within their given areas of specialization. Their prior experience prepares them to meet and overcome the physical and mental challenges they face. Each of them has progressed from novice status to expert status.

Observations made by educators and research conducted by scientists have revealed that learners progress through a predictable series of steps during which the individual acquires skills and the capacity to perform at high levels of proficiency. The purpose of this book is to provide readers with a systematic evaluation of the steps that are involved in learning and performing skills. The overarching theme is that skills are learned and performed as a result of dynamic processes that involve contributions of the body, the mind, and the spirit.

Processes of the Body

Participants in each of the above scenarios evidence a high level of skill and expertise acquired through years of effortful practice and training. The level of performance displayed by professional and Olympic athletes is attained only through systematic training programs that are designed to shape and develop very specific behaviors. Many Olympic women gymnasts, for example, are no more than 14 or 15 years old, but most have been practicing their routines since they were three or four. They are veterans of countless practice sessions and competitive meets. Those who dream of performing at an international level of competition solicit the guidance of teachers and coaches whose job it is to prepare them for elite competition. The same is true for virtually all modern organized competition, regardless of whether the activity is one that is primarily physical, such as sports, or primarily mental, such as chess or bridge. The quality of one's performance is dependent on systematic coaching, instruction, and practice.

Processes of the Mind

The execution of skilled behavior reflects both conscious and unconscious mental processes. When involved in a task such as chess, one analyzes the position of the chess pieces and ponders the outcome of the various moves that are possible in a given situation. Similarly, as the quarterback of a football team prepares for a play, he may analyze the positions of players on the opposing team and adjust his team accordingly. Successful chess players and football players develop the ability to direct their attention to specific game conditions and to solve complex problems in a rapid fashion. Keeping one's attention focused on a task is, at times, exceedingly difficult. Consider that elite chess players often play games that go on for hours and matches that can last months. Football players must keep concentration on every play of a game, even under extreme weather conditions and in stadiums where the noise of the crowd can be deafening. Efficient problem solving can be equally difficult in these situations, as well. Successful performance depends not only on focused and sustained attention but also on the ability to select the best play or move for a specific game situation. Expert chess players make play decisions based on information about chess moves that have been acquired over hundreds or thousands of hours of practice and study. The quarterback selects a particular play based on his experience in similar game situations and the knowledge he has acquired from his coaches. Both the chess player and the quarterback desire to achieve specific goals on each play; they attain these goals by accessing information acquired though practice and experience that has been stored in memory systems. Many sport, play, and work activities center on performance characterized by conscious mental problem solving that stresses speed and accuracy.

It is indeed the case that considerable conscious mental processing takes place in the minds of the chess player and the football player while in the heat of battle. However, it is also true that many other mental processes are active during performance of which the player is not aware or conscious. The manner in which the professional football quarterback positions himself behind the center, places his hands on the ball, drops back, takes a stance to pass the ball, and executes a pass, occurs without conscious effort. He does not have to devote much time and attention to these aspects of his performance; they are habits that have been acquired through hundreds, if not thousands, of repetitions. The expert chess player's mental habits guide her through the multitude of possible moves to a limited number of moves that have the greatest chance for success. Without thinking, she selects only those moves that fit her overall goals of the game; no thought is wasted and no time is lost on the movement of other pieces. One of the characteristics of skilled performance is that it is displayed without apparent effort. Compared to novices, the experienced football player and the expert chess player are fast and accurate. They are able to move and to anticipate the movements of their opponents with little apparent effort. Indeed, it is the expert's ability to perform difficult tasks with apparent ease that classifies him or her as expert.

Processes of the Spirit

Though practice is essential to developing both physical and mental skills, it is not, in and of itself, sufficient for skillful performance. The individual must be motivated to acquire the skills he is taught and able to deal with challenges as they are presented. The physical and mental demands of training and practice are often formidable. An elite gymnast's body, for example, is molded into the coach's vision of the ideal shape through countless hours of stretching and conditioning. Exercises are designed to place the young athlete's body at the very extremes of her range of motion, and then to stretch her body just a little further. Through years of training, the child performs thousands of push-ups, sit-ups, and pull-ups. All of these exercises are designed to help the gymnast attain the level of physical conditioning needed to execute very specific gymnastic routines. The youngster is taught to perform on the balance beam, vault, uneven parallel bars, and on the floor. With practice, she develops basic skills; over many months and years of practice, training routines become increasingly more difficult and challenging. From the very beginning, however, falls and injuries are commonplace. Physical preparation for competition is physically quite punishing. Stretching and conditioning exercises are painful, and falls sometimes result in sprains, bruises, and lasting injury. Anxiety and fear become integral parts of training as the athlete encounters situations of uncertainty in which there are constant possibilities for both success and failure. Progress depends on meeting and overcoming increasingly greater levels of challenge.

Athletes who desire to acquire elite skills must make considerable sacrifices. It is no different for those who want to be doctors, scientists, painters, auto mechanics, or teachers. Indeed, all who are successful in arts, crafts, or occupations have chosen to devote their efforts to the training needed to become skillful. Not everyone attains the level of expertise of a professional athlete or becomes a Nobel prize winner, still, it is characteristic of humans to seek out challenges and to acquire skills. Some skills may appear at first glance to be mundane; for example, the fisherman who makes his own flies for bait. But this apparently simple activity may reflect years of study and preparation. Underlying the creation of the fly is the fisherman's knowledge of the specific stream that will be fished, knowledge of the changes in season that make the fly an attractive bait, and knowledge of the behavior of specific types of fish. In all likelihood, this knowledge was attained from multiple sources—from other fishermen, books on fishing, and months and years of experience. Thus, regardless of the specific task, developing skill requires a certain level of mental preparation and knowledge to meet and overcome the challenges presented during training.

WHAT IS LEARNING?

The ability to perform skillfully demands considerable practice. However, skill is not the result of simply repeating an act over and over. Presently, psychologists define *learning* as "a process that results in a relatively consistent change in behavior or behavior potential and is based on experience" (Zimbardo and Gerrig, 1999, p. 227).

This definition conveys three very important characteristics. First, the term is applied only to situations in which changes in behavior are observed consistently over different occasions. A woman who has learned how to shoot a basketball free throw must be able to demonstrate the appropriate movements each time she steps up to the free-throw line. Second, learning is a process that takes place within the individual and cannot be seen directly. Learning is inferred to take place based on observable behavior. A basketball player can be said to have learned how to shoot free throws only when she can demonstrate the skill or the potential to perform the skill. Once a skill has been learned, it is relatively permanent; that is, it will remain with the person for some time. The performance of our basketball player may deteriorate due to anxiety, lack of motivation, or a layoff from the game, but the skills that she has learned are nevertheless retained. Third, learning occurs only with experience or practice. A novice player may be able to describe what is involved in shooting a free throw and she may understand all of the principles that are involved in the skill; nevertheless, she will not and cannot learn the skill until she has experienced the act of shooting the ball.

THE STUDY OF SKILL

The division that has been made between motor skills and cognitive skills is arbitrary, but the practice of separating skills into different types has had a pronounced effect on the academic study of skill. Presently, there are three separate domains of academic activity. Biophysical scientists interested in skills tend to focus their efforts on studying structures of the body that are related to the control of movement. Cognitive scientists tend to focus on the structures of the body that are related to thinking and problem solving. Researchers interested in understanding motivation have focused the bulk of their efforts on the study of body structures related to survival and emotional behavior. As one of the goals of this text is to help the reader understand skilled behavior in terms of the dynamic interaction of body, mind, and spirit, it is necessary to draw on information provided from each of these research domains.

The Biophysical Approach

All physical movement reflects a coordinated integration of the activity of the nervous system and control of muscle contraction. Physical movement, conversely, affects the activity of sensory and neural systems that send information to the brain. This information is processed and, in turn, guides our actions.

Biophysical scientists tend to focus on the structures of the *somatic nervous system*, a division of the *peripheral nervous system*. (See figure 1.1.) They study how muscles operate and how action is controlled. Typically, the analysis of the control of motor movement involves the study of structures of the *central nervous system*, particularly the spinal cord and structures within the brain stem.

Much has been learned from basic and applied research on the physiology of movement and exercise. A wealth of data concerning the interaction among the structures of the body has expanded our understanding of the complex interrelationships between systems of the body that control how skills are learned and performed. The human capacity to learn and perform skills is linked to biological structures and surges of neural growth that have emerged over millions of years of evolution. Deep within the brain are remnants of the early evolutionary structures that control life-sustaining processes. Structures in the brain stem control basic reflexive behaviors that occur, for the

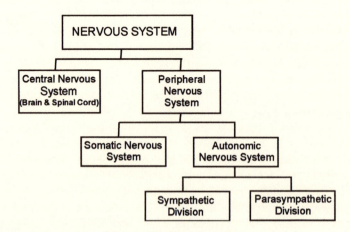

Figure 1.1.   Organization of the Human Nervous System

most part, without conscious awareness. Vital functions controlled by the peripheral nervous system such as breathing, digestion, blood pressure, muscle coordination, and balance are constantly under regulation by brain stem structures. (More will be said of the biophysical approach to the study of skills in chapter 2.)

The Cognitive Approach

Modern humans display the capacity to think, use language, manipulate symbols to solve problems, and plan for the future. The emergence of these abilities corresponded with the most recent structure developed in the brain's evolution, the *neocortex*. The cortex is a convoluted layer of tissue that covers most of the brain; it has evolved in only a few million years, a relatively brief period of time in terms of evolution. The neocortex, sometimes called the *cerebrum*, has two hemispheres within which are located areas linked to the control of thought and action. It has been suggested that the emergence of the structures of the neocortex has freed humans from the constraints of their biological past and provided the means to evolve rationally. Attempts to understand the mental processes involved in skill development and performance have led researchers in psychology, neuroscience, and education to focus on structures of the neocortex and their control of subcortical structures.

At the heart of cognitive science is the assumption that behavior can be understood in terms of the input conditions present in the environment (the stimulus), the internal state of the person (the organism), and the responses made by the individual (*S-O-R psychology*). Cognitive scientists have developed methods of studying the mental processes that are conceptualized to take place *within* the person, events that cannot be observed directly but can be inferred from objective observations of environmental stimuli and their effects on behavior.

Several key assumptions are central to the cognitive S-O-R approach to the study of human activity. At its most fundamental level, the mind is assumed to be a biological processor of information (Ellis and Hunt, 1993; Kellogg, 1995, chapter 1). The mind is hypothesized to work in an orderly and predictable fashion, obeying the same rules that characterize a computer system. Like a computer, the mind is driven to reduce its level of uncertainty about events. Unlike a computer, however, which defines information in terms of mathematical rules, the mind defines information on the basis of meaning. The manner in which the mind derives meaning from the environment is determined by the brain's architecture. Humans are viewed as biological creatures that emerged as a product of evolutionary forces, and the mind reflects the activity of underlying neurological substrates. Specific neurological structures in the brain are hypothesized to dictate the functions of the mind. Perception, memory, and thought are limited by the constraints of the evolution of the central nervous

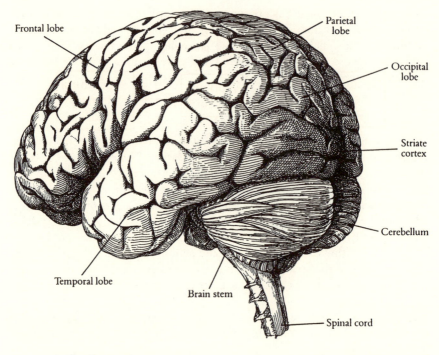

Frontal lobe

Parietal lobe

Occipital lobe

Striate cortex

Cerebellum

Temporal lobe

Brain stem

Spinal cord

Figure 1.2. The Human Brain
From *Eye, Brain, and Vision*, ©1988 by D. H. Hubel. Reprinted by permission of Henry Holt and Company, LLC.

system. The evolutionary forces that molded the body provide the boundaries of the processes of the mind.

An information-processing model is shown in figure 1.3 (Anderson, 1982). The model is characterized by several components that provide a framework for examining the way information is believed to be processed. It is proposed that skills develop from the interaction among four components of the information-processing system:

1. *Processing speed.* A portion of skilled performance can be explained in terms of the speed at which information is transformed and routed through the processing system. The lines and arrows in Figure 1.3 can be viewed as similar to the wiring in a computer system. The amount of information that is transmitted from one component to another is limited by the integrity of the wiring and how much data can be transmitted in a short period of time. Basic sensory information obtained from the environment is organized, transformed into perceptions, and then transferred into working memory. Knowledge gained from past experience and stored in long-term memory is accessed and transferred into working memory. Movement plans developed in working memory are transferred throughout the system and used to initiate action. Thus, the batting performance

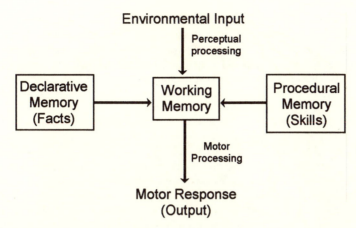

Figure 1.3. Anderson's ACT Model
From "Trainee Characteristics," by P. L. Ackerman and P. C. Kyllonen, in J. E. Morrison (Ed), *Training for Performance: Principles of Applied Human Learning*, ©1991 John Wiley & Sons Limited. Reprinted with permission.

of a baseball player depends greatly on how rapidly he can integrate and respond to a given pitch. Similarly, a child's mathematics performance depends on the speed at which she can extract information from the lines that form the numbers and symbols.

2. *Breadth of declarative knowledge.* Although speed of information processing is important to the execution of skilled performance, skill also depends on an individual's store of declarative or factual knowledge. A portion of a good baseball batter's skill is due to how experienced he is in facing different types of pitchers and differentiating among various throwing styles. Batters must study the throwing techniques of each of the pitchers they face. In the same way, solving algebraic equations demands that a mathematician understand the rules that are used to manipulate and organize numbers. Extended training and practice results in increasingly more sophisticated organization of facts and rules that can be employed to respond to and solve new problems. The experienced batter is able to adjust to the pitching technique of a new pitcher more efficiently than an inexperienced batter. A trained mathematician can solve a novel problem by applying unique combinations of basic rules.

3. *Breadth of procedural skill.* The application of factual information to a problem also involves movement and action. The baseball batter acquires specific, complex patterns for swinging the bat. The steps that are taken to solve a mathematics problem are performed without conscious recognition or awareness of the processes involved. Through repeated practice, action patterns become ingrained and are displayed more and more automatically. Unlike factual information that can be described and defined, procedural skills reflect a type of implicit, nonverbal knowledge. It takes more to perform a skill than just developing an understanding of the actions involved. Skilled performance also involves action; it is only through repetition that procedural skills are acquired.

4. *Processing capacity.* Working memory is the central processing unit of the information-processing model. It is in working memory that information concerning environmental

conditions and possible responses is compiled and possible actions are formulated and considered. Because working memory is limited in capacity, the efficiency of the system is tied to the demands placed on it. Training and practice lead to modifications in the manner in which working memory compiles incoming information and strengthens response productions. Two processes modify working memory efficiency. The *compositional process* collapses long sequences of response productions into shorter sequences. Reducing the number of steps or sequences necessary to formulate a response production reduces the demand placed on working memory; responses are produced more efficiently. Performance of multiple-step mathematics problems occurs more rapidly as individual steps learned early in training are combined and performed later in training as an entire unit. The *proceduralization process* improves working memory efficiency by linking specific environmental conditions to specific responses. Experience and practice lead to problem solving and response selection without going through a series of mental steps. Youngsters' solutions to basic problems of addition and multiplication, for example, initially require them to use some form of counting strategy; however, with repeated exposure and practice, answers come to mind automatically at the sight of a problem. Together, these two processes reduce the demands placed on working memory and lead to efficient and fast mental processing and skilled performance. (More will be said about the cognitive approach to the study of skills in chapter 3.)

The Motivational Approach

Some researchers are interested in explaining not only how the human body functions but also why we behave as we do. Human motivation and emotion play fundamental roles in the development and maintenance of skilled behavior. Developing skills requires overcoming physical and mental challenges. Many who initially desire to become skilled in activities such as chess and basketball find the demands too great to overcome. The physical discomfort and pain may be too great, or the demands on their time may be too much. Central to overcoming these challenges is the ability to muster resolve and attack the task. It is the willingness to act and show spirit that is vital to the execution of skilled performance.

Historically, researchers interested in motivation have been drawn to the study of brain structures and systems linked to emotion, arousal, and stress. The *limbic system*, a network of structures covering and surrounding the brain stem, has been studied extensively. It lies between areas of the brain that control reflexive action and areas that control reasoning and planning. The limbic system performs a number of functions essential to both the acquisition and performance of skills.

Human activity is dynamic; it is more than behavior. It reflects an internal driving force that sparks one to motion. It is goal directed; that is, we all have a purpose for the activities in which we engage. Some motivating forces have a biological basis, such as seeking food when hungry or water when thirsty. Other motivating forces are learned, such as seeking fame or monetary reward. Still other motivating forces are tied to emotional experiences, such as the pleasure derived from the execution of a difficult tennis stroke, or the mastery of the steps required to solve a challenging mathematical theorem, or the exhilaration of falling free during sky diving.

Physiological Arousal

Shifts in physiological arousal occur constantly, every moment of our lives. Some activities produce high levels of biological arousal. Running, wrestling, and playing football or basketball all require a player to exert considerable energy. The circulatory system is called upon to deliver blood to the muscles, and the endocrine system places the body in a state of heightened arousal. Physiological changes also take place when one is concentrating on playing a video game, chess, or a musical instrument. Heart rate and respiration increase, muscles tense, and perspiration increases. Other body systems become less aroused during periods of activity. For example, during periods of exercise, blood flow to the skeletal muscles increases but it decreases to the stomach and intestines. Neuronal activity increases in some areas of the brain during periods of high levels of attention and problem solving but decreases in other parts of the brain. The balance between the excitation and inhibition of physiological systems and cortical areas is influenced by previous experience and training. Thus, the body of an experienced athlete or a master chess player reflects a very different pattern of excitation and inhibition from that of an untrained or novice practitioner of those same skills.

Emotional Arousal

In the scenarios described previously and in countless other examples, participants have reported experiencing changes in their feelings. Individuals who are immersed in an activity or in the heat of competition describe shifts in their emotional state. Many report feelings of exhilaration. Some report a state of mental dissociation during which the mind is relaxed, yet focused on the task at hand. Basketball players often refer to playing "out of the body," giving no apparent conscious thought to a play or the use of a particular strategy, literally becoming one with the game. Movements are made and passes to teammates are made reflexively. Despite what appears to be mass confusion on the court, the basketball player who is "in the zone" plays without rational thought. No mental analysis of the game occurs. The player transcends what his sensory experiences provide. He feels that he is in complete control and that everything is in perfect harmony and order. When the moment comes to take the shot or to execute the perfect pass, the player does not think to act; he acts without thought. This state is described by the practitioners of Zen meditation as "no mind," a transient mental state that is difficult to attain and maintain. For some, the fleeting emotional experiences that come from complete immersion in a task are so extremely pleasurable that they are highly motivated to attain the experience again. These peak experiences are reported by those who achieve them as profound psychological experiences that have lasting effects.

The emotional states experienced during periods of intense concentration and activity are personal and exceedingly difficult for most of us to describe. Consider the avid cyclist who gets up before down to log in a demanding 50-mile bike ride. She may be quizzed by others as to the reason for such behavior. Those who have not experienced the peak experience that such a ride can elicit may look upon the act as bordering on insanity. When pressed for an explanation, the cyclist may be at a loss for words. Similarly, participants in contact sports such as judo and boxing have difficulty articulating why they do what they do. Typically, the response is "Because it feels good," or "I don't know, I just do." The difficulty in explaining the emotional feelings derived from physical and mental activity results largely from the private nature of consciousness. Everyone experiences shifts in emotional states, but the conscious experience is unique to each individual. Emotions and feelings are linked to personal memories that reflect specific episodes of life. (More will be said about the motivational approach to the study of skills in chapter 4.)

All activity is multifaceted; that is, movement and performance reflect the interaction of physical, mental, and emotional systems. These three systems always interact in a predictable and coordinated fashion. A generalist approach will be used to identify the ways that researchers in various domains approach the study and how these approaches parallel and complement each other. Over the past few decades, academic researchers have tended to specialize within specific domains of study. For example, psychologists have come to focus on cognitive skill development; exercise scientists focus on motor-skill development. William Morgan, a pioneer in the field of sport psychology, provided some insight into this dichotomy of research interests when he suggested that psychologists tend to view humans as brains without bodies whereas exercise scientists tend to view humans as bodies without minds (Morgan, 1989).

THE PROCESSES OF LEARNING

Virtually every concept of learning since the time of the ancient Greeks has appealed to some notion of "gluing" or connecting. For many of the natural philosophers of the seventeenth through the nineteenth centuries, knowledge came about through the *association of ideas*. For the behavioral psychologists who emerged in the early twentieth century, knowledge was thought to come about by the *association of stimuli and responses* (Hergenhahn, 1992, chapter 5).

At the heart of the concept of associationism is the assumption that learning is the end result of the way that simple, basic units of the mind are combined. Just how the process of association occurs has been a central topic of discussion since ancient times, and the discussion continues today in the form of various theories of learning.

Behaviorism

The system of experimental psychology promoted by John B. Watson (1878–1958), the father of behaviorism, considered that a true science of psychology deals only with those aspects of human activity that are directly observable. The complex behavior of both humans and animals was assumed to be the end result of combinations of simple reflexes. The belief was that complex behavior could be understood if it could be broken down into its basic element—the Stimulus-Response (S-R) unit. The notion was that an individual acquired all aspects of behavior through experiences that resulted in the association or connection between environmental stimuli and the responses made to those stimuli (Watson, 1913).

Classical Conditioning

Much of Watson's thinking was influenced by methods for the study of learning developed by Ivan Pavlov (1849–1936), a Russian physiologist. Pavlov conducted a three-decades-long study of reflexive behavior, observing that animals and humans are born with sets of unconditional Stimulus-Response reflexes. In his classic example, a dog automatically salivates (the unconditional response) when food (the unconditional stimulus is placed in its mouth. Under specific conditions, however, another stimulus such as a bell (the conditioned stimulus—associated closely in time with the presentation of food—comes to elicit the same response as the unconditioned stimulus (the conditioned response). The development of the relationship between stimuli and the responses to them is referred to as *classical conditioning* (Pavlov, 1928).

Instrumental Learning

Another behavioral psychologist during this period, Edward Thorndike (1874–1949), provided an alternative S-R explanation as the basis for learning. He conducted a number of studies in which he watched how a hungry cat learned to escape from a puzzle box by pushing a pole that opened a door leading to food. Early in training the cat displayed a wide variety of ineffective behaviors; it scratched at the walls of the box, paced, and cried. Eventually the animal brushed against the pole (the correct response) and the door of the cage opened. From that point, Thorndike observed a gradual increase in the number of correct behaviors (pushing the pole) and a decrease in incorrect behaviors (crying and pacing). He then hypothesized that training leads to the strengthening of stimulus-response bonds associated with reward and the weakening of stimulus-response bonds that do not lead to reward. Learning was posited to occur gradually through a number of *trial-and-error* experiences (Thorndike, 1911).

Thorndike's work presaged the work of B. F. Skinner (1904–1996), who proposed that the frequency with which behaviors are performed by animals and humans is dependent on the relationship between a behavioral act and its consequences on the environment. Behaviors that are followed by positive consequences are said to be *reinforced*; behaviors that are followed by nega- tive consequences are said to be *punished*. As behavior is controlled by its consequences, it can be modified through *shaping*, a procedure in which be- havior is modified by the contingent presentation of a reward. Skills were considered to be the result of the arrangement of precise contingencies of re- inforcement.

Cognitive Psychology

The concept of associationism was not abandoned with the advent of cog- nitive, or stimulus-organism-response (S-O-R), psychology. Most contem- porary theories continue to postulate that learning is due to some type of modification in the way that stimuli (incoming sensory/perceptual informa- tion) connect with responses (outgoing motor movement commands). Unlike behavioral-oriented researchers who focus on the measurement of *external* environmental conditions that affect changes in behavior, cognitive re- searchers focus on processes hypothesized to occur *within* the organism (the individual being studied).

Examine the three-stage information-processing model described in figure 1.4. At least three stages of processing take place between the input of environ- mental stimuli and behavioral output. It is in the *stimulus-identification stage* that neural codes are transformed and organized in a manner that allows an in- dividual to derive meaning from sensory experiences. In the *response-selection stage*, specific sensory patterns are interpreted as sounds and visual patterns as figures. What begins as simple variations in sound pressure on the eardrum be- comes a neural code that means, perhaps, one's name. What begins as a pattern of electromagnetic light energy is connected, by association, to the stored image of a friend's face. Response selection involves the retrieval of information stored in memory structures where past experiences are encoded, organized, and maintained for later retrieval and use. Information may be stored for many years, enabling recall of the names and faces of classmates from 20 years ago or an event from childhood. The *response-programming stage* prepares the body for movement. Smiling and waving to an old friend requires the execution of planned physical action.

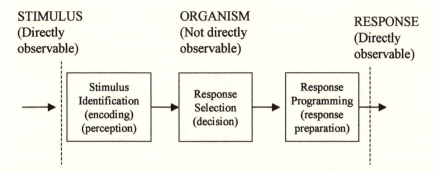

Figure 1.4.   Three-Stage Information-Processing Model

Of the three stages of processing, the response-selection stage appears to be responsible for the interface or mapping of perception onto physical movement. This structure serves as a type of psychomotor workspace where mental action connects with physical action (see overview by Proctor, Reeve, and Weeks, 1990).

Similar stages of processing occur for both a tennis player returning a serve and a chess player selecting a move. Their actions depend on: 1) the information they select from the environment, 2) the decisions they make in selecting specific responses, and 3) the preparations they make in order to perform a given act. Of central importance to the topic of skill learning is the fact that practice and experience affect the manner in which each of the three stages of processing function.

The Learning Curve

Skills, whether they are primarily motor or primarily cognitive, emerge in a predictable fashion. (See box 1.2.) Graphs provide a visual representation of the learning process. An individual's performance is measured during training and then plotted. Data obtained from each member of a group are averaged and then plotted. It is important to remember that graphs represent performance and are only estimates of changes in learning. Measurement of an individual's behavior at any point during training reflects both learning and performance variables. Performance may remain unchanged during successive training sessions; however, learning may continue despite the apparent lack of improvement in performance. Fluctuations in performance during a training session can be attributed to such variables as incentives, motivation, boredom, and shifts in attention.

BOX 1.2   The Power Law of Learning

Researchers who prefer a quantitative approach to the study of nature have attempted to describe their observations via mathematics since the time of the ancient Greeks. Over the past century, a variety of mathematical formulations have been developed to describe learning. Newell and Rosenbloom (1981) evaluated several research studies that assessed perceptual-motor skills, motor behavior, elementary decision-making processes, memory, complex routines, and problem solving. They were interested in identifying mathematical regularities in the processes that underlie the skills developed in these tasks. Newell and Rosenbloom report:

"There exists a ubiquitous quantitative law of practice: it appears to follow a power law; that is, plotting the logarithm of the time to perform a task against the logarithm of the trial number always yields a straight line, more or less. We shall refer to this law as the *log-log linear learning law* or the *power law of practice*" (p. 2).

The power law captures in mathematical terms the changes that are characteristic of skill learning. The greatest improvements in performance occur early in training; the rate of improvement decreases as skills are acquired. Performance eventually nears a point, or *asymptote*, where even slight improvement requires considerable investment of time and energy. Stated in a different way, novices can expect practice to result in large gains in performance early in training; however, as they become more skilled, they can expect practice to result in only small gains in performance. The rate and extent to which skills are learned may differ for any one of a number of reasons, but the pattern of skill development remains consistent.

The power law of practice, historically, was applied first to motor skills. Newell and Rosenbloom suggest that

"Where the general impression seems to have been that the law showed up in perceptual-motor behavior, we think it is clear that it shows up everywhere in psychological behavior—at least it cannot be restricted to some part of the human operation." (pp. 15–16).

Mathematical functions are useful to both researchers and educators because they can be used not only to *describe* the relation between practice and performance but also to provide a means of *predicting* the rate of change in performance that will occur as a function of practice. Teachers and rehabilitation specialists often want to know how much training will be required to bring an individual to a particular level of performance. Mathematical relations such as the power law provide rough estimates of the amount of training required to reach a desired level of performance.

Stages of Learning

The processes that underlie the shift from the novice's slow and laborious performance to the expert's rapid and accurate performance have been foci of interest for several decades. Skilled behavior does not appear without experience. For example, the novice archer who has difficulty hitting a target finds that only with practice will his performance improve. As his accuracy improves and his shooting becomes more consistent, the archer's performance grows smoother; he exhibits less overall muscular tension and experiences fewer feelings of physical or mental effort. It is a generally accepted belief that skill development requires that individuals proceed through a series of stages of learning (Proctor, Reeve, and Weeks, 1990; Salmoni, 1989).

An important early model of the stages of skill acquisition developed by Fitts (1954) and his colleagues (Fitts and Posner, 1967) was expanded upon more recently by Proctor, Reeve, and Weeks (1990). Learning is hypothesized to proceed through three phases of development: the cognitive phase, the associative phase, and the autonomous phase. This model has considerable face validity; that is, most individuals who have learned to perform motor skills agree that the Fitts model describes rather accurately the physical and mental changes that occur as a skill is acquired. The model also dovetails nicely with the three-stage conceptualization of information processing described above. For these reasons, it will be used throughout this book as a framework to describe the processes conjectured to underlie skill learning.

Cognitive Stage

A novel task is, by definition, one that an individual has not performed before. At this stage of skill acquisition, the learner attempts to develop a general understanding of what the task entails, how the task is to be performed, and the goal of the activity.

We have as part of our mental equipment the capacity to make choices, to plan for the future, and to establish goals. We elect to act on the basis of reason and individual problem-solving abilities. The costs and benefits of our planned actions are weighed and judgments are made regarding the merits of behaving or not behaving in a particular way. Behavior tends to follow a general plan or pattern. These organizational plans, referred to by some psychologists as *schema*, are stored in memory. Some schema appear to be innate, as all normally developed humans show similarities in the way they organize information on the basis of order and frequency of events, as well as on the basis of similarity or differences among items and special patterns of stimuli. Perceptual illusions provide straightforward examples of the manner in which innate schemas influence the way we select, organize, and give meaning to what we see and hear. Most schemas are acquired through experience and learning. Through our actions we accumulate information that is stored in memory. Those of us who are taught to drive an automobile, for example, also acquire a general schema for driving other types of vehicles. The schema provides a way to adapt knowledge learned in one situation to different or new situations. The organization of knowledge has been likened to a neural network in which connections are made between the many attributes of events experienced. The sight of a photo of a relative or friend, for instance, brings to mind many associated facts about that person.

Schemas are generalized ways of organizing knowledge. They can be applied to the way we view the world and also used to solve problems. Many complex human activities demand the use of strategic planning, and schemas provide a method of aggregating our knowledge to respond in an adaptive and goal-oriented fashion. Schemas can range from strategies used to solve simple problems governed by well-defined rules (solving an equation or playing chess) to strategies that direct our general direction in life. Schemas help us select from the paths that are available to reach our goals across a lifetime. Some researchers use the term *metacognition* to describe the way individuals make choices and decisions. Metacognition is cognition about memory. It reflects an individual's ability to monitor and control his or her own thoughts and actions. It reflects an awareness of both the nature of demands that are encountered and the ability of the individual to meet the demands. Knowing when to act and when not to act has tremendous adaptive value. Novices, for example, tend to act before thinking, whereas an expert often takes time to consider options before acting.

Associative Stage

With repeated practice, new patterns of responding emerge as effective actions are retained and ineffective actions are eliminated. Humans are biologically designed to be sensitive to particular types and levels of sensory stimuli. Our sensory systems capture and hold information about the environment in terms of spatial data (where things are) and symbolic information (what things represent). The manner and speed in which we encode, classify, and organize sensory information is influenced greatly by our previous experiences. Practice leads to an increase in the saliency of stimuli; that is, with experience, some cues and stimuli become more important than others. For experienced chess players, specific arrangements of certain pieces on the playing board virtually pop out at them. For experienced tennis players, specific movements made by opponents instantaneously draw attention.

A critical component of skill learning is the ability to differentiate between stimuli that are salient and important for performance and those that are not. As a general rule, the greater the number of stimuli in the environment that may be associated with a given response, the longer it will take for an individual to respond to the situation. The novice chess player, for example, may equate the importance of every chess piece and its position on the board. The novice tennis player may respond to all movements of her opponent as being equally important.

The *stimulus-set size* for a novice chess player and novice tennis player is large. Neither have had the experience and practice needed to help them differentiate which cues are more important than others. The slowing of behavioral responding due to stimulus-set size dissipates with practice, however. (See box 1.3.)

BOX 1.3   The Stimulus-Set Size Effect

Stimulus-set size refers to the number of stimulus and response associations present in a task. Take, for example, a multiple-choice examination question: the greater the number of response alternatives, the longer it takes to select one as the correct answer. Practice, however, can markedly reduce the stimulus-set size effect and increase the speed with which choice responses are made.

A classic study by Seibel (1963) provides compelling evidence of the degree to which practice can influence choice-decision speed in complex situations. Three participants were given extensive training on two discrimination reaction-time tasks. In one task, they learned studied patterns of lights presented in 10 different positions and 10 different response keys. This arrangement produced 1,023 possible combinations of light positions and key-press response alternatives. In the other task, the same participants were trained in a situation that had only 31 response alternatives. The participants (Seibel and two research assistants) performed over 200 experimental sessions, usually two per day, each lasting 20 to 30 minutes. The participants' discrimination reaction times during the initial stages of training in the complex condition were, as might be expected, quite long. After 75,000 trials, however, the average discrimination reaction time during the 1,023-alternative condition exceeded the average reaction time during the 31-alternative condition by less than 25 milliseconds.

Expertise is characterized by rapid and accurate performance. Chess players, for example, are able to assess and make virtually instantaneous solutions to highly complex game situations. Practice plays a critical role in the expert's speed.

Autonomous Stage

Experience leads both the chess player and the tennis player to discriminate among many stimuli and to attend to specific cues. With practice, these discriminations are made more and more rapidly and involve less and less effortful thought. Indeed, the expert chess player or tennis player may not even be aware that of extracting useful information. Practice and experience modify the schemas people use to evaluate the tasks they face. Experts tend to approach problems at a more abstract level of analysis than novices. Rather than relying on mechanical task-specific responses to performing a task, experts use general principles to understand the structure of a problem and how it can be solved. Novices and experts evaluate tasks in qualitatively different ways. The expert's rich knowledge base, accumulated through practice, allows a recognition of interrelationships among problem elements that is simply not available to novices. (See box 1.4.)

BOX 1.4   Problem Solving

Chess is a game that involves many possible moves and countermoves. Each stage of the game presents a player with a new problem that must be solved. Part of the challenge is to select a move or combination of moves that will lead to success. Although a variety of mental operations are required to solve a problem, the steps taken are relatively straightforward.

Hayes (1989) suggests that a problem exists when there is a gap, or difference, between an individual's initial state ("where she is") and her goal state ("where she wants to be"). The steps involved in solving problems follow a characteristic sequence:

1. *Finding the problem*: Recognizing that there is a problem to be solved

2. *Representing the problem*: Understanding the nature of the gap to be crossed

3. *Planning the solution*: Choosing a method for crossing the gap

4. *Carrying out the plan*

5. *Evaluating the solution*: Asking "How good is the result?" once the plan is carried out

6. *Consolidating gains*. Learning from the experience of solving (Hayes, 1981, p. 1)

After recognizing that there is a problem to be solved (finding the problem) one conceptualizes its essential elements (representing the problem). A method of solving the problems is devised (planning the solution) and put into action (carrying out the plan). The successfulness of the action plan is then assessed (evaluating the solution) and, if necessary, modifications to the action plan are made (consolidating gains). (Hayes, 1981, p. 1)

The mental processes that underlie each step are complex, and there are considerable individual differences in the way problems are solved. The same problem can be given to two individuals, but each may solve it differently because of such factors as level of cognitive development, previous experience, and domain-specific knowledge.

Factors That Influence the Learning Curve

Understanding how a given person learns a skill is not as simple as the three-stage theory described above may lead one to believe. Skill learning is an extremely complex phenomenon that is affected by many factors. Typically, the roles of three interrelated factors are taken into account: the type of skill being performed (task factors), the effects of practice on the task (practice factors), and conditions that are specific to the learner (subject factors).

Task Factors

In some respects, the tasks that we perform provide a context for our daily activities and constitute the very fabric of our existence. Daily experience for most people is just a long series of individualized tasks: the ritualized morning tasks of washing, grooming, and dressing; the tasks associated with attending school or going to a job; the tasks of preparing meals; and the tasks of socializing with family, friends, and colleagues. The ubiquitous nature of tasks may help to explain the difficulty that educators and researchers face when attempting to classify or categorize the myriad activities that humans can learn to perform.

Task classification systems are—for the most part, driven by the specific interests of various groups of educators or researchers. In the field of education, for instance, teachers often define the tasks within their domain: fine arts teachers have their tasks (e.g., playing musical instruments, painting, singing); physical educators have their tasks (e.g., sports, dance, and exercise); and educational psychologists have theirs (e.g., attention, problem solving).

Practice Factors

Educators have observed that some methods of teaching produce faster learning than others. Researchers who study the processes of learning have identified a long list of factors that influence how well and how fast people learn. Many of these are embedded in the instructional method; for example, the manner in which the learning task is presented, the type of instruction and feedback provided, and the arrangement of practice sessions are all known to contribute to the learning process.

Subject Factors

Individuals do not begin skill training with identical levels of proficiency. Let us say, for example, that ten people who have never used a bow and arrow volunteer to participate in an archery class. Even though all participants are new to the task, considerable differences in performance would be seen even on the first day of training. Overall group performance would be relatively low, but some participants would evidence higher levels of proficiency than others. The observed differences in individual performance reflect the fact that humans bring certain *abilities* with them to the learning situation.

An individual's motivation to learn is another important factor that influences skill development. Becoming skilled at something is not easy. Whether you want to become good in a particular sport or at a particular job, improvement requires practice and extended effort. Consider those who are experts in their fields. How many hours of practice and repetitive drill does it take to become a concert-level pianist, a prima ballerina, or a professional soccer player? Those who excel must be willing to put in considerable effort.

Developmental factors also contribute greatly to skill learning. Throughout life, people are primed to learn specific skills at particular periods of development. There is a dynamic interaction between the individual and the emergence of specific developmental skills. People often display behaviors indicative of the *teachable moment*; that is, they show a natural inclination to learn the skills that they will need to meet and resolve specific developmental tasks. The developmental tasks we encounter throughout the life span arise from several sources. Some tasks are tied closely to biological maturation, others are associated with social and cultural expectations, and still other tasks are linked to the personal goals, values, and aspirations we hold.

The remaining chapters systematically examine many factors that contribute to skill development and its application to problem solving. Research has revealed numerous factors that influence both motor-skill and cognitive-skill learning. Understanding how skills are acquired provides a unique opportunity to examine the interrelationships between three points of view, or philosophies, regarding human behavior. Historically, philosophers and scientists who have attempted to understand human actions have developed explanations that emphasize either the role of the *body*, described in terms of physical structures and biological systems; the *mind*, described in terms of intellect and thought; or the *spirit*, which is described in terms of passions, motives, emotions, and desires.

The analysis of skilled behavior provides a venue for studying the tripartite nature of humans. Each of these three aspects of human nature—mind, body, and spirit—can be viewed as a pillar that supports our capacity to adapt and survive in a constantly changing environment. (See figure 1.5.) When we examine the process of skill learning, the importance of each of these pillars is highlighted.

Consider, for example, a student enrolled in a health and wellness course to learn how to play volleyball. The speed with which she develops skills and the level of proficiency she ultimately reaches will clearly be influenced by how well she can control and coordinate motor movements. The biomechanics involved in learning and playing volleyball are extremely complex. Obviously, deficiencies in any of the multiple hierarchical systems involved in motor movement will impact her capacity to learn the skill. Physical abilities and capacity alone are not sufficient in and of themselves, however. Playing volleyball will require use of her mind to learn proper techniques and then to select and execute specific techniques at the right times. Thus, her skill level also depends

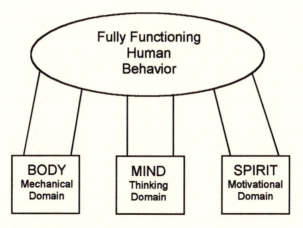

Figure 1.5.   The Tripartite Nature of Human Behavior

on her mental capacities and her ability to reason out solutions to problems encountered when playing the game. Deficiencies in memory and information-processing abilities will clearly impact her skill development. Further, learning a skill such as volleyball requires more than physical and mental abilities; it also demands that the student have sufficient will and intent to learn specific techniques and how the game is played. Without the desire to learn, little improvement will be seen. Indeed, a major source of frustration to educators, coaches, and parents is encountering students who have both the physical and the mental abilities needed to learn but are not motivated to learn or to perform at the levels they are capable of achieving.

The individual differences that make each of us a unique person also make it very difficult for educators, coaches, and trainers to develop skill training programs. For many educators, teaching is a complex endeavor that consists of both science and art. The curriculums used by teachers are based on general principles of learning; however, educators realize quickly that each learner is different and that training programs must be modified to fit each individual's needs.

CHAPTER SUMMARY

Skill is defined as the ability to use one's knowledge effectively and readily in execution of performance. The wide variety of skills that humans learn has resulted in the partitioning of skills into two types: motor skills require movement of the body to achieve a goal; cognitive skills do not emphasize physical action to achieve a goal. The separation of skills into the motor domain and the cognitive domain has had a pronounced effect on skill-related research.

Biophysical researchers tend to focus on the structures of the body that are involved in movement. Cognitive researchers focus on thinking and problem solving. Researchers interested in motivational processes study the goals that people desire.

Skills reflect more than merely learning how to play games and sports; they are integral to human existence from birth through old age. We all progress through a series of developmental stages, each of which presents us with a number of tasks to master. Successful development and aging depends on how well we use the life skills we master to overcome subsequent inescapable challenges that are thrust upon us.

SUGGESTED READINGS

Hayes, J. R. (1989). *The complete problem solver* (2nd ed.). Hillsdale, NJ: Erlbaum.
Proctor, R. W., and Dutta, A. (1995). *Skill acquisition and human performance*. Thousand Oaks, CA: Sage.

Chapter 2

Motor Skills

It is easy to take for granted the movements and actions that we make continuously, throughout our lives. Movement, however, is an extremely complex process that involves both physical and mental processes. Consider, for example, the sport of tennis. A return of service requires the coordination of multiple movement patterns. The skill of swinging a tennis racquet and contacting a ball that travels as fast as 120 MPH involves actions encompassing the player's entire body. A return of service involves the controlled movement of arms, legs, head, eyes, and trunk. The initiation of each of these movements involves preplanning and execution of sophisticated patterns of muscular excitation and inhibition. Equally amazing is the fact that, to be successful, all of these responses have to be organized and performed in a matter of milliseconds. This chapter describes motor skills and how they are learned. When you finish reading it, you will be familiar with the history, research activities, and theories of scientists who are interested in the motor-skill domain.

THE STUDY OF MOTOR MOVEMENTS

Interest in motor skills can be traced to the earliest days of Western civilization. Skilled performance has been critical to human societies for thousands of years. Cultural sport historians have access to well-maintained records of sporting events that occurred during the ancient Egyptian, Greek, and Roman eras. Sport historians have discovered that highly sophisticated methods of athletic training were used during these ancient periods (Poliakoff, 1987).

It was not until the nineteenth century, however, that the structure and functions of the body were studied systematically. The development and subsequent institutionalization of the methods of scientific inquiry led scholars to investigate the nature of biological systems. By the end of the nineteenth century, most physiologists believed that mechanical principles could be used to explain the behavior of all animals and humans. Further, by examining the elementary structures of the human body, insights into the mechanisms of complex behavior and action were thought to be possible.

THE NEUROPHYSIOLOGY OF MOTOR SKILLS

Movement is an extremely complex process that has captured the interest of scientists and educators for centuries. One way that modern researchers study skilled behavior is by examining the physical structures that underlie movement. The sheer complexity of biological motion has led many contemporary scientists to use a research strategy referred to as *reductionism*; that is, the analysis of the individual components of movement. In much the same fashion that a complex automobile engine can be understood by examining its individual parts, so too can complex movements of the human body be understood by examining simple, or individual, movements. All complex movement is thought to be dependent on the execution of collections of simpler movements. The organization of movement is thought to be hierarchical; that is, higher levels of physiological activity control and coordinate lower levels of physiological activity. Thus, the body operates as a whole by smoothly integrating basic units, or modules, that operate relatively independent of each other.

Structure and Control of Movement

All physical movement involves the coordinated integration of activity of the nervous system and control of specific muscle contractions. The human nervous system, as described in figure 1.1, is separated into two parts: the *central nervous system* (CNS) and the *peripheral nervous system* (PNS). Biophysical scientists focus on the mechanisms within the CNS and PNS that underlie controlled movement. All movements, whether the total body movements of an athlete throwing the shot put or the minute finger movements of a child tying his shoestrings, are performed by the contraction of skeletal muscles.

Skeletal muscles are specialized tissues that are designed to contract, or shorten, when stimulated. The contraction of muscles is controlled by nerves that make up the *somatic nervous system*, a division of the PNS. Each muscle of the human body is composed of a number of muscle fibers that are bundled, lying parallel. (See figure 2.1.) Stimulation of a muscle fiber causes biochemical activity within the fiber that brings its two ends closer together similar to the way that one tube of a hand-held telescope slides over another when it is closed.

SPINAL CORD   MUSCLE

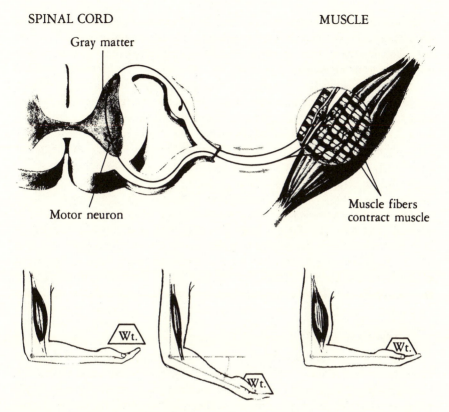

Figure 2.1.   Innervation of Skeletal Muscle
From Neil R. Carlson, *Transparencies to accompany Carlson's Physiology of Behavior.* Copyright 1986. Reprinted by permission by Allyn & Bacon.

When stimulated, typical muscle fibers shorten to 50 to 60 percent of their resting length.

Skeletal muscles (attached to bones via tendons) produce movement by pulling on various parts of the skeleton. The movement of the body's limbs (arms, legs, and fingers) involves coordinated interactions among muscles that attach to the bones. For movement to occur, some of the muscles attached to a bone must be stimulated to contract and pull on that bone. At the same time, other muscles attached to the same bone must relax. The complex processes involved in the excitation of some muscle fibers and the inhibition of others are referred to as *reciprocal innervation.* Movement is an ongoing process in which muscle fibers are signaled at times to contract and at other times to relax (Levinthal, 1990).

Muscle fibers are signaled to contract by *motor nerves* that exit the spinal cord. A *motor unit* is defined as a group of muscle fibers that are controlled, or *innervated*, by individual cells of the motor nerve. The number of fibers controlled by the motor nerve varies considerably from motor unit to motor unit. Muscles involved in precise movements may be innervated by only a few fibers; large muscles involved in gross movements, on the other hand, may have motor units with more than 1,000 fibers.

Movement is, however, much more than simply the excitation and inhibition of muscle fibers. Movement demands that the amount of stimulation be modulated carefully to fit the specific needs of a situation. The muscles involved in the extension of the leg of a ballerina and the leg of a soccer player are the same, but each practitioner trains her body to produce different outcomes. The ballet dancer may seek to produce slow, graceful leg movements, whereas the soccer player wants to perform fast, powerful kicks and thrusts. The rate at which muscle fibers contract is monitored by *muscle spindles* that are located within a particular type of muscle fiber called the *intrafusal muscle fibers*. These intrafusal fibers send information necessary for regulation of muscle contraction back to the spinal cord by way of *sensory nerves*. (See figure 2.2.) The *neural loop* extends from the spinal cord to the muscle fiber and back to the spinal cord; it is fundamental to all movement, regardless of whether the movement is reflexive or voluntary (Levinthal, 1990; Leonard, 1998).

Reflexive Movement

Reflexes are relatively consistent patterns of action that are elicited by a particular stimulus. Some reflexes are innate, occurring without prior experience. An examination conducted by a physician often includes a knee-tap test, which is a simple test of neurological integrity. The procedure involves having the patient sit, with no weight placed on the legs. The tendon is tapped just below the kneecap with a small rubber hammer. The stimulation provided by the tap causes a vigorous extension of the leg by the quadriceps muscle. The leg's rapid response to external stimulation is an example of a *stretch reflex*. The most elementary reflexes are called *monosynaptic*, because the sensory-motor nerve loop that controls the reflex enters the spinal cord and is activated by a single neural event or *synapse*. These reflexes are also referred to as *segmental reflexes* because the resulting muscular action is isolated to that area of the body innervated by a single segment of the spinal cord. The reflex occurs independently of neural activity taking place above or below the segment.

Reflexes can operate relatively independently of the brain; however, generally even the most rudimentary neural activity is part of increasingly larger networks of activity. Groups of neural circuits within the spinal cord known as *central pattern generators* serve to regulate and coordinate movements vital to locomotion (stepping, walking, and running). Neural information is also sent toward the brain. Thus, when a physician taps your patellar tendon with a rubber mallet, you not only react with a reflex but are also consciously aware that your leg has been struck.

Although certain reflexes are inborn, others are acquired by way of experience. Learned patterns of responses elicited reflexively play an important role

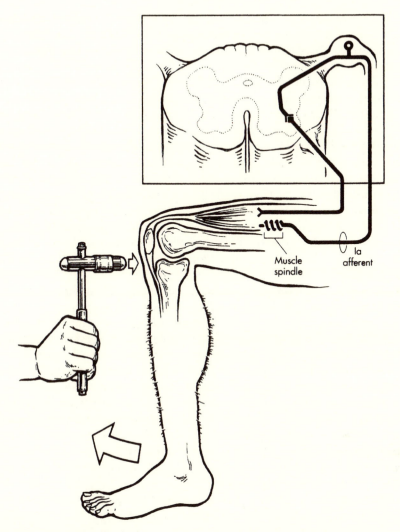

Figure 2.2.   Stretch Reflex
From Leonard, C. T., *The Neuroscience of Human Movement*, 1998, p. 17. Reprinted by permission by Harcourt Health Services.

in adaptive human behavior. They are also central to understanding how skills are developed. How, for example, does a concert pianist learn to control the complex patterns of movement of her fingers and hands? Consider that a trained pianist is able to play certain pieces of music, such as the musical scales, reflexively or without thought. Indeed, she may even be able to carry on a conversation while her fingers continue to move up and down the keyboard with exquisite precision.

The neurological changes that accompany motor-skill learning have fascinated researchers for decades. Considerable efforts have been expended to discover how complex movement patterns or *motor programs* are instantiated
into the nervous system. The brain structure that appears to be most responsible for the control of learned motor programs is the *cerebellum*, a part of
the brain stem that lies underneath the posterior area of the neocortex. (see
Levinthal, 1990, and Rosenbaum, 1991, chapter 2, for overviews). Though the
cerebellum does not initiate movement, it serves as the integrative way station
between the direction of conscious, voluntary movement and unconscious, reflexive movement. The pianist may elect to play the musical scales on the piano,
but the muscular patterns responsible for her precise finger and hand movements are controlled reflexively. The cerebellum is at the center of an immense
feedback system that involves input from the neocortex and input from sensory systems providing information about the position of the body relative to
its environment. Together these sources of information provide the data necessary for the cerebellum to configure a template for comparing the position of
the body to the space that it occupies at any moment.

It would be impossible to coordinate the motor movements necessary for
skilled performance if the nervous system did not have the capacity to compare
the current position of the body relative to a desired position. Playing a musical note on the piano requires the player not only to change the location of the
hand and extend a finger to the appropriate key, but also to use that finger to
depress the key at the desired time, with the desired pressure, and for the desired length of time. As the body moves, the cerebellum receives *kinesthetic*
information provided by specialized neural *proprioceptors* located in muscles,
tendons, joints, and the *vestibular* apparatus of the inner ear. These receptors
give the nervous system the capacity to make real-time analyses of the
movement of body parts. It takes into account the force of gravity, the extent
and direction of movement, the speed and angle of limb movements, and the
characteristics of total body motion.

The cerebellum performs several functions that are critical to the execution
of motor skills. It controls the timing of muscle activity and ensures that patterns of movements are executed in the proper sequence. Motor skills are not
performed in isolation; they occur as continuous chains of movements in which
the initiation of one movement, or link, is signaled by the completion of a preceding movement, or link. The proprioceptive information produced by each
movement is fed back to the cerebellum, continuously updating the progress of
the behavioral chain. Have you ever found yourself unable to recall aloud a
telephone number you wish to dial? Have you then found your fingers automatically entering the entire numerical sequence smoothly and correctly when
your fingers touch the telephone keypad? It is as if your memory resides more
in your fingertips than in your brain. In similar fashion the pianist's fingers follow long chains of movements in which the end of one movement produces the
beginning cues for the next movement.

Another function of your cerebellum is to dampen the momentum created by the movement of your body. Following the laws of physics, a body segment, limb, or digit produces momentum once it is set into motion. Your cerebellum monitors the velocity of your limb as it moves from one point to another. As the limb approaches its terminal location, your cerebellum signals the neocortex to slow or dampen the movement using appropriate muscular contractions. Although skilled performance is often characterized by speed and accuracy of movement, it is also true that control of the force of movements sets the expert apart from a novice. The cerebellum plays a central role in preventing too much or too little force from being exerted during movement.

Perhaps the most fascinating function of the cerebellum is its capacity to look ahead in time to predict where a particular limb is supposed to be in the immediate future. The performance of motor skills involves the execution of a series of movements designed to achieve a particular outcome. The response patterns that have been acquired through repetition and practice provide the cerebellum with a template that dictates the sequencing of body movements that are performed without conscious awareness on the part of the performer. The pianist does not have to think about where each finger needs to go on the keyboard in order to play a particular passage. The cerebellum, via programming achieved through experience, is responsible for monitoring changes in body position and ensuring that the movement pattern is performed smoothly and accurately. Consider that a human can perform as many as 32 separate movements of the 10 fingers in the space of one second!

The capacity of the nervous system to anticipate future needs and to respond reflexively and without conscious thought clearly has tremendous adaptive significance for humans. Damage to cerebellar functions are known to have profound effects on movement and behavior. (See box 2.1.)

BOX 2.1. Trauma to the Cerebellum

Central to skilled movement is the degree of agreement between an individual's intended actions and his actual actions. Goal-directed behavior involves planning, initiation, and execution. Even the most simple of actions, such as pressing a door bell, requires a sophisticated interaction among multiple structures both in the central and in the peripheral nervous system. Instructions from the motor cortex initiate movements of specific muscle groups. The movement of a limb or body segment creates inertia and momentum; information about these changes in the body's position are fed back to the brain. The cerebellum plays a vital role in coordinating the action of muscle movements. It compares simultaneously incoming proprioceptive information concerning the actual body position with information concerning the individual's intended actions, and then attempts to correct discrepancies that exist.

Damage to the cerebellum profoundly affects the execution of coordinated movements. Ataxia is a class of neurological disturbances that follows damage to areas of the cerebellum involved in dampening or
"breaking" the momentum of a moving body segment. The actions involved in pressing a door bell require both the contraction and the relaxation of muscle groups that essentially launch the arm toward its
intended target. Under normal conditions, the limb's momentum is
dampened as the finger reaches the button. Ataxia is a failure in the control of dampening and, as a result, individuals with ataxia "overshoot"
their intended targets. People with ataxia have severe difficulties in performing such basic actions as walking or running. They cannot predict
where their feet will land with each step and, as a result, display uncoor-
dinated gait patterns and have great difficulty maintaining equilibrium.

There are other neurological disorders that are linked to specific cerebellar functions, as well. Damage to specific areas of the cerebellum will,
for example, affect its capacity to predict body position. Normally, the
vestibular system provides information concerning the status of the
body's equilibrium, and the cerebellum uses this information to maintain
balance during and following movements. Loss of this capacity results in
the experience of loss of equilibrium with every movement and the need
to move much more slowly than normal.

Voluntary Movement

Emitted behaviors are actions initiated on the basis of voluntary decisions. You
may emit a response when specific environmental events occur. The competitive
swimmer who is on the starting block, for example, waits for the sound of the start
signal before she dives into the water. You may also emit behaviors on the basis of
internal signals or thoughts. The baseball player may attempt to steal a base on the
basis of his own internal go signal. The initiation of goal-oriented motor-movement
patterns involves neurological processes that take place in the neocortex of the brain.

Areas of the brain that are linked to the control of voluntary movement are located primarily in a band of cortical tissue located in back of the *frontal lobes* and
in front of the *parietal lobe* (see Sage, 1984, and Shea, Shebilske, and Worchel,
1993 for overviews). There is a close functional interrelationship between three
strips of tissues that make up this area of the neocortex. Working from the front
of the cortex toward the back, the *premotor area* is a strip 1 to 3 centimeters wide
that lies just behind the prefrontal area of the frontal lobe; the *primary motor
area* is a strip located immediately behind the premotor area; and the *somatosensory area* is a strip of cortical surface located in the parietal lobe.

These three areas of the brain play a very specific role in the initiation and
control of movement. Each of the three areas of the motor cortex receive input

information from different sources; there are at least twelve different kinds of sensory receptors in the human body. Some of these sensors provide information about the status and operation of processes within the body; others provide information about the status of the external world. The information captured by each type is sent to the brain by a different path, and this information provides the basis for voluntary movement.

The premotor area has anatomical linkages to areas of the neocortex responsible for rational thought, judgment, and decision making. The prefrontal areas of the *frontal lobe* have been implicated in many processes that make our species unique. Experimental and clinical evidence suggests that the prefrontal area is responsible for organizing and planning goal-directed action. The prefrontal area has a multitude of neural connections throughout the brain; some of these connections innervate the premotor area into action. The premotor area appears to assist in regulating movement by translating the plans of the prefrontal area into action. It does so by coordinating elemental motor impulses and integrating them into complex goal-oriented motor plans.

The somatosensory area has inputs that arise from sensory systems that monitor the surface of the body; information concerning touch, pressure, vibration, and position is transmitted to and organized by this part of the parietal lobe. Information generated from sensory receptors in the PNS is sent toward the brain through *affector nerve fibers*. This incoming sensory information allows the somatosensory areas to hold a real time representation of the body's position.

Thus, the premotor areas interact cooperatively with the primary motor areas to initiate muscular movements; in like manner, the somatosensory areas of the cortex interact with the primary motor area to pattern movement. Together these three areas are responsible for the coordinated innervation of single or small muscle groups that are in turn responsible for both voluntary movement and the modification of reflexive behavior. (See figure 2.3.)

Information that is generated from areas within the CNS and sent outward toward target structures in the PNS flows through fibers classified as *effector nerves*. The motor areas of the neocortex send information to skeletal muscles by way of two effector tracts or pathways: the *pyramidal tract* and the *extrapyramidal tract*.

The pyramidal tract is composed mostly of fibers originating from the three cortical areas that are part of the motor cortex. (See figure 2.4.) The tracks descend from the right and left hemisphere of the neocortex to a point in the brainstem known as the *pyramidal decussation*, where the tracts split. About 80 percent of each fiber tract then crosses to the opposite side of the brain and continues downward through the spinal cord as the *lateral corticospinal tract*. The remaining 20 percent of the fibers in each tract do not cross over but continue down the spinal cord as the *ventral corticospinal tract*. The pyramidal tract plays an important role in the control of muscles in our hands and fingers, enabling us to generate incredibly precise and delicate movements.

The extrapyramidal tract is composed of a web of interrelated fibers that originates in areas of the neocortex and descends through a number of structures

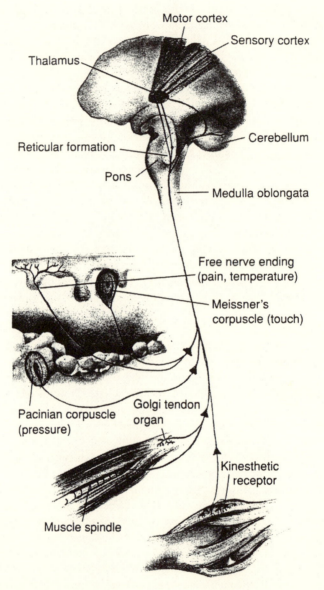

Figure 2.3.   The Motor and Sensory Cortex
Reprinted, by permission, from J. H. Wilmore & D. L. Costill, 1999, *Physiology of Sport and Exercise*, 2nd ed. (Champaign, IL: Human Kinetics), 72.

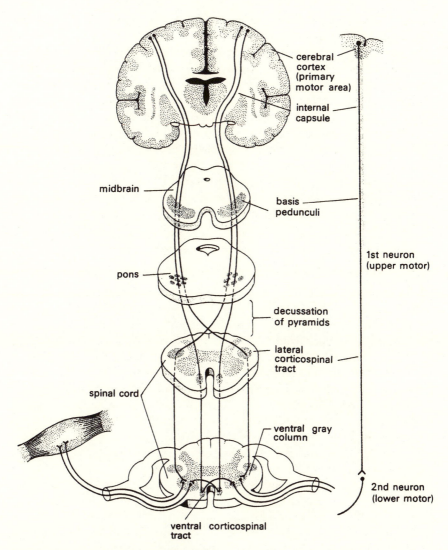

Figure 2.4. The Pyramidal Motor Pathways

deep within the brain. Perhaps the most influential of these subcortical structures is the cerebellum. As discussed above, the cerebellum has the task of controlling well-ingrained learned reflexes and thereby permits structures located
in the neocortex to focus on planning goal-oriented action. The structures that
make up the extrapyramidal system modify and refine movements initiated in
the neocortex and executed via the pyramidal tracts. In a sense, the extrapyra-

midal system maintains the lower-level background conditions that permit the performance of skilled volitional action.

In summary, every movement of the human body reflects vastly complex interrelations between many parts of the nervous system. The physiological basis for movement is not located in one particular area of the brain. Movement, both elicited and emitted, involves a synthesis of multiple neural systems that operate in concert to create action. In much the same way that orchestra music is created by individual instruments, each of which is designed to perform a particular job, human movement is the product of a host of individual systems, each of which is constrained to perform specific operations. When organized properly, these systems enable the exhibition of truly astounding displays of skill. When trauma such as that produced by a stroke destroys areas of the cerebral cortex, the results may lead to marked impairment. (See box 2.2.)

BOX 2.2. The Neuropsychology of Strokes

Cerebrovascular events, or strokes, are defined as localized brain damage caused by diminished blood flow. There are different mechanisms by which strokes influence brain function. Ischemic stroke can occur due to thrombosis the narrowing of a blood vessel, or due to an embolus, in which the release of plaque into the blood stream blocks flow into small vessels. Regardless of the mechanism, the interruption of blood flow for only a few minutes will lead to the degeneration of neurons and their supportive cells. The destructive process is due to damaging cascades of chemical interactions within cells. The tissue damage is essentially irreversible within hours after the onset of a stroke.

The impact of strokes on behavior, cognitive functioning, and learning has been studied extensively (see Delaney and Ravdic, 1997, for an overview). Their effects are multifaceted, resulting from a disorder of movement in initiating and controlling skeletal action. Of the approximately 500,000 stroke cases each year, about 20 to 30 percent become severely and permanently disabled, suffering paralysis, reduced coordination, and loss of sensation. The stroke is also a disorder of cognition, as it can affect general intellectual functioning as well as specific decision-making processes, depending on its location. Finally the stroke is a disorder of emotion, causing a host of affective difficulties. The sudden loss of physical and mental skills is associated first with heightened anxiety and then with apathy, clinical depression, and decreased motivation.

The success of physical and cognitive rehabilitation specialists depends greatly not only on the methods employed to teach new ways of acting but also on participants' motivation and willingness to make the best of their remaining capabilities.

One of the primary challenges faced by researchers who study motor skills is determining how movements are organized and controlled. It is often the case that specific, spectacular actions of athletes, dancers, and actors are celebrated for their uniqueness. Such actions have certainly garnered considerable public interest. However, it is equally fascinating to understand how even the basic and mundane movements involved in walking, running, and writing—all of which are performed daily by almost everyone—are organized and controlled.

HOW MOTOR SKILLS ARE STUDIED

The measurement of human body movement can be performed in many different ways. Historically, the body has been viewed by many as a biological machine; as such, the methods and terminology used to describe its movements and actions draw heavily from such physical sciences as physics and engineering. *Biomechanics* is a branch of study that examines the effects of forces on the human body and the motions produced by those forces.

Traditionally, the study of biomechanics is subdivided into the study of *statics*, which examines how the body retains balance when it is disturbed by external forces, and the study of *dynamics*, which examines forces that cause the body to change speed or direction of motion.

Kinematics is the study of motion in terms of displacement, velocity, and acceleration of limb and body movements without regard for the underlying forces or energy that caused the motion. Kinematics is the study of the geometry of movement. Early researchers employed cinematographic recording methods to capture movements on film. Cinematography is a series of individual pictures taken sequentially at a specific rate; when viewed in rapid succession, the images give the perception of movement. Thus, each picture provides a snapshot of the body in time and space. Movement can be quantified by marking locations on specific areas of the limbs and body and measuring their change in position from frame to frame. Modern kinematic measures have become quite sophisticated; computers are used to store data generated by sensing devices such as light-sensing diodes attached to various landmarks of the body. New technology has provided the means to obtain extremely accurate measures of the position, acceleration, and velocity of limb and body movement.

Biometric measures provide researchers with the means to quantify actions that are directly observable from outside the body. There are also several recording techniques available to provide measures of movement within the body. *Electromyographic* (EMG) methods of recording skeletal muscle activity have provided considerable insight into the manner in which motion is initiated and coordinated. Electromyography is based on the measurement of electrical activity that takes place within muscles as they contract. The method involves placing electrodes on the surface of the skin over the muscle to be measured. When the muscle is activated, a weak electrical signal is produced that is amplified and recorded. The method is unique because it provides a measure of changes in the amplitude and duration of the muscle contraction over time. This type of information permits researchers to analyze the operation of individual muscles and, more important, the way groups of muscles operate to coordinate sequences of muscle inhibition and excitation needed for movement patterns. The EMG has played an important role in evaluating the stages of processing involved in the flow of information from the brain *(central processes)* to the skeletal muscles *(peripheral processes)*.

Researchers have made extensive use of laboratory experiments to describe and explain how movements are learned. The measures that are most often used to study motor skills fall into three general classes: measures of response speed, measures of response accuracy, and measures of response magnitude.

Response Speed

Mental chronometry, a method that provides quantitative measures of the temporal flow of information through the stages of cognitive processing, has been used extensively by researchers to gain insight into how information is processed and translated into action. The method of mental chronometry can be traced to the work of Franciscus Donders (1818–1889) conducted over a century ago. (See figure 2.5.) Donders (1868/1969) demonstrated that the time it took for a person to respond to the onset of a stimulus became longer as task demands were manipulated experimentally. Under laboratory conditions, he first measured the amount of time it took a research subject to press a button when a light appeared. This measure provided an index of the subject's *simple reaction time*. Next, Donders asked the subject to look at a number of different colored lights and to press a button when a specified colored light appeared. This measure provided an index of *discrimination reaction time*. Then he taught the subject to associate a specific response with a specific stimulus (e.g., index finger button press for a green light, ring finger button press for a red light, etc.). Donders then measured how long it took for the subject to respond to each stimulus. This measure provided an index of the subject's *choice reaction time*. Donders observed that subjects' response times became longer as the task became more complex. He proposed that the systematic changes in reaction time (RT) corresponded to various operations of the mind. The simple subtraction of one type of reaction time from another type could yield a quantitative index of a mental process. The importance of this relatively simple experimental method should not be underestimated, as it made possible a quantitative examination of volition (choosing to behave),

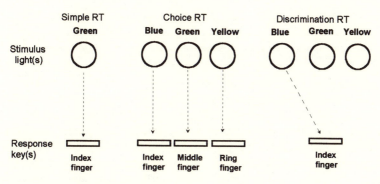

Figure 2.5.   Response-Time Measures

once the subject matter only of philosophers. An inferred state could now be systematically studied by scientists.

Donders's work presaged the scientific study of the mind. Mental chronometry reemerged as a powerful research method for modern scientists. Indeed, one of the most stable and predictable observations of motor performance, *Hick's Law*, is an extension of Donders's research. Hick (1952) and Hyman (1953) conducted a number of experiments that demonstrated an orderly relationship between choice reaction time and the number of stimulus alternatives presented to subjects. Choice RT increased by a nearly constant amount every time the number of stimulus-response alternatives doubled. This relation was expressed mathematically in terms of a logarithmic relation:

$$\text{Choice RT} = a + b[\log_2 (N)]$$

where N is the number of stimulus-response alternatives and a and b are empirical constants.

Researchers who study motor skills have been particularly interested in examining the mental processes that led to the initiation of movement, as well as the processes that occur as movements are executed. Chronometric methods that rely on the measurement of reaction time have provided modern researchers with ways to study mental processes and their temporal order. The time it takes a person to respond to the onset of a stimulus has been broken down, or *fractionated*, into basic units. As seen in figure 2.6, *response time* can be fractionated into *reaction time*, (defined as the time between the onset of a go signal and the initiation of a response) and *movement time* (the time between initiation and completion of a response). Together these two components reflect the cognitive processes involved in stimulus identification, response selection, and response programming.

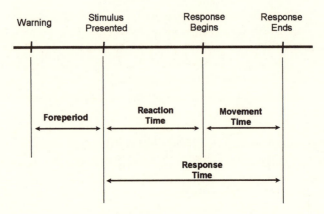

Figure 2.6.   Fractionation of Response-Time Duration

Response Accuracy

Many skills are described in terms of speed of performance. The tennis player who is capable of detecting and preparing his body to return the service of an opponent is more likely to be successful than someone who can't keep up with the serve. Response speed, however, is not the only factor that plays a role in determining the tennis player's success. Motor skills are also described in terms of the *accuracy* of performance. The skilled tennis player cannot be satisfied with just returning his opponent's serve over the net. Skill at playing tennis also requires hitting the ball so that it falls in a particular area of the court.

The goal of many sports is to be as accurate as possible. Athletes may spend months and years repeatedly practicing particular movements in order to increase their accuracy. Indeed, a skilled tennis player may perform tens of thousands of service returns aimed at the edges of the court and designed to bounce past the reach of his opponent. The closer the service return consistently lands near the line that marks the edge of the court, the better the return. Good service returns fall on or very near the line; poor passing shots land beyond the sideline or toward the center of the court, some distance from the line.

Motor-skill researchers often measure differences that exist between desired performance and actual performance. The term *error* is used to describe the difference. Error measurement is a quantitative description of the relation between a goal and actual performance; error in this sense is nothing more than a number, a statistic. It does not mean that a performance is wrong; it merely implies difference. There are a number of ways that response error can be measured. *Absolute error* is an index of overall accuracy in performance. Our tennis player may place some service returns outside the sideline, some inside the sideline, and some directly on the sideline. If the distance between the point where the tennis balls land and the midpoint of the sideline is measured and summed (regardless of the direction of error), then averaged, the result is a single number that reflects the precision of the tennis player's skills. A small numerical value indicates that most of the service returns were close to the target; a large numerical value indicates less precision in performance. *Constant error* provides an index of the consistency of actual performance relative to a desired distance. The tennis player's return of service, for example, may tend to overshoot the sideline. If the distance between the point where the tennis balls land and the midpoint of the sideline is measured and summed (this time taking into consideration the direction of the error), then averaged, the result is a single number with plus or minus sign. The numerical value would indicate the average distance between actual performance and desired performance and the plus or minus would indicate the direction of the difference, providing a summary of the degree to which the tennis player's return of service overshoots or undershoots the sideline.

Response Magnitude

A third measure that captures the characteristics of motor skill is *response magnitude*. Depending on the specific task, response magnitude can be expressed in a number of ways. Some motor skills are described in terms of frequency, or how often a behavior can be performed within a specified period of time. The number of push-ups or sit-ups you can complete within one minute provides an index of your physical fitness, for example. Other skills are defined in such biomechanical terms as force, amplitude, or intensity. Each of these measures has a precise definition that can be applied to specific aspects of movement. Muscular force, for example, provides an index of the effect that the body can exert. The magnitude of muscular force is in direct proportion to the number and size of the fibers that contract within a muscle or group of muscles. A great many sports require that participants exhibit skills that are judged on the athlete's ability to mobilize and recruit muscle fibers. The magnitude of responses may also be measured in terms of duration, or how long behavior can be maintained over time.

There are tremendous individual differences in motor skill performance. Despite the long history of athletic training and preparation, the systematic study of skill development is a relatively recent phenomenon. Research is beginning to provide scientists and educators with an improved understanding of the steps necessary for developing and improving motor skills.

FACTORS THAT INFLUENCE MOTOR SKILL LEARNING

Understanding how motor skills are learned is a complex multifactorial undertaking. The shape of the motor skill learning curve is unique for each individual.

It is determined by the constraints of the learning process (i.e., the stages of learning), the ability characteristics of the individual, and the type of skill being performed.

The Stages of Motor Skill Learning

A novel task is, by definition, one that an individual has not performed before. A young boy who has never ridden a bicycle, for example, may have seen his friends riding their bikes about the neighborhood. Such observations provide him with information about the task and how it might be performed. Indeed, the child might imagine himself on a new bicycle, riding on the street, maneuvering around corners, swerving around people on sidewalks, and gliding in for a controlled stop. The boy may have observed others performing the task but lack any history of direct involvement in its performance. It will not be until the child actually begins to ride a bicycle that the true nature of the task is revealed to him.

The Cognitive Stage

At this stage of skill acquisition, the learner attempts to develop a general understanding of what the task entails, how the task is to be performed, and the goal of the activity. In the case of the young boy, he will probably receive his initial riding *instructions* from adults who will do their best to describe verbally how the task should be performed. Under ideal conditions, the novice attends to what is being said and begins to organize a plan of action. The child sits on the seat of the bicycle, places his hands on the handlebars, and rests his feet on the pedals. Typically, physical support is provided by the instructors or by training wheels to keep the bicycle from toppling. At this point the child begins to initiate movement by pressing his feet on the pedals. It is also at this point that the child may realize a discrepancy between his image of riding a bicycle and the experience of actually riding one. There is a considerable difference between what the child planned and what actually takes place. As he presses on the bicycle's pedals, the force of each stroke results in a slight shift in the position of the bicycle frame and direction of motion. Typically, the child attempts to counter the lateral and wobbling movement of the bike by adjusting the position of the handlebars. Often he overcompensates, loses control and balance, and falls. Experiences such as these lead the young boy to realize that there is a lack of correspondence between his goal and his ability. But despite the lack of initial success and possible bruises to his body and ego, he will try again. With each additional attempt, he will take into account information, or *feedback*, obtained from previous attempts. He will come to match sensory and perceptual information with specific response patterns and develop *psychomotor codes*. These codes provide the backbone for the construction of elementary *motor programs*.

Verbal instructions are particularly important during the cognitive stage of skill development. Faced with the task of learning a new skill, one typically has a general idea of how it is to be performed. The young cyclist, for example, probably has established an image of himself riding his new bicycle. The actual steps required for him to achieve his goal may not be self-evident, however. The process of learning a new motor skill has all the characteristics of problem solving built into it. The learner initiates a journey down a path that will involve a transition from an *initial state* (i.e., incomplete knowledge about how to perform the task) to a *goal state* (i.e., sufficient knowledge to perform the task). Individuals who want to learn a new skill develop a *set of operations* that is created to take them from the initial state to the goal state . One can attempt to solve the problem of acquiring a new skill alone; however, most novices seek out teachers who know how to perform the task at hand, asking for guidance and instruction. (The topic of problem solving is addressed in greater detail in chapter 3.)

Verbal instructions and the manner in which they are provided are known to have a marked impact on how quickly and how well a skill is learned. They affect the learning process in several ways. First, the information presented serves as the basis for the novice's development of a *mental model* of the task. Mental models are constructed on the basis of symbolic codes that are organized and stored into memory. These codes provide information about relationships among environmental stimuli, actions to be taken, and outcomes that are expected from these actions (Proctor, Reeve, and Weeks, 1990). The memory representation that describes the relation between environmental stimuli and behavioral actions is modified as soon as the novice acts. The mental model changes as the results of actions reveal those aspects of the task that are important to desired outcomes and those that are not relevant. The verbal cues provided by a teacher often help the learner to identify the stimulus-response units that are most important, or salient, to learning. For example, a father's instructions to his son to maintain a constant peddling rate isolates one important task component that is vital to learning to ride a bicycle.

Instructions can also have a motivating effect on novices. Initial attempts at learning new skills can be, at times, quite anxiety provoking. Instructions that include information about what the individual can expect as a consequence of his actions may raise his level of confidence and willingness to continue practice. A child who understands that falling off his bicycle will be part of the learning process will be more likely to make constructive use of the information derived from a fall than a child who is not prepared for a fall.

Verbal instructions can, however, be ineffective or even detrimental to the learning process. Their effectiveness is lost when too much information is presented at one time. Human memory systems and attentional processes are limited in their capacities. Teachers who present novices with a long list of facts run the risk of overloading a student's short-term memory capacity. Instructions also lose effectiveness when the information is too complex.

Conceptual information about the underlying principles involved in the execution of a motor task has been found to be less influential than simple concrete information (Wulf and Weigelt, 1997). The effectiveness of verbal instructions is also constrained by the learner's level of cognitive development. To be effective, the level of information presented and the language used should be selected to reflect the novice's developmental and intellectual levels. Too often, adult coaches provide instructions to children that far exceed their understanding. Verbal instructions during the cognitive stage of learning function best when they are presented simply, when they are meaningful to the novice, and when they focus on only a few points at a time.

Feedback is another important factor in the cognitive stage of skill acquisition. The role that it plays in motor skill learning has piqued the interest of both educators and researchers alike. Some have suggested that motor learning cannot occur without some form of feedback. In the example presented above, much of the feedback provided to the novice cyclist is categorized as *extrinsic* or *augmented feedback*; it is information that originates from the environment and indicates or reflects the level of success of a previous response. External feedback is only one source of information that guides learning, however. *Intrinsic feedback* originates from receptors within the body, and it too plays a critical role in the control and acquisition of motor skills. Sensory information generated from the action of the body is transmitted to the spinal cord and brain; together they provide a sense of movement and of the position of the body in space. The young cyclist's body generates a tremendous amount of information during the early stages of learning. Successful cycling will depend on his ability to adapt and ultimately control reflexive input/output systems. Many of the actions that are involved in a skilled performance such as bicycling occur far too rapidly for the person to control consciously. The ability to maintain balance and direct movement during action depends on the organization of stimulus-responses units that occur rapidly and without conscious awareness. The learning process is influenced greatly by the dynamic interaction between extrinsic and intrinsic feedback.

One type of extrinsic feedback is *knowledge of results* (KR). The child's instructor may provide feedback concerning how well the child performed during his last attempt to ride his bike. This type of information gives the child an idea of the errors that were made and how they can be corrected to lead to more efficient cycling. A very large body of research exists that has examined the role of KR on skill acquisition. This work has revealed that KR is an extremely complex phenomenon whose properties are still not completely understood. (See Schmidt and Lee, 1999, chapter 12, and Winstein and Schmidt, 1989, for a critique of KR research.)

There are several issues concerning KR that impact skill learning during the cognitive phase of motor skill acquisition. First, KR can be provided in a variety of ways, and the type of feedback that is given can differentially affect learning. *Qualitative KR* indicates whether a learner's actions were correct or incorrect. *Quantitative KR* provides additional information, such as the magnitude and direction of the error in the movement. *Bandwidth KR* involves giving feedback, but only when performance exceeds a threshold of either good or poor performance. Educators tend to employ the latter method of feedback, giving corrective information when a student's performance is clearly off the mark and supportive information when performance is exceptionally good. The advantage of bandwidth KR is that the threshold for providing feedback can be modified as the learner's performance becomes increasingly proficient.

Second, KR can be given at different points during practice. Feedback can be provided *concurrently* while the learner is moving, *immediately* following action, or it can be *delayed* for some period of time following action. The impact of the timing of feedback on skill learning is not straightforward. Indeed, there are situations in which extrinsic feedback given during and immediately following performance can actually impede learning. It appears that external KR can interfere with or block mental processing that occurs naturally as a learner engages in action (Swinnen, Schmidt, Nicholson, and Shapiro, 1990).

Third, the frequency with which KR is presented differentially influences skill development. *Absolute frequency* refers to the number of times KR is presented during practice (100 percent frequency would indicate that KR was presented following every learning trial). *Relative frequency* refers to the percentage of trials that KR was presented. It would appear at first glance that giving KR following every learning trial would best promote learning. This is not always the case, however, as there are times when learning occurs best under conditions when KR is given on only a portion of practice trials. (See box 2.3.)

BOX 2.3. The Relative Frequency Effect

It makes sense to most teachers that a student will learn best when given as much feedback as possible about his or her performance. Recent research suggests that this assumption may not always be true. A study conducted by Sparrow and Summers (1992) assessed how well young adults were able to perform a line-positioning task. Blindfolded participants were asked to manually move a slide along a metal rod, 400 millimeters from a starting point. One group of participants received 100 percent verbal knowledge of results (KR); other groups received 33 percent, 20 percent, 10 percent, and mixed KR. Each participant's performance was assessed during 100 practice trials and during two non-KR retention tests, one administered two minutes after training and another given 24 hours after training. There were no differences among the groups' performance during practice, but the 100 percent and 33 percent KR groups performed better than lower-frequency KR groups during the first retention test. However, those individuals receiving 10 percent KR and mixed KR outperformed those receiving more frequent KR during the second retention test.

> The results of this and other studies suggest that there are times when it may be beneficial to provide augmented KR following some, but not all, training trials. Giving KR too frequently has been hypothesized to lead learners to depend on extraneous information rather than creating and incorporating their own problem-solving operations (Schmidt and Lee, 1999, pp. 341–342). Learners may benefit most when a relatively high frequency of KR is given early in training but then reduced as the skill is acquired.

Fourth, KR can exert its effects on learning in a number of ways. Feedback serves an *associational function*; it strengthens connections between salient environmental stimuli and specific movements. The cognitive phase of motor skill learning involves developing an understanding of which environmental stimuli are important and which are not and also an understanding of the relation between relevant stimuli and specific motor movements. Feedback also serves an *informational function*. Novices are uncertain about how to plan movements, and feedback serves to help prepare movement plans. Finally, feedback has a *motivational function*; KR energizes learners, promoting interest and willingness to practice with greater effort and intensity.

In summary, the effectiveness of knowledge of results depends on the type of task being learned, the stage of learning, and the mental processing that is involved during practice. Clearly, KR is a powerful factor in learning, and it can serve as a useful tool for educators. Teachers who gain an appreciation of the subtleties of KR will be able to exert considerable influence on novices who are in the cognitive phase of motor skill learning.

Information is gained as an individual interacts with his or her environment. Motor learning involves the connection of stimulus information gathered from the environment with response information gathered from physical movement (*psychomotor coding*). Some aspects of the environment stand out as more important than others, however, and some aspects of responding are more important than others. With each repetition of the task, the learner more effectively codes stimulus elements with response elements. Riding a bicycle, for example, will ultimately be learned by coding and integrating elemental acts into complex goal-directed patterns of movement.

During the initial phase of motor skill training, the learner must become aware of what goes with what; that is, what elements of the environment go with what behaviors. Psychomotor coding provides the learner with a representation of the stimulus-response relationships necessary for adaptive learning. The child on the bicycle quickly comes to realize that there are some aspects of the internal and external environment that are more important (more salient) than others. Motor learning involves the connection of stimulus (S) sets with appropriate motoric-response (R) sets. The emergence of some S-R codes can occur without conscious awareness; typists soon learn the location and arrangement of the keys without having to think about the location of each. This phenomenon is referred to as *implicit learning*, and it has been the focus of considerable research. (see box 2.4.) Learning can also occur consciously, or *explicitly*—for example, when the typist learns that a specific key performs a particular function (e.g., the delete key on the keyboard removes letters). These basic S-R codes play a critical role in determining how rapidly and efficiently behaviors can be performed.

BOX 2.4. Learning without Awareness

Amnesia is a disorder of memory in which knowledge is lost due to physical injury, disease, drug use, or psychological trauma. A classic example of amnesia produced by physical injury was Nick A., who had the misfortune of having a long, thin piece of metal pierce his nose and continue deep into his brain. Following the injury, Nick had great difficulty remembering previously learned information. He lost, for instance, his ability to name the ingredients required to bake a cake. Despite this loss of information, however, he retained the knowledge needed to make a cake. He could not remember what a cake was, but he could remember how to bake one (Zimbardo and Gerrig, 1999, p. 310).

The study of amnesia has led to a better understanding of human learning. Researchers have demonstrated that we acquire *explicit*, or declarative, knowledge about things and we acquire *implicit*, or procedural, knowledge about how to do things. One study found that amnesiac patients could acquire a novel reading skill but later not recall what the skill was or that they had practiced it (Cohen and Squire, 1980). It appears that some aspects of procedural knowledge, which dictates how to perform a skill, can be acquired without the learner's awareness.

Implicit learning occurs when complex information is acquired in an incidental manner; that is, without conscious awareness (Seger, 1994). It has been suggested that this form of learning has been important in human evolutionary history and probably preceded the human capacity to remember symbolic information. Procedural knowledge that is acquired in an incidental fashion is characterized by the long duration of its storage in memory. You may not, for example, have ridden a bicycle in years or even decades, but it all comes back as soon as you mount the bike. This type of enduring knowledge clearly has tremendous importance in many real-world situations.

The cognitive stage of skill acquisition is also characterized by the gradual emergence of *motor programs*, which are prestructured sets of commands that instruct the body to move in specified ways (see Magill, 1998; Proctor, Reeve, and Weeks, 1990; Schmidt, 1988; Schmidt and Lee, 1999; and Summer, 1989, for overviews). There are two reasons why the capacity to organize movement sequences prior to their activation is important to all skilled activities. First, many motor skills involve actions that occur far too rapidly for the individual to make use of the feedback produced by each response. Consider that it takes some amount of time to identify and respond to even the most simple event. Skilled action would be impossible if performers had to stop and consciously analyze the feedback for each response before preparing for the next one. Motor programs provide individuals with the capacity to coordinate and control the multitude of muscle groups that are needed for skilled action.

Central to the development of a motor program is the construction of a response template, which describes the patterns of action that each part of the body involved in performing the skill must take. The movements of muscle groups and limbs are programmed to follow specific parameters of action (force, amplitude, and duration). As actions are performed, comparisons between the targeted goal and actual performance are computed and used to update and refine the response template; thus, motor programs undergo constant revision, or tuning, as a skill is acquired and refined.

Motor programs are often described in terms of a hierarchy (Sage, 1984; Salmoni, 1989; Schmidt and Lee, 1999, chapter 6; Summer, 1989). Low-level programs control relatively limited response sequences. The central pattern generators motor programs described earlier in this chapter provide an example of such motor programs. They are involved in selecting and timing coordinated muscle movements. Higher-level programs deal with progressively more abstract aspects of action; some are goal directed. To achieve a desired goal, higher-level programs instruct lower-level programs to initiate action. Once initiated, long strings of successive movements can be run off to their completion with virtually no interference from higher-level programs. The number of responses that may be strung together can be quite impressive. In some highly predictable situations such as choreographed dancing, performers can execute very long sequences of coordinated movements.

Motor programs also provide learners with a general idea of how to perform a given task. The motor program developed by the novice cyclist, for example, will prepare him to ride not only his own bicycle, but other bicycles as well. Motor programs reflect the adaptive nature of learning; experiences result in relatively permanent changes in processing that provide the means by which past learning is applied to new situations.

The Associative Stage

With repeated *practice*, new patterns of responding emerge as effective actions are retained and ineffective actions are eliminated. Repetition and practice are central to the associative phase of skill learning. The novice bicycle rider, for example, begins to eliminate the inefficient movement patterns that characterize his early attempts at riding. He depends less on verbal instructions and the bonding of specific stimuli with specific responses and more on *proceduralization*; that is, using feedback to solidify the connections between stimulus conditions and patterns of movement. The learner thus increases his speed of action and makes fewer errors—key characteristics of skilled action.

The importance of practice to skill acquisition is unquestioned. Without it, motor skills simply will not be learned. Although there is no debate concerning the importance of repetition of the movement patterns that are involved in performing a given task, there is considerable debate concerning the manner in which practice should be carried out in order to optimize performance. Seven decades of research reveal that practice is a complex phenomenon whose effects on learning are anything but simple. There are several ways that practice can be arranged, or scheduled, and the effects that it has on learning depend on a number of factors (see Magill, 1998, chapter 6, for a summary of practice factors).

Practice schedules are typically arranged in terms of the amount of time (or number of trials) spent on performance and the amount of time between performances. *Massed* (continuous) practice is characterized by long training periods with few periods of rest. The training may extend from a few minutes to several hours; it may occur over few trials or over several hundred. *Distributed* (spaced) practice is characterized by rest periods that are longer than training periods.

Considerable research has been conducted to determine the type of practice schedule that is most efficient for learning motor skills. The results of these studies suggest that the effects of practice distribution depend not only on whether the task is discrete or continuous, but also on whether the effects of a particular schedule are assessed during practice trials or following a retention interval. (See box 2.5.) Despite the complexity involved in assessing schedules of practice, a few generalities can be derived from available laboratory studies. First, it appears that motor skill learning is enhanced by frequent training sessions of a short duration rather than a few training sessions of relatively long duration. Second, distributed practice is more efficient than massed practice when the physical demands of the tasks are high, when the task is complex, or when the learner's motivation is low.

**BOX 2.5. Assessing the Effects of Practice
on Motor Skill Performance and Learning**

Researchers who study skill development make clear distinctions between factors that produce relatively permanent changes in behavior (learning variables) and those factors that have only a transitory effect on behavior (performance variables). Learning is a term used to describe a process that occurs within the individual and cannot be measured directly. Researchers must rely on their observations of overt behavior as indirect indices of learning. Behavior is constantly influenced both by learning variables and performance variables. One of the challenges is to identify and isolate learning and performance variables and to evaluate the manner in which each type of variable affects behavior.

The permanence of skill training procedures is often measured in terms of the degree to which it is retained over time and the extent to which it transfers from one situation to another. *Retention tests* involve measuring performance before and after a delay in time. For example, an individual's performance is measured over a series of training sessions and measured again following a period in which there is no practice. The subject's performance during the retention test provides an index of the durability of training. *Transfer tests* measure the degree to which an individual's practice on one task improves (or interferes with) performance on another task (see Schmidt and Lee, 1999, chapter 14, for an overview).

Recently, researchers' interests have been piqued by the phenomenon of *contextual interference*, which suggests that a practice schedule resulting in less efficient performance and many errors during practice can produce better long-term learning than a practice schedule that results in good performance with relatively few errors. At the heart of the contextual interference effect is the observation that an individual who practices a variety of related skills learns more than an individual who practices a restricted number of skills during a given session (see Magill and Hall, 1990, for a review). For example, baseball players whose batting practices require them to hit fast balls, curves, and change-ups that are thrown in random order perform better in real game situations than players whose practices require them to hit fast balls on one day, curve balls on another, and change-ups on a third (Hall, Dominques, and Cavazos, 1994).

The basis for the contextual interference effect is not entirely understood and several theoretical explanations have been proposed. The effect, however, provides an opportunity to examine the critical role an individual's mental processing plays during the cognitive phase of skill acquisition. The requirements placed on novices during variable practice sessions are more dynamic and unpredictable and require more effortful attentional processing than practice sessions in which task demands are predictable and less mentally taxing. The generally accepted view is that a person learns not only from his or her successes but also by making mistakes; it appears to be supported by empirical research studies. Individuals who practice motor skills in a context that demands adaptation to changing environmental situations are able to transfer what they have learned during practice to new situations. Those who learn in static practice environments may perform well during practice sessions, but they perform poorly in new situations. (Recall those athletes who perform well in practice but who "choke up" during competition.) Practice conditions that are designed to be similar to the conditions of competition may produce effective transfer of knowledge from practice to test situations.

Another aspect of practice that has been studied extensively is the manner in which the task is presented to the novice. The *whole-task approach* involves having the learner perform all components of a task, from beginning to end, on each training trial. The young cyclist's teacher, for example, may ask him to perform the entire task of riding a bicycle all at once. The *part-task approach* involves breaking down the task into its components and teaching them separately. The cyclist may first be taught pedaling motions on a stationary bicycle and later to control the direction of the cycle by moving the handlebars. In general, whole-task training methods appear to be most beneficial when the task to be learned involves continuous movements. Part-task training is desirable when the task is complex and can be broken down into logical subcomponents (see Magill, 1998, chapter 6, and Proctor and Dutta, 1995, chapter 9, for overviews).

There is long-standing interest in whether *mental practice* can improve skill learning and facilitate physical performance. Mental practice, or covert rehearsal, is a symbolic rehearsal of a motor task without making any gross movements. Reviews of research that examined the role of mental rehearsal indicate that it does facilitate motor-skill learning (Feltz and Landers, 1983; Feltz, Landers, and Becker, 1988; Hinshaw, 1991–1992). Individuals who employ mental rehearsal techniques routinely perform laboratory tasks better than those who do not use rehearsal techniques, and the effects of mental practice are greater for tasks with large cognitive components. The reasons for these effects have not been established, however. The lack of a clear definition of what mental practice entails and the lack of reliable methods for assessing the effects of mental practice are reflected in a number of studies whose results are difficult to interpret (Swets and Bjork, 1990).

Mental rehearsal has been conjectured to play an important role during the cognitive phase of motor skill acquisition, when an individual develops a mental map or schema of the task to be learned (Schmidt and Lee, 1999, chapter 11). Theories that explain how mental rehearsal impacts skill learning tend to take one of two approaches: physiological or cognitive. Psychoneuromuscular theories typically evoke an *ideomotor principle* of skill learning, which can be traced back to the late 1800s (Carpenter, 1894). Central to this principle is the assumption that skill learning involves laying down neural pathways that control motor movements. Physical practice results in the excitation of neural pathways that are specific to a given motor movement; mental imagery can also excite these pathways. Excitation brought about by imagery is believed to reinforce neural pathways in the same manner as does physical practice. Early physiological research conducted by Jacobson (1929) supported the belief that muscle activation occurs in conjunction with mental ideation. Similar findings have been obtained in more recent research as well. Suinn (1980), for example, observed that electromyographic (EMG) recordings of downhill skiers' muscle activity changed as they imagined going through various turns and jumps that were part of a highly practiced race course.

Cognitive theories of mental imagery stress the role that memory, attention, and strategies play in learning skills. Mental rehearsal involves the retrieval and manipulation of information that is stored in memory. Some forms of information lend themselves to the creation of images, which can permit the learner to analyze the task repetitively under a variety of conditions. Imagery also provides the learner with a mechanism that enhances how new information is acquired and stored. With imagery, the components of a task can be broken into elements and analyzed from multiple perspectives. Verbal reports of performers indicate that most can control the perspective of the images they create. An image viewed from an external reference point allows the individual to visualize his or her performance as it is seen by someone in an audience. Such images provide for the basis of self-generated feedback similar to the type that would be provided by a coach or teacher. An image viewed from an internal reference point allows one to experience internal kinesthetic and proprioceptive cues that constitute feedback needed to modify the execution of movement programs. External and internal imagery is unique in that it permits learners to vary the speed of their movements, the timing of actions, and the integration of components of movements. It is assumed that all of these aspects of mental imagery can be brought to bear and used to enhance learning beyond that which can be achieved by physical practice alone (Suinn, 1993; Weinberg, 1981).

In all likelihood, both physiological and cognitive mechanisms play a role in determining the effectiveness of mental rehearsal in skill development. Further, the effect of mental rehearsal depends on a variety of factors (Murphy, 1994). The learner, for example, must be able employ imagery techniques. People differ in their ability to control images and the vividness of those images. Children's imagery, for example, differs from the imagery produced by adolescents or adults. The type of task being learned is also important. Mental rehearsal appears to play a greater role in the acquisition of skills that involve multiple steps and complex routines that can be broken down and analyzed, such as figure skating or playing musical instruments, than in simple skills that are characterized by strength and power output, such as weight lifting.

Repetition gradually leads to proceduralization, or increased organization of patterns of muscle movements that control more and more of the basic elements of action. These units of skill come to be proceduralized into holistic action that is hierarchical in nature (Anderson, 1983). The gross movements that characterized the novice cyclist's performance are gradually replaced by responses that are more efficient and lead to a better approximation of the rider's goal. As practice continues, the child begins to ride his bicycle much as he envisioned at the beginning of training.

The coding processes that resulted in the bonding of stimulus-response units during the cognitive phase decrease in importance. The learner no longer focuses on which stimuli go with what responses; during the associative phase the learner strengthens S-R units. Practice leads to a gradual solidification of S-R units which, as a result, can be called into action more quickly and lead to more accurate performance than that observed during the cognitive phase.

The Autonomous Stage

The final stage of skill development is characterized by behavior that is performed in a coordinated and smooth fashion. Many of the elements of behavior that initially required considerable conscious concentration come to be performed with less effort and thought. This shift is referred to as *automatization*. The skilled bicyclist begins to perform as he once imagined he would. He rides his bicycle on streets and sidewalks with complete control and confidence. As he rides, his eyes and ears are free to monitor the environment and he is able to respond to sudden changes that may materialize. He can talk with his friends or he can think about things other than controlling the bicycle. Many of the elemental units of behavior are executed in a *mindless,* habitual fashion. The repression of habits into the unconscious processes of the mind helps skilled performance because it provides the individual with greater opportunity to plan and execute complex sequences of behaviors. The selection of goal-directed behaviors requires mental effort and thought. The young boy may, after extensive training and practice, enter a bicycle race that will require him to use strategy and decision-making processes that involve *effortful* expenditure of mental energy, attention, and the engagement of *mindful behavior*.

Complex behaviors and skills are often described in terms of a hierarchy of habits that are organized through practice and experience (automatization). Motor skills are hypothesized to be initiated by high-level executive processors which oversee the activation of lower-level components. Skilled motor action comes about through the patterning and organization of components of generalized movement programs. Repetition and practice establish series of subroutines that become increasingly longer and which can be called upon and executed with less and less voluntary control (*mindless behavior*). Thus, training leads the pianist to organize patterns of finger movements that, when initiated, are run off to completion, much like a subroutine in a computer program. High-level conscious processing initiates low-level processes, which are run off automatically with little or no conscious awareness.

Considerable research has been conducted on the processes that underlie automatic processing and habit formation. Contemporary theorists have speculated about differences that exist between the *automatic* and *effortful* mental processing that occurs during the performance of a task (Schneider and Fisk, 1982; Schneider and Shiffrin, 1977; Shiffrin and Schneider, 1977). Automatic processing occurs rapidly, without conscious awareness and without intention. (See box 2.6.) Effortful processing occurs slowly, with awareness, and it draws on attentional resources. Automatic processes are of two types: innate and learned. Humans are born to attend automatically to certain types of stimuli (Hasher and Zacks, 1979). We tend to remember, for example, the location of objects without intending to do so. Most of us have experienced automatic memory for location when we take fill-in-the-blank tests. We may not be able to recall the correct information, but we can remember where on the page of text the answer can be found. No effort was made to remember the location of material on the page while studying for the exam; nevertheless, information about its location is stored in memory.

BOX 2.6. Automatic and Effortful Processing

The processes involved in identifying visual cues occur very rapidly, often without the observer's awareness that they are taking place. The selection of stimuli that will undergo analysis and the exclusion of other stimuli from analysis are guided by attentional processes. A series of important studies published by Schneider and Shiffrin (1977) demonstrated that speed of visual detection is influenced by attentional processing. In one of their studies, subjects performed a visual detection task in which they were to report when a specific target character (numbers or letters) appeared on a display amid distractors. Two training conditions were used: in one condition, both target characters and distractor characters were the same (e.g., all numbers or all letters); in the other condition, the target character differed from distractors (e.g., distractor numbers and a target letter). The number of characters on each display varied. Striking differences between the two conditions were found in the amount of time it took subjects to decide if a display included a target letter. When the stimuli were the same (i.e., all letters or all numbers), it took up to 400 milliseconds for observers to decide if target and distractor stimuli were different. The long decision time suggests that observers had to examine and compare each character in a frame before making a decision. On the other hand, when target and distractor stimuli were different, it required observers only 80 milliseconds, on average, to decide if target and distractor stimuli were different, regardless of the number of distractors. In this condition, observers could examine all characters at the same time, automatically. It took up to 400 milliseconds for observers to decide if target and distractor stimuli were different when the stimuli were the same (i.e., all letters or all numbers). The longer decision time occurred because observers had to examine each letter in a frame and compare them.

The distinction between automatic and effortful mental processing has had a marked impact on how researchers conceptualize the processes involved in skilled performance. Automatic processing underlies the development of habits, which are complex behaviors that are executed with minimum voluntary control. Once they are developed, habits are important because they can be performed without drawing on the individual's limited attentional resources. Performers are better able to focus attention on higher-level, goal-directed problems after basic routines of a skill are established. Thus, the basketball player does not have to think about dribbling the ball; that behavior is performed without conscious awareness. Habits are seen as a desirable product of training, and many coaches and teachers strive to establish in their trainees the habits central to performing particular skills.

Learned automatic processing comes about through practice, and it occurs most rapidly when there is a consistent relation between the stimuli that are part of a task and the responses that are required to perform it. Typing, for instance, is a task in which the position of the keys and the responses to be made to them are *consistently mapped*; that is, there is a close correspondence between stimulus and response codes. The typist develops specific motor movements that are linked to a specific cue. Training results in the association and storage of stimulus-response units that can be retrieved very rapidly from long-term memory. Once the finger movements that are involved in performing the mechanics of typing are initiated, they occur without further assistance from higher-level mental processes. Highly skilled typists are able to transcribe words quickly and accurately.

Automatic habits are performed most efficiently when left to run on their own. Indeed, there are times when an athlete's performance deteriorates because he or she begins to think too much about habits that are usually performed without thought. Expert golfers have reported that their putting performance declines when they think too much about the mechanics of swinging the putter. The phrase "paralysis by analysis" is sometimes used to explain what happens when someone "chokes" in this manner; that is, when high-level thought processes interfere with the timing and execution of highly practiced, well-learned behaviors.

Once developed, automatic behaviors can be executed without drawing on the performer's limited attentional resources. The belief is that after the basic routines of a skill are established, the performer is better able to focus attention on higher-level, goal-directed problems (*effortful* and *mindful* behavior). Global mental processes, such as those involved in metacognition, are critical for planning actions and in interpreting the consequences of movements.

The amount of effort and attention that an individual places on preplanning actions is known to have a marked impact on the level of skill that is displayed. Mental rehearsal is often used by performers to prepare themselves to execute well-learned skills. Many highly skilled individuals consider mental rehearsal to be vital to their optimal performance. Olympic-level high jumpers, for example, have often been observed waiting prior to their jumps, apparently going through the jump in their minds before the attempt is made. For decades, coaches and sport psychologists have stressed the importance of thinking it through before initiating physical action. Basketball players are instructed to visualize the flight of the ball and to see it go through the hoop before shooting a free throw. Golfers are urged to imagine the ball crossing the green and dropping into the hole before attempting to putt. Indeed, many coaches place great store on the mental side of performance and suggest that performance is "90 percent mental and 10 percent physical."

Much has been made of the benefits of mental rehearsal and preparatory imagery on the performance of motor skills. Many books describe various psychological intervention programs. These mental training programs typically offer readers a menu of such techniques as attentional focusing, relaxation, cognitive restructuring, imagery, goal setting, and even self-hypnosis (Hardy, Jones, and Gould, 1997).

Mental rehearsal appears to play an important role during both the cognitive phase and the autonomous phase of skill acquisition. It influences skillful performance during the autonomous phase in a variety of ways, some of which include:

1) *Response accommodation*: Mental rehearsal can provide a performer with a way to match his or her skills to actual performance conditions. A boxer may rehearse how he will respond to the tactics used by a specific opponent. A tennis player may imagine how she will adjust her game strategy to accommodate wind and weather conditions.

2) *Attentional focus*: Imagery and rehearsal lead the performer to shift his or her attention to the task to be performed. Concentration on task-relevant aspects of performance reduces the probability of dwelling on irrelevant and potentially distracting thoughts. Many sports, such as springboard and platform diving, require that athletes wait their turn. Mental rehearsal of the task to be performed provides the athlete with a method of filling in the time in task-appropriate ways. When attention is directed toward creating images of failure outcomes, performance has been shown to deteriorate. When attention is directed toward creating successful outcomes, performance is enhanced (Woolfork, Parrish, and Murphy, 1985).

3) *Arousal modulation*: Mental rehearsal can be used to elicit and maintain levels of physiological and psychological arousal that are needed to match the demands of a given task. Some events, like wrestling, demand the mobilization and control of high levels of energy; other events, like tennis, require that energy resources be available over a relatively long period. Mental images of performance may facilitate task-appropriate levels of arousal.

4) *Motivation*: Imagery can be used to reinforce goals established by the performer. A concert-level pianist may see herself receiving applause from an audience, and the image of winning an Olympic medal is a powerful motivator for some athletes (Pavio, 1985).

Metacognition also serves to monitor discrepancies between desired and actual performance, thus playing a key role in the interpretation of the consequences of movements. A comparative *transformational process* utilizes feedback obtained from behavioral action to identify mistakes and to determine strategies for correcting errors (Bandura, 1997, p. 372). Transformational processing assists in the self-correcting refinement of the subcomponents of skills. Discrepancies between desired and actual behaviors are evaluated, and attention can be focused on aspects of behavior that need to be modified in order to perform at a desired level of proficiency.

Despite the fact that people commonly report qualitative changes in the way that they use skills to perform tasks, relatively few research studies have examined how information processing changes with extended practice. The lack of research data is due primarily to the difficulty of studying changes in performance over long periods of time (Ericsson, 1996). As will be discussed in later chapters, expertise within a given domain typically follows a 10-year rule; that is, about 10 years of serious practice is required before expert levels of performance are reached. Nevertheless, the final stage of motor skill development appears to be one in which the learner goes beyond simply producing and controlling motor movements; he or she begins to see unique relationships between actions and their outcomes.

Motor Abilities

Motor abilities have been conceptualized as the building blocks of motor skill development. The extent to which you can learn to perform a given task depends on the presence of genetically linked underlying general capacities. The level of expertise developed by an archer, for example, is determined in part by a specific constellation of basic abilities. The basic abilities required for archery may be similar to those required for other tasks as well (e.g., throwing darts, playing video games, shooting rifles or pistols). On the other hand, the basic abilities required to become a proficient archer may be quite different from those required to be a skilled wrestler. The expertise required of a skilled wrestler is related to a different set or constellation of general abilities.

Motor skill researchers make clear distinctions between *motor skills*, which are specific to a given task, and *motor abilities*, which are general capacities for performance that are related to the demands of a variety of tasks (Magill, 1998, p. 276). Considerable research has focused on the identification and measurement of abilities. The vast majority of this work has involved the development of standardized tests designed to be administered to large numbers of individuals. Perhaps the most well-known research conducted on individual differences in motor abilities was performed for the United States military by Edwin Fleishman. On the basis of thousands of assessments of military personnel, Fleishman developed a classification system of motor abilities that identifies those believed to underlie complex skills (Fleishman and Quaintance, 1984). Table 2.1 lists 11 perceptual-motor abilities and table 2.2 lists 9 physical-proficiency abilities.

Task Types

Researchers who study motor skills have proposed several different classification schemes. These systems reflect various approaches that dominated the theoretical orientation of researchers during given periods. Considerable research conducted from the 1940s to the 1960s, for example, employed a *task-orientation* approach to skill learning. Researchers wanted to know how a particular task was learned and how the performance of that task was influenced by various factors. The popularity of this approach was driven primarily by practical concerns. Much of the early funding for basic research on

Table 2.1
Psychomotor Factors

1. *Multilimb coordination:* The ability to coordinate the movement of a number of limbs simultaneously
2. *Control precision:* The ability to make highly controlled and precise muscular adjustments where larger muscle groups are involved
3. *Response orientation:* The ability to determine and select rapidly just when and where a particular response should be made
4. *Reaction time:* The ability to respond rapidly to a stimulus when it appears
5. *Speed of arm movement:* The ability to make gross, rapid arm movements
6. *Rate control:* The ability to change the speed and direction of responses with precise timing
7. *Manual dexterity:* The ability to make skillful, well-directed arm-hand movements that are involved in manipulating objects under speed conditions
8. *Finger dexterity:* The ability to perform skillful, highly controlled manipulations of tiny objects involving primarily the fingers
9. *Arm-hand steadiness:* The ability to make precise arm-hand positioning movements where strength and speed are minimally involved.
10. *Wrist, finger speed:* The ability to move the wrist and fingers rapidly, as in a tapping task
11. *Aiming:* The ability to aim precisely at a small object in space

Reproduced from Fleishman, E. A., & Quaintance, M. K. (1984). *Taxonomies of human performance: The description of human tasks.* Potomac, MD: Management Research Institute, with permission of the author and publisher.

Table 2.2
Physical Proficiency Factors

1. Static strength: The maximum force that can be exerted against external objects
2. Dynamic strength: The muscular endurance in exerting force repeatedly
3. Explosive strength: The ability to mobilize energy effectively for bursts of muscular effort
4. Trunk strength: The strength of the trunk muscles
5. Extent flexibility: The ability to flex or stretch the trunk and back muscles
6. Dynamic flexibility: The ability to make repeated, rapid trunk flexing movements
7. Gross body coordination: The ability to coordinate the action of several parts of the body while the body is in motion
8. Gross body equilibrium: The ability to maintain balance without visual cues
9. Stamina: The capacity to sustain maximum effort requiring cardiovascular effort

Reproduced from Fleishman, E. A., & Quaintance, M. K. (1984). *Taxonomies of human performance: The description of human tasks.* Potomac, MD: Management Research Institute, with permission of the author and publisher.

motor skill learning in the United States and Great Britain was funded by the military. Military personnel were required to learn and perform very specific tasks under extreme conditions. Consider the plight of the World War II bombardier who, after sitting virtually immobile for hours in freezing cold conditions, found himself in the midst of a squadron of enemy fighter planes or a frightening anti-aircraft barrage. The bombardier had to use a visual sighting device to help him calculate the precise time to release the armaments he controlled. Those who enlisted in the military were trained to perform many tasks that were, to them, strange and novel. Researchers examined these tasks to determine how the specific skills needed to perform them might best be taught.

One way to classify motor tasks is to group them on the basis of environmental conditions. Motor tasks, for example, have been categorized in terms of the degree to which they are *closed* or *open*. A *closed task* is performed under conditions that are highly predictable. Throwing darts, for example, is typically performed in a highly stable environment. The distance from the board to the throwing line and the distance from the center of the target to the floor are standardized. The size of the target and the arrangement of various zones are also standardized. Even the darts themselves are typically matched in weight, composition, and aerodynamics. In a game of darts, each response can be planned in advance, some time prior to throwing the dart. An *open task*, on the other hand, is performed under conditions that are constantly changing in ways that make it very difficult to plan a response. Kayaking down a turbulent mountain stream, for example, requires constant adaptation to changes in water speed and obstacles in the water. A successful kayaker must be able to respond to rapid environmental changes by just as rapidly selecting and deploying specific paddling techniques.

Personality

A general observation is that some people seem to fit some skills better than other skills. It has been suggested that the characteristics associated with long-distance races may be best suited for those who prefer an introverted, solitary life. Team sports may be ideal for those who are extroverted and have gregarious, social, outgoing lifestyles. Observations such as these assume that a relationship exists between personality and performance. *Personality* is defined as "the complex set of unique psychological qualities that influence an individual's characteristic patterns of behavior across different situations and over time" (Zimbardo and Gerrig, 1999, p. 543).

Psychologists study personality in a variety of ways. The approach that is used most by researchers of motor skill learning involves using standardized psychological tests to measure personality characteristics. Hundreds of studies have assessed the relation between personality characteristics and

such variables as general participation in sport, motor ability, and elite athletic skills. These studies, in general, have found that personality does play
a role in skill acquisition and performance; however, the degree of involvement is not clear, and it is clearly task dependent. (The role that personality
factors play in skill development is addressed in greater detail in later chapters.)

THEORIES OF MOTOR SKILL

Some scientists are interested not only in describing how motor skill develops but also in explaining why behavior changes as it does. Since the late
1960s, major motor learning theories have tended to follow three explanatory
trends: 1) closed-loop theory, 2) schema theory, 3) and dynamical action theory. At this time, no one theory of motor learning has emerged that can completely explain how skills are learned. A brief overview of each of the major
types of theories is designed to provide the reader an introduction to issues
and assumptions that are central to contemporary research in motor skill
learning.

Closed-Loop Theory

Theories of this type tend to focus on why we become more accurate in
moving our bodies to attain certain goals. Consider the processes involved in
learning to throw darts to the bull's-eye of a dart board. The movements of
throwing a dart are accompanied with information concerning the accuracy of
the throw. The proprioceptive and visual feedback that are associated by cues
linked to each movement provide the thrower with information that can be
used to modify any discrepancy (error) between desired and actual dart
throws.

Jack Adams (1971, 1976) developed an influential theory of motor learning
that focused on linear-positioning responses—movements that can be influenced by knowledge of results and feedback information. He proposed that
motor learning is the result of two interactive memory states. The first memory
state is a *perceptual trace*, which is developed as the result of body-positioning
movement. The movement of the dart-thrower's arm, wrist, and fingers, for example, lays down a trace within the central nervous system. As every dart
throw will lay down its own trace, practice results in amassing a collection of
traces. The differences that exist among these perceptual traces may change
when the dart thrower employs motion-produced and visual feedback to guide
his throws. Feedback, according to Adams's theory, is fundamental to improvement in skilled behavior. Increases in skill represent the gradual strengthening
of response-specific perceptual traces. The second memory state is a *memory
trace*, which governs the selection of specific behaviors from the collection of

perceptual traces that have accumulated as a function of practice. Learning progresses as the memory trace initiates action and the perceptual trace modifies action on the basis of analysis of the difference that exists between preferred and actual behavioral outcomes.

Schema Theory

Several theories have focused on how people learn motor skills that are executed under variable and changing conditions. Richard Schmidt (1975) introduced a theory of motor skill learning that is based on the concept of the *schema*, which, as described earlier in this chapter, refers to a generalized way of organizing thoughts and behaviors. Many complex human activities involve the development and use of mental maps to organize the relationships that exist between action and outcomes. Schemas provide a method of aggregating our knowledge to help us respond in an adaptive and goal-oriented fashion.

Schmidt hypothesizes that motor learning is an ongoing process in which the selection and execution of behaviors within a given context depends on a number of factors. The flow diagram presented in figure 2.7 describes a central motor response schema and how it is influenced by initial task conditions, actions that are taken, and the consequences of those actions. Goal-oriented movements such as a gymnast's balance-beam routine involve a blend of movements—some of which are executed rapidly, while others are executed slowly. The gymnast begins her balance-beam routine by selecting generalized movement programs that she acquired from previous practice sessions. Her training provides information about the relations that exist among various possible actions and their outcomes. She employs a *recall schema* to plan and initiate action. Her generalized actions are governed by movement parameters such as the selection of muscle groups, the force and duration of muscle contraction, and the spatial location of her body segments. These movement parameters play an important role in the execution of fast, ballistic movements that occur far too rapidly to be controlled by visual or proprioceptive feedback. Once the generalized motor program is initiated, it provides a variety of sensory input that provides the means to match her desired and actual performance. The gymnast employs a *recognition schema* to compare the actual and expected consequences of her actions. Motor learning, from Schmidt's perspective, is based on rules that are generated from the movement of muscles, the sensory experiences that accompany both ballistic and slow movements, and the evaluation of the degree to which those movements lead to desired goals.

The advantage of the schema construct is that it explains how we can apply what we have learned in one situation to new situations and tasks. Thus, the skills we learned in order to drive a car will transfer readily if we are faced with the task of driving a truck.

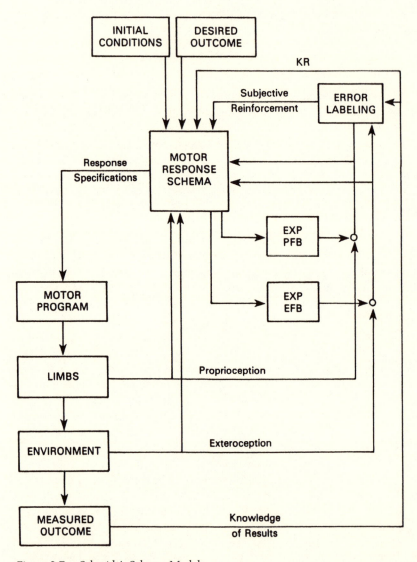

Figure 2.7.   Schmidt's Schema Model
From "A schema theory of discrete motor skill learning," by R. A. Schmidt, 1975, *Psychological Review, 82,* p. 238. Copyright 1975 by the American Psychological Association. Reprinted with permission of the author.

Dynamical Action Theory

An assumption central to both closed-loop and schema theories is that a motor program of some type is represented within the central nervous system and that it controls human movement. Dynamical action theory differs in that it assumes that motor movements are regulated by an on-line interaction between environmental forces and the physical architecture of the human body. Movements, even those that may appear simple (such as reaching for a cup of coffee), are extremely complex. The human body is composed of multiple segments, each of which contains skeletal bones, muscles, and joints. Picking up a coffee cup requires that a multitude of possible movements that segments of the body are capable of making are brought under volitional control and coordinated.

Proponents of dynamical motor learning theories focus on the way that groups of muscles are constrained to act together as part of a complete system. Human action is hypothesized to be constrained at several levels of analysis: 1) the physical laws that govern the movement of objects in motion also govern or constrain the movement of the human body, 2) our intentions to move in a goal-directed fashion are cognitively constrained, 3) the activation of muscles is constrained by neural and metabolic factors, and 4) the manner in which we move is constrained by perceptual factors (Schmidt and Fitzpatrick, 1996).

Karl Newell's (1991; Newell and McDonald, 1992) theory of motor skill emphasizes the role of a *perceptual-motor workspace* that serves as an interface between the individual and his environment. Within this workspace reside the perceptions that define task characteristics and the motor responses that correspond to the task performance. When faced with executing a previously learned task, the demands of the task map closely onto or line up with corresponding motor actions. The degree to which there is a close mapping or lack of overlay will determine the speed and accuracy of movement. When a new task is presented, however, the individual is driven to search his perceptual-motor workspace in order to find solutions that are optimal to performing the task. The search is guided and facilitated by extracting behavioral information from the properties of the environment. Visual and sensory feedback created while actions are underway and immediately after the response has been completed affect or alter the perceptual-motor workspace. Instructional information can also be provided that influences the learner's solution regarding how to perform the task. Practice helps the learner understand the properties of the task, and the layout of the perceptual-motor workspace is the framework through which that understanding is achieved. Skill learning, from this perspective, is a form of problem solving in which the learner actively explores and alters the perceptual-motor workspace until a solution is attained.

CHAPTER SUMMARY

The machinery of the human body represents a remarkable piece of biological engineering. Human action reflects the result of an exquisite orchestration of movements of muscles, tendons, and bone. In this chapter we have seen that even the simplest of actions involves the organization and integrated control of multiple systems. The brain, with its billions of cells, is designed to direct physical movement in an efficient and orderly manner. How the brain controls movement is directly influenced by individual experience. Our bodies are constantly undergoing modification as we learn to adapt to an ever changing world. The finely executed actions of elite performers reflect both evolutionary and learning processes. Scientists will continue to postulate and refine theories and explanations for skilled motor behavior.

SUGGESTED READINGS

Druckman, D., and Bjork, R. A. (Eds.). (1991). *In the mind's eye: Enhancing human performance*. Washington, DC: National Academy Press.

Haywood, K. M. (1993). *Life span motor development*. Champaign, IL: Human Kinetics.

Latash, M. L. (1998). *Neurophysiological basis of movement*. Champaign, IL: Human Kinetics.

Leonard, C. T. (1998). *The neuroscience of human movement*. New York: Mosby.

Levinthal, C. F. (1990). *Introduction to physiological psychology* (3rd ed.). Englewood Cliffs, NJ: Prentice-Hall.

Magill, R. A. (1998). *Motor learning: Concepts and applications* (5th ed.). Boston, MA: McGraw-Hill.

Rosenbaum, D. A. (1991). *Human motor control*. New York: Academic Press.

Schmidt, R. A., and Lee, T. D. (1999). *Motor control and learning: A behavioral emphasis* (3rd ed.). Champaign, IL: Human Kinetics.

Chapter 3

Cognitive Skills

Television game shows are popular throughout the world. Their winners often excel at coming up with correct answers more rapidly than their opponents. The popular game show *Jeopardy!* involves testing how quickly contestants can answer questions in a specific knowledge category. If, for example, the category is *Rivers*, how quickly can you name a river in Brazil? Playing such games successfully requires keen mental or cognitive skills. A player must be both knowledgeable of the topic and able to retrieve the information rapidly. Similarly, the success or failure of many athletes depends on their cognitive skills. Athletes are often required to quickly decide precisely when and how to act. A hockey player, for example, must read his opponents' positions and select just the right time to take his shot at the goal. A golfer prepares his swing to compensate for wind factors and hazards built into the fairway. Skilled performance demands not only a well-trained body, but also a well-trained mind. This chapter builds on the motor skill information presented in chapter 2 and describes how cognitive skills are learned.

THE STUDY OF COGNITIVE SKILLS

The evolutionary success of humankind is attributed to our abilities to think, communicate, and solve problems. The notion that knowledge is power emerged early in the history of our species. We alone among the animals of the world have the unique capacity to use our experiences to modify both the way we act and the environment in which we live. Our minds evolved along with the bodies, helping us adapt to an ever-changing and sometime hostile world (see Mithen, 1996, for an overview of the evolution of the mind).

There has been an interest in *epistemology* (the study of the acquisition of knowledge) since the time of the ancient Greeks. Aristotle proposed in the fourth century B.C. that all objects in nature possess force and emit *eideola*, a type of energy. People who looked at any object were believed to be affected by its energy. Aristotle believed that the eyes literally captured the energy, which was then sent inward into the body, where it served as the basis for knowledge. At the most basic level, knowing was thought to come from sensing the world around us. Indeed, the word *eideola* serves as the basis for the modern word *idea*. We gain knowledge of the world around us by way of our sensory systems. To Aristotle, the memory of an object, a person, or a concept reflected the length of time an *eideola* stayed in the mind and interacted with others that had already been impressed into memory (Hergenhahn, 1992, p. 44).

Psychology, as an area of study within universities, began in the late nineteenth century. Research laboratories opened in Europe and North America, providing students an opportunity to study the processes of the mind. The guiding assumption of much early psychological research was that mental activity could be understood through the application of the principles of the scientific method. The belief that the universe and all things in it, including humans, behave in a mechanical, deterministic way was at the center of the emergence of modern psychology. Participants in the first meeting the American Psychological Association, held in 1892, were of the opinion that the new field of study should be one that focused primarily on conducting basic research regarding how the mind operates. The application of psychological knowledge to clinical populations and the general public was a secondary interest.

The Study of Memory

Although philosophers pondered issues related to the acquisition of knowledge for centuries, it was not until the late nineteenth century that laboratory-based methods were developed to investigate the phenomenon. Hermann Ebbinghaus (1850–1909) is credited with devising the first techniques to measure human memory. He evaluated the basic properties of memory under controlled experimental conditions. In his studies, a research participant was shown a series of words one by one. At the end of the list the subject was asked to recall all the words in the list. Typically, the subject required more than one presentation of the word list before showing perfect performance, which was Ebbinghaus's definition of learning. This relatively simple technique allowed him to study in a quantitative fashion many factors that are related to learning.

The methods developed by Ebbinghaus served for decades as the nucleus of research conducted by psychologists who studied verbal learning. Both basic and applied researchers were interested in understanding the learning process and identifying factors that influence the learning curve. Basic researchers often focused on the development of theories of learning, whereas applied researchers were interested in the implications of these theories to education. The public education system in the United States was formally instituted in the early twentieth century, and thousands of teachers were being trained to teach children. The methods of instruction that emerged in the early decades of the educational movement and continued through the 1960s reflected the widely held notion that repetition and practice were central to learning. Great importance was given to associative memory and the acquisition of elementary units of knowledge basic to higher mental functions, such as thinking and problem solving.

The Study of Information Processing

Research conducted by verbal learning psychologists provided vital information concerning the factors that determine the retention of information. More recently, cognitive psychologists have focused not only on how information is stored but also on how it is processed and manipulated. The information-processing model introduced heralded a major shift in the manner in which psychologists viewed the workings of the mind. Cognitive psychology focused not only on the basic mechanisms of memory, but also on how humans use stored information to think through and solve problems. Numerous theories of memory and information processing have been proposed over the past 4 decades; some of them stress neurophysiological explanations.

THE NEUROPHYSIOLOGY OF COGNITIVE SKILLS

Even in prehistoric times, the brain was seen as the residence of reasoning, problem solving, and emotion. Observations of behaviors before and after brain injury, and personal experiences with wine, beer, and other mind-altering chemical substances, led most to believe that the brain was the place where thoughts, dreams, and actions originated. The focus on the the brain and properties of the brain and their ability to explain behavior, both normal and abnormal, accelerated rapidly since the scientific revolution of the seventeenth and eighteenth centuries. The real breakthroughs in understanding the role of brain structures in human behavior have taken placed only in the past few decades, however.

Structures of Cognition

Attempts to understand the physiological basis of mental processes have led researchers in psychology, neuroscience, and education to focus their attention on structures of the brain, particularly the *neocortex* and its control of subcortical structures. (See figure 3.1.) Of central importance is the study of the hierarchical organization of the brain and how brain systems work together to control sensation, perception, thought, and action.

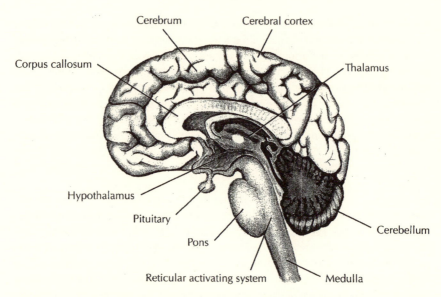

Figure 3.1.   The Neocortex and Major Structures of the Human Brain
From Allyn & Bacon, *Transparency Package to accompany Gerrig and Zimbardo,* Psychology and Life. Reprinted by permission by Allyn & Bacon.

Sensory Systems

Humans have evolved numerous biological sensing devices, or *receptors*, that gather information about the status of events both inside and outside the body. These receptors transmit information to the brain via *affector* neural pathways. This neural information is routed through the brain, with each sensory receptor passing information along very specific pathways. The auditory, visual, and olfactory receptor systems gather information about events that occur some distance from the body; cutaneous receptors in the skin and taste receptors in the tongue gather information about events that come into direct contact with the body; kinesthetic sense receptors located in muscles, joints, and tendons gather information about body movement and position; and vestibular receptors in the inner ear gather data concerning the position of the body relative to the outside world. The human brain evolved over millennia to use the combined input of multiple receptor systems to prepare the body to respond to and interact with the world in which it exists.

The biochemical information that is relayed from sensory receptors to the brain gives rise to *sensation*, an elementary experience of conditions inside or outside the body. The manner in which receptor mechanisms transform raw physical information into biochemical signals that produce psychological experiences has fascinated philosophers and scientists for centuries. A significant amount of experimental research has been conducted for over a century on the physiology of the sensory systems. The physical mechanisms that are responsible for *transduction* (the conversion of physical energy into biochemical neural energy) are fairly well known. Less well understood is how changes in physical processes in the brain give rise to psychological sensory experiences. Brain systems provide humans with the capacity to sense the differences in the quality of a stimulus. Most people, for example, can tell the difference between the visual stimulation that produces a sense of the color red and the stimulation that produces a sense of the color green. The brain also provides us with the capacity to sense differences in the quantity of a stimulus; for example, telling the difference between visual sensory stimulation that gives rise to the sensation of a bright red color as opposed to the sensation of a faded red color.

Psychophysics is a branch of psychology that focuses on the structure and operation of sensory systems. Psychophysics researchers provide fascinating explanations regarding physical energy and how it is converted into the biochemical data that underlies all mental activity. The receptor structures and neural pathways to the brain of each sensory system have been studied extensively, and they provide neuropsychologists with an understanding of the basic architecture of the brain (see Schiffman, 2000, for an overview). Some cognitive psychologists describe sensory receptors as essentially input devices that operate in much the same way that a computer keyboard receives information from the user and sends it to a buffer where, in turn, the incoming stream of information is organized, coded, and sent on to the central processor. The operation of a few of these systems is important to understanding the various types of cognitive skills discussed later in this and other chapters.

The *visual system* has received the most attention of sensory physiologists. The eye is designed to detect specific wavelengths of the electromagnetic energy that constantly bombard our bodies. The *visual spectrum* is a band of energy that stimulates specialized *photoreceptor* cells (termed *rods* and *cones*) that are located in the *retina*, an area of specialized cells at the back of each eyeball. These receptors are sensitive to the light waves that enter the front of the eye through the pupil. When triggered, individual receptor cells transform the physical light energy into neural energy, which is organized by specialized cells in the retina into coded biological data that can be used and interpreted by the brain; e.g., the size, shape, and distance of an object. Visual information is routed via the *optic nerve* to the *optic chiasma*, where optic fibers separate and take two different paths. About 20 percent of the optic fibers proceed to the *superior colliculus*, an area in the brain stem that plays a significant role in controlling orienting reflexes of the eyes, ears, and head toward the source of stimulation. The remaining 80 percent of the optic fibers project to the *thalamus* which, in turn, routes fibers to the *primary visual cortex* located in the *occipital lobe* of the brain.

The sense of hearing is based on the operation of a complex *auditory system* of bones and receptor cells located within the inner ear. Sound is experienced when waves of air pressure flow down the auditory canal and initiate displacement movements of the eardrum (*tympanic membrane*). The movements that are produced are, in turn, transferred to the inner ear by a series of small bones (*ossicles*), and on to a fluid-filled organ called the *cochlea*. The cochlea contains hair cells that are responsible for converting physical energy into neural energy. These hair cells are extremely sensitive; a movement of only 1–100 picometers (trillionths of a meter) is required for some hair cells to activate. The neural activity generated by the hair cells is transported via the *cochlear nerve*, a branch of the *auditory nerve*, to the *inferior colliculus*. From the inferior colliculus, which is located in the brain stem, the activity travels to the thalamus, which routes the information to the *primary auditory cortex* of the *temporal lobes*. Along the way, auditory information is also relayed to the cerebellum and to the reticular activating system.

The *vestibular sensory system* tracks the position of the body, especially the head, and its orientation to the world around it. The vestibular system does not generate a specific sensation in the way visual stimulation produces the sensation of light or auditory stimulation produces the sensation of sound. It does, however, play a role in the control of posture, head movements, eye movements, and balance. The vestibular system is composed of several fluid-filled sacs and canals located within the inner ear. The movement of the head changes fluid flow within the *crista*, which bends hair cells that transform physical energy into neural energy. The information generated by the hair cells is transported by way of the vestibular nerve to the thalamus, where it is routed to the *temporal cortex*, as well as to the cerebellum and spinal cord.

Sensory systems have two roles. First, they provide the central nervous system with information that is necessary to perform low-level, bottom-up reflexive actions; second, they provide the neocortex of the brain with elementary information that is used to perform high-level, top-down mental processes. The dynamic interaction between bottom-up and top-down processes is central to most neurophysiological explanations of how motor and cognitive skills are learned, performed, and maintained (see Posner and Raichle, 1997, for an overview). Understanding how bottom-up and top-down processes interface in the brain can best be achieved by discussing the role of the thalamus as the ultimate switchboard of the brain.

Located centrally in the brain, the thalamus serves as the focal point for most of the sensory systems of the body. The thalamus is composed of a series of separate nuclei that perform several important functions. The first function is to route incoming afferent information to various areas of the brain. The second function of the thalamus is to integrate incoming information. The data that converge from multiple sources undergo the first of several analyses that will eventually lead to the human experience of conscious awareness and thought.

It is within the thalamus that raw sensory input begins to take on the characteristics of *perception*, which is the identification, interpretation, integration, and classification of sensory experiences (Zimbardo and Gerrig, 1999). Visual information, for example, is analyzed and separated in terms of both its pattern and its location and sent to different areas of the neocortex (see Rock, 1984, for an overview). Somatosensory input is analyzed and separated into *percepts*, which give rise to our psychological experiences of warmth, cold, pressure, and pain. The third function of the thalamus lies in its connections to brain structures that are involved in emotion. Projections from the thalamus enter into systems which modulate arousal, motivation, and emotional behavior. The separation of sensory inputs by the thalamus gives rise to perceptions of stimuli as being pleasant or unpleasant. (More will be said about the neurophysiology of motivation and emotion in the next chapter.)

Neural Communication

The description of how neural information is transported from one point in the body to another has been limited to discussion of the interrelation among nerve tracts and fibers. To truly understand the neurophysiology of skill, however, a more detailed examination of the structure and function of individual *neurons* that make up nerves is necessary.

The Nerve Cell

Neurons are specialized cells that are designed to receive, process, and transmit information to other cells in the human body. Over 200 different types of neurons have been identified in the mammalian brain; these cells differ in size, shape, and function. Regardless of the type of neuron, however, all possess similar structural characteristics. The neuron depicted in figure 3.2 shows these common structures. The cell body, or *soma*, contains a *nucleus*, which maintains myriad biochemical processes that take place within the cell and its surface membrane. The neuron is truly an incredible piece of biological engineering when one considers the sheer number of processes that occur when a cell transmits information. The nucleus maintains the energy needed for the cell to live and to perform various protein-based operations that regulate the way the cell functions. *Dendrites* are somatic extensions that receive incoming neural information. The surface of the dendrites and the cell body are sensitive to neurochemicals that stimulate specific types of molecules embedded in the membrane. The *axon* is a tubelike channel that extends from the cell body to the *axon terminals*. Information moves along neural axons, which range in length from less than a millimeter to as much as a meter. The axons of some types of neurons are surrounded by *myelin*, which increases the speed at which information is transmitted down its length. The *synaptic end bulbs* contain vesicles that hold neurochemicals used to transmit information from one cell to the next.

Neurons operate on the basis of biochemical and electrical changes that occur on and within the cell. When a neuron is not active, it maintains an electrical

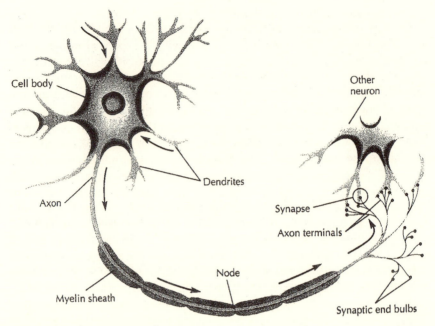

Figure 3.2.   The Structures of a Neuron
From Allyn & Bacon, *Transparency Package to accompany Gerrig and Zimbardo,* Psychology and Life. Reprinted by permission by Allyn & Bacon.

charge, much like the charge that is ready and available in a battery that is not in use. The bioelectrical state of a neuron is altered when its dendrites and soma are stimulated.

The neuron shown at the right of figure 3.2 is depicted with its dendrites and soma being stimulated by the terminal buttons of another neuron. Neural stimulation is of two types: *inhibitory* stimulation produces a bioelectrical potential that makes a neuron less capable of transmitting information; *excitatory* stimulation changes the biochemical state of the soma, making it more capable of transmitting information. A neuron receives both inhibitory and excitatory stimulation from 1,000 to 100,000 other neurons; it is the relative balance of the inhibitory and excitatory processes that determines the bioelectrical state of the soma at any given moment. When excitatory stimulation reaches a particular threshold, multiple processes begin to take place very rapidly within the cell. The neuron is not unlike a bullet resting in the chamber of a rifle. When a bullet is activated by the pressure of the firing pin, an explosion occurs within the casing of the shell that propels the bullet down the length of the barrel. When a neuron is activated, a controlled explosion occurs that sends a bioelectrical charge down the length of the axon. The rate of conduction is determined by the width of the axon and whether or not the axon is myelinated. Axons coated with myelin transmit bioelectrical activity much more rapidly than non-myelinated axons—some as fast as 200 meters per second.

Synaptic Transmission

When the bioelectrical surge arrives at the terminal buttons of the neuron, it causes the vesicles located there to migrate toward the cell membrane and rupture. The vesicles contain *neurotransmitter* molecules that flow out from the neuron into the *synaptic cleft*, a small gap between the terminal buttons of one neuron and the dendrites and soma of another. Neurons do not physically touch each other. Communication between them takes place by means of *synaptic transmission*—the flow of biochemical substances from the terminal buttons of a *presynaptic* neuron, across an extracellular space, to the dendrite surface of a *postsynaptic* neuron. Neurotransmitters function like molecular keys that fit into molecular locks, or receptors, located on the dendrites and soma of a neuron. When the appropriately shaped molecule fits into the receptor, it either inhibits or excites the neuron. Once finished, the neurotransmitter releases from its receptor and drifts back into the synaptic cleft, where it is either decomposed or absorbed back into the presynaptic neuron to be used again later. At a very fundamental level, all thought, feeling, movement, and behavior are the result of synaptic activity.

It is hypothesized that over 60 biochemical substances produced in the body serve as neurotransmitters. The mechanisms that guide the actions of these substances is complex, and they are presently the focal point of considerable experimental research. There are three neurotransmitters, however, whose actions are relatively well mapped out; each is helpful in explaining the neurological basis of both motor and cognitive skills: *acetycholine, norepinephrine,* and *dopamine.*

A neuron transmits only one type of neurotransmitter; thus, entire neural tracts and systems can be defined and classified in terms of the neurotransmitter that is located within the neurons that make up the nerve tract. The *cholinergic* system is composed of neurons that contain the transmitter acetycholine. These nerves are found in both the peripheral nervous system and the central nervous system. In the peripheral nervous system, acetycholine serves two roles. First, it influences the activity of skeletal muscle movement in the somatic nervous system. Every muscular movement in the human body is initiated by information sent from the central nervous system by motor nerves whose neurons synapse at the *neuromuscular junction*, i.e., specialized cells that lie between the motor nerve and muscle cells. These cells stimulate muscle cells via the release of acetycholine, which causes muscle fibers to contract. Second, acetycholine influences glands and structures innervated by the parasympathetic division of the autonomic nervous system. The release of acetycholine is important in maintaining a state of physiological rest. In the brain, acetycholine neurons reside in neural tracts that flow through neocortical and subcortical areas that play important roles in attention and memory (Levinthal, 1990).

Catecholaminergic nerve systems include neurons that contain the transmitter norepinephrine and neurons that contain the transmitter dopamine. Norepinephrine neurons (also referred to as noradrenergic neurons because another name for norepinephrine is noradrenalin) are found in the peripheral nervous system on virtually all of the target glands and structures activated by the sympathetic division of the autonomic nervous system. Norepinephrine neurons are also found in the neural pathways of the brain that interconnect structures in the hypothalamus, cerebellum, spinal cord, and neocortex. The release of norepinephrine is typically associated with increased behavioral activity. Dopamine neurons (also referred to as dopaminergic neurons) are located in several neural pathways that originate and terminate within the brain; they play important roles in the bottom-up top-down neural dialog that takes place among brain systems involved in memory, emotion, and planning. Neurons containing norepinephrine and dopamine comprise a relatively small proportion of the total number of neurons in the brain—about one million of about nine billion total neurons. Nevertheless, these two neurotransmitters play a tremendously important role in brain function. Several neurological diseases impact the central nervous system by affecting the operation or availability of these neurotransmitters. (See box 3.1.)

BOX 3.1. Neurological Disorders

Despite the incredibly large number of cells in the brain, the destruction of a few critical cells can have widespread and devastating effects on brain function. Parkinson's disease is one such debilitating neurological disorder. The effects of Parkinson's disease were brought to the world's attention when Muhammad Ali, former world-champion boxer, moved slowly and with an unsteady balance to light the torch of the beginning of the 1996 Olympic Games.

Parkinson's disease causes the destruction of neurons that send information from the brain stem to areas of the cortex that are responsible for movement control. The neurons most greatly affected by the disease are those that produce dopamine. The *substantia nigra* is an area within the brain stem known to be rich in dopamine neurons; the loss of these cells has a profound influence on a wide range of brain functions. Individuals in the early stages of the disease show rhythmic hand and foot tremors, particularly when the limb is at rest. More severe movement disorders are observed as the disease progresses. Affected individuals have difficulty maintaining balance and rising from a sitting position, and they evidence muscle rigidity referred to as the cogwheel phenomenon, in which their limbs move in jerky rather than smooth patterns. In the latter stages of the disease, an individual's movements may freeze unpredictably. In severe cases, people become stiffly bedridden, frozen in position and unable to speak.

There are a number of diseases that produce their effects by disrupting the operations of neurons and the manner in which they communicate. The skills that are developed over decades of practice can be dealt a severe blow by these neurological disorders. Muhammad Ali, for instance, prided himself as a boxer who could "float like a butterfly, sting like a bee." All of this skill was lost after the onset of Parkinson's disease.

Integrative Systems

Until relatively recently, neurophysiological explanations of higher mental processes were limited to descriptions of areas of the neocortex that are related to particular functions. Early neurological research localized areas of the cortex implicated in language, sensation, movement, and reasoning. For the most part, however, the functions of the cortex were unknown. Most information about the brain was limited to postmortem examination of deceased individuals who had brain injuries. Advances in technology over the past few decades have provided researchers with sophisticated tools to assess the processes occurring within the black box. Although a complete understanding of the functions of the brain is not yet possible, researchers today have a much clearer idea of how the brain operates than they did just a few short years ago.

New knowledge about the brain is accumulating at an extremely rapid pace. Many of these new findings, however, are giving credence to concepts about the organization of the central nervous system that have been articulated for decades. Perhaps the most enduring generalization made about the higher processes of the brain is that they follow a pattern of hierarchical organization. Areas of the brain are designed to perform very restricted mental operations that are carried out in a very specific manner. Vision, for example, is a process that involves multiple levels of analysis. As incoming visual information undergoes analysis, information is routed to different locations in the cortex. Some visual information proceeds to the primary visual cortex, while other information is sent to the parietal lobe. Vision does not reside in the occipital lobe, nor does it reside in the parietal lobe. It is a combined product of a number of modules of the brain that carry out highly specific functions; the operations of basic modules are controlled by higher-level modules that are, in turn, controlled by even higher-level modules. (See box 3.2.)

BOX 3.2. Functional Organization of the Brain

General principles derived from biological research (Posner and Raichle, 1997, pp. 242–245):

1. *"Elementary operations are localized in discrete neural areas."* Researchers are finding that components of the cognitive processing system (such as vision, motor control, and memory) are localized in particular areas of the brain.

2. *"Cognitive tasks are performed by networks of widely distributed neural systems."* Although the components of processing may be localized, cognitive processes involve the interactions among many cortical and subcortical areas.

3. *"Computations in a network interact by means of 'reentrant' processes."* The interactions among areas of the brain are not serial, and information is passed back and forth among groups of neural areas. Information is often fed back, reentering an area of the brain that is involved in neural computations.

4. *"Network operation is under hierarchical control."* Higher-level systems typically inhibit the activity of lower-level systems.

5. *"Once a computation is activated, the threshold for its reactivation is temporarily reduced."* Once a brain area has been active, it becomes easier for a stimulus to reactivate it.

6. *"Less effort and attention are required to repeat a computation."* The efficiency of an operation improves with repetition; as a result, the overall activity that accompanies the computation is reduced. Blood flow to the involved area of the brain is reduced, electrical activity declines, and there is less interference between repeated computations.

7. *"A computation activated from the bottom up by sensory input involves many of the same neural systems as the same computation activated from top down attention systems."* The areas of the brain that are activated by stimulation of environmental events via incoming sensory nerves may also be activated internally by high level brain systems.

8. *"Practice in the performance of any task will decrease the number of neural networks necessary to perform it."* Repetition of events leads eventually to their becoming more automatic and performed with less attention.

9. *"The mind becomes capable of performing behaviors through the development of specific pathways connecting local computations."* New skills can be developed at any point during the human life span.

10. *"The symptoms of mental disorders may result from damage to localized computations, to pathways connecting these computations, or to the attentional networks and neurochemical systems that modulate the computations."* Illness and disease can influence cognitive processing in a variety of ways.

Presently there is a great deal of debate among cognitive researchers concerning the existence and location of high-level "executive" modules. Brain action is a dynamic ongoing process in which multiple mental operations are occurring in real time. Although information-processing models give the impression that cognition is the product of the flow of information from point to point within the brain, in reality, many processes occur in unison. How the brain is able to coordinate this mass neural action is just beginning to be understood by scientists. New research tools are revealing how the mass action of the brain is controlled.

Neurophysiological Measures of Cognition

Several methods are used by cognitive scientists to map regions of the brain that are correlated with specific mental processes and overt behavior (see Posner and Raichle, 1997, for an overview).

Electroencephalography (EEG)

One of the first methods developed, electroencephalography involves measuring electrical activity in the brain. In much the same way that the activity of skeletal muscle activity, which takes place under the skin, can be measured by way of EMG electrodes, the activity of the brain can be measured by electrodes placed on the skull. The EEG technique involves recording changes in the electrical activity in the brain from multiple electrodes placed on various locations on the head. The EEG has been of great value in mapping the temporal course of event-related potentials; electrical changes in the brain follow stimulation of sensory receptors. When a light or sound affects a receptor, information is conducted along sensory pathways to the brain. Neural electrical activity that occurs within individual neurons aggregates and produces changes in electrical potentials that are strong enough to be detected by electrodes located on the surface of the skull. Thus, electrodes pick up neural information as it travels through the nervous system.

Imaging Techniques

The capacity to measure the structures and functions of the brain was improved considerably by the introduction of brain imaging techniques in the early 1970s. The first method, *x-ray computed tomography*, involved passing focused beams of x-rays through the brain at various angles. The manner in which x-rays pass through the brain is affected by the density of the tissue. As a result, information can be gathered via powerful computers that produce images of the structures at a specific level of the brain. A major technological advance was achieved a few years later with the introduction of *positron emission tomography* (PET), which used autoradiography techniques rather than x-rays to construct brain images. The importance of the PET method lies in its capacity to identify structures as they operate in the living, functioning brain. The greater the level of involvement of a particular area of the brain in performing an operation, the greater the need for blood in that area. A PET image provides cognitive researchers with a visual display of the relative amounts of blood flowing to various regions of the brain as it functions. The PET method provides a powerful tool to examine how the brain functions when it is in the process of performing specific operations such as examining pictures, listening to music, or performing mathematical operations. These techniques played a key role in identifying the neural networks hypothesized to be involved in high-level mental processes such as attention and memory.

An important addition to the cache of methods available to cognitive neuroscientists is *magnetic resonance imaging* (MRI). This technique takes advantage of the effects that magnetic fields have on the behavior of molecules in the brain or any other part of the body. MRI techniques provide very clear and highly defined images of the brain and organs of the body. New generations of MRI tools, such as functional MRI (fMRI), designed for very fast image acquisition, are providing additional information about brain function by producing images of blood flow and chemical metabolism within the brain.

The EEG, PET, and MRI methods of measuring brain structure and function complement each other. The event-related potential that is measured by the EEG and some types of MRI provide measures of the temporal sequence of information processing. The images provided by PET and fMRI show the processes of the brain in action. The data now made available to researchers by these techniques provide the means to examine not only how the brain operates but also how operations of the brain come to be modified by learning and experience. Indeed, the brain undergoes tremendous changes throughout the human life span.

HOW COGNITIVE PROCESSES ARE STUDIED

As stated at the beginning of this chapter, many television game shows center around players' ability to answer questions as quickly as possible. In similar fashion, games of strategy such as chess require the application of highly sophisticated problem-solving skills. It is of course true that some motor movement is involved in these situations; answering questions requires the initiation and control of muscles involved in articulation and speech production, and playing chess involves moving game pieces from one position to another. Cognitive skill researchers are interested in how we extract information from the world around us, hold or remember that information, and use it to guide our actions (see Anderson, 2000, for an excellent introduction to cognition). Three internal mental processes—*memory, attention,* and *metacognition*—are of most interest to those who study cognitive skills.

The Structures of Memory

Memory can be conceptualized as environmental information, or data, that is held for some period of time. Cognitive scientists have determined that there are three types of memory (Solso, 1995). Each of the three types of memory can be described in terms of how much information it holds and how *long* it can be held it.

Sensory Memory

The human body is equipped with a variety of ways to sample what is taking place in the world around it. We are constantly being bombarded by physical energy—light energy, sound energy, and forces that place pressure on our bodies. Each of our sensory systems is tuned to receive incoming energy in much the same way that a radio can be tuned to pick up either AM or FM electromagnetic energy waves. Our sensory systems not only pick up information from the outside world but also grab and hold it for brief periods of time. It is the persistence of stimulus information that provides the beginning of the transformation of sensation to perception—the change of raw physical energy into a form that has meaning.

Our visual and auditory organs are constantly active and busy scanning the outside world. As you read the words that are printed on this page, your eyes are not examining each letter of each word. Rather, they are skipping over areas, stopping or *fixating* momentarily to grab an eyeful of visual data. The visual snapshots that are taken provide the basis for *iconic memory storage* that lasts for only a brief period of time—about 250 milliseconds. Your ears scan a multitude of sources of sound energy all around you, taking in an earful of auditory data that are the basis for *echoic memory storage*, which lasts 2 to 20 seconds.

Although sensory systems store data for brief periods only, they have the capacity to funnel a tremendous amount of information into the body's processing system. A large proportion of this sensory information is ultimately deemed irrelevant, and it decays without being processed. Relevant information, however, activates a series of transformations that results in our awareness of the world.

Short-Term Memory

In a very general sense, short-term memory holds the data of which we are aware at any given moment. It can be conceptualized as operating like the central processing unit (CPU) of a computer. Information enters short-term memory storage from the sensory systems. While it is held there, information that is stored in long-term memory is accessed and retrieved. It is the flow of information from the sensory system that provides information concerning sights, sounds, colors, and spatial location, and it is the flow of information from long-term memory that gives meaning to the sensory experiences.

The short-term memory system is rather limited in the amount of information it can hold at any given time. The short-term memory storage in adults is seven items, plus or minus two items (Miller, 1956). It is also the case that data are held in short-term memory only briefly, 15 to 20 seconds at most, under normal conditions. (See box 3.3.) Most people have experienced the frustrations of loss of short-term memory. For example, after going to the trouble of looking up someone's telephone number, we frequently forget it after using it only once.

BOX 3.3. Short-Term Memory Retention

Everyday experience provides many examples of the fragility of human memory. Forgetting the name of the person to whom you were just introduced, losing a telephone number from memory within seconds of looking it up in a phone book, or losing track of the transfer truck in the next lane are events that many people experience on an everyday basis. Laboratory studies of short-term memory provide compelling support for the supposition that humans have, at times, great difficulty retaining information.

Our understanding of the properties of short-term memory was advanced considerably by classic research studies conducted independently by Brown (1958) in England and by Peterson and Peterson (1959) in the United States. These two studies provided the basis for what is now known as the Brown-Peterson paradigm. The method, which is procedurally quite simple, provided the basis for many studies of short-term memory. It involves briefly showing an individual three letters of the alphabet that have no apparent meaning (e.g., ZPK) and asking him or her to remember the letters for periods ranging randomly between 0 and 18 seconds. During this retention period, the participant is asked to perform a rehearsal prevention task, such as counting backward from 99 by threes. Although it would seem easy to maintain letter triads in memory for only a few seconds, the counting task exerts a profound effect on how long the letters are maintained in memory. Participants forget almost half of the information after a delay of only 3 seconds; approximately 60 percent is forgotten after 6 seconds, and about 93 percent is lost about a delay of 18 seconds (Peterson and Peterson, 1959).

Results such as these identify two aspects of memory that are important to understanding cognitive skill development. First, information stored in short-term memory is lost very rapidly; second, memory can be kept active in memory by way of mental strategies, such as rehearsal. Strategies help to maintain information in short-term memory and increase the likelihood that it will be transferred to and made a part of long-term memory. Thus, what an individual elects to do with information during the first few seconds after it enters awareness plays a critical role in remembering. The vast majority of those who exhibit exceptional memory skills were not born with these abilities; rather, they have learned to use specific techniques that enhance memory storage and retrieval.

Long-Term Memory

Humans have the remarkable capacity to benefit and learn from their experiences. These experiences are catalogued and stored in long-term memory. The total storage capacity of the brain is not known precisely, but the general consensus is that it is huge and that some memories can last for decades. We are capable of storing several different types of information. Most cognitive psychologists agree that there are two general categories of memory. One is *declarative memory*; it encompasses information about events, facts, and concepts—it represents what we know. There are two forms of declarative memory. *Semantic memories* are generic and categorical, such as the meanings of words and concepts; they are the facts that are available to everyone within a particular group or culture. Knowing who is the Queen of England, for example, is information that is available to virtually everyone. *Episodic memories* are those that are unique to the individual; they are acquired from personal experience. Someone who has had the privilege of meeting Queen Elizabeth will store many memories about this particular and unique experience. The second general category of memory is *procedural memory*; it encompasses information about skills—it represents our knowledge of how to do things. There are many mental operations that we perform without thinking about them. Experiences result in memories that permit us to perform such cognitive skills as reading, adding a two-digit series of numbers and using grammatical language, and also to perform such motor skills as riding a bicycle, walking up a flight of stairs, and playing a musical instrument.

It must be emphasized that these descriptions of the storage capacities and the duration of retention of information in each of the three memory systems (sensory, short-term, and long-term) are drawn from studies that measured the average performance of young adults. As will be described later, the manner in which information is transformed, stored, retrieved, and manipulated can be modified considerably through experience and training. Indeed, it is the malleability of each of these memory structures that provides the basis for the acquisition of cognitive skills.

Attention

In much the same way that memory is no longer viewed as a single entity but rather as a number of different systems, *attention* is viewed as a multidimensional process (Kahneman, 1973; Parasuraman and Davies, 1984; Wickens, 1992) that influences the operation of memory systems in three ways. *Focused attention* involves selective identification and processing of information. Its role is to analyze incoming sensory information and to determine what is relevant and what is not. We exist in a "noisy" environment that provides a huge amount of information, only some of which may be important at a given moment. This sensory information arrives simultaneously from multiple sensory channels and bombards the information-processing system. Focused attention provides a type of bottleneck where the incoming stream of data is organized into patterns that can then be perceived as meaningful. *Divided attention* involves processing two or more sources of information simultaneously. Short-term memory is limited in the amount of incoming data it can hold and manipulate; as a result, competition for processing takes place. Attention serves to determine the importance of the information that is held and worked on in short-term memory. A trade-off takes place in which some information is given more priority than other information. Several theories of cognition focus on the role of *working memory*, which emphasizes the relation between attention and short-term memory storage (e.g., Anderson, 1982; Baddeley, 1990). *Sustained attention* involves vigilance and the maintenance of information in memory, particularly short-term memory stores. Everyone has experienced the sensations of boredom, monotony, and difficulty in keeping on task; when attention is not sustained and does not remain focused, our information-processing systems can wander.

Metacognition

Metacognition is referred to as cognition about memory; it reflects our awareness of the skills we have and how they should be applied to solve a specific problem. A skilled chess player, for example, responds to the arrangement of chess pieces; her attention is focused on some pieces and patterns of pieces and away from other pieces. The processes of selective attention lead her to consider only information that is relevant to this particular game. The manner in which attention shifts to some, but not all, chess pieces is determined at least in part by processing that examines the chess match at a global or molar level. The skilled player has experienced many games and learned much concerning the execution of techniques that lead to winning the game. This information, which is stored in the master player's long-term memory, is activated by the meta-cognitive game plan and brought into working memory where lower-level processing occurs (see Flavell, 1985, for an overview).

FACTORS THAT INFLUENCE COGNITIVE SKILL LEARNING

Much of what constitutes contemporary research and theory in cognitive skill acquisition can be linked to the pioneering work of Sir Frederic Bartlett in the late 1950s. He was one of the first researchers to define explicitly a framework that could be used to assess thinking and cognition. He contended that the development of cognitive skills, like motor skills, relied on the way information is extracted from the environment and used to satisfy a goal (Bartlett, 1958). The study of *problem solving* was central to Bartlett's work, and problem solving continues to be the central focus of study for many researchers who followed him (Hayes, 1989).

One of the advantages to the view that both cognitive skills and motor skills have similar underlying properties is that the two types of skills can then be evaluated via a common framework. We will now examine how cognitive skills are acquired and performed by exploring the role of three interrelated factors: the constraints of the learning process (i.e., stages of learning), the ability characteristics of the individual, and the type of skill being performed.

The Stages of the Learning Curve

You may not remember very clearly what kinds of learning activities you performed in elementary school when you were six to ten years old. If you were to visit an elementary school today, one thing that you would find are children who are learning to read, write, and perform mathematics. Further, the methods used to teach children these skills typically involve practice, practice, and more practice.

Consider, for example, the way that most children are taught the rudiments of arithmetic skills (addition, subtraction, multiplication, and division). A portion of almost every school day is set aside for repetition and memory drills. Often, flash cards depicting individual mathematical problems are shown and the student is expected to solve the problem as quickly as possible. The child's progress is typically measured by the teacher in terms of the number of problems solved correctly within a given period of time.

Mathematics is usually taught in sequence; children learn addition, subtraction, multiplication, and division in that order. They exhibit very predictable behavior while mastering each of these mathematics tasks. A young girl who is introduced to the methods of subtraction, for example, may initially struggle to acquire an understanding of the difference between the concepts of adding to and taking away, through demonstration and examples. Once the child appears to understand the concepts, she is given the first of many hundreds of subtraction problems she will be expected to solve. At first, the child's performance may be laborious and excruciatingly slow. To help her visualize the solution to $8 - 3 = ?$, she may resort to using her fingers and toes. Nevertheless, she will eventually produce a response and then move on to the next problem; she may initially complete only a few problems during each class period. However, as she performs the same mathematics problems over and over, day after day, quantitative changes in her performance are typically observed. Both her speed and her accuracy improve. She no longer has to use her fingers or some other overt counting device to assist in solving the problem; everything is accomplished covertly in her head. With hundreds and hundreds of repetitions, the child may be able to solve problems extremely rapidly and accurately, almost without having to think about them. Solving the problem $8 - 3 = ?$ becomes routine.

You will notice that progress in learning to subtract progresses through a series of stages similar to those used to describe motor learning in the previous chapter: a cognitive stage, an associative stage, and an autonomous stage.

The Cognitive Stage

From the outset, learning involves mental activity that follows a plan of action. The young girl's ability to learn subtraction skills hinges on her capacity to reorganize her previous knowledge of one type of mathematical operation (adding to) to comprehend the premise of another type of mathematical operation (taking away from). For the child, previously learned and stored *mental representations* that are involved in solving one type of problem are critical to the development and storage of new representations essential to solving different types of problems. The human mind is prepared, either through innate programming or through prior experience, to solve problems.

Once a plan of action is initiated, attention is focused on the task at hand. The child may be given a page of problems arranged in rows and columns. Each problem must be scanned visually in order to associate a particular value to each of the numbers in the equation. The shape of the components of each numeral is integrated and gives rise to a percept and its associated numerical value (e.g., 8 and 3). Early in training, the child may have to analyze each number and think about its value before applying any mathematical rule. Repetition, however, results in increasingly efficient *perceptual learning*, and the student requires less and less time to identify individual numbers. She gradually begins to perceive them automatically, without conscious awareness. Further, her expectancies begin to *prime* her to respond, without thought or hesitation, when specific types of stimuli are presented. As with motor skills, the initial stages of cognitive skill learning involve figuring out what goes with what and establishing elementary stimulus-response units.

The way in which a learner approaches a problem (his mental representation) often determines whether or not it will be solved. Having access to and use of mental representations is perhaps the most critical factor in developing cognitive skills (Newell, 1980; VanLehn, 1989). If a learner, regardless of age, cannot understand the underlying rules that apply to a given problem, it is unlikely that he will be able to learn the task. Developing a useful mental representation is a dynamic process that integrates environmental information with knowledge that is stored in memory.

Not all problems are as well-defined as those found in mathematics; indeed, most of the problems we face are not. Luckily, humans possess the capacity to examine problems from a variety of points of view. Adaptive learning involves being able to modify one's perspective concerning how a problem can be analyzed and approached. If one approach fails, the individual may be able to reorganize his or her perspective to come up with a better solution. Many times it falls to teachers and parents to arrange and rearrange environmental conditions in ways that best permit the learner to attack a problem and succeed. Everyone has faced tasks that seemed at the onset to be formidable and unsolvable. As it happens, we have all been shown ways to organize a problem so that the solution is obvious and easily attainable.

A voluminous body of literature deals with the manner in which a person's capacity to extract information from the environment becomes more efficient as a result of experience and practice (see Gibson, 1969, and Treisman and Galade, 1980, for details). A large portion of this literature focuses on how humans are able to detect, select, and combine specific environmental elements in ways that lead to unified perceptual experiences. This is called *perceptual learning*. It appears that our perceptions of the world around us are based on combinations of the elemental features of stimuli that we sense. (See box 3.4.) Thus, when we read words, the letters of each word are perceived as horizontal lines, diagonal lines, and vertical lines that are arranged in specific ways. Before the young girl can subtract 3 from 8, each of the numbers must be perceived on the basis of the integration of their features.

BOX 3.4. Perceptual Skill

Take a moment and attempt to read the text below. Kolers (1975) conducted a series of studies that evaluated how people become skilled at reading typographically inverted text. As you might expect, participants initially found the task to be extremely difficult; their rates of reading inverted text ranged from 8 to 22 times slower than their reading rate for normal text. Practice led to substantial changes in performance, however.

> Recognition seems so simple, direct, immediate. The
> skilled processing of information that must be involved
> is not itself apparent, for the object seems familiar
> as soon as the eye encounters it. In part, recognition
> seems so immediate because we spend most of our time in
> familiar surroundings. We work in the same rooms, see the
> same people, walk the same streets, live in the same
> houses for long periods of time. The perceptual
> information we receive each originally day is usually
> repetitions and redundant.

After about two months of training during which participants read aloud a total of 160 pages (about 300 words per page), their reading rates improved to the point that they could read the inverted text about as rapidly as they could read normal text. Kolers demonstrated that the basis for the improvement in reading occurred as a function of the participants' experience with specific letter patterns. He suggested that novices attack a novel perceptual task by using such tactics as visual exploration, problem solving, and geometric analysis in an attempt to isolate relevant information. Practice leads readers to change in two ways: they become more selective in sampling information in the visual field and identifying relevant targets, and they alter their subjective representation of what they see.

Perceptual skills are part of everyday life. We make many decisions that require choosing between or among alternatives. Going shopping, for example, consists of one discrimination and selection task after another. We consider a bin of apples and look for just the right one, we select one tomato over another on the basis of its color, and we select one brand of soap on the basis of a particular packaging label. Over time we become more skilled in our choices; the consequences of our selections teach us to avoid some products and to choose others.

Inverted Reading Text. From R. W. Proctor and A. Dutta, *Skill acquisition and human performance*, p. 54, ©1995. Reprinted by permission of Sage Publications, Inc.

The processes involved in distinguishing visual elements can occur very rapidly, without the observer even being aware that they are taking place. The selection of a target stimulus to undergo later analysis and the exclusion of other distractor stimuli from analysis are guided by attentional processes. The speed of visual detection is influenced considerably by experience. Practice, under certain conditions, leads to a gradual shift from effortful to less effortful and more automatic attentional processing (Hasher and Zacks, 1979; Schneider and Shiffrin, 1977; Shiffrin and Schneider, 1977).

The selection and processing of specific parts of the stimulus environment are also influenced by an individual's expectancy regarding how specific stimuli relate to specific responses, preparing him or her to act. Effects of expectancy, or *priming*, occur when previous exposure to a stimulus results in increases in the speed, accuracy, or probability of a response (Posner, 1980; Posner and Snyder, 1975). When the young girl is given a sheet of mathematics problems and expects to perform subtraction operations, she will evidence positive priming; if given subtraction problems, her initial calculation speeds will be faster than if she did not know what kind of mathematics problems to expect. Priming occurs extremely rapidly and without conscious awareness. Nevertheless, it can have a profound effect on the way in which individuals construct their perceptions and respond automatically to cues in a given environment.

The Associative Stage

The associative phase of learning is characterized by a shift from slow and laborious mental processing to rapid and smooth processing. In the case of the young mathematician, practice helps her solve more arithmetic problems in a set period of time. Changes in her processing speed are linked to the modification of mental operations taking place in her working memory. *Chunking*, which involves the integration of multiple discrete items into larger groups, has been hypothesized as one way that working memory processes may be modified. For example, most people find that it is easier to remember a new telephone number when the digits are grouped. Which of the memory tasks listed below do you think would be easier to perform?

3523752407

or

(352) 375-2407

Research has shown consistently that the capacity limitations of short-term memory (seven items, plus or minus two) can be overcome by using chunking operations (Newell, 1990; Newell and Rosenbloom, 1981). Working memory speed is increased because fewer chunks of information have to be manipulated to solve a given problem. Practice at chunking information can result in profound changes in the amount of information that can be held in working memory.

The way that the young girl practices her subtraction or multiplication problems will contribute greatly to her ability to retrieve correct responses. It is more than sheer repetition that determines whether or not the problems she practices will be stored and retrieved. There are a variety of factors that are known to affect memory processes. Research has shown clearly that the amount of information stored depends on the manner in which the material to be remembered is processed, or worked on, by the learner. There is considerable and convincing evidence that the manner in which information is *rehearsed* plays a key role in whether or not it gets memorized. Consider how you might go about trying to remember a telephone number. If you want to order a pizza, you may look in a telephone book for the number you need. After locating a suitable pizza shop, you may use a technique referred to as *maintenance rehearsal*, which is to repeat the shop's seven-digit telephone number over and over in order to keep it in memory long enough to dial it. Once the call is made, the number is quickly forgotten. On the other hand, you may meet someone at a party and find him or her to be incredibly interesting. You ask for a telephone number. Since you may have no paper and pencil and you do not want to forget the number, you may elect to use an *elaborative rehearsal* or some form of *mnemonic* technique to enhance memory storage and retrieval (see Craik and Lockhart, 1972, for an overview of rehearsal processes).

A mnemonic is any method or procedure that facilitates the storage and retrieval of information from memory. The use of mnemonics greatly influences memory processes. Some mnemonic techniques employ *mental imagery*, which involves creating a mental picture or representation that connects pieces of information in long-term memory. Mental imagery is a particularly powerful psychological process that has been pondered by philosophers for centuries and has been studied extensively by cognitive researchers (e.g., Pavio, 1986; Tarr and Pinker, 1989). Perhaps the best-known mnemonic device is the *method of loci* (method of places). This technique was described by ancient Greek orators and poets as a way to remember long passages. The method involves having the speaker first imagine a room or some open space with numerous features, such as a pot, door, window, table, etc. As the orator learns the material to be spoken he mentally associates various parts of his speech with features in the room. As he speaks, he visualizes himself walking from one area of the room to another and from one topic to another. Thus, the mental path he creates keeps the story he must remember in its correct order; nothing gets left out of his presentation.

Other mnemonics, such as the *peg-word system*, employ both imagery and a rhyme scheme to order and remember material. Memory experts often use this technique to demonstrate remarkable feats—for example, remembering the names of dozens of strangers. The mnemonists typically greet members of an audience as they enter, one at a time. The memorization procedure involves associating a word or number (a peg) with each person's name. This peg, along with a visual image of something particularly distinctive about the person, can help the expert recall well over 100 names, in their correct order (see Chase and Ericsson, 1981, 1982, for an example of expert memory). Regardless of the memory techniques employed, however, elaboration has the effect of making material more distinctive than if it were memorized simply by rote.

Another way to enhance memory storage is to impose some form of order on the information being learned. The young child learning basic mathematics skills is typically taught addition, then subtraction, and then multiplication. Teachers know that students will learn more efficiently when problems are grouped according to their common operations. Organization groups individual items on the basis of some specific relationship. The effect of grouping items so that they can be remembered has been well researched (see Ellis and Hunt, 1993). You will be able to memorize and recall more words when they are presented according to categories than when they are presented in random order.

Each of the elaboration techniques described above has been shown to enhance the storage and recall of memory. You might ask, of course, whether one technique is superior to the others. The answer is that the effectiveness of each technique depends on the type of task being performed. For some tasks, it is easy to employ imagery (such as imagining a cow standing in a pasture in order to remember to buy milk at the market); for others, however, imagery works less well (such as imagining the concept of freedom in order to remember to let the cat out when you get home). The effectiveness of organization and mnemonic techniques are task dependent. It is also the case that the learner must elect to invest the mental effort required to initiate and maintain working memory processes for these tasks to work.

The Autonomous Stage

Practice provides the learner with the basic building blocks needed to deal with complex problems. At some point during training, the learner begins to perceive relationships that go beyond basic stimulus-response relationships. As a child proceeds through years of mathematics training, for example, she may begin to apply elementary rules to increasingly more complex problems. She no longer struggles to perform basic operations; they take place virtually without thought. The removal of the burden of performing routine operations allows her to consider mathematics problems in terms of abstract *reasoning*. Problem solving is goal-directed behavior. Information stored in long-term memory is of little value unless it can be brought to bear at the right time and used effectively to solve a problem (Sternberg, 1986).

We encounter many problems that require us to make decisions by weighting various factors that can be used to predict the likelihood of one outcome over another. We address complex problems by using two interacting reasoning processes. *Inductive reasoning* requires logical thought and the evaluation of a number of specific factors to reach a general conclusion. A chess player may evaluate the position of the chess pieces on the board in order to generate a general rule that will guide his next move. *Deductive reasoning* involves thought that proceeds logically from a general premise to a specific conclusion. Part of playing chess involves mentally working through possible outcomes to a given move; for example, "if I move my queen to this position, then my opponent will respond by ... " The problems that people encounter in their real lives involve many possible moves and countermoves. Adaptive behavior, regardless of whether it involves playing board games or playing the game of real life, is dependent on the amount of game knowledge an individual has accumulated and his or her ability to use it at the right time and in the right way.

Cognitive Abilities

Researchers who study cognitive skill development, like those who study motor skill development, distinguish between cognitive *abilities*, which are general capacities related to the demands of a variety of tasks, and cognitive *skills*, which are specific to a given task. Considerable research has been conducted to identify and measure ability factors that underlie adaptive behavior. Many *psychometric tests* have been developed over the past 100 years that provide measures of cognitive abilities. Statistical techniques are used to identify and determine the relations that exist among various ability factors measured by a given test.

General Cognitive Ability versus Specific Cognitive Abilities

Some theorists propose that complex behavior is governed by a unitary *general cognitive factor* that provides a template for mental functioning. *General intelligence*, in these theories, is viewed as genetically based and influenced little by environmental experience. In much the same way that some people appear to be endowed with natural athleticism, some seem to possess native intelligence. These individuals seem to be able to learn many cognitive skills rapidly and with little effort.

Other theorists emphasize that cognitive skill learning involves *specific cognitive factors* that combine in unique ways to determine how one learns a given skill. Cattell (1963), for example, suggests that intelligence reflects the interaction between two factors—*fluid intelligence* determines one's ability to adapt and to solve all kinds of problems, regardless of previous experience with them, and *crystallized intelligence* reflects one's accumulation and use of factual information. Other researchers suggest that intelligence may reflect over 150 specific abilities (Guilford, 1967).

One way theorists have evaluated the relation between general factors and various specific factors has been to arrange them in a hierarchy. As seen in figure 3.3, a general cognitive factor resides at the top of the hierarchy, and major factors (such as fluid intelligence, crystallized intelligence, and short-term memory) are placed in the second tier of the hierarchy. Minor factors (such as verbal reasoning, number abilities, and spatial abilities) are located on the third tier. These low-level ability factors are related to performance on specific test items. Notice that general factors located higher in the hierarchy can be explained in terms of specific factors that are located lower in the hierarchy.

Predicting Cognitive Skill Learning

Educators, like sport coaches, are interested in predicting how well a student can learn and perform new skills. *Standardized tests* are administered to students at various points throughout their academic training. These are used both to assess an individual's current level of performance and to predict his or her future levels of performance. The scores that high school students attain on tests such as the Scholastic Achievement Test are often evaluated by college and university administrators and used to identify those students who will be admitted. It is assumed that the scores obtained on standardized tests reflect the applicant's basic abilities and that these scores predict future performance in college-level courses.

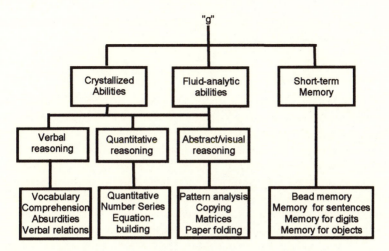

Figure 3.3. Factors Tested by the Stanford-Binet Intelligence Scale
From Allyn & Bacon, *Transparency Package to accompany Gerrig and Zimbardo,* Psychology and Life. Reprinted by permission by Allyn & Bacon.

Measures of basic cognitive abilities, like measures of basic physical abilities, are not perfect predictors of a student's future learning and performance, however. There are some high school students who perform well on standardized tests but do not succeed in college; other students perform well in college classes despite attaining lower scores on standardized tests. Measures of cognitive abilities can only provide educators with rough estimates of a student's future performance (Sternberg, 1985). There are many noncognitive factors, such as level of motivation and persistence, that are not assessed directly by standardized tests. (More will be said about the role of noncognitive factors on skill learning and performance in the next chapter.)

Task Types

There is no generally agreed-upon classification system that is adhered to by researchers interested in understanding cognitive skill development. It is clear, however, that cognitive skills are limited to specific types of tasks; like motor skills, they are *domain specific*. This means that an individual's training will not produce improvements in all aspects of cognitive function; rather, training will enhance only certain aspects of mental activity. A tennis player's practice at serving improves only one aspect of his game; a student's practice at remembering names will result only in improvement of a specific type of memory.

The scientific study of the mind has led researchers to develop a multitude of mental tests. The vast majority of these tasks fall into one of three categories, however: those that measure the *speed* of mental processing, those that measure the *amount of information* that can be stored in memory, and those that evaluate *problem solving*.

Mental Speed Tasks

Skilled individuals are often described in terms of how fast and accurate they are on given tasks. Both motor and cognitive performance can be evaluated in terms of the information one selects from the environment (stimulus-identification stage), the decisions made in selecting specific responses (response-selection stage), and the preparations to perform a given act (response-programming stage). Consider a reaction-time test in which a subject's choice between making one of two possible responses is based on which of two stimuli are presented. Although the task appears simple, there are a number of information-processing steps before a response is executed. The stimulus must first be processed perceptually and recognized. Then, based on the categorization of the stimulus, a response is selected and initiated.

Researchers have developed tasks that isolate, to some degree, the operations of each stage of processing. The *additive factors method* developed by Saul Sternberg (1969) is one task that is used widely to measure information-processing speed. The role that each stage plays in processing information can be evaluated by manipulating specific test conditions. Alteration of physical characteristics of stimuli, for example, impacts the speed with which environmental information is extracted, whereas manipulating the similarity among stimuli impacts decision-making speed. The additive factors method is discussed in chapter 10). Laboratory tests that provide measures of mental speed consistently show that human performance can be altered markedly by practice and experience.

Memory Tasks

A large number of tasks have been developed to evaluate how memories are stored and retrieved (see Puff, 1982, for an overview). Two broad classes of memory tasks dominate the cognitive research literature: those that focus on short-term memory and those that focus on long-term memory. Short-term memory tests evaluate how people retain information that persists in memory for one minute or less. The *digit-span* test described previously is the best-known test of short-term memory. It and other tests of short-term memory provide researchers with ways to examine both how information is stored and retrieved and how memory is influenced by other factors. Long-term memory tasks deal with information that is stored for more than a few minutes. Typically, tests of long-term memory assess an individual's semantic memory, which includes knowledge that is common to those who live in a given culture, or assess an individual's episodic memory, which includes knowledge about specific events that he or she experienced during his or her life.

It is known that both short-term memory and long-term memory are susceptible to the effects of outside interference. *Proactive interference* occurs when our memory performance is disrupted by previously learned material. Consider the situation when you are given a new telephone number. You may have difficulty remembering your new number because of the memory of your previous telephone number. *Retroactive interference*, then, occurs when our memory of previously learned material is disrupted by newly learned material. Using the telephone number example again, consider that after you have learned and used your new telephone number, you may find it difficult to remember your old number, even if you have used it for years.

Problem-Solving Tasks

Cognitive scientists are interested in how we use strategies and goal-oriented plans to solve complex problems. In general, problem-solving tasks fall into two categories: well-defined problems and ill-defined problems (Newell and Simon, 1972; Newell, 1980). *Well-defined problems* are characterized by having an initial condition, a goal condition, and path constraints. Chess is an example of a well-defined problem. The initial condition, or state, is defined by the position of the chess pieces on the chessboard, and the goal state is a checkmate position. The manner in which we move various chess pieces is limited by a set of rules, or constraints. The color of the squares and the type of movement allowed each chess piece provide the player with elementary information needed to develop a plan of attack and a plan of defense. Each time a chess piece is moved during the game, the player encounters yet another problem to be solved. Thus, games like chess involve a series of *problem space states*, each of which requires the player to make judgments concerning the most appropriate path to take. The paths selected to reach goals in well-defined problems are guided by *heuristics*, or strategies. The strategies that can be employed to solve well-defined but complex problems vary considerably. One person's strategy may be based on objective logic and analyses, whereas another's heuristics may be based on subjective personal beliefs, hunches, or initial impressions.

Ill-defined problems are characterized by the lack of a definite starting point and the lack of a clearly stated goal. Most problems that we encounter in life are not like the clearly defined tasks encountered in chess; the rules that guide choices in ill-defined problems are usually vague. Solving them requires generating a problem space that best suits the situation. We then formulate strategies on the basis of our past experiences and the information available to us at the moment. Often we respond to ill-defined problems in terms of previously encountered problems with similar characteristics. Thus, we develop problem-solving strategies on the basis of *analogy*; that is, contrasting the characteristics of a current problem with previous problems. Solving problems by analogy, however, is effective only when there is a true correspondence between past and present problems. At times problems may appear on the surface to have structural similarities when in fact the problems are fundamentally different ones that require different strategies. The repeated but ineffective use of a previously used strategy to solve a new problem is referred to as *functional fixedness*; it reflects our failure to recognize fundamental differences that exist between two ill-defined problems (McKelvie, 1985). Insight occurs when an individual reorganizes or restructures a problem and recognizes the solution to a problem (Kaplan and Simon, 1990).

THEORIES OF COGNITIVE SKILL LEARNING

The rapid expansion of cognitive science has fostered numerous studies that describe how the body and mind function; dozens of theories have been promoted to explain the operations of the mind. The sheer volume of information flowing from the research laboratories of cognitive scientists may overwhelm those who are just beginning to explore this domain of investigation. An overview of several theories of cognitive skill acquisition is presented here to introduce the reader to issues that are of central interest to contemporary cognitive psychologists.

Problem-Solving Theory

Allen Newell (not to be confused with Karl Newell, whose theoretical work in motor learning was described in the previous chapter) presented in 1990 a review of a body of research conducted over a 15-year period by researchers interested in modeling cognitive learning in terms of artificial intelligence (AI), which is the study of information and how it is processed from the perspective of computer science. Several key assumptions are made by researchers who use an AI approach to the study of human cognition. It is hypothesized that AI provides a framework for understanding the cognitive mechanism that underlies human intelligence. Computers can be programmed to function as do human operators; both use symbolic information to learn, store information or knowledge, and apply that knowledge to solving problems.

One of the goals of AI-based computer programs has been to determine how cognitive skills are learned. Computers have been programmed to respond to problems such as those encountered in chess. Software programs that provide computers with sufficient information to understand and solve basic problem sets have been designed; for example, some programs enable computers to master the rules for moving various chess pieces. The configuration of the chess pieces and the legal operations that can be performed with each piece describe a problem space. The computer program's solution to a chess problem involves first searching the problem space for possible outcomes and then selecting a move. The computational steps taken by the computer program to solve the problem modify how the computer will respond to future problem sets. The computer program learns from its actions; less computational time is spent on inefficient task solutions and more computational time is allocated to task solutions likely to achieve a successful outcome.

Computer programs, much like humans, can learn by acquiring information and organizing it into units, or chunks, of knowledge. The chunking process is hypothesized to underlie the improvements in speed and accuracy of action that define skilled behavior. Expert chess players, for example, are capable of rapid decision making and superior response selection. This is due, at least in part, to their organization of and access to thousands of chunks of information concerning specific game situations (Newell and Rosenbloom, 1981).

Parallel Distributed Processing (PDP) Theories

Rumelhart and McClelland (1986) introduced a computational theory of cognition modeled on the neurophysiology of the brain. The incredible speed with which the brain operates led them to propose that it cannot operate in the linear and serial stagelike manner that is at the heart of many information-processing models of cognition. Their theory hypothesizes that information courses through multiple pathways distributed throughout the brain. Environmental information is viewed as an *input* that surges through the architecture of the brain, affecting tens of millions of individual neurons. Each of these neurons, in turn, influences other neurons which together form a huge interactive network that produces an *output*.

The PDP model uses computer programs to simulate how the brain is believed to operate. These programs are based on the arrangement of units that are hypothesized to operate in the same fashion as individual brain neurons. These units are seen as basic elements of knowledge (e.g., rules of language, plans for movement) and are the building blocks of complex thought and action. Units are arranged into modules, which distribute information throughout the brain. Environmental stimuli influence units that comprise an input layer and interact with multiple layers of intermediate units, which influence output units that result in observable behavior. Suppose that someone asks you to name your closest friend. The question serves as an input that leads you to access multiple units containing knowledge (e.g., how you define "friend," who your friends were at different periods of life). During the process of accessing the one person who stands out as your closest friend, you also access knowledge that you have accumulated about her (e.g., her physical characteristics, attributes, behaviors). These hidden mental operations lead you to select the person who best fits the question presented to you. All that is left is to initiate an output. Due to the complex nature of the brain, tens of millions of neurons may be involved in the multitude of possible pathways for information throughout the processing system.

Connectionist models such as PDP have been used to explain how cognitive skills are learned. As units (neurons) interact, they are hypothesized to leave a trace that simultaneously strengthens connections among some units and inhibits the connections among other units. Practice causes specific pathways to become increasingly stronger and more efficient. A computational system weights the importance of various pathways that lead to outputs designed to achieve a desired goal. Over repeated trials, the weighting process results in increases in processing speed and decreases in error. The PDP model views skill learning as the result of a self-correcting system.

Adaptive Control of Thought (ACT*) Theory

John Anderson (1982, 1983) developed a general theory of cognition that addresses directly the learning process and how experience alters information-processing operations. ACT* theory has undergone a number of revisions since 1982 (Anderson, 1987); however, the primary operations of his system remain essentially the same. Performance output is the result of operations within working memory on two sources of stored information. The first is a long-term declarative memory storage structure that holds information in a semantic net, a network of nodes of knowledge linked together by associations. Semantic nodes contain information *about* a given task, such as images, sequences, and logical propositions. The second is a long-term production memory storage structure that holds information concerning *how* actions are to be executed. The activation of working memory by environmental cues prompts a rapid search of both declarative and procedural memory systems. Performance depends on *production rules* that specify the pairings of specific conditions in working memory with specific actions.

Anderson suggests that skill acquisition is analogous to developing production rules that fit domain-specific task conditions. Solving mathematics problems such as addition, for example, involves matching declarative knowledge gained from previous experiences and applying it to the specific problem at hand. Performing actions in a new domain, however, requires development of production rules that fit new tasks.

The ACT* theory proposes that skills are developed and refined in three stages. The first stage involves problem solving. When faced with a novel task, the learner initiates actions based on general problem-solving strategies. The strategy of analogy, for example, gives the learner an opportunity to transfer declarative knowledge accumulated from performing tasks in one domain to a new task in a new domain. Other strategies include the use of instructions, feedback, and analysis of subcomponents of the task. The importance of these strategies decreases quickly as practice provides the basis for the creation of production rules, however. The second stage is characterized by the construction of goal structures that provide a framework for organizing the declarative knowledge accumulated from practice. Knowledge compilation processes play a critical role in organizing information. Compilation includes chunking, in which small units of information are rearranged into larger units, and composition, in which multiple-step operations are collapsed into fewer steps. These compilation processes reduce the amount of information that enters working memory and as a result, improve the efficiency of working memory and lead to fast and accurate responding. The third stage is characterized by the strengthening and tuning of production rules. Practice that leads to favorable outcomes results in the strengthening of specific production rules.

CHAPTER SUMMARY

Philosophers once believed that the human mind was too complex to study. Researchers today have found that the mind can be analyzed and studied in a rigorous, scientifically valid manner. Advances in instrumentation and laboratory methodologies have provided researchers with insights into mental operations. Powerful new tools provide the means to examine structures of the brain involved in thinking and problem solving.

The mind is no longer a black box in which processes take place that we do not fully understand. Researchers are beginning to understand how the mind functions and how it changes as a result of experience. The rigorous study of memory, attentional, and metacognitive systems provide increased understanding of how the learning process takes place. We are beginning to map out and analyze the dynamic interactions that take place between the processes of the mind and the processes of the body, a unique point in the history of humankind.

SUGGESTED READINGS

Anderson, J. R. (2000). *Learning and memory* (2nd ed.). New York: Wiley.

Baddeley, A. D. (1990). *Human memory: Theory and practice*. Needham Heights, MA: Allyn & Bacon.

Ellis, H. C., and Hunt, R. R. (1993). *Fundamentals of cognitive psychology* (5th ed.). Madison, WI: Brown and Benchmark.

Kellogg, R. T. (1995). *Cognitive psychology*. Thousand Oaks, CA: Sage.

Newell, A. (1990). *Unified theories of cognition*. Cambridge, MA: Harvard University Press.

Posner, M. I., and Raichle, M. E. (1997). *Images of mind*. New York: Scientific American Library.

Schiffman, H. R. (2000). *Sensation and perception* (5th ed.). New York: Wiley.

Chapter 4

Motivation and Skill

Humans are motivated to perform amazing feats. We have climbed the world's highest mountains, explored virtually every mile of its land mass, and descended miles below the surface of the sea. We have even been to the moon and walked on its surface. Humans are by nature motivated to overcome difficult challenges and barriers to attain our goals.

There have been individuals throughout history who have made careful observations of behavior in war, birth, death, love, and other human dramas. People are driven to explain why humans behave in the ways that we do. Descriptions and explanations of human actions are found in stories and poems from preliterate times and extend through the ages to the writings that fill modern libraries. This chapter describes how motives energize and drive us to learn skills that allow us to overcome challenges and meet our goals.

THE STUDY OF MOTIVATION

We often describe those who are active, inquisitive, and outgoing as "spirited." Conversely, those who elect not to put much energy into their actions are described as spiritless. The word *spirit* is derived from the Latin word for "breath." Early philosophers reasoned that all living things have the breath of life placed in them. This spirit was thought to be infused at birth and taken away at death. From the time of the ancient Greeks to the seventeenth century, philosophers and theologians considered the spirit and the mind to be one and the same. Many people who lived during this period accepted the notion that events in nature were predestined. Everything was part of a great plan devised by God, who manipulated and controlled all events.

The Age of Enlightenment, which historians place in the seventeenth century, was hallmarked by a fundamental shift in the way that Western civilization began to view nature and to explain what caused events to happen. The emergence of democratic nations in Europe led political and social philosophers to promote views that championed the value of rational thought. René Descartes (1596–1650), an influential philosopher and mathematician, was responsible for a pivotal moment in the development of thought and academic inquiry in Western civilization. He proposed that the soul and the mind were separate entities; thus, they could be examined individually. The soul was the object of study by theologians and the mind was the subject of scientists. For Descartes, the mind was a nonphysical entity that controlled the movement of humans. He developed a *dualistic* model of human behavior in which thought and action emerged as the product of *interaction* between the physical world and the psychic world. The mind and body worked together in a deterministic and machinelike way to make sense of everyday experiences and thoughts.

Descartes developed the first physiological theory of behavior that explained action in terms of an interaction between the mind and the body. Movement was thought to be initiated by the flow of "animal spirits" through hollow tubes that ran from the brain to the muscles. Limb movement was conceptualized in terms of hydraulics; the ebb and flow of animal spirits caused pressure that resulted in muscle movement. The mind, which was nonphysical and permeated the entire body, was said to be in control of the allocation and flow of these spirits. Humans, unlike animals, were said to have the capacity to act voluntarily, choosing to initiate or to inhibit action. Emotions were conceived by Descartes as reflecting the amount of animal spirits that the mind allocated to perform actions. Human passions such as hate, love, and wonder were present in everyone; however, the amount of spirit (and thus the level of emotion) could be controlled by the mind. If allowed to proliferate unabated, the presence of animal spirits would lead ultimately to irrational actions. Although the Descartes model is clearly rudimentary, it has two elements that have been retained in modern theories of motivation: 1) behavior is energized, and 2) humans have control over their actions.

Modern Perspectives of Motivation

Contemporary psychology, as a field of study, is fragmented. Psychologists differ considerably in the way they view the nature of humans. Consider the case of a young man seen riding his mountain bicycle down the stairway of a multilevel parking garage at a rapid speed. At the bottom of each set of stairs, the rider's momentum caused him to hit the wall and carom off at an angle that helped propel him onto and down the next flight of stairs. After riding/falling down five flights of stairs, the young man sprinted on his bicycle through the parking garage to the top level, where he proceeded to ride/fall down the steps once again. Some psychologists would explain the young man's behavior in terms of an unconscious death wish; others would posit that he was training for bicycle races that may lead to fame and fortune; still others would suggest that he did it simply because it felt good. Regardless of its specific theoretical orientation, however, each explanation of the activities observed involves identification of what energizes behavior, and each explanation details how those behaviors are controlled.

DYNAMIC PSYCHOLOGY

Central to understanding motivation is the notion of *energy*. The performance of a task, whether physical or mental, demands the mobilization and expenditure of physical and mental effort. Skilled performance is often discussed in terms of drive, spirit, or motivation—dynamic forces that energize the individual. Indeed, motivation is often used to help explain why people differ in how quickly they learn new skills, persist at the practice of skills, and maintain their interest in performing skills.

Some explanations postulate sources of energy that exist within the individual. Humans are often conceptualized as decision makers who make judgments affecting their willingness to expend effort. Teachers encounter students of all ages who may physically be in class but elect not to actively participate and show little desire to learn. Other explanations revolve around the manner in which the immediate environment comes to control individual action. From this perspective, decisions to act are not made by the person; rather, the environment draws behavior out of the individual. Teachers have long observed that the activity level of students can change markedly when class material is modified.

In reality, motivation reflects a *person-environment interaction*—the actions of an individual are instigated by changes in the environment; these actions, in turn, influence and modify the environment in ways that affect the person's ongoing thoughts and behavior. To truly understand behavior, three questions must be addressed. First, what are the conditions that instigate behavior? Second, why do people select and engage in specific behaviors? Third, what effect do a person's actions have on his or her environment?

Conditions That Energize Behavior

Modern behavioral scientists make clear distinctions between two terms that are central to the study of motivation: motives and needs. A *motive* refers to a psychological state or physiological disposition that energizes behavior. A need is the object of a motive; it is the specific thing (e.g., food, water, money), event (e.g., praise), or psychological state (e.g., well-being, happiness) that is desired by an individual (Deci and Ryan, 1985). Psychologists describe three categories of motives and needs that affect human action.

Physiological Needs and Motives

Like a machine, the human body requires fuel to function, and without a steady supply of fuel it stops working. Thirst is a motive to satisfy the body's need for water. Loss of body fluids through sweating and other biological processes leads to the activation of systems designed to control the body and return it to a physiological balance. Some of these regulatory systems are embedded within the central nervous system. Loss of fluids trigger centers of the brain that, in turn, signal the production of specific hormones that influence the activities of the autonomic nervous system. The internal state of the body continues to change as fluids are lost and not replenished. As the need for fluids increases, so too does the person's level of motivation to locate and drink water.

Biosocial Needs and Motives

Normal development throughout the life span requires that many needs, both physical and psychological, be met. It is clearly the case that infants require more than nourishment and a safe environment in order to mature successfully; they also need intimate social contact with parents or other caregivers. Humans are driven to secure such social needs as acceptance, affection, and love throughout their lifetimes. Thus, people are constantly motivated to acquire both *viscerogenic needs*, which are directly related to survival, and *psychogenic needs*, which are not strictly needed for survival but are nonetheless critical to well-being.

A biosocial need state creates a feeling of disequilibrium. A worker who spends most of the day performing routine tasks in an understimulating office environment may feel a strong need to get out and talk to friends at the end of the workday to increase social stimulation. Conversely, someone who spends each workday in a noisy public environment may seek a quiet, secluded place in order to regain a sense of balance and psychic equilibrium. For most people, states of disequilibrium are experienced throughout most of the day, while periods of equilibrium are typically brief in duration and occur infrequently.

Psychic Needs and Motives

Humans possess unique experiences and perceptions of the world. Most people believe that they have the capacity to think independently, to make up their minds, and to control their destinies. The motivation to secure creative fulfillment and personal growth has been the center of philosophical discussion for centuries. When the source of the individual's motives to act is within, it is referred to as *intrinsic motivation*. This is contrasted with behaviors driven by *extrinsic motives* that have their sources in the person's environment. A baseball player who practices in order to become a highly paid professional athlete is motivated by extrinsic rewards. Another player who practices for the sheer pleasure of playing the game is motivated by intrinsic rewards.

Some suggest that we are aware of our need for individuality and that we make conscious decisions leading to personal fulfillment. *Existential-humanistic* philosophy suggests that we have the capacity to make choices. We elect to go down one of several paths of life, each of which will lead to unique experiences and feelings. Thus, one may be motivated to spend years struggling to achieve the experiences unique to being an artist. The needs that fuel the behaviors of the artist may not be fame or fortune but rather the act of painting, playing music, or carving wooden dolls. Each of those who lives an *authentic life* chooses for himself or herself the life path that leads to experiences that provide meaning to existence. It is the individual who ultimately determines the value that an experience or action holds. Those who elect to go down paths of life chosen by others lead *inauthentic lives*; they may be successful in achieving social rewards and goals, but they fail to attain the experiences that they truly desire, those that would provide real meaning to their lives (see Hergenhahn, 1992, chapter 7, for an overview of existentialism).

Selection of Action

Motives, in and of themselves, are directionless. A dynamic force given direction through experience and learning, they serve only to energize an individual into action. Motivated action provides the drive needed to learn a skill. Adaptive behavior represents a gradual accumulation of knowledge and skills throughout life. A skill, once learned, is made part of an increasingly enlarging repertoire of skills. The mature human adult, who has accumulated a lifetime of specific skills, possesses a wealth of behavioral options. Compare this to a child's relatively impoverished repertoire of skills.

Regardless of the type of learning procedure that modifies an individual's behavior, learning provides options that have the potential to achieve needs and goals. Motives energize the behavioral patterns (skills) that are instrumental to reducing needs. Thus, skills function to help us adapt and survive. When we experience a need, there exists a condition of *disequilibrium* (a discrepancy between our current state and our desired or ideal state). Actions that reduce the discrepancy between current and ideal states are then selected and performed so that we can achieve a state of *equilibrium.*

Psychologists have employed the concept of *negative feedback* to describe the dynamic and interactive relationship between an individual and the environment and to explain how actions are directed toward achieving a *homeostatic balance*, or state of equilibrium. The psychological concept of negative feedback was modeled on mechanical *control systems* designed by engineers in the early twentieth century (see Cziko, 1995, p. 106, for an overview). Much like mechanical systems that respond to ever-changing conditions, humans must be able to sense changes in their environments and to select behavioral actions best suited for each situation. Human behavior, however, is not controlled only by the environment; it is determined by the interaction between the environmental information obtained by the individual's sensory systems and an internal reference point. Unlike mechanical servomechanisms that have reference values set at a factory or user, human behavior is controlled by instructions provided by the individual. The *voluntary* and *conscious* decisions a person makes to initiate specific actions, and the intensity and persistence of those actions, represent a significant portion of human behavior (Carver and Scheier, 1981).

Effects of Action

Once a behavioral act has been put into motion, it affects both the environment and the actor. Like a mechanism, behavior regulates environmental conditions toward a determined reference point. Unlike mechanical devices, however, humans experience *feelings* and *emotions* as they act. Disequilibrium and changes in homeostatic state result in complex reactions involving both the body and the mind. With every act arise sensations and associated feelings that serve as the basic building blocks of emotion, which goes hand in hand with motivation (Cofer, 1972; Parkinson, 1995). The infant who misses a scheduled feeding senses hunger, engages in increasingly loud and longer lasting crying, and displays clear signs of frustration and emotionality. As the baby is nursed, its emotional pattern changes rapidly, and signs of contentment dominate. Similar changes in emotional patterns are seen in athletes training for competition. The high school spring board diver may experience frustration when introduced to a new dive. At the beginning of training, there is typically considerable difference between a diver's desired and actual performance. Even though the diver can rationally understand what steps must be performed to execute the dive, he will still experience a variety of emotions as he learns it. Negative emotions such as fear and anxiety may dominate his thoughts early in training; with practice and feedback, however, these negative emotions decrease, and positive emotions such as exhilaration and joy are experienced more frequently.

The notions of *tension* and *tension release* are found in many theories of motivation and emotion. It has been suggested that the drive created by motives and needs instills a state of physical and mental tension that can be reduced only through action and behavior. For example, take the social situation in which the behavior of one roommate is a constant source of irritation to another. The one who is being annoyed may try several methods of dealing with the source of the irritation. However, if these coping strategies fail, tension increases. At some point, she may fly into an emotional rage. Although becoming irrational may not be the best solution to a problem, it often results in a reduction in tension and a sense of relief. The tension experienced during periods of disequilibrium can range from mild to intense and thus plays an important role in determining the level of effort allocated to learning a given task or solving a particular problem.

The examples of goal-directed action provided thus far have focused on situations in which motives energize behavior that leads to reduction in disequilibrium. Often, however, the goals people set are not met, and in some cases, behaviors result in greater discrepancies between actual and ideal states. Consider a student enrolled in an upper-level mathematics class who has not acquired the basic skills required to solve complex problems. The student may indeed be extremely motivated to perform, yet he receives increasingly lower scores on tests as the term goes on. Performance in some cases, no matter how motivated, may fail to effect desired environmental changes. Lack of success can have profound effects on our motivational and emotional states. There is considerable research evidence to suggest that when we are unable to control or to effect changes in our environment, it can result in decreased levels of motivation (reduced intensity and persistence of behavior), impaired learning, emotionality, and depression.

Motivation is a multidimensional construct; it can be described in terms of *overt behavior, covert thinking,* and *emotional status*. It is easy to see the energized activity of a young child who has just learned that pushing a button on a soft-drink machine can lead to the presentation of a favorite soda. The depression of the button is an *overt act*—one that can be observed directly. Motivation can also be described in terms of the mental processes that underlie overt action. Consider the mental activity that is involved when playing chess. Players may expend considerable mental energy in *covert thinking* while considering the pros and cons of various moves before actually physically moving a chess piece. Motivation is also linked to an individual's *emotional status*. Consider the behaviors of the child who puts all the coins in her purse into a drink machine that refuses to operate or to return her money. Her cries of despair and the force of her fists pounding the buttons of the drink machine provide clear evidence that humans do not act like robots. Feelings, moods, and emotion are an inescapable part of human behavior.

THE NEUROPHYSIOLOGY OF MOTIVATION

The emergence of mammals about 150 million years ago marked the beginning of many new animal species, including those who would eventually become members of the species *homo*, the ancestors of modern humans. The selection of a species, both then and now, depends on the capacity of its members to fit into a particular environmental niche and to thrive long enough to produce offspring. Mammalian species that evolved successfully did so because they possessed physiological structures and behavioral characteristics that were a good fit with the environment. One characteristic of mammals that has aided the survival of many species is a reproductive strategy that differs from that of other animals. Nonmammalian species typically survive on the basis of sheer numbers. A single female may have the capacity to produce hundreds or even thousands of offspring. The main reproductive effort of many nonmammals is confined to producing offspring which, once born, are left to fend for themselves. The majority do not live to maturity. Because of their overwhelming numbers, however, a few do live long enough to produce offspring of their own, thus assuring the survival of the species. Mammalian species employ a reproductive strategy in which few offspring are produced but tremendous effort is directed toward nurturing the young and ensuring their safety.

Perhaps the most important characteristic of mammals is their dependence on social interrelationships. In a dangerous environment, an individual who is part of a larger group has a better chance of living to reproductive maturity than one who lives in isolation. Many changes in mammalian physiology occurred in concert with reproductive strategies that focused on the evolutionary benefits of maternal bonding and socialization. Profound changes took place within the lineage of the emerging human species. Multiple systems evolved that were vital to surviving in a harsh, demanding environment. Some systems enabled humans to sense the environment and respond to threatening situations by fighting or fleeing; others controlled the need to obtain food and water required for survival. Still other systems focused on procreation (i.e., finding mates, producing children, and ensuring their survival). Researchers interested in the neurophysiology of motivation tend to focus on how various systems of the human body function interactively (Levinthal, 1990; MacLean, 1970, 1990).

The Limbic System

The *limbic system* plays a key role in the integration of motivation, emotion, and behavior. It is a diffuse web of structures and nuclei located deep within the brain. (See figure 4.1.) The limbic system can be conceptualized as a layer of brain tissue between the phylogenically "old" part of the brain (the brain stem, which controls reflexive functions necessary to life), and the phylogenically "new" part of the brain (the neocortex, which controls thinking, memory, and problem solving). The main structures of the limbic system include the *septum*, the *amygdala*, and the *hippocampus*. In modern humans, the limbic system has extensive connections to cortical systems such as the prefrontal region of the *frontal lobe*, and to subcortical structures, such as the *hypothalamus* and the *thalamus*. Through these connections the limbic system plays a key role in motivation and emotion.

The structures of the limbic system figure significantly in behaviors that, on one hand, are critical for survival and, on the other hand, promote pleasure. The human body has been exquisitely designed over millions of years of evolution to respond to environmental challenge and demand. It acts in a coordinated and reflexive fashion when faced with a threat or challenge and can learn from its experiences. The body has also evolved structures within the brain that reward actions that perpetuate both the survival of the individual and the survival of the species. People experience pleasure from drinking water when thirsty, from eating food when hungry, and from engaging in sexual activity when aroused.

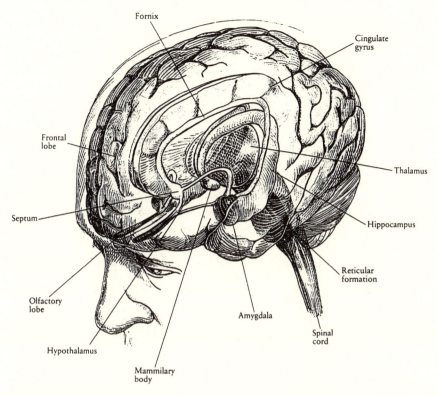

Figure 4.1.   The Limbic System
From *Brain, Mind, and Behavior* by Floyd E. Bloom, Arlyne Lazerson, and Laura Hofstadter. Copyright 1985, 1988, 2000 by W. H. Freeman and Company. Used with permission.

The septum and amygdala are regions of the limbic system that are activated predominantly by sensory pathways linked to *olfaction,* or smell. These two structures are known to be involved in reflexive patterns of feeding, fighting, self-protective, and mating behaviors. Injury or damage to either area in animals results in very profound changes in behaviors. Monkeys who have damaged amygdala areas become either hyperaggressive or hypoaggressive and display nonfunctional mating behaviors. The hippocampus receives inputs from visual nerve pathways and areas of the brain that are involved in forming memories. It has also been implicated in the storage of very basic types of memories tied to emotional events. The limbic system is influenced not only by direct sensory stimulation of the present environment, but also by emotional memories of past environments.

The real workhorse for the limbic system is the hypothalamus. It is a small but very complex structure that contains numerous nuclei that receive input not only from the limbic system and other areas of the brain but also from bloodborne molecules that flow into the brain via the circulatory system. It lies at the base of the brain, under the thalamus, which is the sensory switchboard of the brain. The hypothalamus controls and organizes behaviors instrumental for survival—fighting, feeding, fleeing, and mating. Alteration of some hypothalamic nuclei in laboratory rats modifies their eating and drinking behaviors; alteration of other nuclei modifies courting and sexual behaviors. Direct stimulation of specific hypothalamic nuclei of laboratory cats elicits instantaneous stalking and attack behaviors.

The electrical stimulation of areas of the hypothalamus and other areas of the limbic system has been found to be rewarding for many species of animals, as the limbic system appears to contain the pleasure areas of the brain. Animals with electrodes implanted within specific areas of the hypothalamus are highly motivated to behave in ways that will result in electrical stimulation. Indeed, studies of animal learning have demonstrated that hungry or thirsty laboratory animals choose brain stimulation over food or water in some conditions. These observations have led some researchers to hypothesize that mammals evolved neurological reward systems to reward behaviors that are essential for survival and, as such, are fundamental to motivation (Heckenmuller, 1985).

The hypothesis that there are natural reward centers in the brain was provided considerable support by the isolation of *endorphins*, a class of naturally produced opiatelike substances that circulate through the brain and function as both neurotransmitters and hormones. Receptor sites, which become stimulated by the presence of endorphins, are located throughout the neocortex and limbic system and in the pituitary and adrenal glands. The precise mechanisms by which endorphins have their effect on the body are still under investigation; their roles are vigorously debated. It appears, however, that the various substances that make up the class of endorphins influence behavior in a variety of ways. Perhaps the most well known is their *analgesic* (pain-reducing) effect. When these substances were first discovered, they were called *endorphins* to reflect their naturally occurring opioid qualities. Since then, they have been implicated in a variety of functions ranging from the modulation of emotion, social behavior, and general physical and mental health and well-being.

Endorphins have been argued to have evolutionary significance because many of the experiences that are part of normal human development are potentially painful (Panksepp, Herman, Vilberg, Bishop, and De Eskinazi, 1980). Activities such as fighting to survive, competing for a mate, and bearing children are physically and mentally effortful and take us to the limits of our endurance. Early in the history of human evolution, endorphins may have served primarily to reduce the perception of pain, allowing one to fight on regardless of physical injury. As the physical structures of the brain evolved in concert with mammalian development, endorphins came to be involved in the physiological mechanisms that underlie the emotions experienced with social bonding and attachment. Their role in modern humans may be even more widespread, influencing the emotions we experience in complex social situations such as play, socialization, and mental well-being. Pain and pleasure are part of normal life-span development. The bonds between parents and children, husband and wife, and friends become strong, and the pleasures they engender are beyond measure; however, the child's separation anxiety or the loss of friend or mate can be equally emotionally devastating. The capacity to cope with both the pleasures and pains of life have been linked to the properties of the brain and the role of endorphin production.

The physiological mechanisms that have evolved to drive humans to secure food, water, and mates also motivate us to acquire skills. Physical and cognitive skills provide the ability to master the challenges and demands of our complex social environment and ensure our survival and psychological well-being. In the same way that pleasure is derived from securing basic physiological and biosocial needs, humans are hypothesized to be rewarded for acquiring skills required for normal development, by the sheer pleasure derived from their execution.

Regulatory Systems

The limbic system is intimately related to two systems that are vital for normal body functioning and for survival: the *autonomic nervous system* a subdivision of the *peripheral nervous system* which regulates functioning by way of neural stimulation, and the *endocrine system*, which regulates organs via the release of hormones. These two systems interactively control physiological levels of arousal and the energy that drives motivated action.

The Autonomic Nervous System

The *autonomic nervous system* (ANS) controls glands and muscles that are important in maintaining a state of internal biological equilibrium. The ANS is composed of two fiber systems: *sympathetic fibers* designed to prepare the body to deal with emergency situations, and *parasympathetic fibers* designed to maintain physiological rest and calm. As seen in figure 4.2, the vast majority of the organs, glands, and muscles of the body are innervated by nerve fibers of both the sympathetic and parasympathetic systems. When faced with an emergency situation, the sympathetic fibers assume dominant control over these targeted structures. They excite and increase the activity of some and inhibit and decrease the activity of others. All of us have experienced events that lead to sudden and rapid changes in heart rate, respiration, and mental disorientation. Losing one's balance on slippery ice, a near hit by a passing car, the sight of a charging vicious-looking dog, and the nasty alien that pops out from nowhere on a movie screen can all provide the stimulus needed to initiate instantaneous arousal. Under these conditions the sympathetic fibers increase the activity of some structures (e.g., the cardiorespiratory system) and decrease the activity of others (e.g., the stomach, intestines, and salivary glands). Following the removal of a threat, parasympathetic fibers assume dominance over these targeted structures; the activity of the cardiorespiratory system decreases and the processes involved in digestion increase. The parasympathetic system brings about a vegetative state of biological calm and rest.

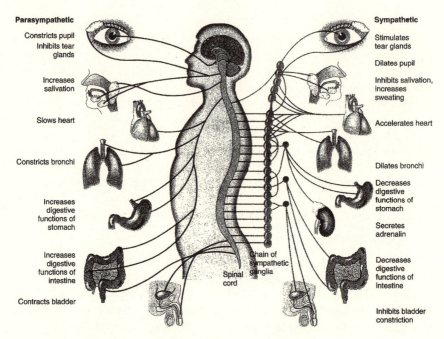

Parasympathetic

Constricts pupil
Inhibits tear
glands

Increases
salivation

Slows heart

Constricts bronchi

Increases
digestive
functions of
stomach

Increases
digestive
functions of
intestine

Contracts bladder

Sympathetic

Stimulates
tear glands

Dilates pupil

Inhibits salivation,
increases
sweating

Accelerates heart

Dilates bronchi

Decreases
digestive
functions of
stomach

Secretes
adrenalin

Decreases
digestive
functions of
intestine

Inhibits bladder
constriction

Chain of
sympathetic
ganglia

Spinal
cord

Figure 4.2.   Major Structures of the Autonomic Nervous System
From Allyn & Bacon. *Transparency Package to accompany Gerrig and Zimbardo,* Psychology and
Life. Copyright 1996. Reprinted by permission by Allyn & Bacon.

The *sympathetic-adrenal-medullary arousal system* links the structures in
the hypothalamus to the inner section, or medulla, of the adrenal glands. When
the limbic system is activated, the hypothalamus is stimulated, innervating a
neural path of the sympathetic system that activates cells located in the adrenal
glands, located near the kidneys. Each is composed of two parts: a central medulla
and a surrounding layer of cells referred to as the cortex. The hypothalamus, via
the sympathetic system, stimulates cells located in the medulla. These cells in
turn lead to the secretion of neurohormones (adrenaline and noradrenaline) from
the medullar region of the gland into the bloodstream. These molecules perform
a role in arousing the body that cannot be accomplished entirely by neural stimulation. They increase the energy production of skeletal muscle fibers by signal-
ing the cell to convert glycogen into glucose, the basic fuel for movement.

The Endocrine System

The *endocrine system* is composed of a number of glands that interact with
each other and with structures of the body by way of chemical substances called
hormones. Table 4.1 lists several of these glands and their functions. Hormones
are often described as molecular keys that flow through the bloodstream and

Table 4.1
Major Endocrine Glands and the Functions of the Hormones They Produce

These Glands:	*Produce Hormones That Regulate*
Hypothalamus	Release of pituitary hormones
Anterior pituitary	Testes and ovaries
	Breast milk production
	Metabolism
	Reactions to stress
Posterior pitutary	Water conservation
	Breast milk excretion
	Uterus contraction
Thyroid	Metabolism
	Growth and development
Parathyroid	Calcium levels
Gut	Digestion
Pancreas	Glucose metabolism
Adrenals	Fight or flight responses
	Metabolism
	Sexual desire in women
Ovaries	Development of female sexual traits
	Ova production
Testes	Development of male sexual traits
	Sperm production
	Sexual desire in men

From Philip G. Zimbardo and Richard J. Gerrig, *Psychology and Life, 15th ed.* Copyright 1999. Adapted by permission by Allyn & Bacon.

open biological locks that are located on or within specific target structures. These chemical keys contain messages that signal organs to respond. Hormones do not initiate the activity of targeted structures; they modify and regulate ongoing biological processes.

Two structures are central to the functioning of the endocrine system: the *pituitary gland*, which is referred to as the master gland because of its widespread effect on the endocrine system, and the *hypothalamus*, which produces hormones that are transported to the pituitary gland to be released into the bloodstream. In a way, the hypothalamus serves as a bridge between the activities of the nervous system and the activities of the endocrine system. Biological well-being depends on an intimate, interactive relationship among the various systems of the body. The control of target tissue and target organs by both neural and hormonal communication provides a vivid example of the synergy involved in human action.

The pituitary gland secretes at least 25 *tropic* hormones; that is, hormones that travel through the bloodstream and affect specific targets. There are systems that regulate the homeostatic balance of the body, systems that regulate biological arousal, systems that regulate responses to environmental demands and challenges, and systems that regulate sexual behaviors.

Another system that has received considerable attention from researchers interested in motivation is the *pituitary-adrenal-cortical arousal system*, which links the release of *adrenocorticotropic hormone* (ATCH) from the anterior area of the pituitary gland to the outer layer, or cortex, of the adrenal gland. When the outer layer of the adrenal gland is stimulated by ATCH, it varies the amount of *glucocorticoids* (steroids) released into the bloodstream. These molecules have the capacity to enter cells and direct their nuclei to increase protein production and energy supplies—processes vital to the repair of damaged tissues.

The Fight-or-Flight Response

Many of the behavioral manifestations of motivation and emotion can be understood by examining the relation between brain structures and the processes of the autonomic nervous system and the endocrine system. The fight or flight response has been viewed as a critical survival mechanism. When humans are faced with threatening situations, they respond automatically with a highly orchestrated pattern of physiological responses designed to aid in survival. When danger is sensed, the limbic system is activated.

Through its neural connections, the limbic system innervates pathways of the *sympathetic-adrenal-medullary system* that release adrenaline and noradrenaline into the bloodstream. These hormones play a critical role in quick preparation of the body to meet environmental challenges. Circulating adrenaline stimulates the release of glucose into the bloodstream and increases the amount of blood that flows to the brain. The brain, a major consumer of energy, benefits from the increased availability of energy supplies, particularly when its structures are responding to threatening environmental situations. The brain is known to consume approximately one-fifth of the body's available oxygen when an individual is in a relaxed or resting state. However, when environmental conditions change and one is challenged, blood flow to the brain can increase by 20 percent and brain oxygen use by 30 percent over resting conditions. Corresponding with these changes is a brief spike in instantaneous increased awareness, focused attention, and physical readiness to respond (Dienstbier, 1989, 1991).

At the same time that circulating adrenaline benefits the brain, the body's muscle tissue is benefiting from circulating noradrenaline. When faced with a potential threat, the muscular system increases its activity. The mobilization of the body for rapid action draws on available energy supplies. Noradrenaline helps skeletal muscle tissue by increasing blood flow to muscles and aiding in the release of free fatty acids, which are broken down and utilized by muscle cells as fuel (Levinthal, 1990).

This surge of neurohormonal activity lasts only briefly, however. But threatening situations may demand prolonged periods of physiological arousal and preparedness. This longer-lasting arousal is instigated by the pituitary-adrenal-cortical system. Signals from the hypothalamus cause the pituitary to secrete ATCH, which flows from the pituitary gland to the adrenal gland's cortex and stimulates it to release glucocorticoids into the bloodstream. Such steroids tend to reduce the sensitivity of the body's joints and musculature to shock and damage; it is a type of natural pain suppressor that remains active for a relatively long period of time. (Consider the amount of physical punishment the body of a football player or boxer can absorb during competition without experiencing a level of pain that would lead him to quit playing.)

The time course of arousal systems that constitute the fight-or-flight response is important to understanding both the physiology and the psychology of threat-produced arousal. When stimulated, the sympathetic-adrenal-medullary system evidences a rapid onset, with maximal release of neurohormones and then a relatively rapid return to baseline levels. The surge of activity has been linked to optimal physical and mental performance and is associated with pleasurable emotional feelings. The pituitary-adrenal-cortical system maintains a low base rate and a slow release of glucocorticoids into the bloodstream. The accumulation of steroids has been linked to the development of negative feelings such as anxiety and depression (Levinthal, 1990). The fight-or-flight response has figured prominently in many modern theories of stress and emotional well-being. These issues will be described in depth in chapter 5.

HOW MOTIVATION IS STUDIED

Recall that skill was defined previously as the ability to use knowledge effectively and readily in execution of performance, and that both motor skills and cognitive skills are performed to achieve a goal. Whether skills are overt (involving body or limb movements) or covert (involving problem solving and memory), they are linked to achieving some type of goal.

Goal-Directed Action

A *goal* is a need that an individual identifies in terms of an *end state*; that is, the end result toward which he or she is moving. In some cases, there may be a clearly defined end state (e.g., being able to perform 50 successive push-ups); in others, the goal state may be defined only vaguely (e.g., to become a better person). The goals that individuals develop are determined by a variety of factors categorized in terms of physiological, biosocial, or psychic needs. Studies reveal that multiple factors energize behavior and drive individuals to act and that these factors influence how people think and how they feel.

Motivation and Consciousness

Researchers tend to define goals in terms of what individuals consciously try to do (Weinberg, 1994). Regardless of the type of goal, attaining a goal requires that higher-order mental processes select, organize, and direct lower-level processes. Cognitive psychologists recognize that the machinery of the information-processing system does not operate blindly; it must be directed by a global processor that evaluates the costs and benefits of actions in specific situations. *Consciousness* has been proposed to be a type of executive processor that is at the top of the hierarchy of the information-processing system.

Early Twentieth-Century Views of Consciousness

Perhaps the most influential U.S. philosopher to address the phenomenon of consciousness was William James (1842–1910). His *Principles of Psychology* (1890) addressed the topic of consciousness, and his views of the characteristics of consciousness are echoed in many of the present-day debates among scientists and philosophers interested in the role of consciousness and human thought.

James proposed that consciousness is characterized by four elements (Hergenhahn, 1992, p. 306):

1. Consciousness is a uniquely personal activity. No one else can truly appreciate what is in the forefront of your consciousness, as no one else can think your thoughts or feel your feelings. You might guess or hypothesize what someone else is thinking or feeling, but you can never known for certain. Further, our ability to communicate our thoughts to others is always limited by our language and its grammar structure. A psychological experience may be generated as we engage in some game or sport activity, but we can never truly communicate the essence of the experience to another individual.

2. Our conscious state is constantly changing. James compared consciousness to a river, which is constantly in motion, heading toward the ocean. Our thoughts join in a stream of consciousness, which is changing constantly in its form.

3. Consciousness, although changing continuously, still maintains a sensible theme that connects various ideas that emerge in the flow of consciousness. Ideas in the normal mind are not random; they reflect our ongoing physical activities, the environment, and the mind's attempt to make sense of sensory information that is being channeled toward the brain.

4. Consciousness is an adaptive activity. We live in potentially dangerous environments that demands that we be aware of hazards and ready to respond accordingly. Consciousness drives the attentional mechanisms that coordinate thought and behavior.

Consider the thoughts you might enjoy as you walk across an open field on a summer day. Your mind jumps from one idea to the next. Ideas are maintained in conscious awareness only with effort. You must deliberately and consciously focus on an idea for it to be sustained in your immediate awareness. The consciousness state is like the surface of a pot of boiling water. Heat and

steam are released from the surface because of the energy produced by movement of water molecules beneath the surface. The unconscious state, on the
other hand, is like the heated water below the surface. It is constantly in motion, moving and swirling toward the threshold at the surface. At times, energy
builds up and causes a release of heat energy into the air above the boiling
water. In the same way, ideas, images, emotions, and bits of knowledge swirl
around in the unconscious mind. Individual psychic elements combine or break
away from others. When a number of elemental ideas unite, their combined
mass increases and begins to challenge other conglomerations of psychic elements for entry into consciousness.

Contemporary Views of Consciousness

Recent advances in cognitive science, neuropsychology, computer science, and
cognitive psychology have provided new approaches to understanding consciousness. Researchers from many different backgrounds are actively pursuing scientific examinations for consciousness. Most champion the view that the secrets of
consciousness can be understood by examining the physical and chemical properties of the brain and the basic components of the brain that organize and make
sense of information provided by both the internal and external world (Crick,
1994).

Today, consciousness is described as an *emergent property*, meaning that it
originates in the workings of the brain. Once consciousness is realized, it interacts
with and affects the activity of the brain itself (Baars, 1988). Thus, although consciousness arises from the activity of the 55 billion cells that constitute the brain,
it is more than just a side effect of neurological activity. The dynamic, emergent
properties of consciousness direct brain function and, in turn, our behavior.

Consciousness is the module at the top of the hierarchy of the mind. It plays
a more general role than that of metacognition, which is a lower-level module
of the mind that is domain specific. Mental modules are viewed as independent
systems that perform selected and relatively restricted operations. Thus metacognition, at the direction of consciousness, has a very specific job to perform; it
constructs patterns of behavior that are designed to achieve specific goals. Metacognitive processes produce patterns of behaviors by directing attentional processes (viewed as a lower-level module) to affect memory structures.
Attentional processes are designed to perform a number of specific tasks by directing the actions of sensory memory, short-term memory, and long-term memory structures—the basic modules of the mind.

Thus, a major contributor to an orderly mind is the degree to which consciousness directs the activation of the modules that comprise the hierarchy of the mind.
Skilled performance demands that task-relevant information be selected and
brought into consciousness. Athletes who can't keep their minds on track often
find that their performance suffers. Irrelevant thoughts surface into consciousness

and interfere with task-related decision making. The truly skilled individual is one who is best able to bring a disordered state of awareness under control.

Motivation and Feelings

Over the centuries, numerous philosophies have emerged concerning the conscious experiences described by humans. *Phenomenology* is an attempt to explain consciousness in terms of feelings an individual derives from experiences (Stanage, 1987). Each movement or action taken and each thought is loaded with meaning beyond that which is provided by the sensory systems of the body. Because everyone possesses different histories, the meaning attributed to each sensation varies from individual to individual. The qualities of these experiences are directly dependent upon the individual's interpretation of them; thus, what each person feels during participation in games, sports, music, or work is unique. Further, the experience that is derived is ultimately determined by the individual. One person may view the sensations produced by skydiving as positive, whereas another who performs exactly the same activity could view it as a terrifying event, never to be undertaken again. The point made by phenomenologists is that experiences obtained during activities have value in and of themselves; experiences are a source of knowledge that is fundamental to an individual's personal growth and well-being.

Emotion

Modern researchers define *emotion* as short-term, positive or negative affective reactions to real or imagined objects (Wells and Matthews, 1994). The scientific study of human emotion typically involves examining the components of emotional experiences and relating them to other psychological states such as cognition and attention. Parkinson (1995) has identified four components of emotional experience:

1) *Situational awareness.* Emotional responses are linked to an individual's evaluation of specific situations. Before an event can be responded to emotionally, there must be some interpretation of the meaning of the event. Events that are not appraised as either positive or negative elicit little emotion.

2) *Arousal.* Changes in the activity of the autonomic nervous system occur during periods of emotional experience. The specific emotion state that accompanies changes in generalized sympathetic arousal depends on how the individual interprets and evaluates the physiological signals he or she senses as they become emotional.

3) *Facial expressions.* Considerable cross-cultural research provides support for the hypothesis that some facial expressions are innate. It appears that, regardless of cultural heritage, people are equipped with the ability to recognize basic emotional states in others' facial expressions, such as contempt or joy.

4) *Action readiness*. Changes in physical arousal that are part of our emotional experiences prepare us to act. For example, fear and anger are emotions that set the conditions for movement; conversely, the emotions of sadness and despair are associated with withdrawal, lethargy, and lack of movement.

Mood

Modern researchers define *moods* as general and pervasive negative or positive affective states that can influence thought and behavior (Morris, 1989). Unlike emotions, which bring about rather circumscribed patterns of responses, moods possess the capacity to affect a wide variety of behaviors. When one is in the mood to be entertained, any one of a number of activities may suffice. Moods affect individuals for relatively long periods of times. *Depression*, for example, is a mood state characterized by lowered levels of motivation during which people experience feelings of helplessness and a pervasive sadness. Some people experience depression for months or even years. Mood states can serve as a type of background filter that colors how people perceive and act upon environmental stimuli. You may experience a piece of music, for example, as either pleasant and enjoyable or grating and irritating, depending upon the particular mood state you are in while listening.

Thus, moods influence what we attend to and how we evaluate those things. They influence how we remember past events and how we expect to perform in the future. An individual's past sport performance, for example, may be viewed in either a positive or negative light, depending on his or her mood state at the time the act was performed and when the memories are retrieved. The manner in which past performances are evaluated is extremely important, as it can set the tone for how an individual expects to perform in the future. The way in which people interpret past behaviors and anticipate future behaviors plays a fundamental role in determining how motivated they are to learn new skills. Mood states are linked to how people appraise their abilities to meet and overcome the demands that are part of learning new skills. Those who perceive themselves as helpless are not motivated to learn skills.

MOTIVATION AND SKILL LEARNING

The role of motivation in skill acquisition is extremely complex; there are multiple interacting factors that influence the initiation and persistence of behaviors. Some of these factors are environmentally based; others reside within the individual. Learning occurs within the context of a person-environment interaction. Skill learning takes place within social and cultural environments that promote specific kinds of actions. Consider the parents of a newborn infant who may have great plans for their child. In some households, parents will place balls, gloves, and sports equipment in the infant's crib; in other homes, the crib may be strewn with books and surrounded by replicas of famous artwork. From the outset, a child is affected by the intent of his or her parents to promote behaviors that they perceive to be important for the future. These early attempts to guide and motivate a child's behaviors have profound effects on some children, but negligible effects on others. Not everyone who begins life with a golf club in the crib will become another Tiger Woods. The manner in which an individual (regardless of age) responds to prompting within a given social climate is also shaped by personal wishes, desires, and goals.

One way to evaluate the role of motivation in skill acquisition is to examine the learning histories of experts. This research tactic involves analyzing the training histories of accomplished performers in various skill domains. Evaluating the background experiences of numerous sports figures, chess players, and musicians who are acknowledged experts in their fields reveals a number of common factors. All highly skilled people proceed through a series of distinct stages as they make the transition from novice to expert.

The Stages of the Learning Curve

The stage model of learning is particularly important when attempting to understand how specific motives influence skill acquisition. This is because the impact of a given motivational factor often depends on the practitioner's particular stage of skill development. The motives that drive a person to learn skills while in one stage may not have the same effect on behavior in another stage of skill development. Consider that many skills require years of practice before mastery is reached. In modern educational systems, for example, students are expected to spend years practicing and refining academic and sports skills.

The Cognitive Stage

Typically, those who become elite performers were introduced to the activities at which they excel at an early age, usually between three and nine years of age. Initially, they engaged in these activities as play. The notion that playful experiences lead to the selection of activities into which an individual will later channel his or her resources is important. Play (discussed in detail in chapter 7) appears to be essential for normal development. Play is thought to be innately motivated behavior that is important in determining how well humans adapt to their environment. Playful activities occur throughout the life span. Although there may be some advantage to learning some skills early in life, this does not mean that play activities that reveal new domains of knowledge and skill development cannot be experienced later in life. Play provides an opportunity for anyone, at any age, to become involved in a naturalistic form of problem solving; tasks are constructed, deconstructed, and reconstructed without relying on external rules or giving in to structure or demands.

Play is generated internally, but it is usually influenced by outside factors. The manner in which a young boy or girl elects to play soon comes to be guided by the culture in which the child lives. It is not long before the child's play is affected by the rules and constraints of society. Nondirected play leads to rule-directed games; in such games the child must learn the relation between specific actions or skills and specific outcomes or goals. A cognitive threshold is crossed when the child realizes that attaining goals is related to practice. The child may come to this conclusion on his own, as when a boy realizes that he will have to learn many different ways to control the movement of a soccer ball to become a professional soccer player. This conclusion may also be reached on the basis of information provided by others, as when he realizes that becoming an astronaut will require that he learn mathematics. Regardless, attaining such insight is not a trivial matter. The mental processes that occur during the cognitive stage determine our aspirations and goals.

The transition from play to actual skill learning is marked by the introduction of specific training activities taught by a teacher or coach. A young girl may ask her parents to find someone to teach her how to play basketball, or an adult interested in learning yoga may search the telephone directory for a class in which to participate.

The Associative Stage

A teacher or coach introduces the training methods required of novices to achieve their goals. The teacher describes the steps involved in learning the skill and introduces a practice regimen. The novice is expected to arrange his or her daily routine to accommodate the need for practice drills and exercises. Parents often become highly involved in the learning process by ensuring that their child practices regularly. Even at this early stage of instruction, several motivational factors interact to determine how the learner will respond to training.

One motivational factor to be considered is the goals of the learner versus the goals of the teacher. Some people may elect to pursue a training program designed to prepare them for competition and for public recognition of their skills; these individuals have a *task-mastery orientation* (Roberts, 1989). Their primary interests lie in making comparisons between their performance and the performance of others. Training and practice are seen as a vehicle for overcoming opposition and winning. Others are not interested in competing with others; they are more interested in improving their personal competency. These individuals have a *mastery-goal orientation*; their goals are subjective and internalized. For them, it is the process of learning, not the outcome of their practice, that is important (Nicholls, 1989).

A novice's goal orientation will determine to a great extent whether or not a particular training approach will instill the motivation necessary to engage in prolonged and deliberate practice. The novice's goals may differ dramatically from the teacher's or coach's goals. The youngster who maintains a mastery-goal orientation toward learning to play baseball may quickly disengage from participating in practices that are designed around drills to prepare players for competitive play situations. Likewise, a young ballplayer who envisions himself playing professionally as an adult may have difficulty learning in training environments that merely use baseball as a vehicle for fostering general health and wellness.

The term *deliberate practice* has been used to define the type of practice that people engage in because they expect that it will lead to the development of specialized skills. Unlike leisure activities and play, deliberate practice is performed in utmost seriousness, with high levels of focused attention and concentration, and with the singular intent of improving performance (see Ericsson, 1996, for an overview of deliberate practice).

Improvement in both motor performance and cognitive performance occurs when an individual is pushed toward his or her capacity limits. The human cardiovascular system and muscular system adapt to the demands that are placed on them, and people become stronger and perform faster when they train within a *training zone*. This zone is defined by a specific level of intensity and duration of activity. Indeed, physical training has become an exact science in which very specific training regimens have been developed to produce very specific effects.

To make progress in the performance of any skill, one must gradually increase training demands. A historical review of elite performers reveals that their training regimens increased considerably in both frequency and duration, with some individuals engaging in deliberate practice as much as four to five hours per day, as many as six days per week (Starkes, Deakin, Allard, Hodges, and Hayes, 1996). Further, training is performed consistently for years by some individuals and for decades by others. The ever-increasing intensity, frequency, and duration of training designed to promote improvement in skilled performance can, however, overwhelm some individuals. Deliberate practice is both physically and mentally taxing. Too much can lead to fatigue, exhaustion, and burnout in some individuals. Successful training involves a careful balance between periods where considerable energy is expended in order to produce improvement and periods where the body and mind can recover from such exertion.

Time is a valuable commodity to most people in modern society. Thus, the training time needed to improve skill can compete with other activities that may also be important to the learner. Take, for example, an aspiring teenaged gymnast who may be faced with giving up a portion of her social life in order to train for competition. Conflicts may arise when she is expected to perform tedious, repetitive, and effortful practice drills instead of spending time with family and friends.

Training demands do not necessarily take their toll only on the student. Demands are placed on the student's family, as well. Increased training time equates to increased costs for training, equipment, and travel. Further, the time required to transport students to and from classes and competitive events can also be considerable. Researchers have noted that only one child in families with several children typically is singled out for advanced skill training because of the financial and time costs involved.

The challenges and difficulties that face students during the associative stage of skill learning may be considerable. It appears that many students draw upon various sources of motivation to fuel their behavior during this very difficult stage of learning. One explanation for the persistence of training during the associative stage of skill acquisition is that there is a distinctive change in the source of the drive that motivates the practitioner. Rewards that are gained from practice become associated less with external rewards and more with intrinsic rewards. Early in training, such external rewards for performance as medals, ribbons, certificates, and praise may be potent sources of motivation, particularly for children. However, as the learner matures and gains more experience, external rewards lose their capacity to motivate and sustain practice behavior. The rewards that drive some individuals to continue practicing day in and day out become increasingly more intrinsic in nature. Instead of focusing on *outcome goals* (such as winning an Olympic event), these practitioners focus more on *process goals* (such as the improvement of specific performance components). This is not to say that outcome goals become a totally ineffective source of motivation; rather, the types of goals that are important to a person may shift over time under specific environmental conditions (Deci and Ryan, 1985, 1991).

Learners who internalize the source of their motivation may have an advantage over their competition, however. Researchers have observed considerable differences in the amount and quality of practice performed by people who are motivated primarily by extrinsic rewards and those who are motivated primarily by intrinsic rewards. When students perform tasks in order to achieve external rewards, their behaviors are guided and judged by others. External guidance is not necessarily bad, as part of the educational process involves a teacher who directs students toward the most efficient ways to solve problems. Indeed, it is particularly important to provide guidance during skill acquisition's cognitive stage. However, external guidance imposed later in training may actually limit or interfere with the student's approach toward problem solving; the coach's or teacher's way may be perceived by the learner to be the only acceptable way to perform a task. Students may come to depend too much on their teachers for guidance and fail to explore new ways to behave. As a result, the student's sense of self-competency and control may not adequately develop, as he or she perceives that actions are linked to some outside force or condition. Further, if a student's motivation is merely to attain an external reward, practice becomes rather mechanical. Practice behavior is signaled by the availability of an external reward, and it terminates as soon as the reward is obtained. The student is motivated in these instances only to do the minimum that is required to attain his or her goal (Condry and Chambers, 1978).

Those who are intrinsically motivated tend to focus on the *process* of training rather than on the *product* or outcome of training. They tend to examine a problem from multiple perspectives and to think through alternative ways in which a problem can be solved. Instead of waiting to be instructed how to respond, they initiate their own search for ways to solve a problem. Typically, people who are intrinsically motivated are more flexible in terms of the strategies they employ during practice than are those who are extrinsically motivated. Further, because they initiate their own actions, intrinsically motivated individuals tend to persist in effortful behavior; practice tends to terminate once they are satisfied with their performance, not simply because the training session is at its end or the coach is satisfied with their performance.

Thus, at least part of a learner's motivation to persevere during the associative stage of training—and the hours of deliberate practice he is willing to invest—may be due to *self-involvement*. The guitarist who spends hours practicing scales, the ice skater who does hundreds of figure eight repetitions, and the man who won't put the Sunday crossword puzzle down until it is completed all do these things because their actions are meaningful to them.

It is interesting to listen to the goals of young children who are interested in learning a new skill. Some will say that they want to be professional baseball players, or astronauts, or neurosurgeons, or prima ballerinas. You will notice that the reality of what is involved in achieving their lofty goals does not seem to enter their minds. However, the rigors of training experienced during the associative stage typically helps to focus learners on the discrepancy between their current skill proficiency levels and those required to meet their level of aspiration. The way that individuals modify their goals during the associative stage of skill acquisition may differentiate between those who persevere and those who quit.

There is a large literature that addresses issues surrounding adherence to exercise programs and identifies those factors determining who continues to exercise and who drops out (Dishman, 1988). Studies on exercise adherence support the complexity of the issue and posit many reasons to explain why some individuals continue to exercise and others do not. One important factor is the match between an individual's perceptions of his or her abilities and the level of the goals that are set.

The feedback that a learner obtains from practice during the associative stage of skill acquisition reveals information regarding the degree of discrepancy between his or her actual level of proficiency and the level of proficiency that is needed to achieve a particular goal. If an individual's goal is to become a professional golfer, but he has a difficult time achieving par even after years of practice, it is unlikely that his goals will be achieved. When an individual's goals are thwarted or blocked, negative emotional responses are produced. The *frustration hypothesis*, which is based on many studies conducted with both animals and humans, has been used to explain two ways people may respond to frustrating situations. Some people see the gulf between their present skill level and the level of skill needed to attain their goals as too great; they are most likely to elect to drop out. Others elect to keep their unrealistic goals and work hard on attaining them by devoting all of their energy and resources to trying to attain the requisite skills.

Part of maintaining the proper motivation to acquire skills and to persist at training regimens appears to be the ability to constantly adjust and modify goals. Adaptive goal setting requires reasonable and rational decision making about goals and the appropriate level of effort needed to achieve those goals. This is particularly important when you consider the tremendous physical and mental changes that occur throughout our life spans. Goals change as individuals progress from childhood, to adolescence, and to young and older adulthood.

The Autonomous Stage

The sources for the motivation behind the perseverance of people who are already accomplished in their fields are complex and interactive. Two main themes emerge when researchers have attempted to explain what motivates people to practice their crafts for decades on end.

Some researchers suggest that the primary motivation for the persistence of deliberate practice is competitive success. The study of elite performers suggests that the time an individual spends in deliberate practice decreases very rapidly once he or she chooses to withdraw from competition. Without a competitive situation to fuel the desire to succeed, motivation to maintain or improve performance decreases. It appears that, for some people, if they can't run with the "big dogs," they will not run at all.

Elite performers choose to pursue virtually a full-time involvement in their area of specialty. At this decision point, a student may see his or her skill as the basis of a vocation or career. Often students who elect to press onward at this point, to hone their skills with the hope of entering the upper echelon of performance, will move to new geographical areas to be close to master teachers. They may have to petition for the attention and instruction of these master teachers. In many areas of sports, the arts, music, and academics, the selection process at this level is highly competitive; only a few individuals are selected from many applicants. The demands subsequently placed on these select few may be incredibly taxing. The goal that characterizes practice at this level of study is to improve constantly.

People often continue to persist in actions, not because they are linked to goals and outcomes, but because they are linked to the feeling generated while in the act of performing. Experiential motivation provides the basis for the positive emotional experience. Activity, for some individuals, leads to joy and a heightened state of well-being (see Csikszentmihalyi and Csikszentmihalyi, 1988, for an overview). Two individuals, for instance, may be equally skilled at playing a musical score; however, one may perceive that playing the piece is a chore and merely a way of acquiring fame and fortune, whereas the other may view playing the score as great fun and something to be enjoyed simply for its own sake. The motivation to practice and perform is not related to extrinsic external rewards but rather to intrinsically generated emotions.

Research conducted on expert performers suggests that while many elite performers do, in fact, decrease the amount of time they engage in deliberate practice after they retire from competition, there are some who continue on. This persistence has been explained in terms of *internalization of reinforcement*; that is, they find practice itself to be inherently enjoyable. Enjoyment in the field of sport has been defined as "a positive affective response to the sport experience that reflects generalized feelings such as pleasure, liking, and fun" (Scanlan and Simons, 1992). Enjoyment is conceptualized as a general state that reflects the feelings derived from both extrinsic reward (such as the enjoyment of receiving a Nobel prize) and from intrinsic rewards (such as the phenomenological experiences derived from mere physical movement).

In summary, it is clear that individuals come to a number of decision points during the stages of skill learning. At each decision point, a person may opt to 1) mobilize resources to meet new challenges and press on regardless, 2) to modify training goals and practice intensity, or 3) to disengage from the activity entirely and quit. The basis behind the decisions that are made at these points are incredibly complex and depend on multiple factors. Nevertheless, the decisions that are made will shape the trajectory of the individual's rate of skill acquisition and, ultimately, the level of skill the person attains.

THEORIES OF MOTIVATION

Many theories have been proposed to explain why people behave in the ways that they do. These theories tend to reflect the three sources of motivation introduced at the beginning of this chapter: physiological, biosocial, and psychic.

Physiological Theories

Behavioral theories of learning and motivation that predate the cognitive revolution continue to exert a strong influence on contemporary educators. These theories explain motivation in objective terms, on the basis of the strength and persistence of action. Clark Hull (1884–1952) developed one of the most influential behavioral theories of the twentieth century. Hull (1952) suggested that the motives of all organisms (animals and humans alike) could be explained in terms of biological adaptation. A biological drive state is produced when an organism's homeostatic balance is disrupted. Tissue needs (such as food, water, and sex) energize the organism into action and goad it to seek out whatever is necessary to maintain the organism's homeostatic balance. The organism's history of learning and experience dictate the specific actions that are taken to satisfy these basic physiological needs. In the most simple situation, hunger is a stimulus that arises from metabolic processes that use the body's energy stores. The student who skips breakfast may feel increasingly clear sensations of hunger as the day wears on. The drive for food energizes the student and makes her more active and aroused. The choice that she makes to satisfy her hunger will depend on her past learning. She may have learned where candy and soft drink machines are located and she goes there to secure those things that will satisfy her cravings.

Hull hypothesized that behavior is motivated by *primary drives,* which are stimuli that ensure biological survival, and *secondary drives,* which are stimuli associated with the reduction of primary drives. A hamburger can serve as a primary reinforcer for someone who is hungry; however, because of its association with access to a hamburger, money comes to serve as a secondary or learned reinforcer. We learn through the process of association that money can provide access to those things that reduce our primary needs.

Behavioral theories in general and Hull's drive-reduction theory specifically view human behavior from a mechanistic perspective. Humans are considered to be completely self-maintained, biological robots whose actions are as predictable as all other events in nature. Motivation is understood in terms of the impact of environmental stimuli and reinforcers. Drives are posited to lead to increasing levels of biological tension, and drive reduction leads to a return toward homeostasis (decreased tension levels). The objectivity of behavioral theories (such as those developed by Edward Thorndike, John B. Watson, and B. F. Skinner) have been embraced by many who were looking for ways to modify and control people's actions. Considerable efforts were made to apply the principles of conditioning and learning developed under laboratory conditions to education, labor organizations, business, and mental health domains.

Biosocial Theories

A number of theories of motivation address the impact of social factors on persistence and learning. The extensive work of Alfred Bandura has had a pronounced effect on contemporary views regarding how skills are learned and the factors that motivate behavior. Central to Bandura's theory (1977, 1997) is the assumption that our actions are the result of complex interactions between our thoughts, the context of the environment in which we act, and the effect of our actions. Bandura's notion of *reciprocal determinism* blends the elements of information processing and the dynamics present within social settings. Our behaviors are posited to be self-activated; that is, we do not act in a robotlike manner when specific stimuli are presented to us; rather, we are consciously aware of how our actions best fit the present situation. Human behavior is adaptive. There are times when we perceive it to be to our advantage to engage in a given manner. In school settings, for example, a teacher may ask students a question. Some children may raise their hands to signal their intent to answer the question, not only because they believe they know the answer, but also because they understand the social rewards that are associated with their participation. Students who answer a teacher's questions correctly demonstrate competency, not only to the teacher, but to classmates as well. There may be other children, however, who hesitate and elect not to raise their hands. Some of these children may know the answer but perceive that it is to their advantage not to participate in class activities. Their past experiences have led them to perceive themselves as ineffective and unskilled; these self-perceptions lead them to withdraw from classroom participation.

According to social cognitive theory, our motivation to behave is linked to what we have learned about ourselves and to our perceptions of our abilities. Several different cognitive structures guide our actions, but Bandura suggests that *self-efficacy* plays the central role in determining our willingness to engage in action, the level of intensity of our actions, and the persistence of our actions. Self-efficacy reflects our beliefs about our abilities and capacities to deal with problems within a specific domain. Unlike the notion of confidence, which reflects a global belief that we may have about our abilities to deal with problems in general, self-efficacy beliefs are tied closely to specific types of tasks. A student, for example, may have a sense of high self-efficacy when it comes to playing soccer but a sense of low self-efficacy when it comes to solving an algebraic equation.

Self-efficacy beliefs represent a combination of multiple sources of information. The manner in which we assess our ability to perform a task depends on both personal factors and environmental factors. Our self-efficacy is determined by: 1) our personal histories of success and failure; 2) vicariously watching the successes and failures of others; 3) verbal encouragement and persuasion, and 4) our interpretation of our physical arousal. These factors work together to determine *outcome expectations*; that is, what an individual anticipates will be the result of his or her actions. Self-efficacy precedes behavior and outcome expectations follow behaviors. Outcome expectations play an important role in determining whether we will develop positive, adaptive views of our abilities and skills, or negative, maladaptive views.

Psychic Theories

Humans appear at times to be driven by forces that defy rational thought. Why would someone choose to climb mountains, skydive, or swim in shark-infested water and thereby place herself in a position of real danger? Several theories have been proposed to explain these seemingly irrational acts. Sigmund Freud (1856–1938) became interested in understanding what motivates human behavior. His *psychodynamic theory of personality* was based on the premise that humans are driven by unconscious motives that are grounded in our biologically based need for procreation. Freud was trained both as a research physiologist and as a medical doctor and was much influenced by the Darwinian theory of evolution. He conceptualized humans as being in a constant state of anxiety brought about by the drive to procreate that arose from an unconscious psychic force called the *id*. The libidinal energy of the id, to Freud, was a blend of the drive for life (*eros*) and the drive for death (*thanatos*). As conceptualized, this unconscious force reflected millions of years of evolution that preceded the advent of modern man. The motivations for the behavior of prehistoric man were simple—survival and procreation. Activities that led to the survival of the individual and the survival of the species dominated all other activities (Freud, 1910/1949).

Freud posited that it was not until recently in the evolutionary history of humankind that the neurological structures responsible for the control of the basic libidinal impulses developed. Paralleling structural changes within the brain were changes in the environments in which humans lived. Social systems began to emerge in which members of a community were taught the rules of behavior. It became necessary for humans to control their instinctual urges. Freud hypothesized that the conflict between humans' instinctual urges and the demands for social order and conduct place everyone in a constant state of psychological tension and anxiety. He proposed that this undesirable psychological state is reduced by various defense mechanisms that we use to keep unconscious wishes and desires in check. Some of these defense mechanisms are behavior patterns that set the stage for peak experiences. Individuals driven to perform athletic activities or games of chance serve to reduce, at least for a while, the anxieties experienced by the ceaseless driving force of the id.

Freud's psychodynamic theory was initially looked upon with considerable skepticism when it was first introduced to the medical and scientific community. By the mid-1920s, however, his views gained widespread acceptance, and by the 1930s his theory was an established doctrine. Today the language of Western civilization is filled with terms introduced by Freud and others who have followed the psychodynamic tradition. Freud's view of the dynamic forces that drive and motivate humans has had a tremendous influence. His theory of motivation has been criticized extensively by many contemporary researchers and practitioners; nevertheless, he stands in a class of his own when one considers how the views of a single individual have had such an enduring impact on psychology.

Abraham Maslow (1907–1970) proposed that everyone is naturally motivated to become *self-actualized*; that is, to become the best that we can be. Self-actualization is a psychological state that is experienced when we attain our full potential, personal growth, and creative fulfillment (Maslow, 1968, 1987). This state is attained only after we meet and overcome a series of needs, which are arranged in a hierarchy. In Maslow's system, basic needs must be met before progress can be made toward self-actualization. All humans are motivated to secure physiological needs that are necessary for survival—food, water, shelter, and clothing. When basic needs are met, we are then driven by a need for security; an environment that is safe and stable. Next, social acceptance, love, and affiliation are sought out. If all of these lower needs are achieved, we are driven to seek the esteem of others and to experience autonomy, competence, and independence. It is only then that we begin to experience the psychological state of self-actualization, which is characterized by a transitory period of feelings of inner peace, transcendence, and harmony with all nature.

Much of Maslow's work focused on understanding how people deal with adversity, yet retain the qualities that make humans unique. People are often blocked from achieving the needs that they are innately driven to achieve; individual experiences, social situations, or historical events such as war, famine, and economic upheaval all affect the likelihood that we can become self-actualized. The essence of Maslow's humanistic theory of motivation deals with how people cope with these adversities and maintain the will needed to continue toward self-actualization.

CHAPTER SUMMARY

In this chapter, we evaluated motivation in terms of a type of energy that can arise from a number of different sources. Our level of motivation can be energized by physiological, biosocial, or psychic needs. We examined several neuroanatomical systems that are involved in the regulation of motivation and our ability to adapt to environmental demands. The human mind and body have evolved together to help us meet our needs and to overcome the challenges we face. Our bodies are equipped with a variety of mechanisms that can be brought to bear in fight-or-flight situations. Our minds are equipped with mechanisms that help us consciously evaluate the problems that confront us and how they can be resolved. The mind was presented as a problem-solving system that mediates among our needs, goals, and actions.

Skill learning can be thought of as a problem in need of resolution. If a novice's goal is to become skilled, he or she will allocate the energy needed to complete the arduous training that is required. We have learned in this chapter that many factors can influence our level of motivation as we strive toward our goals in life.

SUGGESTED READINGS

Bandura, A. (1997). *Self-efficacy: The exercise of control.* New York: W. H. Freeman.
Crick, F. H. C. (1994). *The astonishing hypothesis: The scientific search for the soul.* New York: Scribner.
Frijda, N. H. (1986). *The emotions.* Cambridge: Cambridge University Press.
Heckenmuller, J. (1985). Cognitive control and endorphins as mechanisms of health. In J. E. Birren and J. Livingston (Eds.), *Cognition, stress and aging* (pp. 89–110). Englewood Cliffs, NJ: Prentice-Hall.
Maslow, A. H. (1968). *Toward a psychology of being.* New York: Van Nostrand.
Wells, A., and Matthews, G. (1994). *Attention and emotion: A clinical perspective.* Hillsdale, NJ: Erlbaum.

Chapter 5

Skills, Challenge, and Survival

We confront challenges every day of our lives. You do not have to be a mountain climber or an explorer to be challenged. We confront each day knowing that we have a series of tasks that we need to accomplish. Each day may involve attempts to perform well in school, at work, in social situations, or in sports. We live within social communities that expect us to perform in certain ways at certain times. Young children are expected to learn to play games and get along with others; older children are expected to attend school and learn basic academic skills; adolescents are expected to begin to integrate themselves into the adult world with its responsibilities of working and starting a family. Adults are expected to deal with adversities of the real world.

Our ability to meet these challenges depends greatly on the skills that we have learned. Parents put in a tremendous amount of time and effort to teach their children how to behave; teachers provide students the opportunity to benefit from education; coaches provide instruction in playing games and sports. We are provided opportunities to acquire skills throughout our lifetimes. How well we learn these life skills may well determine our success in life and how we feel about ourselves.

In this chapter you will be given a brief history of the evolution of our species and how social structures emerged that placed great emphasis on the acquisition of knowledge and skills. When you complete this chapter, you will understand how the human body and mind evolved and how they prepared our ancestors to survive the demands of a hostile world. You will find out that the mechanisms and processes that helped our ancient relatives meet and overcome the stresses of their world are not always well suited for modern humans to use to deal with the stresses that are encountered in an increasingly technological world. Finally, you will see that a variety of theories focus on skill learning and how skills are vital to our ability to cope with and overcome the challenges of everyday life.

THE FUNCTION OF SKILL

Skills, at their most fundamental level, have one purpose: they are vital for survival. It is sometimes easy for those of us who live in safe and stable homes to forget that the world in which we live can be exceedingly harsh and dangerous for other members of our species. Members of the human race have always faced life-challenging situations. It was a constant, mind-numbing challenge for our ancient ancestors to obtain the necessities of life—food, water, shelter. Those who lacked the skills needed to obtain these necessities perished. Dangers and challenges confront modern humans, as well. Although most of us have the luxury of a steady supply of the necessities of life, our world demands that we have certain technical skills in order to function successfully.

Early Humans

There is considerable debate among anthropologists concerning the beginnings of our species—*Homo sapiens*, or modern humans. Although the specific details concerning the exact evolutionary history of humankind are debated, there is general agreement among most scientists that our ancestral roots can be traced back to a group or genus of early hominids (Tattersall, 1995). This group included at least three species: *Homo habilis, Homo erectus*, and *Homo sapiens*.

Several characteristics made the genus *Homo* different from earlier groups of hominids such as *Australopithecus*. Although *homo* exhibited the erect bipedal movement displayed by members of *Australopithecus*, members of the *Homo* group had larger brain cavities and brain volume (600 to 750 cubic centimeters) than did the earlier genus. Brain volume has been implicated as a crucial factor in the evolution of our species (Holloway, 1979). A functioning human brain consumes considerable energy. Supplying the brain with the energy necessary to function efficiently led members of *Homo* to gradually alter their dietary intake from the herbivorous plant-based diet that was characteristic of *Australopithecus* to a meat-based diet rich in calories. Obtaining such food required them to hunt, kill, and eat animals.

The hallmark accomplishment of *Homo* over 2.5 million years ago was to create tools that could be used to hunt and survive. The capacity to create and use tools reflects the emergence of complex cognitive and motor skills in the species. Stone tool production required that a particular type of stone be selected for a particular use; shaping the stone into a useful tool required the maker to understand something about the properties and characteristics of different types of stone and methods of chipping. As these tools were made for specific tasks, the earliest were probably used to smash bone to remove calorie-rich marrow or to dig for roots and tubers (Washburn, 1979). Over time, however, tool production became more sophisticated, and simple tools were crafted to cut the meat and hide of animals (see Mithen, 1996, chapter 6, for an overview of tool development).

Over hundreds of thousands of years, the physical and mental characteristics of *Homo* slowly changed (Cosmides and Tooby, 1994). *Homo habilis* was a relatively small hominoid who scavenged for food and used fist-size hammerstones and small, sharp flakes as tools. Members of the later species *Homo erectus* (1.5 million years ago) were tall and lean. The gradual shift over time to a high-calorie diet resulted in changes in the manner in which food was metabolized by *Homo erectus*. The size of the gut was smaller and muscle mass and brain volume were larger in this species. *Homo erectus* was fast, lean, and mean; his brain, however, was still primitive compared to that of modern-day humans. Most of his actions were limited to responding to threats, searching for food, and finding mates. Most likely, members of this species lacked the emotional traits that are traditionally associated with humanity.

Evidence of migration patterns suggests that *Homo erectus* learned not only how to deal with the immediate challenges of the environment, but also how to plan for future events. Migration requires acquiring and using knowledge about changes in terrain, weather patterns, sources of food and water, and shelter. Further, the species developed social organization as the advantages of group hunting and the need to defend resources were recognized (Isaac, 1979). Between one million and 700,000 years ago, *Homo erectus* migrated from Africa into Europe (see "Human Evolution: Migration," *Science* 291:1721–1753, 2001).

Europe was cohabited by *Homo erectus* and a group called the *Neanderthals* for over 500,000 years. Both groups lived in small migrating social units organized around hunting. Their hunting activities were directed toward locating large prey such as bison and elk, which could provide considerable calorie-laden food for a group of individuals. Hunting large animals required planning, the use of tactics and strategies, and possession of effective weapons. Hunting of this type was decidedly not a spur-of-the-moment act. The men involved in tracking herds of animals had knowledge of an animal's general behavior and how it would react when attacked. The hunt usually involved leading a solitary animal into a cul-de-sac or trap that allowed the men to surround and confuse the animal. Attacks were coordinated and brutal. The animal was charged repeatedly, brought down with long wooden spears, and killed at close range using handheld weapons—a dangerous enterprise to say the least. Such methods of hunting led to frequent serious injuries to those who made up the hunting party. It might be expected that the preparation for such events was anxiety-provoking for those who participated in the hunt. Anthropological evidence suggests that preparatory rituals preceded some hunts and that successful hunts were followed by ritual acts. No one knows for certain, but it stands to reason that there was a tremendous amount of emotional release associated with group hunting. During the attack, younger members of the group watched older and more experienced hunters and learned those techniques that were critical to a successful hunt. Memories of the attack, the skills that were necessary for success, and the physiological-emotional state experienced during the hunt came to be part of the collective history of the group.

The Neanderthals were known to craft tools and weapons from flint; the stone could be worked into specific shapes that could hold a sharp edge. The cognitive development of hominoids of the period was clearly reflected in the technology required to make tools. Crafting flint tools and weapons demands considerable mental processing and skill. A Neanderthal would have to be able to differentiate among various types of stone and to identify flint. Further, the toolmaker might have to travel considerable distances to locate the flint. Once the stone was found, the toolmaker was required to consider how the flint could be shaped into a specific type of tool. Shaping, or flint knapping, is not easily performed. It requires knowledge of the shape of the core of the stone and the manner in which sections will flake off. A piece of flint struck incorrectly will shatter. Thus, the toolmaker had to remember how to strike the flint in a manner that would produce a usable product. Anthropologists have discovered hand axes—a type of multipurpose tool used for cutting, scraping, and defleshing— that required as many as 300 strikes to shape. The skills involved in creating a simple tool might have required years to develop. Toolmaking was probably a social activity, one that allowed members who had acquired the skill to pass the knowledge to younger members.

For reasons that are not well known, members of the Neanderthal culture disappeared about 30,000 years ago and *Homo sapiens* came to the forefront (Tattersall, 1999; Tattersall and Matternes, 2000). *Homo sapiens* emerged as the dominant group due to the command of complex language, a skill not possessed by the Neanderthals. Early human artifacts reflect that *Homo sapiens* possessed considerable physical and mental skills. Weapons and tools became increasingly more sophisticated. The invention of the throwing stick, for example, increased the distance that a spear could be launched. Cultural products also reflected the expanding mental abilities of early humans. Cave paintings reveal that early *Homo sapiens* had the mental skills required to reproduce three-dimensional figures and the motor skills necessary to paint scenes that recreated events.

Modern Humans

Early civilizations began to emerge approximately 10,000 to 13,000 years ago. At about the same time, groups of people in Southeast Asia, the Fertile Crescent of mideast Asia, and central Mexico elected to give up their nomadic hunter lifestyle and began to invest their collective efforts in planting and harvesting food crops and domesticating animals (Stoskopf, 1993). The shift from a transient, hunter-gatherer existence to one that depended on cultivation of crops and domestication of animals had a profound impact on the evolution of the human species. Mutual cooperation among individuals led to the development of villages, then cities, and, eventually, to nations and empires that depended on the diversification of the skills of its members. The social dynamics of civilization created different roles for individuals who required specialized knowledge. The relative stability of civilization permitted the opportunity to pursue activities fundamental to the development of technology, education, arts, and crafts.

The advent of civilization heralded a significant change in which survival of the community began to outweigh the importance of the survival of individual members. Increasingly larger numbers of people became dependent on their capacity to work together cooperatively to acquire, store, and protect food. Intense pressure was placed on those responsible for maintaining stable sources of food and this led to the rapid acceleration and accumulation of cultural knowledge. Groups of individuals sharing common goals worked together to solve complex technological problems (Hole, 1992).

The problems faced by early farmers were particularly daunting. Consider, for example, what was required to cultivate rice, perhaps civilization's first food staple. Successful rice farming requires that specific steps be taken during specific seasons of the year. Seedlings must first be grown from rice; then, at the right time, they must be dug up and transplanted to a flooded field or paddy. After the tender plants grow for several months, the rice paddy must be drained. Two to three weeks later the rice is laboriously harvested. The rice stalks are cut, bundled, and allowed to dry before the rice grains are removed from the stalk. Clearly, agricultural practices are complex endeavors that require considerable agrarian knowledge about plants and their growth patterns, as well as knowledge about seasonal changes in weather and temperature. Deviation from the time-honored steps or miscalculations of seasonal weather conditions could lead to a failed harvest and severe hardship. Crop catastrophes could cause the death of an entire community.

It was also vital for early communities to ensure that the food grown during one season of the year was somehow made available throughout the entire year. The need to preserve and store food led to the construction of buildings and the development of techniques designed to protect food from spoilage. Food was an extremely valuable and precious commodity; the very survival of a community depended on its access to a continuous supply of it. Once safely stored and protected from spoilage, food had to be protected from those who were not part of the community that produced it. The first evidence of organized warfare emerged during this period of human history. War was, and continues to be, a form of organized and sanctioned theft (see Bronowski, 1973, chapter 2). Communities soon surrounded themselves with walls and other fortifications erected by builders and engineers. Other members of the community began to specialize in crafting both defensive and offensive weapons to protect their precious stores of food.

Thus, with civilization inevitably came the division of labor. People who had specialized skills in farming, engineering, or warfare were needed to help maintain the continued existence of a community. Individual community members, regardless of their roles, were important to the continued survival of the group. Members who performed military duties were deliberately putting themselves at personal risk to ensure the continued survival of the group. Being part of a community became a powerful incentive for individual actions. Success at farming, building, or soldiering led to social recognition and reward for having contributing to the continued success of the community.

Cultural Knowledge

Since the earliest civilizations, an individual's capacity to be successful and the benefits that success brought to the community, have been greatly enhanced by the ready availability of *cultural knowledge* accumulated from previous generations. Rituals designed to perpetuate communal practices acquired through trial-and-error learning are found in all civilizations (Cziko, 1995). Ancient farmers clearly did not understand *why* certain planting practices yielded superior crop growth, nor did engineers understand the structural and chemical dynamics of various materials used to build walls and structures. Nevertheless, the practices that successful farmers used to grow crops enabled them and their communities to survive and thrive. It was critically important that they pass these practices on to the next generation of farmers. Those who employed unsuccessful cultivation methods failed to support their communities, and as a result, these communities failed and died out.

The fact that some procedures worked and others failed led to the emergence of highly structured and rigid cultural practices. It did not matter that the people did not understand why one practice worked and another didn't. These practices often took on religious and mystical characteristics. The art of forging a traditional Japanese sword, for example, involves a long series of steps in which metals are repeatedly heated, hammered, treated, and cooled. Each step taken toward creating the weapon is precisely controlled and timed by ritualistic actions. Even today, skilled traditional swordmakers follow age-old rituals that can be traced back for hundreds of years. The result of the ritualized construction process is a sword that has the properties of both flexibility and strength. The ancient swordmaker may not have understood why the methods he used produced a weapon so highly valued by warriors for its strength and fine cutting edge. He did, however, recognize the differences between a sword that was brittle and likely to shatter during battle and one that gave its user a reliable advantage over his opponents.

It was not until the advent of the scientific revolution in the seventeenth and eighteenth centuries that people began to understand why nature works as it does. Today, modern rice farmers understand those processes of nature that underlie superior crop, yields; modern engineers create structures designed using principles that reflect their understanding of the physical and chemical structure of building materials. It should be remembered, however, that the advance of civilization continues to require the transmission of cultural knowledge from one generation to the next, regardless of the advances achieved by the use of modern scientific methods. Even today, rituals link people to the skills they need to manipulate and control their environments. The manner in which such information is passed from one generation to the next has been the subject of considerable attention by biological and social scientists alike.

EVOLUTIONARY PSYCHOLOGY

The political revolutions that characterized many European nations in the seventeenth and eighteenth centuries were paralleled by intellectual revolutions. New governments fostered the growth of new ideas. People were given greater freedom in expressing their views. Treaties were written describing the nature of governments, societies, and the rights of individuals.

This newfound freedom of inquiry led some to ponder questions that had been suppressed for centuries. One of the most explosive topics was the history of humankind. Explorers and naturalists who traveled the world returned to England and Europe with information about people and strange-looking animals in exotic lands. Early scientists were eager to study and to explain the diversity seen in nature and the world around them. Explanations of human diversity were offered for the first time. Evidence was beginning to accumulate from a variety of sources to suggest that the human species came to exist as a result of the same environmental pressures that led to the survival or extinction of other species.

Darwin's Theory of Evolution

During the five-year voyage of the British ship, HMS *Beagle*, a young British naturalist named Charles Darwin (1809–1882) had an opportunity to visit and explore many new and exotic lands. His copious observations of geological formations and animals and their behavior led him to develop a general theory of evolution. His book *On the Origin of Species by Means of Natural Selection* (1859) described a view of the world that stirs controversy even today. Darwin proposed that all living species, including humans, emerged in response to environmental demands and pressures. Central to Darwin's thesis were three principles of evolution:

1. *The Principle of Natural Variation.* Darwin, like many observers throughout history, noted that offspring are not identical to their mother or father. There may be similarities between successive generations, but there are always differences between parents and their offspring. The genetic mechanisms that produced the variability observed in offspring were unknown to Darwin; however, his observations led him to hypothesize that an element of *randomness* is part of evolution.

2. *The Principle of Super Fecundity*. Adult members of all species produce more off-spring than can be supported by their environment. Thus, there is competition among offspring to acquire sufficient resources to survive and mature.

3. *The Principle of Natural Selection*. Environmental conditions set into motion the pro-cess of *elimination*. Those individuals equipped to obtain available resources are those best able to mature and live long enough to have their own offspring; individuals who lack the characteristics necessary to obtain the resources required for survival do not live long enough to procreate. The evolution of every species, according to Darwin, depends on random variation and, as a result of *selection*, a steady accumulation of beneficial characteristics that result in a fit between members of a species and their environment.

The concept of survival of the fittest was popular even before Darwin pub-lished his theory of evolution. His work, however, is considered to be the most scientifically influential because of the ease with which it can explain many nat-ural observations (Cziko, 1995).

Intergenerational Transmission of Information

Darwin's theory of evolution began a furor of discussion and argument con-cerning human nature that continues to the present. One component that at-tracted considerable attention was his view of the mechanism responsible for the evolution of human thought and behavior. Darwin was concerned primar-ily with biological evolution. He noted, however, that evolution resulted not only in animals with specific physical structures, but also in animals with spe-cific behavioral patterns. Darwin hypothesized in *The Expression of Emotions in Man and Animals* (1872) that behavioral patterns exhibited by our species, such as displays of threat and aggression, exist because of their importance to our early predecessors. He conjectured that aggressive and threatening behav-ior was instrumental to their survival. Individuals who displayed such behav-iors were most likely to mature and have offspring of their own who, in turn, evidenced similar behavioral patterns. These deeply ingrained behavioral pat-terns, developed over many generations, continue to be displayed by modern humans, despite the loss of their importance to survival because of changes in the social environment. Emotions, for Darwin, were the expressed remnants of behaviors whose importance had been preeminent in the distant past.

The notion that humans possess *innate behavioral patterns* linked to our evolutionary history is a strong and compelling one, still articulated in the writings of modern researchers and philosophers. *Sociobiology* is a contempo-rary version of Darwin's theory that emerged in the 1970s as an attempt to ex-plain the social behavior of insects, animals, and humans (Wilson, 1975, 2000). A central assumption of sociobiology is that the continued survival of a species is dependent on *inclusive fitness*, which is described as the extent to which members of a social community act in concert to ensure that genetic codes im-portant to that social community are passed on to the next generation. Indeed, individuals within a social group may forfeit their lives in some cases to ensure that others in the group will be able to pass on genes important to species survival. Sociobiologists see human acts such as altruism, warfare, religion, child-rearing, and mate selection in terms of genetically based behavioral patterns.

There is, however, a logical inconsistency in the traditional Darwinian view regarding how the behaviors of members of one generation can be passed to the next generation. In order for behavioral patterns to be passed on via some genetically based mechanism, an individual's behavior during his or her lifetime must have a direct effect on the transmission of the genetic code that is present only in the *germ cells* of males (sperm) and females (ova). The biological development of every cell in the human body is controlled by the information present in his or her *genetic code*, which is composed of sequences of genes unique to each individual. Of course, the specific actions that one takes can have very profound influences on the body. Skeletal muscles can be enlarged through exercise, cardiorespiratory efficiency can be increased, and joint flexibility can be improved. These changes, however, affect only *somatic* (body) cell systems. No matter how much a man alters his physique through weight-lifting regimens, he will not effect changes in the germ cells that are responsible for sexual reproduction. His sons and daughters can inherit only the coded information that exists in the germ cells of their father and mother; they cannot inherit their father's exercise-altered physique.

The study of genetics has revealed that the human capacity to behave and think reflects two basic evolutionary processes. *Phylogenetic processes* are those that constitute the unique genetic heritage of an individual. Every newborn member of a species will repeat the stages of growth and development experienced by all previous members of that species. The developmental patterns of infants and children are well established, and changes occur in a highly predictable fashion. Indeed, the emergence of specific movement patterns and physical and mental capacities are used by physicians and educators as indices of normal development in infants and children. Changes in phylogenetic development occur slowly, as they reflect the selective processes of evolution on the species as a group.

Ontogenetic processes are those that occur within a single individual's lifetime. The actions we take provide us an opportunity to cope with rapid environmental changes. Acquiring safety habits during childhood (such as always buckling seatbelts in an automobile) allows us to adapt to the demands we will encounter during adolescence and adulthood. These behavioral adaptations will directly increase the likelihood that we will survive to have children of our own.

Humans have only limited control over the phylogenic processes that guide the development of members of our species; however, we do have the capacity to modify and adapt ontogenetic processes. One explanation for the rapid and successful evolution of the human species over the past 5,000 years is our use of *cultural knowledge* and our capacity to capitalize on the experiences of other members of our species to help our individual members meet and overcome survival challenges.

Richard Dawkins (1976, 1986, 1995) introduced a radical view of evolution that has become a theoretical cornerstone for the work of *neo-Darwinian* researchers. He proposed that the rapid evolution of human civilization and culture could be better explained in terms of the variation, selection, and propagation of *beliefs* and *practices* than in terms of gene modification. This cultural knowledge can best be understood by studying the objects constructed by individuals who make up a community, the thoughts they think, and the actions they take. Dawkins suggests that genes are not the only mechanism by which evolution occurs; genes may have been the dominant form of intergenerational transmission of information for three million years, but this does not mean that rival forms of evolution cannot emerge.

Dawkins terms the basic unit of replication of cultural knowledge a *meme;* he describes it as a permanent pattern of matter or information intentionally produced by a human act. The term was derived from the Greek word *mimesis,* or imitation, and it was coined to convey the importance of learning by example and of imitation as a mechanism for passing information from one individual to another or from one generation to the next.

In a very general sense, a meme can be thought of as analogous to an idea. You will recall that information competes for entry into short-term memory and awareness. In the same way that biological selection depends on variability and super fecundity, mental selection depends on an ongoing competition among ideas and thoughts. Many of the thoughts that come to mind may have little evolutionary significance or value. Being able to remember the words to a popular song written in the 1960s, for example, may capture one's attention, but it has virtually no importance in the broad scheme of evolution of the human species. However, many of the billions of members of the human species are continually faced with environmental problems that demand creative solutions; for example, there is a need for better methods of health care, nonpolluting automobile engines, and long-lasting energy sources. Many different solutions to the same problem could be generated by many different minds; some ideas will be better than others. Consider the number of failed attempts at designing a functional aircraft before the Wright brothers succeeded with their design. For every successful inventor, there are many whose ideas never prove successful (see also the views of Csikszentmihalyi, 1993, 1999).

The replication of memes requires that an idea be transmitted from one brain to another. In the same way that a song whistled or hummed in a crowded elevator can be picked up and carried to other places by other people, ideas about creating a better source of engine fuel can be transmitted to the brains of those who listen or read. Some memes are powerful enough to enter and control consciousness. The little tune that gets stuck in your head and keeps repeating throughout the day and the mathematical solution to a sticky problem that evokes the comment, "Why didn't I think of that?" are examples of ways memes come to be part of cultural knowledge. Some have short-term but massive effects on a culture. Platform shoes and minidresses had their moments of fashion glory;

both represent memes with short life spans. The effects of other memes are more long lasting. Concepts of good and evil, accepted rules of social conduct, and civil law are examples of ideas that have been maintained across generations.

Dawkins emphasizes that the meme can be regarded as a living structure, and that it operates in much the same way as a virus that can affect one's brain, as well as the hard drive of the computer. The meme is an actual structure of the human nervous system; once activated, it modifies the consciousness of the person who thought of the idea and those who come into contact with it. The traditions that characterize a culture or community, the behaviors of its members, and the skills that are taught reflect the accumulation and selection of shared beliefs. The continued success and survival of a community depends on how efficiently cultural knowledge, which accumulates on the basis of variation and selection, makes the jump from the collective minds of one generation to the next.

The evolution of brain structure, cognitive processes, and skilled behaviors occurred interactively; each is positively related to survival. Over millions of years, the physical structures of our ancient ancestors gradually changed. Structures of the body and brain that did not benefit the species were modified or lost. The mind and consciousness emerged in humans because they, like other structures of the body, played an important role in the survival of both the individual and the species. Modern humans, like their ancient ancestors, are predisposed to behave in ways that enhance the likelihood of survival. One way that humans have come to increase the likelihood of their survival has been to acquire skills that are based on the cultural knowledge of a community.

Throughout the history of humankind, education has been fundamental to the progress of our species. Education provides younger members of a culture with the opportunity to learn from previous generations and to add to the store of knowledge and invent new ways of meeting the challenges of survival. It is also a way of providing members of the social group with perceptions of what constitutes normal or acceptable behavior. From the earliest days of an infant's life, its behavior is guided by a set of socially determined constraints. As the child grows, she learns to adapt her biological needs to the rules of family and the social group. As she learns, she recognizes that there is a purpose for the skills she is taught to perform. As she matures, her skills come to determine her social identity. The skills acquired during a lifetime provide her with the means to meet and overcome the stresses and challenges that are part of life.

STRESS, SKILL, AND SURVIVAL

The term *stress* is perhaps one of the most overused words in the vocabulary of modern civilization. It has a negative connotation; drawn from the lexicon of mechanical engineers, it conveys a notion of a structure that is under great pressure and on the verge of collapsing and breaking down.

Modern Civilization

The history of Western civilization is characterized by a progression of increasingly stupendous inventions and the evolution of new technologies that have helped humans to control their environments, attain a stable supply of food, reduce the chance of premature death, and multiply. Since the 1870s, science and technological advances have led to a civilization largely characterized by city dwellers. In the early decades of the twentieth century, the mass production of such products as clothing, automobiles, home furnishings, chemicals, and tools required large numbers of workers who performed routine assembly-line tasks. The more recent high technology industries (such as computer and information processing, for the most part) continue to require large work forces. Today, as in previous decades of this century, many citizens are drawn to live in urban environments and work at jobs that resemble the assembly-line tasks that faced factory workers at the turn of the last century.

Early twentieth-century philosophers pondered the effects that the stresses of urbanism and industrialized society have on the psyche of the individual. A central theme expressed by many of these was that the human species evolved gradually over millions of years and was designed to function in an open environment much different than the environment found in an industrialized city. The patterns of behaviors that, for countless years, were fundamental to survival of the individual are, of necessity, suppressed in an industrialized society.

William James was influenced greatly by the writings of Darwin and others such as Herbert Spencer (1820–1903), who promoted biological evolution as a way to explain human social systems (Spencer, 1870). James proposed that the evolutionary constraints that resulted in the physical characteristics of modern human beings were instrumental in the selection of the mental characteristics of humans as well. He stated that the human mind is as important to the survival of an individual as any physical structure. In the same way that the heart, brain, stomach, and muscles have specific functions that help to adapt and survive, the mind has a function.

In James's view, the function of the mind is to mediate between individual needs and environmental demands. The survival benefits of the mind were described by James in a scenario in which a hiker walking through the woods is confronted by a bear. The sight of the animal evokes changes in the hiker's level of physical arousal. The level of arousal evoked is critical to the survival of the hiker. If he is too physically aroused, he may become rigid with fear and be unable to select an adaptive response. A lower level of physical and mental arousal permits the hiker to make a clear assessment of the situation, select the appropriate response, and execute a successful escape. The hiker lives another day. Thus, optimal performance demands not only a well-trained body, but also a well-trained mind. James made extensive use of the concept of the *habit* as a mechanism to explain how the mind is influenced by experience and assists in survival.

Physiologists during the early decades of the twentieth century also became interested in the effects of stress on the body and mind. Walter Cannon was the first to employ the term *stress* to describe physiological changes experienced under threatening conditions. Cannon (1929) proposed that the body responds to emergency situations with increased arousal of the sympathetic nervous system and subjective emotional experiences. These changes elicit a fight-or-flight response that helps the individual to overcome or escape from the threat. Cannon (1935) also introduced the concept of physiological homeostasis and how stress affects our physiological functioning. The ideas and work of James and Cannon provided a framework for the study of stress and emotions that is evidenced in modern neurological theories and psychological theories of stress.

The Neurobiology of Stress

The modern conceptualization of stress and its effects on the body and mind can be traced to the work of *Hans Selye* (1907–1982), a neuroendocrinologist who, beginning in the 1930s, conducted a number of classic studies that described the effects of stressors on laboratory animals (Selye, 1976). Selye's early laboratory research demonstrated that animals exposed to stressors responded physiologically in very predictable ways. They evidenced enlargement of the adrenal cortex, which continuously released stress hormones; the lymphatic glands (thymus, spleen, and lymph nodes) shrank or atrophied; the production of white blood cells decreased; and, under extreme conditions, the animals died.

Selye noted that, regardless of the type of stressor, animals displayed similar patterns of responding. Selye coined the term *general adaptation syndrome* to describe these patterns. Organisms proceed through three distinct physiological states when exposed to a stressful event. (See figure 5.1.)

The first stage is the *alarm stage*, in which the stressor activates the body's fight-or-flight reflexes. Heart rate and respiration increase and the blood vessels in the cardiorespiratory system enlarge. This causes a shift of blood flow to the muscles. Blood flow to the digestive system decreases at the same time. Patterns of neural activity shift in the brain, and these pattern shifts signal changes that will occur in the autonomic nervous system. The interior tissues of the adrenal gland signal a release of hormonal substances (adrenaline and noradrenaline) that circulate through the bloodstream, stimulating the body and preparing it for action. The brain also directs the release of hormones from the pituitary gland; one of these is adrenocorticotropic hormone (ACTH), which flows to the exterior tissues of the adrenal glands and stimulates the release of anti-inflammatory substances (corticosteroids) throughout the bloodstream. These find their way into muscle tissue and joints. During the alarm stage, the individual is on full alert and is preparing either to engage in the rigors of combat or to mount an all-out effort to evade the situation.

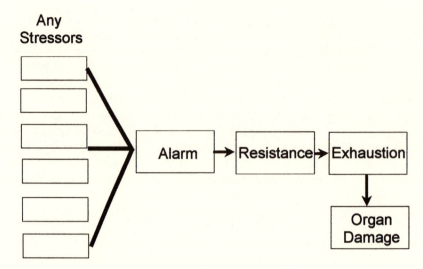

Figure 5.1.   Elements of the General Adaptation Syndrome

When stressors are chronic and do not dissipate over time, individuals shift to the *resistance stage* of the general adaptation syndrome. The body continues to battle the stressors in this stage. Arousal levels are maintained and biological systems are called upon to maintain their heightened state of readiness. Central to this prolonged state of arousal is lymphatic activity, which plays a major role in fighting disease and infection. When stimulated, the lymphatic system releases lymphocytes into the bloodstream to attack invading cells. The effectiveness of the lymphatic system declines over time as biological resources are depleted, however. If stressors are not reduced or removed, an individual's biological coping mechanisms gradually become less efficient, and the likelihood of illness and disease increases. Also, the long-term presence of previously health-promoting biological substances released by glands during the alarm stage begins to have a detrimental effect on the body; for example, stomach ulceration can occur.

As physiological defense systems are depleted, the individual enters the *exhaustion stage*. At this point, clear physical damage can be seen in the adrenal glands, lymphatic structures, and the stomach. Individuals become increasingly susceptible to illness in this state and, in extreme cases, death may occur. Selye noted that humans and animals progress through the three stages of the general adaptation syndrome whether the stressor is biological (infection), physical, or mental. It is for this reason that he defined stress as the *nonspecific* response of an organism to any demand made upon it.

Since Selye's landmark publications, a great amount of research has been conducted to assess the effects of both physical and mental stressors on skilled human performance. The physiological reactions of humans during stressful conditions have been found to be the same as those experienced by laboratory animals.

The Psychology of Stress

Given the degree of public concern with the effects of stress on physical and mental well-being, it may seem odd that the systematic study of the psychological factors central to the stress response is a relatively recent phenomenon. The notion that stress can influence thought and behavior can be traced back to the ancient Greek physician, Hippocrates, but the scientific study of the psychological effects of stress on behavior began with basic research following World War II (Newton, 1995). Many soldiers exposed to combat experienced short-term psychological distress and reduced combat efficiency as well as long-term psychological trauma and depression. The men and women who were pressed into military service were, before combat, normal people who evidenced few signs of psychological problems. Clearly, then, it was the physical and mental demands of wartime conditions that extracted a toll on some of these individuals.

Research on the effects of war conditions on human performance led to the first systematic study of psychological stress. The pioneering work of Richard Lazarus, which began in the 1950s and has continued to the present, provided the impetus for many contemporary theories of stress. Stress, as conceptualized by Lazarus (1993a), is defined by the presence of two conditions; first, a *judgment* is made regarding whether an agent (external or internal) is threatening or noxious. Second, an *appraisal* is made of the situation to determine how to cope with the agent. Although people differ considerably in their judgments of and responses to given events, they tend to employ similar appraisal processes. The *appraisal process* begins with the *primary appraisal stage*, during which the individual evaluates the significance of a given event to his or her safety. The primary questions posed during this stage revolve around the personal significance of the event at that particular moment ("What do I have at stake in this encounter?"). The *secondary appraisal stage* is characterized by the individual's evaluation of the resources and skills he or she possesses and how they can be used to deal with the event ("What can I do?"). The *reappraisal stage* is characterized by the individual's modification of the initial appraisal. The ongoing person-environment relationship provides a constant stream of new information that may be used to update a prior evaluation of the event (Lazarus, 1993a).

Central to much of Lazarus's research on psychological stress is a focus on individual differences that exist among our appraisal of and response to stressful conditions. The way that people judge events to be threatening or not can differ tremendously. For example, final examinations may be judged to be harmful or threatening by some high-school students and challenging by others. The negative judgments of harm and threat produce unpleasant mental states linked to distress, and distress ultimately impairs performance. The positive judgment of challenge, conversely, brings about pleasant mental states linked to feelings of exhilaration. These feelings foster and promote optimal performance.

Lazarus's research revealed that judgments of stress and the appraisal process are influenced by myriad factors. He and his colleagues (Lazarus and Folkman, 1984) concluded that stressors can be grouped into three categories: 1) *Cataclysmic agents* such as war or natural disasters that affect large groups of individuals; 2) *personal agents* such as the sudden death of a friend or family member; and 3) *background agents* that reflect the daily hassles of everyday life. Within these categories, stressors are subtyped as *acute* (temporary) events and as *chronic* (long-term) events. Both acute and chronic stressors can exert powerful influences on our emotional states. How we respond to stressful events was linked by Lazarus to characteristics of the *situation* and characteristics of the *person*. Situational factors such as the nature of the threat, when the event occurred, and its intensity and duration modulate the judgment process. Personal factors such as beliefs about abilities, skills, and social resources contribute to the stress response; similarly, motivation and level of commitment to deal with stressful events affect coping.

Early research on stress by Lazarus and others revealed that psychological stress is not a condition confined only to military personnel who were caught up in wartime situations. Rather, stress is ubiquitous and can affect any one of us at any time of our lives. Theories of stress derived from laboratory studies of human performance under stressful conditions were perfectly suited for the *health psychology* movement that emerged in the 1980s (Seaward, 1997). Unlike human-factor-oriented researchers whose interests lay in examining the dynamics of job demands on workers' stress, health psychologists were interested in holistic issues such as *wellness*, or how people establish a balance or harmony among the physical, mental, emotional, and spiritual aspects of the human condition.

Stress and Emotion

The commonsense view of human emotion is that it is a state during which actions are performed without rational thought. Most of us have at one time or another said or done something during the heat of the moment, only to regret our actions later on, after giving the situation more careful deliberation and thought.

Modern researchers define *emotion* as short-term, positive or negative affective reactions to objects (either real or imagined). The scientific study of human emotion involves examining the components of emotional experiences and relating those to other psychological states such as cognition and attention.

Motives for action based on our emotional state are thought to be *prepotent*, (more powerful) than motives based on thinking, cognition, or rational problem solving (Frijda, 1986). From the position of evolutionary psychology, it makes sense that humans respond quickly to threatening situations (LeDoux, 1997). Innate action without thought would seem to have high survivability importance. Thus, when we are in an emotional state, we may act before we think. Recent neuropsychological research has provided a structural basis for the speed with which humans display emotional behavior. Incoming sensory information is routed to the thalamus, an area of the limbic system that controls many of our reflexive behaviors. The thalamus has been likened to the switchboard of the brain, as virtually all sensory data is routed through the thalamus and on to other areas of the brain. Information is sent to lower-level, reflexive systems responsible for maintaining the body's functions (heart rate, breathing, etc.) is sent as well as to higher-level cortical systems that are important in thinking and reasoning. The stimulation of lower-level systems produces behavioral responses more rapidly than the stimulation of higher-level systems. As a result, reflexive changes occur in the body before the higher-level cortical systems of the brain have an opportunity to ponder the meaning of environmental events.

Stress and Cognition

People placed in stressful situations often describe how their capacity to think is diminished or altered; they become disoriented. A common complaint voiced by students who perform poorly on examinations is that they knew the material but just couldn't think straight during the exam. More serious examples of the distorting effects of stress are the automobile and airplane accidents that are attributed to momentary lapses in thought and actions that occur before completely thinking through the situation. Military psychologists have noted that many soldiers never discharge their weapons during actual combat situations. After major Civil War battles, for example, muzzle-loading rifles filled with load after load of powder and shot were found on the battlefield, many of which had never been fired. The soldiers evidently continued to go through the highly practiced skills of loading their weapons but, during the emotionally charged heat of battle, never actually fired them.

Stress extracts its toll on cognitive processes, specifically on the processes of attention and mental effort (Schonpflug, 1983). Attention has several properties, one of which is to select the object of our state of awareness. The object may be a physical stimulus such as a blinking light on the flight-control panel of an airplane, or a mental stimulus such as the memory of a line from a popular song. When faced with a problem to be solved, optimal performance depends on the selection and utilization of task-relevant information. For example, successful negotiation of a bicycle through a crowded college campus depends on the rider's awareness of many obstacles that may be present. The cyclist must be vigilant for pedestrians, cars driving by or stopping to let people out, other cyclists, and other stimuli. The cyclist who focuses her attention on task-irrelevant stimuli (such as waving to a friend or letting her mind wander to the test she just took) is setting the stage for disaster.

Stress and Arousal

Several theories have been proposed to explain how stress affects selective attention. Central to most theories is the assumption that stressful situations result in changes in physical arousal, and that the physical and mental reactions to arousal play a key role in performance. Yerkes and Dodson (1908) developed one of the first theories to address the relation between arousal and performance. They studied laboratory animals' escape behaviors while the animals were at various levels of arousal. Rats were trained to escape an electric shock by turning small wheels located in their cages. The rats performed most efficiently under moderate levels of shock arousal and poorer under both low levels and high levels of shock arousal. These observations led Yerkes and Dodson to suggest that an inverted, U-shaped function could predict the level of performance under arousal conditions (see figure 5.2). The *Yerkes-Dodson Law* has fostered considerable research since it was posited, and it has maintained a prominent place in the vast majority of textbooks that address topics related to the effects of arousal on human performance (see Hardy, Jones, and Gould, 1996, chapter 5, for a review of arousal).

Attention's role in the performance of tasks under stressful conditions was expanded upon by Easterbrook (1959), who proposed that both task-relevant and task-irrelevant environmental cues are present whenever a task is performed. In the example of the cyclist, there are cues in the situation that are relevant to negotiating a bicycle through traffic, such as visual and auditory stimuli generated by the movement of people and cars. There are also irrelevant cues, such as who the pedestrians are and how they are dressed. Under conditions of low stress, the cyclist may be able to attend to both relevant and irrelevant cues while riding through a crowd. However, when the cyclist is aroused such as she might be if under time pressure to get to class, riding through a crowded area requires narrowing her attentional focus. Under increased but still relatively low levels of stress, the range of cues on which she can focus narrows, and task-irrelevant information begins to be discarded. All the while, the more task-relevant information continues to be processed. The cyclist may be able to wind her way rapidly through traffic when she attends primarily to relevant cues and devotes less attention to distracting, irrelevant cues. According to the *cue-utilization hypothesis*, performance begins to break down when arousal levels increase to the point that we begin to discard both task-irrelevant and task-relevant information. Attention becomes focused on fewer and fewer cues as arousal levels increase. As a result, important information such as a dog darting into traffic may not be attended to and could result in a nasty tumble.

Research driven by the Yerkes-Dodson Law and Easterbrook's notions of attentional narrowing has provided data to suggest that the relation between arousal and performance is not as simple as initially conceived. Contemporary theories of stress that are based on information-processing models conceptualize attention as only one of several cognitive processes involved in the

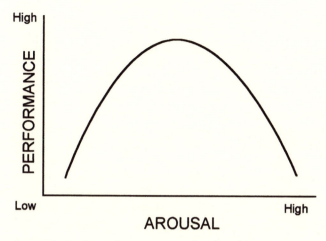

Figure 5.2.   Inverted-U Relation between Arousal and Performance

stress response (Wells and Matthews, 1994). Threatening agents come to be the primary objects of our attention; however, the perception of threat leads to attempts to stabilize or control the environment. We draw on past experiences and knowledge to counter the physical and mental imbalance central to the stress reaction. Responding involves the allocation of resources needed to activate short-term and long-term memory structures and integrate information in ways that lead to efficient problem solving.

Self-focus has been used to describe how attention can be directed inwardly on our thoughts and memories and outwardly on events on the environment. Shifts of attention toward internal mental activities and the external situation provide us with the capacity to control a stressful situation and regain physical and mental stability when in those situations. Successful control of cognitive processing during stressful conditions requires an optimal blend of internal focusing and external focusing that fits the specific situation at hand. Stress conditions, however, may elicit memories of an individual's past experiences and his success or failure at regaining stability. Our individual beliefs about our ability to meet the demands of the situation come into play during this stage of the stress response. Self-focus on negative thoughts, worry, and self-concern may flood memory systems and interfere with coping strategies. Errors in performance mount under these conditions. We may select well-learned skills that are inappropriate, and/or we may generate problem-solving approaches that are ineffective for the situation. The likelihood of behavioral withdrawal and mental disengagement increases with our perception that the gulf between the demands of the stressor and our skill in reestablishing physical and mental stability is increasing (Carver and Scheier, 1981, 1988).

Wells and Matthews (1994) systematically reviewed research and concluded that stress can affect cognition in several ways.

- *Stress may impair overall attentional efficiency.* The physiological consequences of arousal and the accompanying energy expenditure, coupled with negative thoughts of worry and anxiety, reduce our cognitive resources to attend to and respond to environmental conditions.
- *Stress may limit the selectivity function of attention.* Narrowing of attention can cause a failure to detect useful information by focusing too much on specific parts of a situation rather than viewing the event in its entirety.
- *Stress may reduce motivation and effort.* Failed coping behaviors can lead to withdrawal and total disengagement; stressful situations are studiously avoided.

In summary, the stress response is a complex and dynamic interaction between a person and the environment. In the real world, responses to mild stressors may vary considerably from one person to another.

LIFE-SPAN COPING SKILLS

Skills have both function and purpose. The process of learning *coping skills* is a fundamental strategy for dealing with stresses, tasks, and challenges encountered throughout life. Regardless of the type of stressor, people come to rely on learned coping skills to manage stress. A great deal of research has been conducted over the past two decades that describes the relation between life events and wellness. Unfortunately, relatively little attention has been placed on *how* the process of skill learning impacts the ability to adapt to the stressors.

Developmental Tasks

The manner in which people face *developmental tasks* by drawing upon physical and mental skills may set or modify the trajectory of their life course (Havighurst, 1972). A child's history of success or failure at learning the tasks of early life affect how well she handles the learning tasks of adolescence. The skills developed in adolescence influence how the socially maturing person meets the developmental tasks of adulthood. And the skills developed over decades of practice play important roles in how older adults deal with physical and mental changes that accompany the aging process.

How we face the developmental tasks encountered as we navigate the courses of our lives has been proposed to be intimately linked to continued physical and mental growth and, ultimately, to happiness and wellness. These tasks are unavoidable; they constitute a basic part of individual growth and reflect the very fabric of society. The way in which skills are acquired and performed serves as the basis for judging ourselves and provides each of us with a method for approving or disapproving of our own and others' actions.

Some developmental tasks are associated with particular stages of maturation. Learning a language is a task associated with childhood. It is of utmost importance that this skill be acquired during the teachable moments of the early years of life; failure to acquire language can have long-term consequences that are not easily overcome later in life. Other developmental tasks are *recurrent* and encountered in different forms throughout the life span. Social skills, for example, are established through training and practice. The way these skills are employed is essential for satisfactory social growth and development.

The acquisition of skills is fundamental to the successful adaptation of both the individual and the individual's culture. Skills are neither simply the means to an end nor just mechanical actions that achieve a specific goal. Skills are absolutely necessary for advancement (Csikszentminalyi, 1997, 1999). The skills that we acquire during our lifetimes provide the flexibility and capacity needed to adapt to an ever-changing world. The psychological wellness and evolution of the human species depends on skills; without them, each of us as individuals and our collective culture will stagnate, and we will eventually lose our place in nature.

The Stress of Learning

Consider that the very process of learning new skills can be conceptualized as a stressful event. Many learning theories view the initial stages of skill acquisition as a period during which the learner faces a problem to be solved. Several of the classic theories of learning described in previous chapters suggest that skills are acquired gradually and that learners go through three distinctive stages: cognitive, associative, and autonomous. During the cognitive phase, the learner is forced into a situation in which she must appraise the task at hand to determine the level of effort and attention that will be delegated to the task. It is at this moment that her appraisal process sets the learning trajectory. She asks, "What is the significance of this task?" Her appraisal process will dictate the quantity and quality of the effort expended to accomplish the task. The next questions asked are, "Do I have the ability to learn this task?" and "How much effort should I put into this problem?"

The associative phase of the skill acquisition process is characterized by practice and repetition. These conditions elicit such internal questions as, "Is learning this skill worth the amount of practice that is required of me?" and "What benefits will I gain from this practice?" The answers to these self-generated questions may determine to a great extent the effort and willingness extended to cope with the frustration of trial-and-error learning. No one becomes an expert without experiencing the emotions associated with failure and those associated with success. The costs of continued practice are high, because most of the emotional feedback from performance is negative. With persistence, however, the frequency of errors decreases and the positive emotions linked to success begin to exert their control over the learner's willingness to continue.

Even when skills have become automatic, performers continue to generate questions such as, "Will my performance continue to improve?" "Can I get any better at this task?" At some point, the gains of practice gradually begin to lessen. Despite considerable effort, the performer may feel that he is not getting any better; indeed, declines in performance levels may be observed. The personal choices revolve around withdrawing from the task (retiring) or reformulating the task-skill relationship. The motivation to continue to practice and to refine and hone skills becomes linked more to the psychological gains that are derived from practice. A threshold will be reached in skill level for each person. The individual's personal internal appraisal processes continue to determine the degree of willingness to persist in search of psychological growth.

CHALLENGE THEORIES OF STRESS MANAGEMENT

Stress is often thought of as the great evil of the modern industrial world. There are those, however, who point out that stress can have positive consequences as well. *Eustress*, a term originally coined by Selye, is often used to describe a biologically advantageous state in which people are confident that they have the skills and resources necessary to meet and overcome potentially stressful situations (Selye, 1974).

Hardiness Theory

Historians have noted that people differ considerably in the ways that they cope with such cataclysmic stress conditions as concentration camps or being held as prisoners of war. Researchers who study the trauma individuals suffered during the Holocaust, for example, found that some individuals succumbed quickly to the strain of being imprisoned, abused, and under the constant threat of death. Others, however, were able to somehow overcome this stress, maintaining perspective on the situation, as well as their dignity. Psychologists and philosophers have been interested in why (and how) some of us are able to overcome situations of extreme hardship and others are not (Frankel, 1984). The construct of *hardiness* has been used to describe the personality and characteristics of those who can stay psychologically healthy even under unbelievably stressful conditions.

Kobasa (1979) and her colleagues (Kobasa, Maddi, and Kahn, 1982) conducted a series of studies that evaluated how business executives were able to deal with the threat of losing their jobs during a period of economic downsizing. Her studies provide evidence to suggest that hardy individuals can be differentiated from those who do not satisfactorily adapt in three distinct ways. Hardy individuals: 1) maintain a belief that they have an element of control over events that affect them, 2) demonstrate deep levels of commitment to activities they perceive to be important, and 3) show the ability to see change in situations as a source of challenge.

On the basis of her research, Kobasa hypothesized that the elementary structures of hardiness are innate; however, the expression of hardiness traits can be directly affected by education. Our commitment, perception of control, and need for challenge can be modified through learning. Kobasa and her colleagues conducted an intervention study to determine the degree to which hardiness could be increased in a group of business managers and executives. Participants in this study were taught the skills of *focusing*, or learning to recognize the physiological changes that occur during periods of stress. They were also taught to *reconstruct* or to view a potential stressor from multiple perspectives. Finally, they were taught to *compensate*, or to draw on personal experiences and skills to change a negative situation into one they perceived as positive. This intervention produced marked and lasting changes in the way many of the workers responded to their working condition.

Several national educational programs (Outward Bound, Project Adventure, National Outdoor Leadership School, etc.) have developed curricula based on the assumption that hardiness can be developed. Participants in these programs are exposed to psychologically and physically demanding situations such as rock climbing, seafaring, wilderness camping, and isolation under controlled and supervised conditions. Skills that will help students meet and overcome obstacles that most would have perceived as overwhelming are taught under real world conditions. The positive experiences gained from dealing successfully with environmental demands are believed to generalize to the home environment. Some educational programs designed around the hardiness construct are specifically geared to individuals who face certain life-span tasks, such as adolescents with adjustment problems, new business executives, teachers, and those with progressive or debilitating diseases.

Toughening Theory

Dienstbier (1989, 1991) has proposed that controlled levels of physical or mental stress promote a type of toughening that leads to improved physical and mental health and increased capacity to deal with the rigors of life. Central to his theory is the view that coping responses are modified when one rises to meet challenges. He draws upon research conducted with animals and humans that demonstrates the effects of early experience and stimulation on behavior.

Several studies have shown that rearing laboratory animals in exciting and stimulating environments has a profound affect on their development. Animals who receive enriched life experiences early in life exhibit greater stress tolerance and a more even emotional temperament than animals not provided such early experiences. There is also evidence to suggest that early stimulation will accelerate the physical and mental development of human infants. Stimulating environments have positive effects on mature adults, as well as children. The stimulation produced by physical exercise such as running and mental exercise such as problem solving is hypothesized to be related to the development of improved stress tolerance.

Toughening manipulations are thought important because they alter neurohormonal processes that underlie successful coping behavior. The toughened individual, when compared to individuals who are not toughened, evidences lower overall base rates of autonomic nervous system activity. Further, when these individuals encounter novel stressful situations, they experience a rapid onset of neurohormonal systems that produce increased awareness, focused attention, physical readiness to respond, and the delayed onset of neurohormonal systems that are linked to reductions in performance levels and the development of negative feelings. When the stressor is terminated, the toughened person's autonomic nervous system returns to baseline levels more rapidly than does the less tough person's. Further, when stressors are presented repeatedly over a period of time, the toughened person adapts quickly to the stimulus and displays increasingly less arousal with each presentation. Thus, those who have histories of experiencing and dealing with stressors are physically and behaviorally more relaxed or seemingly unresponsive, yet they are very quick to mobilize their resources to defend themselves when the need arises.

Toughened individuals are thought to be better able to evaluate and extract information from environmental situations than others. For instance, both toughened and nontoughened individuals may initially appraise an event as potentially stressful. However, toughened individuals are more likely than others to modify their initial appraisal and change their perceptions of a stimulus situation from a threat to a challenge. This secondary appraisal process is fueled by the toughened individual's recognition that he or she has the necessary skills and resources to meet the challenge.

The appraisal process is critical to the development of toughening. An individual's perception of an event as a stressor leads him to decide, "This is too much for me—I'm going to lose." Conversely, an individual's perception of an event as challenging leads him to decide, "I can take this on—I'm going to win." The psychological process of decision making also explains why toughening cannot occur by simply changing the activity level of the body by way of drug injections or mindless physical or psychological activity. Simply going through the motions of physical or mental training programs is not enough; the individual must view the task at hand as one that, while demanding, can be successfully overcome by employing his or her skills and abilities. The belief that one can cope with challenging situations results in positive feelings of control over the environment. Overcoming challenging tasks reinforces our emotions and produces expectations of future success.

Toughening experiences have positive short-term and long-term physiological and psychological benefits. Experiencing a challenging situation increases a person's energy and arousal levels, which set the stage for him to meet and overcome task demands. The person's newly acquired history of success, in turn, motivates him to continue to engage in challenging activities. This continued performance of challenging activities instigates practice, and it is associated with maintenance of skilled behavior. When faced with a potentially stressful situation, those who have histories of toughening show low levels of fearfulness, anxiety, sadness, and distress. They are characterized by being calm under fire and able to perform efficiently, even under hazardous conditions. Paralleling these psychological and behavioral changes are corresponding improvements in the individual's immune system and his capacity for toughness. The positive physical and psychological changes associated with mastering challenging tasks lead the individual to seek out the very tasks that served as a toughening manipulation.

There is a wealth of information suggesting that there is a connection between our motivation to be actively engaged in solving the day-to-day problems of life and our physical and mental heath. The remaining chapters of this book describe how skills are acquired in different ways at various stages along the life course, how skills are important to our success at meeting the stress and challenges of life, and how skills are vital to wellness.

CHAPTER SUMMARY

Skills are not limited to those that are used to play games of sports; they are fundamental to our very survival. Humans have evolved physical and mental structures and processes designed to prepare us to meet the immense challenges imposed by a sometimes hostile world. The human body has been engineered to respond in a predictable fashion when danger is sensed, and the human mind provides us the flexibility we need to respond adaptively to dangerous situations. Surviving a threatening encounter depends on our ability to execute in a timely fashion the skills we have learned.

The evolutionary success of the human species is due, in part, to our ability to transmit cultural knowledge and skills from one individual to another and from one generation to the next. Through training and education we have the unique opportunity to acquire the physical and mental skills that we need to meet and overcome the challenges and stresses of modern life. Our ability to play a role in society as fully functioning individuals hinges on the skills that we acquire over a lifetime. Learning life-span coping skills demands careful instruction and requires considerable practice and effort, however.

SUGGESTED READINGS

Bronowski, J. (1973). *The ascent of man*. Boston: Little, Brown.
Cziko, G. (1995). *Without miracles: Universal selection theory and the second Darwinian revolution*. London: MIT Press.
Dawkins, R. (1995). *River out of Eden*. New York: Weidenfeld and Nicolson.

Lazarus, R. S. (1993). From psychological stress to the emotions: A history of changing outlooks. *Annual Review of Psychology, 44,* 1–24.

MacLean, P. D. (1990). *The triune brain in evolution: Role in paleocerebral functions.* New York: Plenum Press.

Mithen, S. (1996). *The prehistory of the mind: The cognitive origins of art and science.* New York: Thames and Hudson.

Seaward, B. L. (1997). *Managing stress: Principles and strategies for health and well-being.* Boston: Jones and Bartlett.

Selye, H. (1976). *The stress of life* (Rev. ed.). New York: McGraw-Hill.

Tattersall, I. (1999). *The last Neanderthal: The rise, success and mysterious extinction of our closest human relatives.* Boulder, CO: Westview.

Wilson, E. O. (2000). *Sociobiology: The new synthesis.* Cambridge, MA: Harvard University Press.

Chapter 6

Teaching Skills

Education is a systematic method of transmitting information from one individual to another. In the history of humankind, it has been fundamental to the progress of our species. Education provides younger members of a culture with the opportunity to learn from previous generations and to add to and invent new ways of meeting survival challenges. It is also an important venue for providing members of the social group with perceptions of what constitutes normal or appropriate behavior. From the earliest days of an infant's life, his or her behavior is guided by a set of socially determined constraints. A child learns to adapt biological needs to the rules of family and social group. An adolescent is constantly challenged to learn new behaviors and skills as he or she matures toward adulthood, which brings with it a host of life-span tasks and demands.

This chapter addresses how a teacher's understanding of the interrelationship among a student's body, mind, and spirit can be used to set the stage for efficient and effective skill learning. When you complete this chapter you will see why the processes involved in education have played pivotal roles in the success of the human species. You will also see how modern educators blend time-honored methods of teaching, which have evolved over thousands of years, with advances in modern research. Today's educators have a better understanding of the learning process and the conditions that motivate students to learn than at any point in history. New multidisciplinary approaches to understanding the processes of the body and the processes of the mind provide teachers the capacity to develop optimal learning environments. Developmental and life-span research have helped teachers to modify their instructional approaches to accommodate the many differences that exist among students.

THE TEACHER-STUDENT RELATIONSHIP

Educators are valued members of every society. In all cultures there are long-standing institutions of learning. Traditionally, teachers are seen as individuals who perpetuate the ideals of a culture from one generation to another. A successful teacher is more than just a person who presents information to students. Teachers take on multiple roles as they prepare their students for the future.

Ancient Views of Education

Consider the behaviors of people living 50,000 years ago. Survival was clearly difficult. The environment was hostile and daily life was extremely harsh, with most of the behaviors of group members revolving around strenuous activities designed to obtain sufficient amounts of food to sustain life. Many groups lived a nomadic-type existence that involved following animal herds. Division of labor existed even during the earliest days of humankind. Those who were physically the largest and strongest participated in group hunts while others performed tasks that involved searching for alternative sources of food.

The groups of this period were composed of small extended families that included adults, adolescents, and children (Dunbar, 1992, 1993). Adults who participated in animal hunts constructed and prepared the tools and equipment necessary to kill, dismember, and transport the animal back to other members of the group. Adults who searched for plants and berries developed methods for holding and carrying food. Successful hunting and gathering required complex mental abilities. Hunters had to acquire knowledge of the behaviors of the animals they were tracking, the terrain on which the hunt was taking place, and methods for selecting, isolating, and attacking an animal. Gatherers had to be able to discriminate between edible and potentially deadly plants, bushes, fungi, and berries.

It was probably the case that most survival skills were passed from older to younger individuals by way of modeling. Younger individuals observed the actions of adults and noted the relationship between those actions and their outcomes; that is, adults' successes or failures. Those young members of the group who stayed close to and were attentive to the actions of older, more skilled members were more likely to acquire survival skills. The strong bond that linked the infant to its mother may initially be explained in terms of nurturing and protection; however, as the child matured, strong bonds developed between the child and productive members of the social group. Children were assimilated at a young age into hunter-gatherer activities, and the fact that they stayed close to adults and watched the successful and unsuccessful behaviors of adults probably played a key role in their own survival to adulthood.

The switch from a hunter-gather lifestyle to one based on agriculture and commerce had a profound effect on the evolution of humankind. Within a relatively brief period of time (only a few thousand years) humans emerged to dominate and control natural events. The development of language and methods of writing have been viewed as critical factors in the emergence of civilization (Dunbar, 1993). Acquiring the ability to communicate by way of symbols reflects a major leap in the method of transmitting knowledge from one individual to another. The invention of numbering systems and methods for recording transactions greatly enhanced trading and bartering for goods and services. These developments were central to educating individuals destined to perform specific roles in society and ensuring that they acquired the specialized skills they would need in those roles.

Groups of individuals developed the skills needed to create the tools, build the cities, and carry on commerce and trade. The craftsmen learned their trades through systematic training. In some cases, skills were passed from parents to children; in other cases, children received instruction from teachers. Regardless of the skill taught or the source of the instruction, however, teaching came to be a serious and highly ritualistic endeavor.

Highly skilled craftsmen, then and now, have often been looked upon as special people. Whether a craft involved shaping a piece of hot metal into a plow or sword or weaving a basket from slender reeds, a skilled craftsman could create products so quickly and efficiently that it seemed that he or she had some type of mystical or magical power. Some of the attraction of a novice to a master teacher can be attributed to the belief that the master has knowledge, power, and insight that others do not possess. A master teacher's hidden knowledge played a role in the development and strength of the teacher-student relationship in early civilizations. The methods of training some trade skills became more ritualistic and secretive as time passed. Master craftsmen began to organize the manner in which they selected and taught novices. As the behaviors and performance of students reflected the quality of instruction, teachers began to develop methods for ranking and certifying students' skill levels. Indeed, even today, there are fraternal societies such as the Masons that trace their origins back to master guildsmen who first established the standards for defining the quality in their craft and who defined the stages of training demanded of students who wished to become builders.

Students in emerging cultures throughout the world began to turn to masters for enlightenment. Those novices who met a master's selection criteria were often willing to follow the instructions of their teacher without question. Novices, believing that their master had special and mystical insight, assumed that there was a purpose for every activity required of them. They were willing to participate in training that was often effortful, discomforting, confusing, and, at times, humiliating. As their skills developed, however, the students experienced the positive emotions related to overcoming challenges and associated with success. Often, students bonded emotionally with their teacher and emulated him or her. As part of a student's pledge to his teacher to obey and follow directions, the novice became a member of a community of craftsmen who were recognized for their specialized skills. Thus, from the earliest days of civilization, training and education has been a ritualistic endeavor that leads to the inculcation of a social identity.

Modern Views of Education

One of the hallmarks of the late nineteenth and early twentieth centuries was the introduction of public education. With the onset of industrialization came increasing urban development; it became clear to those in political power that a successful nation was one whose members acquired specific skills and trades. The *progressive education movement* in the United States provides an example of the fundamental changes occurring during this period in the way education was conducted. Laws that limited child labor were passed, and education was made compulsory for all children. New universities and colleges were constructed and programs designed to train those who would educate students in public elementary and high schools.

The relationship between students and teachers in many educational settings today differs from that seen during earlier periods of history. Modern teachers face students who differ widely in their motivation or drive to learn. One of the greatest challenges a modern teacher faces is to develop classroom teaching techniques that challenge individuals to expend the effort necessary to acquire new skills. Effective education occurs when a student sees his or her teacher as an individual who possesses specialized skills and recognizes the importance of having or acquiring those skills. Further, the student must be willing to face the demands and challenges that are part of the educational process. Without an implicit agreement and the development of an emotional bond between student and teacher, learning will be slow and unpleasant for the student and a source of annoyance for the teacher.

The approach taken to teaching skills has also changed over time. Contemporary educational systems are often *noncontextual*; that is, teaching takes place in a classroom that is physically removed from the real world environment in which students will be required to perform the skills they have been taught. In the past, students learned their skills and crafts in apprenticeship-type environments in which they could see the reasons for learning to perform a task in a particular way. The natural teaching environment provided students with multiple sources of information they could use, not only to develop skills, but also to learn how those skills could be applied. Further, methods of instruction tend to be *modularized*; that is, instruction is focused on the component parts of complex skills. A student is often required to meet a specific level of performance on one part of a task before moving on to the next. Compared to earlier periods in history, the focus of most modern teachers is on the instruction of abstract knowledge that is designed to provide students with basic skills that will be applied later in life. For example, basic mathematics and reading skills are taught under the assumption that a student will apply the newly acquired skills to problems encountered later in life outside the classroom. Students are trained to meet the demands of an ever-changing, increasingly technological world. The drawback of this approach, however, is that abstract skills taught out of context may appear meaningless to some students (Bailey, 1997; Evers, 1998).

THE APPRENTICESHIP MODEL

There has been a resurgence of interest in using an apprenticeship model in education that emphasizes the bond between an expert teacher and a novice apprentice. The *cognitive apprenticeship model* developed by Collins and his colleagues is based on the concept of modeling expertise (Collins, Brown, and Newman, 1989). According to this model, the teacher is viewed as a master of the craft who imparts mastery to students through systematic modeling and feedback. Modeling involves teaching by showing; that is, demonstrating those actions and behaviors that are central to executing specific skills. Modeling is a means of communicating that is, in many ways, superior to verbal descriptions of how to act. In much the same way that a photo is worth a thousand words, the actions of a model provide a learner with a mental image that can be used to create a cognitive map or schema of the skill to be learned. The learner's observations of an expert model provide an opportunity to see and understand relations that exist between actions and their outcomes.

Educators have for centuries relied extensively on methods of modeling and feedback to teach physical skills. The premise of the cognitive apprenticeship model is that the methods that are effective in teaching physical skills are also effective in teaching cognitive skills. However, the methods of modeling and feedback are applied somewhat differently during mental skill training because of the internal nature of cognitive processing.

Apprenticeship and Physical Skills

One of the reasons why the apprenticeship method is so successful in teaching motor skills is that the teacher's actions are overt and observable. A soccer instructor, for example, teaches by showing the body actions that are involved in kicking the soccer ball in a particular way. A student can observe and then attempt to emulate the teacher's actions. Although a student's attempt may be crude and inefficient, it approximates the behavior that is desired by the coach. At this point, feedback can be provided by the teacher to guide the learner, over many practice trials, toward the desired response goals.

Application of appropriate feedback is critical to a learner's skill development, and the technique of *scaffolding* is central to the apprenticeship model. The role of the master teacher is to provide the support, or "scaffold," to ensure that a learner progresses in skill development early in training. The amount of support provided by the teacher decreases as a student acquires skill proficiency. Manipulating a student's scaffolding requires a teacher to be acutely aware of the student's *zone of proximal development* (Vygotsky, 1978) or *region of sensitivity to instruction* (Wood and Middleton, 1975), which means that teachers should take into account the factors that impact an individual's skill development. The rate and level of skill development depends on a dynamic interaction among task factors, subject factors, and practice factors.

Apprenticeship and Cognitive Skills

Modeling one's expertise in mental skills is not as straightforward as demonstrating expertise at physical skills. Unlike motor skills such as soccer, students cannot directly observe each of the steps that a master teacher uses to solve a problem. Collins and his colleagues suggest that educators who attempt to teach cognitive skills face two problems. First, it is difficult for students to generate a mental map or schema of cognitive skills. Unlike physical activities in which students can develop a mental map or schema that describes the relation between actions and outcomes, the steps that are required to perform certain problem-solving activities are difficult for some students to visualize. Second, it is difficult to provide a clear rationale for the steps taken to solve a cognitive problem. There are, for example, a number of ways in which the components of an algebraic equation can be broken down or simplified. The selection of the correct method may be perfectly clear to an expert but may be totally baffling to some novices. As a result, a student may learn to solve specific algebra problems without truly understanding the reasons for his or her actions.

The apprenticeship model describes six components of cognitive-skill teaching that are critical for ensuring that information flows from a master teacher to his or her students.

1. *Externalized modeling.* The actions of the teacher must be made as directly observable as possible. This requires the teacher to articulate clearly the mental steps she takes to solve a particular problem. The instructor should, in a sense, talk out loud as she solves a problem; she should describe each step taken and, most important, *why* that particular step is taken. There are a variety of ways that a teacher can model cognitive skills; for instance, she can describe particular strategies, she can "walk through" methods that can be used to decompose large problems into smaller and easier to manage subproblems, or she can identify cues that are critical to the selection of particular solution pathways. These descriptions provide the student with a glimpse into the reasoning processes that guide the teacher's mental actions. They also serve as the basis for a student's mental map of the actions that are involved in performing a cognitive skill.

2. *Coaching.* The validity of a student's mental model can be tested only when attempts are made to use skills to solve a problem. A student, for example, may have a mental map that guides his approach to solving a particular type of algebraic problem. A teacher who monitors how a student solves a problem actually serves as a coach. Requesting that the student explain his actions provides the teacher with an estimate of the student's mental

model and a means of measuring his understanding of the characteristics of the task at hand. The teacher can then provide feedback and guidance as the student goes through the steps involved in performing the task.

3. *Scaffolding*. Effective teaching requires that teachers provide the support necessary for students to make the transition from novices to skilled performers. Considerable scaffolding may be needed early in training; however, the level of support needs to be gradually reduced as a learner's proficiency increases and he or she is able to perform more independently. Ensuring that an optimal amount of scaffolding is provided requires an ongoing dialogue between a student and his or her teacher. The interplay between apprentice and master transforms a student's mental map from one that is only a rough approximation of relationships between actions and outcomes to one that is increasingly more precise, sophisticated, and similar to the mental map employed by the teacher.

4. *Articulation*. It is important that students learn skills that prepare them to meet the demands of the world. Experts are characterized by their capacity to adapt their skills to situations that are novel or unique. This capacity is derived from an expert's extensive learning experiences. One of the challenges of teaching is to provide a novice with the information that has been gained by the expert through years of experience, without having the student physically repeat those experiences. Recall the role of the meme. Humans are unique in that we can use language and memory to learn from the experiences of others without having to repeat those experiences. As a result, a young soccer player can learn much about the game through the descriptions of the experiences of others, and a novice mathematician can advance in understanding by listening to experts.

Master teachers recognize the importance of requiring students to explain how and why they would approach a task in particular way. The creation of hypothetical situations, which require novices to describe and articulate how they would respond, leads to the formation and expansion of their knowledge bases. In order for them to achieve the expert teacher's skill level, students must develop rich caches of knowledge that can be drawn upon when needed. The development of such knowledge bases, however, involves continued mental effort for both teacher and student. It is the obligation of the teacher to continually probe and question students. When students are required to describe and support their reasoning, they are forced to reorganize, restructure, and edit the information they have stored in memory. As a result, students' long-term memory systems are enriched and their speed of processing is enhanced. It is the obligation of the novices to expend the mental effort required to solve the problems that are presented by their instructors.

5. *Reflection*. Education typically involves placing increasing demands on students. The idea is to challenge students without overwhelming them. The tasks that novices face are often simplified by their teachers. It makes sense that higher-level algebra problems are not given to elementary school children, because they have not yet acquired the skills needed to solve the problems. Teachers change the demands of their training programs as students acquire the necessary skills. What this change in demand means to the novices is that the mental maps they used successfully early in training may not be successful later in training.

It is vital that a student compare and contrast his mental map to those used by his teacher and by other students. The apprenticeship model stresses the role that social dynamics play in furthering the educational process; knowledge is shared and disseminated freely. Open debate and discussion fosters and fuels continuous academic challenge and opportunity to learn new ways of dealing with problems. The process of reflecting on the merits of our approach to problem solving is not limited to the academic educational setting; it is important throughout life.

6. *Exploration*. The acquisition of skills is a liberating force. As discussed previously, skills can be seen as tools that are needed to adapt and survive in a potentially hostile world. The act of executing a well-honed skill elicits an emotional experience in many people, and it provides the potential to experience life to its fullest. Apprenticeship models of education stress the freedom that students experience when they gain mastery in a given domain. The distinction between the role of the student and the role of the teacher lessens; indeed, a collegial relationship emerges in which the student and the teacher work together as experts to expand the boundaries of their knowledge.

The cognitive apprenticeship model has been applied successfully in a wide variety of situations to teach both physical skills and mental skills. The method of apprenticeship has been found to be effective in teaching elementary and high-school students mental skills that are essential to understanding and solving academic problems. Equally important, however, apprenticeship techniques have been shown to be useful for instructing children, young adults, and older adults in the skills that are needed to deal with developmental tasks encountered outside the academic classroom. Expert modeling and feedback have been applied to teaching such diverse skills as socialization, parenting, life adjustment, and retirement.

Teaching is a difficult but highly rewarding experience. Its difficulty lies in the creation of environments that match a student's unique motivation, goals, personality, and stage of physical and mental development with the task to be learned. A successful educator is a keen observer of human behavior and is sensitive to the range of individual differences that students possess.

EDUCATION AND MOTIVATION

The acquisition of skill requires that a learner become involved in the educational experience. Whether the skill taught is primarily physical or primarily mental, learning depends on students' allocation of effort to the task at hand. Educators and coaches are well aware of the importance of the role of motivation in the learning process. Indeed, throughout history teachers have encountered students with a "rage" to learn, those who are drawn to the activity and put forth high levels of effort (Winner, 1996). Teachers also face students who are apathetic, distractible, and lack the drive to learn. Teachers spend significant amounts of their time attempting to arrange learning environments that increase the level of motivation and effort of their students.

Individuals are said to be driven to action by three sources of motivation: external reward, internal reward, and phenomenological experience. Although these sources of motivation are typically described as separate processes, all three are present in every learning situation. Further, whereas each source of motivation can instigate action and behavior, the source that dominates may vary as a skill is acquired. Understanding the multiple sources of motivation helps to understand the reasons why individuals engage in activities, disengage from activities, and reengage in them.

External Rewards

Central to the study of learning is the notion of *associationism*; that is, learning occurs because connections are developed between events in nature. The pioneering work of Ivan Pavlov (1928) and Edward Thorndike (1911) provided empirical support for the long-held view of philosophers that actions are set into motion by environmental conditions. For the dog in Pavlov's laboratory, the sound of a bell came to be associated with food. Each presentation of the bell and the presentation of food strengthened the association between the bell and the food; after a time, the animal came to respond to the sound of the bell in the same manner as it had to the food itself. The sound of the bell became a reward that elicited predictable changes in behavior. Stimuli that occur closely in time with a reward come to be connected, or associated, with the reward. Pavlov's laboratory research led him to propose what is referred to today as the classical conditioning model.

The cat in Thorndike's "puzzle box" could escape from the box and attain food by moving a lever within the box. The animal quickly learned to associate the lever-press response with escape and food reward. The repeated demonstration of rewarded behavior led Thorndike to posit a generalized *Law of Effect*; that is, behaviors are performed when they lead to a satisfying state of affairs. In both Pavlov's experiments and Thorndike's cat in the puzzle box, the behavior of the animals changed in a predictable fashion when the stimuli in the environment signaled the onset of a rewarding event.

Early behavioral psychologists applied Pavlov's classical conditioning model and Thorndike's Law of Effect to education. John B. Watson saw the classical conditioning model as a way to predict and control all action. All that were required to teach were the right environmental conditions. His views are embodied in his most quoted comment, "Give me a dozen healthy infants, well formed, and my own specified world to bring them up in and I'll guarantee to take any one at random and train him to become any type of specialist I might select—a doctor, lawyer, artist, merchant-chief and, yes, even into beggar man and thief, regardless of his talents, penchants, tendencies, abilities, vocations and race of his ancestors" (Watson, 1926, p. 10).

B. F. Skinner advanced Thorndike's view that behaviors could be modified by arranging the relation between action and reward (Skinner, 1938). His method came to be labeled *behavior modification*. It had a profound effect on the U.S. educational system. The *token-economy system* became a mainstay in many classrooms, educational institutions, and work organizations (Kazdin, 1994).

Central to this system is the exchange of rewards for behaviors. In an elementary school setting, appropriate behaviors may be rewarded with a sticker or star. When the child earns a sufficient number of these tokens, they are exchanged for a desirable toy or food. Inappropriate behaviors lead to *time-out from reinforcement;* that is, the withdrawal of the opportunity to obtain tokens or rewards. Even today, the time-out principle is used widely in education and home settings to control and shape the behavior of children (Lutz, 1994).

The effectiveness of external rewards to motivate behavior has been studied extensively in both laboratory and applied settings. Controlled laboratory conditions have been used to demonstrate repeatedly that specific environmental events will set conditions for an animal to engage in action. A light that signals the availability of food will prompt an animal to become more active and to engage in behaviors (such as pressing a lever) that reliably lead to food reward. However, if the contingency between lever pressing and reward is removed, a procedure referred to as *extinction,* the animal will disengage from lever pressing. When the contingency is reinstated, the animal will reengage in lever pressing (Williams, 1973). A teacher's verbal directions set the conditions for children in the class to behave in a specified manner. Appropriate actions such as engaging in classroom activities will be maintained when rewarded by praise or tokens. Disengagement from classroom activities will occur when the possibility of earning rewards is removed; reengagement in activity occurs when reward systems are reinstated.

The strict stimulus-response orientation of early behaviorism changed to a more cognitive orientation in the 1960s and 1970s. One of the reasons for this fundamental shift in explaining behavior came from behavioral research that focused on *purposive behavior;* that is, behavior that is engaged in to attain a goal. General theories of behavior attempted to explain how internal motivational forces interacted with previous learning to instigate behavior. The idea that internal psychological states energize purposeful behavior is reflected in more contemporary views of learning and education. The early work of Alfred Bandura (1977), for example, led teachers to focus on the power of modeling to motivate students. Bandura stressed that humans learn not only from their own actions, but also by watching how the actions of others lead to reinforcement. Children acquire knowledge about their world through observational learning; their own behavior is motivated by noting relations that exist between the behaviors of others and the effects of those behaviors. A child who sees other children receiving praise and rewards for staying in their seats and raising their hands will engage in the same actions. If a child observes a classmate receiving attention (a type of reward) for acting in an unruly fashion, he or she may engage in similar actions. For Bandura and other social cognitive psychologists, behaviors are the result of *reciprocal determinism,* meaning that the dynamic interaction among one's attributes and beliefs concerning a particular social situation, the behaviors one emits in that specific environmental context, and the rewards that are obtainable in that setting.

Internal Rewards

External rewards can come to control the behavior of animals and humans. The effect is not universal, however. Some students who engage in learning activities do not appear to require external rewards. Indeed, some will disengage from training when their behaviors are followed by external rewards. Observations of this type of action have led some psychologists and educators to develop an understanding of *intrinsic* (self-generated) *rewards*.

A basic assumption articulated by those who are interested in motivation engendered by intrinsic rewards is that there is a difference between actions that are engaged in with the intent to develop a product and actions engaged in for the processes involved in performing a given task. For some, the goal of action is not the termination of action and acquisition of a reward; rather, the reward is satisfaction with a job well done.

Intrinsically motivated people often see the tasks they are asked to perform as problems to be solved. Unsolved problems are, by their very nature, tension producing; humans are driven to structure their world and to reduce disorder or disequilibrium. Thus, the drive to engage in a learning task is controlled by the student's perceptions. If teaching involves a problem to be solved and a student has the prerequisite skills to attack the problem, she will engage it. One of the more influential theories of intrinsic motivation (Deci and Ryan, 1985; Deci and Porac, 1978) views the drive to solve problems as an important evolutionary mechanism. The challenges of independently solving a problem helps to develop competence and self-determination; these psychological characteristics are vital to operating in and adapting to a complex and possibly hostile environment. The mental processing that takes place as a child thinks through a problem is instrumental to the development of the cognitive structures that will be needed throughout his or her life span.

Deci's model suggests that a student's motivation to learn is determined by his or her perceptions of the challenges involved. If the task is too simple and affords little challenge, a student will disengage and seek other activities. If the task is too difficult, a student will disengage until such time that he or she has the prerequisite skills. Reengagement involves not only changing the characteristics of the task but also an appraisal of the demands of the learning task. Motivation is thought to be cyclical in nature; that is, as people develop skills, they go through periods of engagement, disengagement, and reengagement that are influenced little by external rewards. The level of motivation at any given point reflects an individual's choice.

The general theme of theories of intrinsic reward is that the act of choice is critical to the learning process. Overuse of extrinsic reward and control limits students' actions in some cases. When a teacher implements an educational program designed to produce a specific product, she restricts the options for solving problems to those she selects. As a result, students attend only to the elements of a given task, and they fail to understand that problems can often be solved in a number of ways. Further, the steps involved in learning are predetermined and shaped by the teacher's external contingencies. This cookbook approach lessens a student's opportunity to develop a sense of control and self-determination, and he quickly loses interest in the task. Actions that are intrinsically rewarding are proposed to lead students to attempt challenging tasks that require novel approaches to achieve solutions (Deci, Vallerand, Pelletier, and Ryan, 1991). Students work at developing logical and coherent methods of problem solving that draw from a wide array of information.

Psychic Rewards

Models of motivation that stress either external or internal reward have in common the assumption that behavior is always directed toward some future goal. The rat that presses the lever does so to reduce its physiological need for food or water. The act of pressing a response lever does not lead to immediate satiation, however. It takes time for the food to be eaten and digested before the act returns the animal's system to a homeostatic balance. The animal's learned responses are linked to changes that will occur in the future. A child in the classroom may be intrinsically motivated to perform a task in which a series of steps that are linked to solving the problem must be discovered. He may entertain numerous possible actions and evaluate the costs and benefits of the various ways in which the task may be solved. The steps that are taken while solving the problem are linked to the future goal of completing the task, attaining stability and organization, and reducing psychic tension.

There are situations, however, when people and animals are motivated to act in seemingly purposeless ways, performing activities that have no clear goal. Imagine a toddler who spends hours stacking blocks, knocking the blocks down, and restacking them. It is difficult to imagine that she is motivated by applying some mental problem-solving heuristic to the task. It is easy to imagine, however, that she is lost in the moment of stacking blocks because it is fun and pleasurable. Although it may be that she, by interacting with her environment, learns to control movement and develops psychomotor skills, she is not involved in a systematic training program. She is simply enjoying the experience.

The emotional feelings that accompany action can serve as potent motivators. If you are caught in the act of singing a tune when no else seems to be around, a common response is, "I don't know why I'm singing; it just feels good." It is unlikely that you are singing in preparation for your musical debut; it is more likely that you are merely experiencing the moment. This is not to say that an opera singer who has spent years training her voice cannot experience enjoyment while singing on stage, or that a baseball pitcher cannot experience enjoyment as he throws a fast ball over the outside corner of the plate. Indeed, both the singer and the athlete may derive phenomenological experiences from their actions, regardless of the millions of dollars paid to them to perform. For some individuals, it is the act itself—not the outcome or goal of the act—that is important, and they are highly motivated to engage in actions that produce pleasurable feelings.

Those who advocate using phenomenological experiences as a source of motivation suggest that virtually any activity has the potential to engender positive emotions and enjoyment. We derive enhanced pleasure from activities when we possess skills that are needed to perform them, however (Csikszentmihalyi, 1975a, 1978, 1990; Csikszentmihalyi and Csikszentmihalyi, 1988; DeCharms, 1968). The problem encountered in many educational settings is that skills are not viewed as an end in themselves; rather, skills are seen only as a means to an end. Students need to become engaged in the educational experience for its aesthetic—for the beauty and the creative feelings it produces. There is evolutionary significance in learning for pleasure. When people develop a passion for learning, they add new dimensions and unique ways to solve problems and meet challenges to their lives. The human species continues to move along an evolutionary pathway, and the survival of our species depends on variation and the ability to respond creatively to new challenges.

Educators can structure teaching environments to promote positive emotional experiences in students. A positive learning context is one in which there are clear criteria for performance of the task to be taught, and the student is provided unambiguous feedback concerning his or her actions. Tasks should also be designed so that there are qualitatively different levels of challenge that require students to draw from multiple sources of their knowledge base. Most important, it is the student, not the teacher, who has the capacity to increase or decrease the level of challenge present in a task. The control of the student is critical, as there must be an exact match between skill level and the demands of the task. These conditions are believed to set a context for the student to obtain an accurate estimate of the *self*; that is, a concept of his abilities and capacities. Teachers should strive to develop environments in which students are provided the opportunity to face controllable levels of challenge (Csikszentmihalyi, 1978; Stanage, 1987). From this perspective, people are innately motivated to seek out and engage in activities that are challenging.

EDUCATION AND GOAL SETTING

When teachers set out to help students acquire skills, they seldom ask the students what goals they wish to attain. In most school settings, students' advancement is made on the basis of achieving predetermined quantitative criteria—number of correct problems solved, time required to read a passage from a book and answer a set of questions, or number of free-throws made. The focus of education is primarily on the development of skill levels that are adequate for students to solve the problems they will encounter outside the school setting. If a student desires to become better than average at a particular skill, he often is required to seek specialized instruction from an expert in that skill domain.

Expertise

Literature has emerged during the past few years that addresses directly the role of practice on expertise. It has been known intuitively for a long time that there are individual differences in the extent to which practice improves performance. Two individuals may spend the same amount of time perfecting a task, yet considerable differences in skill level may be seen upon execution of the task. Ericsson and his colleagues (Ericsson, Krampe, and Heizmann, 1993; Ericsson, Krampe, and Tesch-Romer, 1993) reviewed many studies of expert behavior from a variety of domains and concluded that the critical variable in expertise is *deliberate practice*. They suggest that truly exceptional performance occurs only when certain conditions are met. First, the task to be learned must be well defined and it must provide the learner with an opportunity to repeat the task and to receive clear, coherent feedback and knowledge of results. Further, the level of difficulty must be appropriate for the individual. Finally in Ericsson's view deliberate practice is not necessarily enjoyable; people practice because it leads to improvements in performance, not because practice is fun. The level of attentional effort demanded during effortful practice that leads to expert performance differentiates deliberate practice from play. Play may lead to improvements in performance, but not to expert levels of performance.

Experts are not necessarily more intelligent than novices; they are just more practiced. Indeed, Ericsson (1996) holds a strong environmentalist position that suggests that practice far outweighs the role of native intelligence in developing expertise. He cautions that the practice that results in progress must be deliberate, however. It must be conducted with mental effort, concentration, and motivation. Simply going through the actions is not sufficient to develop expertise. Practice must be serious and understood as necessary for attaining specified performance goals. Deliberate practice produces *domain-specific* improvements in performance. (See box 6.1.) Expertise is limited only to those skills that are practiced. Becoming an expert in chess will not make one an expert in backgammon or checkers. Further, high levels of skill come only with practice that is consistently performed over thousands of training trials. In most domains, the number of training sessions required to develop expertise may take years. Ericsson and his colleagues suggest that it takes approximately 10 years of systematic, deliberate practice to become an expert in most cognitive and motor skills.

BOX 6.1.   Expert Children

Expertise is often domain specific, which means that an expert's specialized skills are limited to a particular area of performance. A world-class basketball player, for example, may not perform at the same level of excellence on a baseball field. The phenomenon of domain specificity is demonstrated clearly in studies that have examined the performance of children who are expert chess players. It is almost always the case that adults perform better than children on memory and problem-solving tasks. However, there are situations in which children outperform adults.

A classic study conducted by Chi (1978) and a more recent one by Schneider, Gruber, Gold, and Opwis (1993) compared children's and adults' performance on two types of memory tests: a traditional digit-span test of short-term memory and a chessboard reconstruction task that assessed memory of the arrangement of pieces on a chessboard. The children in the Schneider et al. study were about 12 years old, and one group was composed of highly ranked chess competitors. The expert children's performance on the two memory tests was compared to the performance of children who were novice chess players, adults who were experts, and adults who were novice players. Children, regardless of their level of chess skill, performed more poorly than adults on the short-term memory test, a common and expected finding. However, expert children's memory and expert adults' memory for the position of chess pieces were significantly better than the memory of both novice children and novice adults. In this restricted situation, the player's training and experience, not age, was critical to exceptional memory performance, as this was a test of domain-specific memory skills.

The topic of expertise has recently become an area of research interest. Experts from many domains have been identified and evaluated, with the speed and accuracy of skilled performers being of particular interest. Experts' superior performance has been attributed, at least in part, to memory organization and function. Experts not only possess more domain-specific knowledge but also organize their knowledge in ways that allow them to access more information and to make decisions more rapidly and accurately than novices.

Training for Expertise

Most of the research on expertise has been descriptive in nature; comparisons have been made between the performance of experts and the performance of novices. These differences are then explained in terms of a retrospective evaluation of the experts' training history. There are probably as many training approaches as there are experts. Glaser (1984) and his colleague (Glaser and Bassok, 1989) have attempted to apply to the educational setting what has been learned through the study of experts. He suggests that the key to successful training lies in the transfer of training control from the instructor to the student. During the initial stages of training, the teacher should maintain a structured educational environment that provides students with unambiguous information concerning the components of complex skills, how the components relate to the outcome of practice, and how they relate to the terminal skill. With the acquisition of basic components, the teacher charges the student with increasing responsibility for self-monitoring his or her practice performance and for establishing a system to regulate the criteria used for practice. At the same time, the level of environmental support provided by the instructor decreases. The goal is to have the student become self-directed and to control his or her level of involvement during practice sessions, using instructors primarily as a source of feedback for competitive performance. When the student is allowed the opportunity for self-interrogation and self-evaluation, he or she is able to modify goals and expectancies.

Individual Goal Setting

Society provides great rewards to some who are experts. Considering the amount of money paid to experts in sports, music and entertainment, and business, it may seem that the only acceptable level of performance is elite, expert behavior. However, external rewards for performance are only one source of motivation. Internal rewards and phenomenological experiences also play a significant role in motivating behavior and acquiring skills. The psychological pleasures attained from action do not necessarily demand world-class levels of expertise. Indeed, individuals who have acquired elite skills are a rarity. If one considers the amount of practice and the time needed to become an expert, it is easy to explain why only a few reach the level of world-class athletes or performers in a given domain. Most will not attain the proficiency expected of world-class performers.

The point has been made that successful performance is bound to the psychological concept of self-efficacy. There are elite athletes and professional businessmen who, despite reaching the pinnacle of success in their areas, continue to hold negative views of their performance. Others, however, may derive great psychological pleasure and enhanced self-efficacy when they attain personal goals that do not even approximate expert performance. The role of skill as a route to good physical and mental health was discussed previously. It may be that the most important knowledge that can be transmitted from teacher to student, regardless of the student's age, is that pleasure, feelings of worth, and self-control can be gained from actions that lead to realistic and attainable goals—even if the goal is simply to perform the act itself.

Ultimately, it is the individual who selects his or her goals in life and the manner by which those goals will be achieved. *Existential-humanistic* philosophers who have addressed the topic of education stress repeatedly that students will experience a form of *personal alienation* if they give up the power to choose for themselves. The essence of being human is having personal choice, and the value of the mind is that it permits personal choice. It is the greatest violation of the human spirit for some outside force, society, or person to dictate what one's goals and aspirations should be. As what is of value is unique to the individual, nothing could be worse than requiring someone to achieve goals established by others.

External control creates an environment in which students engage in mindless actions that provide little in the form of psychological rewards. The controlled student who aspires to the goals of others is prevented from using her own mind to engage in training activities as a type of solvable problem. If all the steps are identified and the student is forced to follow them precisely, she is not provided with an opportunity to tap her creative resources and potential. When students select their own goals and paths of skill development, they display an openness to divergent ways of thinking and behaving and evidence a willingness to experiment and to enjoy the emotions attached to both failure and success. Practice generates situations with powerful emotional impact. The potential threat of harm, discomfort, or humiliation during training is enough to create an alteration of physical and mental states. Through repeated and focused practice, students learn to harness their emotions and they are able to cultivate the creation of mental conditions conducive to enhanced performance.

At first glance, the behavioristic notion of deliberate practice and the existentialist notion of self-directed learning appear to be mutually exclusive approaches to education. Both approaches, however, have a place in the learning process. There are expert musicians who report peak experiences when they perform. They often thank their mothers or fathers for forcing them, as children, to practice their music when they would have preferred to be outdoors playing with their friends. Without external control, these musicians would not have acquired the basic skills needed to be able to play automatically without effortful attention. As a result, the musicians would not be able to perform challenging pieces of music. These musicians also thank their teachers for providing them with the freedom to experiment with their music. Without freedom of choice, the musician is not able to reinterpret and modify standard pieces of music into new and unique arrangements. The enjoyment derived by creating new approaches to playing music is what makes one an artist, as opposed to a skilled technician. Artistic expression, regardless of whether it is playing a musical instrument, playing chess, or ice skating, comes only after we acquire basic skills and then have the freedom to choose our own methods of practice and performance.

Teaching Styles

Two approaches are often used to teach skills. One approach advocates the use of *toughening manipulations*; that is, placing people in challenging situations that evoke strong physiological responses. Advocates of this position believe that people who learn to overcome moderately stressful situations develop the physical and mental resources required to act adaptively, and in doing so acquire a sense of competence and a positive self-image. The other approach, advocates the development of *autotelic behavior*; that is, self-selected. Advocates of this position believe that forcing people to participate in activities they find undesirable can lead to negative psychological and behavioral consequences. These two approaches may, however, be conceptualized as representing two sides of a coin. Effective teachers recognize the value of each approach but also are cognizant that each has its strengths and weaknesses.

One of the greatest difficulties of teaching is knowing when to control the learning environment and the behavior of a student and when to allow the learner to take charge and to choose his or her own path. An important factor in helping teachers to determine the right mix of control and freedom is the learner's perceptions of the skill to be learned, and whether the learning situation elicits positive or negative emotions. Learning situations that are perceived as challenging are accompanied by positive emotional affect and the desire of the learner to *approach* and participate. Learning situations that are perceived as threatening are accompanied by negative affect and the desire to withdraw and to *avoid* participation. Observing a student's approach or avoidance behaviors reveals a great deal. Although an individual's perceptions of a learning situation may be caused by any one or a combination of factors, ultimately these perceptions are translated into approach or avoidance behaviors.

Common to both the toughening view and the autotelic view of teaching is the notion that successful training depends on a match between the demands of training and the individual's skill level. From an information-processing perspective, students will approach and engage in training when the learner has the declarative and procedural knowledge that are necessary to fulfill the demands of a task. If one has insufficient knowledge of or experience with a given task, he or she will perform poorly and will begin to withdraw the cognitive resources required to perform the task. Thus, an ineffective teaching environment is created when a teacher provides a student with information that is too complex and the learner does not understand how to behave; when a teacher presents information too rapidly and overwhelms the student's capacity to encode and transform it; or if too much information is provided and overwhelms the learner's processing capacity.

When students are placed in learning environments where they are provided the opportunity to explore and to solve problems, they have fun. A coach or teacher can make skill development enjoyable by capitalizing on the innate motivation to seek challenging tasks. There are several ways that structure can be provided to game and play activities so that children acquire essential skills without making learning tasks boring and monotonous. Through play and structured games, a child can be provided opportunities for action. Gross-motor physical activities such as dance, tumbling, and yoga permit a child to experience the pleasures of movement and body control. Fine-motor activities such as crafts, painting, model building, and pottery let a child experience the pleasure of creating an object or image. Activities such as singing, shouting, and reciting poems provide a child with the opportunity to make use of and enjoy knowledge. Learning how to play with words, to make puns and analogies, can make the educational process challenging and fun for children. Children who are given the opportunity to experience and learn from their own actions evidence a lifelong motivation for creativity. Autotelic children develop into autotelic adults (Csikszentmihalyi, 1990). Those who learn that they can derive pleasure through their own actions are seldom bored. They constantly manipulate and search out activities that present challenges. As adolescents and adults, their drive to play and experience the pleasures of new challenges continues.

A LIFE-SPAN APPROACH TO TEACHING SKILLS

Historically, the study of skill development has focused on the first two decades of life. When one thinks about skills, the first pictures that come to mind are a child taking his or her first steps, or a girl learning to ride a bicycle, or a boy kicking a soccer ball. This conceptualization of skill learning is similar to that of many educators and researchers interested in child development during the early decades of the twentieth century. The history of modern developmental psychology began with the work of G. Stanley Hall (1844–1924) in the late 1800s. The academic field of psychology was just emerging during this period and teachers and researchers were beginning to specialize in different areas of study.

Child Development

Several assumptions guided the objective and scientific study of child development during the first half of the twentieth century. One pervasive belief was that the majority of physiological and psychological development was linked to genetic background. The study of development has always been tied closely to the fields of biology and genetics; the belief held by many early psychologists was that child development was synonymous with biological maturation, which unfolds in a predictable fashion (see Baltes,

Staudinger, and Lindenberger, 1999, for an overview of life-span development issues).

Growth, both physical and mental, was assumed by early teachers and researchers to be a progression of highly predictable changes. These changes
were often described in terms of a series of developmental *milestones* (Clarke-
Stewart, Perlmutter, and Friedman, 1988). Development was assumed to be
uniform and *unidirectional;* that is, every child changed in essentially the same
way and these changes reflected a natural progression toward complete maturation. Numerous psychological tests and inventories were developed during
the early 1900s that measured the processes involved in the physical, mental,
and social maturation of children.

The first two decades of life were believed to be the most critical period in a
person's lifetime. It was assumed by many early researchers that childhood experiences during the *formative years* inexorably set the adult life course.
Drawing again from the conception of growth developed in the biological sciences, psychologists and educators believed that a child had to achieve certain
levels of functional capacity and skill at each stage of childhood development
to grow into a fully functioning adult. Some psychologists posited that there
are critical periods when children must be exposed to specific kinds of learning
experiences. If the child does not have these experiences during these time-
frames, the window of opportunity bypasses them. Failure to develop appropriately during an early phase of development was thought to negatively
affect the child's capacity to develop completely during later phases of growth.
Ultimately, adult behavior was tied to childhood patterns of growth. An adult's
behavior was often explained by carefully examining what transpired during
his or her formative years (see Maier, 1969, for an overview of classic developmental theory).

The rapid expansion of public education in the United States during the early
decades of the twentieth century led to tremendous growth in child development studies. Psychologists, educators, and researchers were trained to describe
and to explain the process of human development. Today, child psychologists
continue to study and document physiological, cognitive, and emotional
changes that accompany *chronological aging;* that is, the passage of time from
the moment of conception to the point where the individual becomes a fully
functioning mature person.

A vast amount of data have been collected to document the way that children
change as they age. These *normative* data provide the basis for describing specific characteristics at a specific point in time. *Norms* are standard patterns of
development of achievement. These measures provide researchers with a way
to plot an individual child's developmental progression and as a way to compare
his or her progression to that of other children who are the same chronological
age (see Haywood, 1993). Parents, for example, are often interested in the age
at which their child should begin to take his or her first steps. A child's developmental age can be derived by comparing the age when a particular behavior

(such as walking) emerges and the norms that have been established for that behavior.

Life-Span Development

Relatively recently, some researchers and educators have begun to think about human development in term of changes that occur from the moment of conception to the moment of death or, in the terms of some life-span psychologists, "from sperm to worm" (Hetherington and Baltes, 1988, p. 3). The studies conducted by life-span developmental researchers are similar in many respects to those conducted by child-development researchers. There are, however, several key assumptions that guide the work of life-span developmental researchers that differ from the assumptions held by researchers in other fields.

Life-span researchers assume that development is a multidirectional process, one in which the *trajectory* of one's life path can be influenced at virtually any point during the life span. The factors that influence the developing child are indeed important to his or her future; however, there are factors that affect people throughout their lives that can be equally important to their continued development. Our lives are not fixed on the basis of what happens to us during our first two decades. It is simply not the case that there is a unidirectional and positive acceleration in children's capacities and skills during the first decades of life that peaks in young adulthood, which is then followed by unavoidable declines in abilities and skills with advancing age. There are multiple physiological, cognitive, and social variables that direct how we act.

Several life-span theories of development describe the passage from birth to death in terms of a series of stages. A stage of life is defined as a naturally occurring level in the developmental process that is separate from other levels. There are two assumptions concerning the nature of progression through the life span. First, the stages of life are hypothesized to be sequentially ordered. Second, the developmental progress that occurs during one stage sets the conditions that are necessary for the individual to make a transition to the next stage.

Psychosocial Theory

Erik Erikson (1950, 1963, 1968) proposed an important stage-centered theory of life-span development. His theory emphasizes the relationship between the developing person's psychological growth and the society in which he or she lives. Erikson postulated that psychological development depends on the resolution of a series of *social crises* that emerge during specific stages of the life span. These crises are critical to the individual, because they ultimately determine the role that he or she will play within society.

Table 6.1
Erikson's Psychosocial Stages of Development

Approximate Age	Stage	Effect of Resolution
0–1½	Trust vs. Mistrust	Drive and hope
1½–3	Autonomy vs. Self-doubt	Self-control and willpower
3–6	Initiative vs. Guilt	Direction and purpose
6–puberty	Industry vs. Inferiority	Method and competence
Adolescent	Identity vs. Role Confusion	Devotion and fidelity
Early adult	Intimacy vs. Isolation	Affiliation and love
Middle adult	Generativity vs. Stagnation	Production and care
Later adult	Ego-Integrity vs. Despair	Wisdom

From Bem. P. Allen, *Personality Theories: Development, Growth, and Diversity* (3rd ed.) Copyright 2000. Adapted by permission by Allyn & Bacon.

Erikson outlined eight stages of life-span development. These stages are summarized in table 6.1. At each stage, positive life-span development hinges on the ability to master and resolve a central problem. These problems emerge from a dynamic interplay between an individual's *ego* (how one views himself or herself) and social and cultural constraints and expectancies. A *personal dilemma* is experienced when an individual's psychological forces conflict with the rules and obligations imposed by society. Erikson proposes that life-span problems can be responded to in one of two ways. One leads to positive outcomes and personal growth and the other to negative outcomes and physical and psychological deterioration. It is our capacity to *synthesize* (merge our personal needs with the constraints of society) that determines the trajectory of our psychological development.

Erikson's theory is quite popular, not only in the social and behavioral sciences, but also in specialized fields that deal with age-related issues. The broad-based psychosocial orientation of the theory, with its integration of anthropology, literature, the arts, science, and history, has made it a useful tool to examine many issues that arise in the study of human development.

Developmental-Task Theory

In some life-span theories, skills are viewed as mastery of *developmental tasks* that are encountered as they progress through life. The notion that life is a series of tasks has been popular in psychology and education for many decades. Robert Havighurst (1972) listed a number of developmental tasks that parallel Erik Erikson's eight-stage theory of development. Havighurst defines a developmental task as one "which arises at or about a certain period in the life of the individual, successful achievement of which leads to his happiness and to success with later tasks, while failure leads to unhappiness in the individual, disapproval by the society, and difficulty with later tasks" (1972, p. 2). Thus, the manner in which we deal with a given developmental task sets the direction of our life's trajectory. Developmental tasks reflect a given society's or culture's core beliefs; they reflect aspects of behavior that are deemed to be important for group membership and physical and mental health.

Havighurst compares the path of life to the paths up a mountainside selected by a mountain climber. Sometimes the climber traverses areas of a mountain range that are level and easy to cross; at other times, she encounters parts of the mountain that are steep and require skill and effort to negotiate. Like the mountain climber, we enjoy periods of our lives when we can go though our daily routines with minimal effort; however, at various times of our lives we encounter challenging situations that demand specific skills and mustering of the effort needed to overcome them. Failure to develop the requisite skills leaves us unable to reach the summit of the mountain, stranded on the mountainside.

An integral part of life-span development is education. Learning is not confined simply to academic training given early in life. It is a lifelong process in which an individual must be actively engaged in the learning process in order to acquire the skills needed to resolve life's tasks. Fortunately, the structure of the family and society have evolved in ways that provide opportunities to learn life skills from others. Formal education is provided to children, adolescents, and young adults in modern industrialized nations. Further, people learn many skills in an informal manner. We draw on the knowledge gained by others who have successfully confronted their own developmental tasks.

Havighurst emphasizes also that people are often primed or prepared to learn specific life skills at particular periods of development. There is a dynamic interaction between the individual and the emergence of specific developmental tasks. People often display behaviors indicative of what Havighurst describes as the *teachable moment*, a natural inclination to learn the skills that they will need to meet and resolve developmental tasks. The teachable moment is, however, transitory. Successful development often hinges on the timing of a student's readiness to learn and the teacher's readiness to impart knowledge.

The developmental tasks we encounter arise from several sources. Some tasks are tied closely to biological maturation; others are associated with social and cultural expectations; and still others are linked to the personal goals, values, and aspirations we hold. A list of the developmental tasks described by Havighurst is seen in table 6.2. There are particular tasks at each stage of development that we encounter. Our ability to resolve these tasks requires the acquisition and performance of motor, cognitive, and even social skills.

Table 6.2
Havighurst's Developmental Tasks

Developmental Tasks of Infancy and Early Childhood
1. Learning to walk
2. Learning to take solid foods
3. Learning to talk
4. Control/elimination of wastes
5. Sex differences and sexual modesty
6. Forming concepts and language to describe reality
7. Getting ready to read
8. Learning to distinguish right and wrong and beginning to develop a conscience

Developmental Tasks of Middle Childhood
1. Learning physical skills necessary for ordinary games
2. Building wholesome attitudes toward oneself
3. Learning to get along with age-mates
4. Learning an appropriate masculine or feminine social role
5. Developing fundamental skills in reading, writing, and mathematics
6. Developing concepts for everyday living
7. Developing conscience, morality, and a scale of values
8. Achieving personal independence
9. Developing attitudes toward social groups and institutions

Developmental Tasks of Adolescence
1. Achieving more mature relations with age-mates of both sexes
2. Achieving a masculine or feminine role
3. Accepting one's physique and using the body effectively
4. Achieving emotional independence from parents and other adults
5. Preparing for marriage and family life
6. Preparing for an economic career
7. Acquiring a set of values and an ethical system as a guide to behavior—developing an ideology
8. Desiring and achieving socially responsible behavior

Developmental Tasks of Early Adulthood
1. Selecting a mate
2. Learning to live with a marriage partner
3. Starting a family
4. Rearing children
5. Managing a home
6. Getting started in an occupation
7. Taking on civic responsibility
8. Finding a congenial social group

Table 6.2
(Continued)

Developmental Tasks of Middle Age
1. Assisting teenage children in becoming responsible and happy adults
2. Achieving adult social and civic responsibilities
3. Reaching and maintaining satisfactory performance in an occupational career
4. Developing adult leisure-time activities
5. Relating to one's spouse as a person
6. Accepting and adjusting to the physiological changes of middle age
7. Adjusting to aging parents

Developmental Tasks of Later Maturity
1. Adjusting to decreasing physical strength and health
2. Adjusting to retirement and reduced income
3. Adjusting to the death of a spouse
4. Establishing an explicit affiliation with one's age group
5. Adopting and adapting social roles in a flexible way
6. Establishing satisfactory physical living arrangements

From R. J. Havighurst, *Developmental Tasks and Education* (3rd ed.). Copyright 1972. Adapted by permission by Allyn & Bacon.

CHAPTER SUMMARY

There will be periods in our lives when we are students, and there will be times when we are teachers. Think about your own past for a moment. Have you shown a brother, sister, or friend how to perform a skill? Perhaps you have already worked in your community to teach sport skills to children. You may have been an instructor at summer camp or in a program that provides educational services to children or adults. We cannot avoid the role of teaching as we progress through our lives.

Teaching is a difficult but highly rewarding experience. Its difficulty lies in the need to create environments that match students' physical, mental, and emotional characteristics with the tasks to be learned. This chapter focused on the processes of the body and the mind and how our understanding of these domains can help to create conditions optimal for skill learning. Recent theory and research have provided educators with a better understanding of the many factors that impact how people learn skills. The reward of teaching is that we provide a new generation of people with the skills that they will need to improve their lives and the world in which we live.

SUGGESTED READINGS

Collins, A., Brown, J. S., and Newman, S. E. (1989). Cognitive apprenticeship: Teaching the crafts of reading, writing, and mathematics. In L. Resnick (Ed.), *Knowing, learning, and instruction: Essays in honor of Robert Glaser* (pp. 453–494). Hillsdale, NJ: Erlbaum.

Ericsson, A. A. (Ed.). (1996). *The road to excellence: The acquisition of expert performance in the arts and sciences, sports, and games.* Mahwah, NJ: Erlbaum.

Erikson, E. (1963). *Childhood and society* (2nd ed.). New York: Norton.

Erikson, E. (1968). *Identity, youth, and crisis.* New York: Norton.

Evers, W. M. (Ed.). (1998). *What's wrong in America's classrooms.* Stanford, CA: Hoover Institution Press.

Havighurst, R. J. (1972). *Developmental tasks and education* (3rd ed.). New York: David McKay.

Maier, H. W. (1969). *Three theories of child development.* New York: Harper & Row.

Chapter 7

Skills of Childhood

Childhood is a period of life dominated by massive amounts of skill development. The newborn comes into the world possessing only a few basic reflexes but quickly demonstrates the capacity to learn a multitude of skills needed to adapt and survive in a new environment, almost from the moment of birth.

Children are characterized by their natural drive to acquire new knowledge and skills. This chapter focuses on children's learning and how it is affected by the physical, mental, and emotional changes that occur as they mature. It examines the impact of early experience on skill development and whether or not specialized instruction can accelerate learning. When you complete this chapter you will be more aware of the differences that can exist among children and why they differ in their capacity to learn.

HISTORICAL VIEWS OF CHILDREN

Developmental psychologists are interested in the role of children in modern cultures and society. The study of children and childhood is, however, a recent phenomenon. Few distinctions were made between the needs and motives of children and adults prior to the nineteenth century. Children were often thought of simply as little adults. The world of the child and the world of adults were thought to be the same. Any child who survived infancy was quickly pressed into services that contributed to the survival of the family and the wider social group. There was little notion within the typical family that children thought, learned, or should act differently than adults (see Borstelmann, 1983, for a description of early views of childhood).

During the Age of Enlightenment in the seventeenth and eighteenth centuries, social philosophers engineered new systems of government and reanalyzed the nature of human rights. Children and their role in society became a keystone of the plans developed by the architects of the new order. Men like John Locke (1632–1704) in England and Jean-Jacques Rousseau (1712–1784) in France espoused ideas concerning the nature of humans that had tremendous impact on developing democratic governments throughout Western civilization. Both Locke and Rousseau emphasized the uniqueness of children and how their abilities differed from those of adults. Locke realized how important individual differences are in children and advocated the development of educational methods that would permit children to learn useful skills by doing and practicing.

During the nineteenth century, two forces emerged that shaped modern perspectives on the nature of children and their role in society. The first was the scientific method and its acceptance as the preferred way to understand, predict, and control nature. The use of methods of science provided a means whereby the forces of nature could be contained, manipulated, and controlled. Humankind was thought to be capable of mastering the natural world. The very nature of humans was envisioned to be understandable through precise study. The emerging scientific study of nature and the corresponding optimistic belief that behavior could be controlled had a profound effect on parents and educators alike. The second force was Charles Darwin's theory of evolution. Social philosophers such as Herbert Spencer (1820–1903), who espoused the concepts of evolution, contended that the principle of survival of the fittest applied not only to individuals within a species but also to human societies and cultures. The societies that were composed of members who were the most physically and mentally capable of meeting the demands of changes brought about by industrialization and urbanization would survive. Books instructed parents how to teach their children how to learn the skills necessary to be a contributing member of society. Central to the *eugenics* movement was the notion that humankind should strive to develop children who are physically, mentally, and morally strong.

Public education was seen as a vehicle for ensuring that all members of society would have the skills necessary to meet and overcome the challenges posed by international industrial competition. The *progressive education movement* led by John Dewey (1859–1953), reflected the spirit of the times in the United States. The population of cities in North America increased dramatically with the influx of immigrants from all parts of the world. America and Canada were expanding from the east to the west coast, and a widely held notion was that anyone could be successful if given the opportunity. As the nation experienced an explosion in the growth of democratic ideals, the process of education underwent dramatic transformation. The new approach to teaching was characterized by a shift from an autocratic style of instruction that emphasized rote memorization to a democratic style of instruction that emphasized the role of adaptive problem solving. Children were no longer viewed as passive recipients of facts gained by way of drills; they were viewed as continually growing, changing, and adapting individuals. Instructional theory focused on harnessing this natural growth and change and guiding each student to engage in actions that would help him or her acquire knowledge.

The new approach to education centered around allowing the child to be an active participant in the learning process. It was only through action and experience that useful knowledge was acquired. Progressive education was formulated on the concept of evolution. People were assumed to be motivated innately to learn the skills necessary for individual survival; it was the task of the educational system to direct and guide their need for activity in ways that would benefit the development of society and promote the continued evolution of the human species. The accumulation of knowledge was not limited only to children, however; it was vital to individuals across the lifespan. The progressive educational theory and its focus on developing children's functional life skills provided a model that has been adhered to by many U.S. educators to the present time (Borstelmann, 1983; Brant, 2000).

DEVELOPMENTAL PSYCHOLOGY

The concept of evolution had a marked impact on psychologists who were interested in the scientific study of children. G. Stanley Hall (1844–1924), considered to be the father of developmental psychology, was a proponent of *recapitulation theory* (Hall, 1904). This theory proposed that every child goes through stages of development that parallel the evolution of the entire human species. The unfolding of biological structures and the appearance of their functions during the early *ontological* development of every human child repeats or *recapitulates* the biological changes that occurred over the millions of years of *phylogenetic* development of modern humans. Hall hypothesized that a child evolves from a single cell to a multicelled organism that becomes increasingly differentiated and complex in much the same way that the entire human species evolved from a simple to a more complex organism. Further, Hall believed that the behaviors of modern children reflected the behavioral characteristics of our early human ancestors. His observation that children can evidence cruelty and impulsiveness was assumed to reflect the types of behaviors engaged in by early humanoid species. Games of war and mock battles were thought to reflect the aggressive nature of humans exhibited during early civilization. Although recapitulation theory did not stand the test of empirical verification, it does provide a vivid example of the extent to which the theory of evolution was embraced as a modern view of the nature of children and how they develop.

Many early twentieth-century developmental psychologists focused their efforts on studying and describing how children mature and develop over time. *Maturation* reflects biologically based changes in the structure and functions of the body that are linked to genetically based directions or codes. Maturational processes are essentially the same for all members of a given species. These biological changes are, however, influenced by an individual's environment and learning experiences. *Development* refers to an orderly sequence of physical, mental, and emotional changes that emerge through the interaction of the child and his or her environment.

Developmental psychologists measure and describe in great detail the changes that children undergo during the first few years of life. The clockwork regularity of the emergence of specific physical structures and behavioral patterns lies at the heart of stage theories of child development. As discussed in chapter 6, there are three core assumptions of most child development theories. First, developmental progression is uniform and unidirectional; all children change in essentially the same ways and change is always an accumulative process of increasing complexity. Second, the interactions that occur between children's biological maturation and the environment in which they live prepare them to move from one stage of development to the next. Third, children's behavior at one stage of development can be explained in terms of what occurred to them during previous stages.

Researchers have developed growth models that describe children's physical, cognitive, and emotional development—the three pillars of human behavior. Understanding why and how children learn skills is intimately related to understanding the developmental changes that occur within each of these areas.

Physical Development

Biological changes begin at the moment of conception and continue at a phenomenal pace during the next two decades of life (see Berk, 2000, for an in-depth description of physical development). Patterns of growth follow two themes. First, biological changes follow the *law of developmental direction*. The direction of growth proceeds *cephalocaudally*, from the head toward the feet, and *proximodistally*, from the center of the body to its periphery. Second, biological changes in growth are *asynchronous*, meaning that the systems and structures that comprise the human body develop at different rates and at different times. The genetic codes that control the activity of cells determine when cells remain stable, when they become active, and when they divide. As a result, one part of the body may be undergoing extremely rapid growth and change while other parts of the body remain relatively unchanged.

The nine-month period of prenatal development that precedes an infant's birth is divided into three stages. The *germinal stage* is characterized by two weeks of rapid cell division and the creation of rudimentary neural organization. The *embryonic stage* begins during the third week following conception and continues through the seventh week of gestation. The blueprint of genetic codes found within the DNA of the developing organism's cells initiates and directs the creation of physiological structures such as the central and peripheral nervous systems, the glands of the autonomic nervous system, and the skeletal muscles that will eventually come to control movement. In a few short weeks of growth, neural connections that will integrate the multiple systems of the body are formed. The *fetal stage* is characterized by the continued growth and organization of structures that emerged during previous developmental stages. The brain, for example, grows initially at a rate of 250,000 neurons per minute, and reaches its full complement of over 100,000 billion neurons by the time birth occurs.

Motor behavior occurs in the developing child even before birth. The study of prenatal development reveals that the fetus has developed many of the motor reflexes that will be needed to deal with the world by the fifth prenatal month. A description of some of these reflexes is seen in table 7.1. At birth, the infant is wired and primed for survival.

Infancy is a period of about 18 months of development that is characterized by the newborn's total dependency on the care of others. Much of the infant's existence during this period of life involves motor learning. Infants become increasingly mobile and interact more with their environment. The progression of infant movement follows the same cephalocaudal-proximodistal pattern seen during prenatal development. For example, infants first control their shoulder movements, then their elbow movements, followed by their hand movements and finally their finger movements. Thus, the infant's control of gross-motor movement precedes control of fine-motor movement.

The shift in control and precision of movement parallels the growth of the brain and the central nervous system. A baby's head in infancy is already about 60 percent of its adult size, and the brain's growth in mass accelerates rapidly during the first two years of life. The developmental processes that began in the brain prior to birth set the conditions for tremendous growth. Neural pathways are established and information is processed as the nerve cells become sensitive to neural and hormonal signals. The complete complement of neurons that a person will ever have are present at the time of birth. However, the ultimate architecture and specific function of the brain and spinal cord of each individual will depend on several factors. Brain function is made more efficient with the growth of cells that enhance neuronal activity by transporting metabolic products and by providing structural support to neural pathways. Further, the size of individual nerve cells increases and their structure becomes more complex. The axons of some cells become covered by myelin, a white fatty substance that improves the rate at which information can be transmitted from one point to another. The interconnections of some neural pathways become more complex while other neural pathways weaken. The newborn is equipped with many more neural pathways than are needed for adaptive behavior. Cells that are part of redundant and inefficient neural circuits die off as environmental conditions

Table 7.1
Infant Reflexes

Reflex	Time
Tonic neck reflex—arms extend, legs flex	Prenatal to 7 months
Palmar grasping—hand closes around object	Prenatal to 4 months
Moro—fingers spread	Prenatal to 3 months
Babinski—toes extend	Birth to 4 months
Sucking—sucking motion	Birth to 3 months
Rooting—head turns to side stimulated	Birth to 1 year
Plantar—toes contract around object	1 to 3 months
Startle—arms and legs flex	7 to 12 months

Reprinted, by permission, from K. M. Haywood and N. Getchell, 2001, *Life Span Motor Development* (3rd ed.). (Champaign, IL: Human Kinetics), 90.

have their impact on the child. This neurological *pruning* has been linked to the infant's individual experiences and the learning process (Kolb and Whishaw, 1990).

Early childhood is a period lasting from about 18 months to 6 years of age. The period is characterized by rapid improvements in the control and expression of motor movements. The child engages in extensive practice of gross-motor movements that have important roles in play and, later on, in games and sport. The actions of the child are paralleled by asynchronous brain development. The two hemispheres of the cortex come to control different functions at different points in time. Areas of the left hemisphere in most children begin to control the production of speech sounds, for example. Areas of the right hemisphere are linked to nonspeech sounds, emotions, and the organization of spatial information. The two hemispheres of the brain are linked by the *corpus callosum*, a large neural pathway. The effects of practice, along with changes within the developing cortex, come to control a child's ability to initiate, time, and execute motor skills. Control of the movement of minute muscles that are involved in the production of speech sounds stands as a testament to the level of motor control that emerges during the first few years of life.

Motor skills become more refined during *late childhood*, which extends from about 6 years to about 13 years of age. A child's rate of physical growth begins to slow during this period. Play behavior begins to be replaced by practice at specific types of skills. Children become interested in many different types of physical and mental activities during this time of their lives. They often sample different sports and games and pursue those that match their emerging physical and mental abilities. The physical activities that children engage in during this period are important, because they often set the tone for the kinds of activities they will pursue as adults.

Cognitive Development

Several researchers have proposed that mental development, like physical development, is characterized by a progression of distinct stages through which all children go before reaching maturity. Jean Piaget (1896–1980), a Swiss psychologist, proposed a highly influential theory of children's mental development in the 1920s that continues to impact many modern educators and researchers (see Maier, 1969, and Wadsworth, 1976, for excellent reviews of Piaget's work). Piaget was interested in the link between the biological and psychological development of infants and children. He believed that the primary developmental task of childhood was adaptation. Piaget's research technique involved making detailed observations of individual children and how they solved problems. His theory focuses on the way that children behave as they adapt to environmental demands.

Piaget proposed that children's adaptation was the net result of two opposing processes that pulled them from one level of understanding of how the natural world works to the next level of understanding. The process of *assimilation* reflects a child's conception of his or her world at a particular moment in time. Assimilation is a force that directs a child to establish an equilibrium (balance) between his or her physical world and mental world. The process of *accommodation* reflects a child's attempts to deal with the world as it really exists. A child's world is not static; it is constantly changing. The changing world provides children with new experiences and new information that must be incorporated with previously learned knowledge and organized into patterns or schemas that fit the world as it currently exists. Schemas, according to Piaget, are psychological patterns of intellectual behavior that emerge as a result of the processes of assimilation and accommodation. Schemas link previously learned ways of viewing the world with new potential ways of viewing it.

The ongoing dynamics of the real world impact the developing child; they create a disequilibrium that forces the child to continuously reorganize and restructure perceptions of nature. Assimilation and accommodation simultaneously push and pull on the child's cognitive schemas of the world. Piaget posited that childhood is characterized by constant mental activity directed toward restructuring and modifying the child's view of his or her place in nature.

Piaget suggested that children's *experience*, rather than *maturation*, is the key to their cognitive development. It is only when we are faced with the challenges imposed by the real world that we are forced to reorganize our thoughts. The processes of mental organization that occur as a child attempts to obtain a sense of equilibrium push him or her toward more complex levels of cognitive organization. He described four stages of cognitive development that occur in a set sequence during particular age ranges. Each stage is characterized by patterns of thinking about nature and how it works. There is a *continuous* change in the complexity of children's thinking within each stage of development. The movement from one stage to the next is *discontinuous*, however. Cognitive growth leads children to a threshold that, when crossed, enables them to view nature in a qualitatively different way than they did during previous stages. The transition from one stage of cognitive development to the next depends greatly on a child's experiences. Those that are part of problem solving push the child to search for new and more complex ways of understanding and adapting to the world. According to Piaget, progression occurs as we attempt to balance *what we know* with *what we are experiencing* at a given time.

1. *The sensorimotor stage* (birth to 2 years). Piaget's theory focuses considerable attention on the first two years of life, when an infant faces multiple developmental challenges. Central to this stage of cognitive development is the building of relationships between the infant's actions, which are almost exclusively in the form of motor movements, and internal sensory experiences that are derived from those actions.

Making physical movements and repeating them comprise the bulk of a baby's day. These movements, which were initially elicited reflexively, come to be initiated voluntarily by the child. Through practice, the infant begins to understand the relationship between movements and their effects on the environment. Patterns of mental and behavior action set the stage for play behaviors through which the child develops rudimentary concepts of causality, spatial orientation, and the permanence of objects. The maturation and refinement of locomotor skills provides the child with even more opportunity to experience and experiment with his world. The capacity for intelligent reasoning rapidly propels him toward the next stage of cognitive development.

2. *The preoperational stage* (2 to 7 years). Mental operations are defined as the ability to organize and reorganize knowledge. The child in the preoperational stage of development is capable of representing objects mentally that are not physically present. Children of this age can imagine all sorts of things. They often employ *animistic thinking* in which life and mental processes are given to physical, inanimate objects. A child's favorite teddy bear, for example, does indeed come alive for him. Although he may be able to imagine the existence of objects, he has yet to develop the capacity to understand how objects can change their appearance and still *conserve* their basic attributes. To the child, a ball of clay that is rolled into a tube of clay, even before his eyes, is not the same object. The ball and the tube are two different objects.

It is also true that children within this age range tend to be *egocentric*; that is, they are unable to view events in nature from the perspective of other people. The child has only one perspective: his own. The dynamic of language skills, play, and social interactions, however, provide him the experiences that force him to abandon this self-centered view of nature and move toward the next stage of cognitive development.

3. *The concrete operational stage (7 to 11 years)*. This stage is characterized by the child's display of *logical reasoning skills*. The child is able to employ mental operations, such as those that underlie conservation, to objects that are tangible, real, concrete. Children who have mastered conservation are aware that the physical properties of an object are not changed even when the object's appearance is altered. A child will recognize, for example, that the amount of a ball of clay remains unchanged despite changing its form into a cylinder or cube. The capacity to employ reasoning skills provides children with a powerful tool to help them understand the world in which they live. They become increasingly aware of the rules that govern both nature and their own lives.

4. *The formal operational stage (11 years and older).* The final stage in Piaget's theory is characterized by the ability to perform the type of logical problem solving performed by scientists. Advanced *deductive logic,* in particular, provides the child with the ability to generate and test hypotheses about events that occur in nature. This form of reasoning involves the capacity to develop and manipulate knowledge in symbolic form. These newly developed cognitive skills provide children a way to see linkages among environmental events or objects that appear, on the surface, to have little in common. The capacity to use mental operations to manipulate knowledge also permits the child to begin to view the world from multiple perspectives.

Piaget's views sparked considerable debate that continues to the present day. Not all aspects of his theory have withstood the rigors of empirical tests; nevertheless, his theory of cognitive development is considered a classic by many contemporary researchers. Piaget's approach to examining individual children and how they perform specific types of mental tasks is similar to the approach that many educators take in assessing a student's classroom performance.

Emotional Development

Early twentieth-century views of emotion and its development were aligned with behavioristic orientations of child development. John B. Watson, for example, proposed that all human emotions are based on reflex patterns (Watson, 1930). In the same way that children are born with a number of innate motor reflexes, they also begin life with three emotional reflexes: rage, fear, and love. At birth, these behavioral patterns occur when a specific stimulus is presented: a loud noise elicits fear; restricting freedom of movement elicits rage; and stroking or patting elicits love. Through conditioning and learning, infants learn to respond emotionally to other stimuli. The emotions of developing children were assumed to reflect increases in their capacity to differentiate among stimuli that have the potential to elicit emotional patterns. Watson's form of behaviorism viewed emotion simply as learned behavior; little was made of the sensations that accompany emotional responses.

The view that complex emotions are based on prewired sets of reflexes continues to hold a place in modern psychological theories of emotion. With the rise of cognitive psychology, however, greater emphasis has been placed on understanding how emotional development is tied to cognitive development and the acquisition of language (see Mussen, Comger, Kagan, and Huston, 1990, for a detailed description of emotional development).

A child's emotional development is particularly sensitive to the social environment. Infants learn quickly the impact that smiles, frowns, and cries have on parents. Indeed, a child's smile plays a big role in determining the frequency of pleasurable physical contact with adults. Infants are capable of modifying reflexive emotional patterns within the first two years of their lives. Their capacity to control some aspects of emotional behaviors are enhanced as they develop language skills and are able to attach descriptive labels to their feelings.

The pattern of emotions that a child adopts during childhood may be affected by the style of parenting employed. Research evidence suggests that parents who use an *autocratic style* (punitive, unaffectionate, detached, and unsympathetic) teach their children to control emotional displays. Children who perceive themselves as under constant threat of punishment are often fearful, submissive, and slow to explore their world. A *permissive style* of parenting (characterized by a lack of clearly stated rules and responsibilities), on the other hand, leads children to be social and outgoing. Children exposed to this type of parenting style, however, may tend to be emotionally immature and to lack persistence and self-reliance. An *authoritative style* of parenting, which balances the needs of the child with the rules of the family, prompts children to express their emotions in ways that are viewed as friendly, cooperative, and socially responsible (Clarke-Stewart, Perlmutter, and Friedman, 1988, chapter 10).

It must be emphasized, however, that a specific parenting style will not necessarily cause a child to behave in a particular way. Behavior is the result of an exceedingly complex interaction between the developing child and the environment. Multiple factors determine the extent to which a child will respond to the rules that govern display of emotional behavior. What is important, however, is that patterns of emotional behavior, such as being submissive and controlled, or friendly and self-reliant, play a role in the way that a child will respond when required to learn motor or cognitive skills.

In summary, the points at which children reach specific developmental motor, cognitive, and emotional milestones can vary considerably. Recognizing the sources of individual differences in developmental progress can provide teachers, parents, or coaches with insight regarding how to structure a given youngster's skill-training programs for best results.

EARLY EXPERIENCE AND THE MIND-BODY RELATION

Throughout history there have been *child prodigies;* that is, children who show exceptional talent and skill at a very young age. These children evidence abilities that are remarkable even by adult standards. Wolfgang Mozart was considered a prodigy because he was already playing, writing, and orchestrating excellent music at the age of seven. There are many examples of successful men and women in the arts, politics, and business who showed remarkably advanced abilities as children.

Various explanations for child prodigies have been offered, with considerable debate among psychologists, educators, and parents about advanced skill development in childhood. Some explain such gifts in terms of genetic factors and propose that children's abilities are linked to the abilities of their families. Others explain this in term of environmental factors and suggest that all children have the capacity to learn a tremendous amount of information at an early age

(Winner, 1996). The idea that a child's skills can be accelerated through rigorous training programs instituted early in life has had a marked impact on developmental specialists and some parents.

The Body's Effect on the Mind

In the nineteenth century, it was virtually axiomatic that exercising the body developed the "organ" of the mind as surely as it developed the skeletal muscles. Early medical texts suggested that exercise promoted the growth of the central nervous system and improved mental abilities. The presumed relation between physical fitness and mental fitness was a cornerstone of the view that physical activity could contribute to the improvement of participants' moral qualities. Children who experienced vigorous activity were believed to develop brains that relayed information more quickly and efficiently than did the brains of inactive children. This view of the body-mind relation became instantiated in America's emerging public educational system. Teachers from grade school through college were charged with instructing pupils in matters of the mind and the body; thus, the study of physical education came into existence in U.S. schools.

The Mind's Effect on the Body

The proponents of Darwinian evolution had a marked influence on modern psychology. William James, reflecting the spirit of the theory of evolution, considered the mind to be as much of an organ of the body as any physical organ. In his view, the processes of the mind are shaped by environmental pressures and designed to serve very specific functions important for survival. Perhaps the most important function of the mind, to James, was the creation of *habits*; that is, reflexive patterns of behavior. James posited that habits are formed through repetitive actions that cause neurological pathways in the brain to develop, resulting in increasingly rapid flow of energy. Through repetition, he said, the brain would perform optimally in guiding the body's actions, with less effort and fatigue. Habits were likened to instinctual patterns of action that do not require conscious effort or attention to be executed (James, 1890). As described in the first section of this text, the concept of habits has played a central place in most contemporary theories that attempt to explain how motor and cognitive skills are acquired.

James's philosophy had a marked influence on the general public as well as academic fields such as psychology, education, and exercise studies. Dynamic changes were taking place in the United States, and social engineers were quick to take up his recipes for the development of a sound mind and moral character. His views and the views of behavioral psychologists such as John B. Watson dovetailed with the growing eugenics movement and the institutionalization of methods designed to develop the backbone of the country by instilling good habits in children at an early age. James provided rules of conduct that were simple to understand and made sense to the general public.

Critical Period Concepts

Even the casual observation of children's behavior reveals that the first few years of life are characterized by tremendous physical, cognitive, and emotional change. The acquisition of many skills seems to take place almost without conscious effort. The development of language, for example, begins slowly about the second year and then accelerates rapidly. Children have the capacity to learn multiple languages and the motor skills needed to speak fluently by the time they are 10 years old. However, those introduced to a second language after the age of about 14 appear to have more difficulty with its acquisition than if it is introduced earlier in life. And in extreme cases when a child has been deprived of the opportunity to develop a language, he may never successfully acquire the ability to communicate orally with others. Such observations have led some to suggest that there are *critical periods of development* linked to skill acquisition. Coaches and teachers often emphasize that children will benefit most when training is introduced within a particular period (see Lerner, 1986, for a discussion of the critical period concept).

The concept of the critical period suggests that maturational processes produce physiological changes within the developing organism that can be influenced markedly, in a positive or negative fashion, by the presence or absence of a particular stimulus or event. Support for the existence of critical periods comes from observations of embryonic development. It is clear from these studies that specific organ systems have only one chance for normal development. If an organ system is not stimulated in a certain fashion at a specific point in the developmental sequence, it will be permanently affected. (If the needed environmental stimulus is applied at a later point in development, the affected organ system will be atypical.) A classic series of Nobel-prize-winning studies by *David Hubel* and *Torsten Weisel* in the 1970s demonstrated the importance of stimulation at critical periods in the development of the brains of laboratory animals (See Hubel, 1988, for a review of this research). In these studies, the processes that are typically present in the normal development of laboratory animals' visual systems were blocked during the period when the visual cortex should have been undergoing rapid growth and development. The visual cortex of those who did not experience visual stimulation developed abnormally; they displayed visual impairments that were not reversible.

Research studies such as these support the case that the normal biological development of an organism is linked to specific environmental events. There has been debate, however, as to how far the critical period concept can be applied to motor and cognitive skill development. The tremendous success of professional golfer Tiger Woods, for example, has been explained by some as relating directly to his father's introducing him to the techniques of golf at an early age.

On the other hand, there are professional golfers, such as Greg Norman, who did not begin playing the game until much later (Greg was 16), yet they have still become highly successful golfers. The nexus of the debate revolves around just how fixed critical periods truly are. When it comes to the development of motor and cognitive skills, there have been enough exceptions to the rule to lead some to propose a *sensitive period concept*; that is, there may be an optimal period for a particular intervention to affect development, but it is not critical that the individual experience that intervention (Lerner, 1986). It may help to introduce children to grammar, language, or sport skills at an early age, but this is not necessarily demanded. It is recognized, however, that children who miss early experience during sensitive periods of development will have to engage in deliberate practice in order to achieve the level of performance of those who learned the skill during optimal periods of development.

The Enrichment Concept

Use of *early stimulation interventions* to maximize a child's abilities and skills has been promoted vigorously in modern society. The observation that the presence or absence of a specific environmental event (whether that be a hormone, a protein, tactile, or sensory stimulation) can, under certain conditions, have a considerable effect on animal growth and development has led some people to generalize the effectiveness of early experience to human development. Parents have been introduced to methods of exposing children in the womb to music and language programs. Infant stimulation products have been developed that are intended to advance children's mental and physical development. In the United States, legislative bills have been introduced that would require parents to play classical music to their infants. In fact, some parents feel that if their child is not in enrichment programs designed to accelerate skill development, he or she will fall behind the rest.

Systematic examination of enrichment programs reveals that a case can be made for the beneficial effects of these programs under certain limiting conditions. However, there is sufficient evidence to suggest that the majority of such interventions do not promote fundamental and long-lasting changes in motor and cognitive abilities (see Druckman and Bjork, 1991, for an evaluation of enrichment programs). The notion that general stimulation and intervention programs will affect all children in the same fashion has been found to be too simplistic. Missing from consideration are multiple factors that exist in a child, his family, and his environment. One of the major limitations of many enrichment programs is the belief that limited exposure to a training intervention can "inoculate" the child for the remainder of his or her life. Skill development is characterized by effort and extended practice. The belief that a child's brief exposure to Mozart's musical works will set the conditions necessary to develop musical skill demands a rather large leap of faith. A second shortcoming of most enrichment programs is that they are based more on individuals' opinions of how children learn skills than on fact. These programs are rarely designed to be adapted to the needs of an individual child. Little thought is given to individual differences in the maturation of motor, cognitive, and emotional capabilities.

This is not to say that children cannot acquire skills at an early stage of their development. Children can, and do, learn! What is emphasized by those who have conducted systematic evaluations of the effects of enrichment programs is that the one-size-fits-all method of teaching is neither effective nor desirable (Wachs, 1982). A better understanding of the factors related to motor and cognitive skill development will enable parents and teachers to design interventions that are sensitive to the tripartite nature of children. From the first moments of life, children acquire knowledge based on the interactive properties of associative learning, thinking and problem-solving learning, and emotion.

SKILL LEARNING IN CHILDREN

Skill development is a dynamic process that reflects the interaction among the *biophysical domain*, which includes aspects of behavior that are mechanistic, habitual, and automatic; the *thinking domain*, which includes aspects of behavior related to conscious problem solving and thought; and the *emotional domain*, which includes aspects of behavior classified as motivation and feeling. Children differ from adults both quantitatively and qualitatively in the manner in which they acquire skills. The bases for these differences may be elucidated by examining each of the three characteristics of human behavior. Understanding the contribution of each of these facets of behavior provides insight into the processes involved as children acquire motor and cognitive skills.

The Biophysical Domain

The accumulation of habits is essential to children's survival. The world they are born into is hazardous and their actions determine whether they live or die. A young child in the process of learning to walk who is left alone in a kitchen faces many real and potentially life-threatening dangers. Hot stoves, stored chemicals, and sharp utensils are present and can pose real threats. Parents are quick to recognize these dangers and attempt to minimize the dangers that lurk in each room of their house by restricting the child's access and by teaching the child avoidance habits. The child who has learned the unconscious habit of stopping and looking in both directions before crossing the street has acquired an essential survival skill. Habits are unconscious, automatic responses incorporated into routine by way of practice. They are the building blocks for complex skilled behavior.

Educators and psychologists have been extremely interested in how children acquire habits. Researchers have found a number of differences between children's and adults' encoding, transformation, and utilization of information in memory (see Gallagher, French, Thomas, and Thomas, 1996, for a review). Perhaps the most robust finding is that young children's speed of processing is slower than older children's (Kail and Bisanz, 1992). Even on simple reaction-time tests, children take longer to respond than adults. There are several reasons for the age-related differences in response time. Young children have more difficulty than older children in extracting information from their environments. When a young child is faced with a task that requires responding to a complex environment, he has more difficulty focusing on the elements of the task than does an older child. A younger child also takes more time inspecting individual elements of a complex stimulus than an older one. Young children's performance is less efficient than that of older children, when shown stimuli for a brief period of time. Further, young children are more likely to be distracted by the nonrelevant elements of a task. Until age five or six, children often display *overexclusiveness*—the tendency to focus on only a few cues that may not be related to the task at hand. Between the ages of about 6 and 12 years, however, they tend to show *overinclusiveness*—attending to both relevant and irrelevant cues. It is during this period that children are most likely to be easily distracted from the task at hand. By the time they are 11 or 12, most have developed the ability to discriminate between relevant and nonrelevant cues and demonstrate efficient performance (Kaye and Ruskin, 1990). Findings concerning the age-related differences in encoding information suggest that optimal performance occurs when there is a match between a child's information-processing characteristics and the environment. Encoding is inefficient when information is presented too rapidly or too slowly.

Children are also slower than adults in their ability to retrieve information stored in memory and to use that information to make decisions (Chi, 1976, 1977). It has been suggested that children have fewer areas in short-term memory available for storing information retrieved from long-term memory. Their mental processing can be overwhelmed when they attempt to deal with too much information. These observations suggest that optimal performance occurs when tasks are simplified and children are given adequate time to process both information that is presented to them and information that they have stored in memory.

Although children's basic mental machinery may work more slowly than that of adults, both acquire learned automatic responses in much the same fashion. Training results in increases in speed and accuracy in executing physical and mental skills. Children, like adults, benefit from domain-specific training and experience. As children acquire more task-specific information, their memory structures for the task become more elaborate, and the number of pathways by which information can be retrieved increase. These changes permit more rapid transmission of information within the processing system and lead to faster performance. Even without specific training, however, children evidence increased processing speed. They show faster response speeds on a wide variety of tasks (Kail and Bisanz, 1992). These observations suggest that the capacities to perform tasks mature with age and are related to the growth and development of systems within the central nervous system.

The Thinking Domain

Children, like adults, acquire habits through experience. A child's ability to acquire automatic responses is essential to the development of physical and mental skills. The young baseball player is taught to hit a pitch by first learning to swing his bat in a specific manner and then by repeating the swing until the proper action is expected without concentration on the position of his arms and legs. Learning to swing a bat correctly without having to think about it allows him to concentrate and focus attention on other aspects of playing the game, such as evaluating the motions of the pitcher, listening to and following the coach's directions, and evaluating and responding to specific game situations. These higher-order mental processes control the execution of lower-level, previously learned, and well-developed patterns of behavior.

Metacognitive processing, which controls the actions of basic information-processing systems, reflects our knowledge about our abilities and capacities. Metacognition is central to the identification of goals and the selection of strategies that can be used as methods to solve problems. Young children are less able to select and utilize strategies than are older children and adults. Researchers have examined how mental strategies such as rehearsal, chunking, and labeling can be used to help solve problems. In general, children below the age of six who have not learned specific strategies to solve problems can be taught to do so. Many research studies have demonstrated that children can learn to perform laboratory tasks more effectively after being taught a specific strategy to use in problem solving. However, children of this age are usually not able to call up and use strategies to solve similar problems when those problems are encountered outside of the laboratory situation. Young children often fail to transfer their knowledge from one situation to another. Thus, teaching a child a strategy to solve a problem or to make decisions that may be useful for an adult will not necessarily mean that a young child will employ the strategy in a novel situation (see Flavell, Miller, and Miller, 1993, for an overview of metacognitive processes).

The ability to produce and use problem-solving strategies increases with age. As children mature, they are capable of invoking increasingly more sophisticated rules to understand and solve problems. Experiences provide them with knowledge about the tasks they face. Older children are more likely to generate their own unique mental associations regarding aspects of a given problem. Rather than depend on external sources to provide ways to solve problems, older children begin to elaborate and work through problems on their own. The older child begins to construct a unique framework for selecting the physical and cognitive skills needed to solve specific problems or to perform specific actions. These problem-solving skills become more complex and grow increasingly richer with each new experience. The child's past experiences provide a framework for responding to novel situations, and the experiences derived from facing and overcoming new problems alters his or her mental framework.

With experience also comes a decrease in the amount of mental effort required to act skillfully. Older children learn to control the allocation of their attention with increasing precision. Research assessing the allocation of attentional resources indicates that young children must exert greater mental attention to perform a task than older ones. The more efficient use of attention that accompanies maturation and experience permits them to perform with increasing efficiency and less mental effort.

The Emotional Domain

It has been suggested that children possess an innate drive to master their environments; the steps that children go through to achieve mastery engender powerful positive emotional states. Children at play are *autotelic*; they seek problems to be solved and in doing so acquire the skills that are necessary to be successful. The processes of play and problem solving are highly pleasurable. Recent studies have focused on the motivation exhibited by precocious children who have learned skills at a very young age (Winner, 1996). Some stand out because of their rage to master specific artistic skills such as drawing, music, and sport. Precocious children are characterized by their intense drive to learn. Some children view the practice required to learn to play the guitar as drudgery and akin more to work than to play. The engaged child makes no distinction between play and work. For some, the drive to learn the skills to play music, games, or sports is all-consuming. Some Little League baseball players become totally absorbed with their sport. They sleep with their gloves and baseball hats, practice throughout the day and have to be literally pulled home from the ball field by their parents. Further, they show their irritation and displeasure when not permitted to practice or play. The total involvement of these children in their activities produces rapid skill acquisition, as they learn the structure of their art or sport and approach it in unique ways. They discover new solutions to problems and invent new ways of performing. What is unique about these children is that they do not perform because of extrinsic rewards or to achieve personal intrinsic goals; they appear to perform and practice for the pleasure of the actions. These children may well achieve goals and be given recognition for their accomplishments, but these sources of reward play a secondary role to the subjective experiences brought about by action and skill.

Although some children are drawn innately to some tasks, others experience anxiety, boredom, and monotony when participating in skill-development activities. One reason some experience these negative emotions is that their choice of participation was determined by their parents or teachers (see van Wersch, 1997, for a discussion of children's motivation). Existentialist philosophers have long stressed that individual happiness comes by way of individual choice. Without the capacity to choose for oneself, the activities of life are prefabricated. The child who agrees to participate in skill training because it is required, gives up her individual freedom, she feels as if her value has been diminished. She may begin to perceive herself as living an inauthentic life. It is the individual who ultimately determines the worth or value of the activities he or she pursues and the skill that he or she learns. From the existential perspective, nothing could be worse than requiring someone to participate in skill-training activities.

Other points of view exist concerning participation in skill-training activities, however. The source of motivation for a child to initiate skill training is not intrinsic (Magill and Anderson, 1996). Some may initially resist because of preconceived negative ideas about the task. Under these conditions, a child may need to be involved in training in a way that demonstrates the positive benefits of a given task. For instance, a young girl who sees the physical demands required of gymnastics training may fear that she will be unable to perform as well as others. However, once she participates in a beginner class, she will probably begin to enjoy the process of learning new skills.

PLAY, GAMES, SPORT, AND DEVELOPMENT

Different cultures hold very different ideas about what constitutes acceptable behavior and actions in their members. Despite tremendous differences that exist among cultures, virtually all promote play, games, and sport as positive experiences, particularly for children.

Play

Play provides perhaps the clearest demonstration that complex human behaviors are tied to the evolution of our species (see Hughes, 1999, for an indepth evaluation of play). Play has been observed in virtually every human culture, past and present. It also provides an example of a link between actions and sensations of pleasure and is defined as an activity freely chosen by a child that is intrinsically motivating and pleasurable. During play a child is actively and totally engaged in an activity that often involves make believe and a distortion of reality. Although there is a general consensus among researchers as to what constitutes play, there is less agreement in explaining play behavior. Several theories focus on play as instrumental to skill development.

Play and Cognitive Skills

It has been proposed for over a century that play is critical to developing the skills and knowledge required of children in later adult life (Johnson, Christie, and Yawkey, 1987; Kretchmar, 1994). More recently, developmental psychologists have emphasized that play serves as a vehicle for learning problem-solving skills (Seefeldt, 1996). Play provides a relatively safe opportunity for a child to use emerging cognitive capacities to solve naturalistic problems in a variety of ways. It is characterized by an element of make-believe and the capacity to construct, deconstruct, and reconstruct problem-solving activities. There are no exterior rules of play; a child constructs his or her own form of reality. Opportunities to play provide an opportunity to exercise and practice ways of mentally manipulating the world. The manner in which children deal with problems encountered during periods of play change as a child matures neurologically and cognitively.

Recent neurologically based theories of play suggest that the manner in which a child's brain is formed is related to play activities. There is some evidence to suggest that certain functions of the brain are localized in each hemisphere of the cortex. Cognitive functions that are responsible for analytical processing of environmental information and for the control of language are located in the left hemisphere, and functions that are responsible for nonverbal abstractions and affect are located in the right hemisphere. The two hemispheres are connected by a wide band of neural tracts called the corpus callosum. The integration of the two hemispheres is believed to be enhanced through play activity (Vanderschuren, Niesink, and Van Ree, 1997). Through play, a child employs functions of both hemispheres to solve play-generated problems (Panksepp, 1998; Panksepp, Siviy, and Normansell, 1984).

Play and Physical Skills

Physical activity and stimulation early in the life of laboratory rats and mice is known to result in increased brain size, neuroendocrine reactivity, and a better capacity to deal with environmental stressors, as opposed to outcomes in animals that have not been exposed to early stimulation. Observations such as these led to the concept of mental and physical toughening. Several researchers suggest that the rough-and-tumble play behavior of children serves to prepare them for the rigors of the real world. Rough-and-tumble play differs from vigorous play in several ways. Although vigorous play appears to serve as exercise, rough-and-tumble play is primarily a social activity in which two or more children feint aggressive acts. Fighting, hitting, and wrestling are part of rough-and-tumble play; however, this form of play differs from true aggression in a number of ways. Real fighting is usually limited to two children who display serious threatening gestures and use their maximum strength. Rough-and-tumble play can involve many children, who restrain their strength and are more likely to smile and laugh while being active (see Hughes, 1999, for an evaluation of rough play).

Rough-and-tumble contact play provides children with a mechanism to establish an accurate assessment of their skills relative to the skills of other children. Children typically engage in this sort of play only with peers who possess a specific level of play-fighting skill. Children will avoid contact play with those who have considerably higher or lower strength. Play fighting with peers similarly matched in skill level provides a child with two sources of information. First, through contact play, children are given an opportunity to recognize their limitations. Second, they establish positions within a social hierarchy based on individual skill and competence.

It must be stressed, however, that although the toughening explanation for rough-and-tumble play has intuitive appeal, it is only one of several plausible explanations for play. Not all children engage in rough-and-tumble play. Those who seldom participate in contact play may still become group leaders.

Play and Emotional Experience

Perhaps the most obvious explanation for the motive to engage in play is that it is an innately pleasurable act. Children often appear to be in a constant state of action and movement directed toward play. Some researchers have proposed that when a child is absorbed in play, he or she has achieved an optimal state of arousal. The innately pleasurable state that is associated with optimal arousal is thought to motivate a child to action. In a sense, the child seeks stimulation. *Arousal modulation theory* focuses on the reciprocal relation among physiological arousal, motivation, and play. The central premise of arousal modulation theory is that children are innately driven to attain an optimal level of arousal (Berlyne, 1960; Zentall, 1975). A predictable and unchanging environment is boring and monotonous. Play provides a vehicle for altering the environment so that it becomes unpredictable and uncertain. The physical and mental tension created by this unpredictability motivates a child to action, and he or she is driven to reestablishing a state of organization and predictability. Thus, play first creates disequilibrium; then it restores balance. The act of attaining equilibrium produces powerful positive psychological feelings in a child. Success in attaining harmony and order then produces an environment once more unchanging and predictable, which elicits feelings of boredom and monotony and motivates the child to renew the play cycle.

Some suggest that play is the basis for all skill development (Csikszentmihalyi, 1975b, 1981; Csikszentmihalyi and Bennett, 1971). Through play, a child learns to recognize the multitude of opportunities for action afforded by the surrounding world. Instead of being a passive recipient of stimulation, a child learns to interact, modify, and manipulate the environment. He learns that the world affords multiple sources for potential flow experiences. Parents often accuse their children of having short attention spans because they move from one activity to another, only staying with each for a brief time. It may well be that engaging and reengaging in a variety of tasks serves to establish lifelong behavioral patterns. A child learns to modify his world in such a way that action produces a flow experience. This pleasurable psychological state is attained when he is in control and actively manipulating his environment. When absorbed in play, he is learning to utilize developing skills to meet the challenges provided by the world around him. Children are able to use their developing mental skills of imagery and problem solving to take virtually any object or situation and turn it into a play activity. Parents often find that their children have more fun playing with the box that enclosed an expensive toy than with the toy itself. The flow experience that is attained through action is a powerful, innate reward for engaging in behaviors that are important for normal physical and mental development.

Skill at manipulating the environment to attain positive outcomes is central not only to theories of play, but also to theories of intelligence (Sternberg, 1988). One component of intelligence is the capacity to modify the environment to maximize the utilization of skills. Thus, the instinctual patterns of play serve as a cornerstone for the development of intelligence and patterns of behavior that are used throughout life.

Games and Sport

Games have been described as a form of competitive play characterized by established rules and set goals (Hughes, 1999). At the heart of every game is a process of overcoming obstacles. Whether a youngster is playing a video game, chess, or soccer, she places herself in a contrived environment in which she uses very specific behaviors to achieve success. The player agrees to limit her actions to those that are dictated by the rules of the game.

Sociologists and anthropologists have suggested that games provide children with an introduction to social rules. The manner in which games are played teaches the values that are attributable to success. Some societies present games as highly competitive activities in which individual success leads to rewards and social status. Others employ games as a method of teaching cooperation and the value of group decisions. Still others reward players for working together to overcome a challenge. For children, games represent the beginning of lifelong rituals. The games that a child plays are similar to those of her parents and grandparents, providing a vehicle for the transfer of knowledge of skill and performance from one generation to the next. Playing games involves psychological tension and requires high levels of emotional arousal. Children quickly experience the excitement of playing games and the emotions that are tied to both success and failure. The memory of a specific game, the people with whom the game was played, and the emotions that were experienced during the game may be retained throughout a person's lifetime. This can result in long-lasting bonds between the players. The games played early in life serve to establish the stories that are shared with others later in life. Those who attend high-school and college reunions many decades after graduation are quick to discuss shared experiences in games that were played.

Sports have also been viewed as a vehicle to introduce children to important adaptive skills. In the latter part of the nineteenth century, sport was seen as a way to develop character and to promote strong moral values (Mechikoff and Estes, 1993; Swanson and Spears, 1995). With the growth of cities, the rise of industrialization, and immigration of large numbers of families into the United States, organized sports were thought by social welfare agencies to keep boys busy, off the streets, and out of trouble. These early programs were designed not so much to teach sport skills but rather to instill values and inculcate beliefs that were in line with social changes that were taking place. In the 1920s, however, programs emerged for children below the age of 12 that focused increasingly on the competitive aspects of sports. This change paralleled the explosive growth of professional sports. Children's sports teams were formed that involved leagues, playoffs, and championships. Little League baseball was introduced in 1939 and, within a few years, there were organized competitive programs for children in numerous sports (see Wiggins, 1996, and Ewing and Seefeldt, 1996, for overviews of children and sport).

There has been controversy from the earliest stages of organized children's sports concerning the effects of competitive sport activities on developing children. As early as the 1920s, educators grew wary of and distanced themselves from organized sports due to its overemphasis on winning and the emotional strain placed on children to play like adults. The withdrawal of professional educators resulted in many programs being led by volunteers who lacked training in teaching methods. Nevertheless, youth sports programs have emerged as a multibillion-dollar industry in which over eight million children between the ages of 6 and 16 participate (Berryman, 1996).

Proponents of organized competitive sports for children have traditionally stressed that sports benefit participants by increasing physical skills, enhancing social competence and teamwork skills, and building character. Research conducted to examine the relation between sports and these purported benefits is equivocal; there is evidence that early sports participation can provide positive benefits, but there is also evidence it can have detrimental effects on childhood development.

Sport and Physical Skills

There is every reason to believe that general activity promotes health and physical fitness. Highly active children are more efficient in using their physical resources than those who are not active. Under normal conditions, there is little reason to believe that sports will be detrimental to a child's physiological development and function. It is only in situations in which extreme training demands are placed on a child that normal development may be negatively affected. Sports that require repetitive actions such as swimming, tennis, and baseball have been found in some studies to compromise children's skeletal growth and integrity (Lord and Kozar, 1996; Malina, 1996).

Although team sports have been promoted as a way to teach specific skills, it has been observed that children involved in traditional sports such as baseball, football, and soccer receive relatively little skill training per se. Young children have been found to spend more time engaging in competitive game conditions than in preparing for competition through skill training. The vast majority of coaches employ a learning-by-doing approach in which children are placed in competitive situations and expected to acquire proficiency through trial and error. Few coaches have developed the expertise or experience necessary to apply research-based information concerning learning principles and child development in training their young athletes.

The situation is quite different, however, for children who participate in sport-specific training programs designed to develop elite performers, and more children are being channeled at very early ages into such programs. Children as young as four are pressed into daily training regimens designed with one goal in mind: to produce optimal performance. Young runners may log 80 miles of training per week in preparation for marathon races. Aspiring swimmers log up to 20,000 meters per day and execute up to a half-millions strokes per year. Some elite gymnastic programs require young children to perform daily training sessions, each lasting several hours. These programs are designed by coaches and teachers who often have vast personal experience in their sports and employ research-based teaching techniques. The products of these intensive training programs provide clear evidence that children can acquire highly sophisticated skills through systematic instruction and practice.

Sport and Competence

The success of the British military in the nineteenth century was once said to be founded on schoolyard playing fields. Boys who grew up to be competent military men learned the value of teamwork, leadership, and command through competitive sports. There is little doubt among researchers that children's perceptions of their abilities and competence can be affected greatly by game and sports experiences, as well as by academic ones. *Perceived confidence* is defined as belief in one's ability to perform particular activities (see Horn and Harris, 1996, for an overview). Researchers often examine discrepancies that exist between perceived competence and actual competence. A child's perception of his abilities and skills plays an important role in the feelings generated by participation in sports or academic activities. Those who view themselves as competent typically describe challenging situations as enjoyable and fun; those who doubt their competence often report negative feelings toward challenging situations. Children's perceptions of competence carry on throughout their lifetimes. Adults who rate their skill levels as high also report that they have control over their environments and can influence the outcomes of problem situations. Individuals who perceive themselves as less competent are more likely to feel controlled by the environment and that they have little autonomy.

Sport and Character

Historically, participation in competitive sports at a young age has been seen as preparation for a child to withstand the stresses of adult life. Success in competition requires emotional control so that effective decision making can occur. A young baseball player batting with the bases loaded in the final inning is more likely to be successful when he is in control of his emotions. Children's experiences in situations like these are thought to result in a fundamental change in the way they deal with competitive situations, both on and off the playing field. Controlled competition may serve as a toughening manipulation for young children that will have positive effects on their ability to deal with the stresses they encounter throughout life.

There is little doubt that competitive sports are anxiety-provoking for many children (Smoll and Smith, 1996). Numerous studies have identified a relation between high levels of sport-induced stress and the onset of physical illness and psychological dysfunction in children. However, the strength of the relation is modest, and it is not possible to predict whether a specific child will suffer negative consequences from sports competition. Children, like adults, differ in their evaluation and appraisal of environmental stressors. One child may view batting with the bases loaded as a positive situation; another child may view the situation as physically and psychologically overwhelming. These two children may also interpret the outcomes of their batting performance much differently. Thus, the potential for psychological harm is exceedingly difficult to predict. Also, the pressures children face in organized sports do not appear to differ from those encountered in other realms of education.

There are many possible reasons to explain differences among children's perceptions of and responses to stress. Motivation for participation has been identified as an important contributor to these individual differences. Sports participation differs from play activity in that children's engagement in sports is directed more by external than internal motivation. Often a child's parents make the decision for their son or daughter to participate in a sport. Examination of the reasons why children disengage from competitive sports has revealed that anticipation of stress contributes significantly to the decision to withdraw. Further, those who engage in sports to please their parents evidence greater levels of stress and drop out of sports programs more frequently than children who make independent decisions concerning sports participation (Smoll and Smith, 1996).

INDIVIDUAL DIFFERENCES

Not all children mature and develop in exactly the same way or at the same rate. Researchers have taken two approaches to the study of individual differences. One approach focuses on the use of statistical concepts that are central to the *normal curve model,* a mathematical representation of the characteristics of an infinitely large number of measures that make up a population. *Psychometrics* is a branch of psychology that specializes in the development of tests used to measure mental characteristics (Anastasi, 1982; Kline, 2000; Murphy and Davidshofer, 1994). Tests have been created to measure specific *constructs* such as intelligence, aptitudes, personality, and beliefs. These constructs are often assumed to be normally distributed; that is, the frequency of scores is predicted by the normal curve model. For example, when a test for competitive anxiety is given to a sample of five-year-old children, most of them will have scores around the average and very few will have extremely high or low anxiety scores. A test of short-term memory will reveal that the capacity of most to remember information is about the same; however, there will be some five-year-olds who have a memory capacity more like that of an average eight-year-old, and there will be some whose memory compares to an average three-year-old. Researchers point to these normally distributed individual differences in basic abilities to explain why children learn skills in different ways and at different rates. The milestones of motor, cognitive, and emotional development provide estimates of the points when basic abilities are first observed. In reality, there is considerable variation in the emergence of basic abilities and, as a result, considerable variation in the manner and rate that children acquire physical and mental skills.

The second approach to the study of individual differences focuses on the effects of *information-processing characteristics* and their impact on skill acquisition (see Sternberg, 1986, chapter 1, for an overview). Researchers who employ this approach conduct laboratory-based experiments designed to isolate the basic components of the processing system. Participants in these studies are often grouped on the basis of some identifiable characteristic. For example, children diagnosed with dyslexia, a specific type of learning disorder, may comprise one group, and children with no learning disorders may comprise another group. Both groups of children are then given tests that measure specific information-processing components. The performances of the two groups are then compared. If differences are detected, researchers point to information-processing deficits to explain why children learn skills in different ways and at different rates (Baumeister, 1984).

Readiness to Learn

Skill development depends on factors related to the task to be learned and on factors related to the individual learning the task. Successfully teaching children is often a matter of being aware of their readiness to learn skills. Readiness for training is a multifactorial issue; a child's chronological age should not be used as the sole determinant of when skill training should begin. A coach or teacher needs to examine the physical and cognitive demands engendered by the task at hand. The demands of a given task must match the learner's physical and mental skill levels. A child's readiness to benefit from training will depend on the level of physical maturation, prerequisite skills, and motivation. Maturation does not refer only to physical abilities; it reflects changes in the physical, cognitive, and emotional domains. For example, a boy may have sufficient physical ability to play contact sports such as football, but he may lack the cognitive ability necessary to understand the coach's directions or to deal with the social dynamics of a team sport that focuses on competition. Another child may have developed the cognitive abilities to execute the skills needed to play football but lack the physical abilities needed to execute those skills.

Researchers who assess individual differences in readiness for skill development suggest that teachers and coaches strive to create a *mastery motivational climate* (Ames, 1984) in which a child's progress in skill development is evaluated in terms of individual progress rather than by group averages or optimal performance. Teaching environments that promote positive emotions and the motivation to learn are characterized by a focus on children's execution of the components of a skill rather than the outcome (success/failure) of an entire action. Examining the components of a task can lead teachers to provide children with response-appropriate feedback for learning correct techniques. Effective feedback is information that is unambiguous and easy for a child to interpret and understand; it relates directly to the components of the task at hand; and it corresponds to the amount of effort exerted by the learner.

The importance of contingent feedback on skill learning was discussed in previous chapters. As children develop, they readily learn to discriminate between feedback that is accurate and truthful and feedback that is inappropriate. Children as young as four years of age begin to make comparisons between their performance and the performance of their peers. As they grow older, they begin to judge the credibility of their teachers. Teachers who provide blanket comments such as "good job" for everything a child does may run the risk of losing his attention. When a teacher's credibility as an information provider is diminished, children seek performance feedback from other sources. Young children look to adults for information and guidance, but older ones look to their peers for feedback. During early adolescence, cognitive skills develop that are important in abstract reasoning, problem solving, and using declarative knowledge. Learners begin to establish internal criteria for performance and to provide their own performance feedback. Maturation and experience produce children and adolescents who change qualitatively over time.

Effective skill trainers develop instructional techniques that take into consideration these natural changes that occur throughout the life span. It is a natural consequence of development that children experience the learning process differently than adolescents or young adults. Methods of instruction appropriate for young children may be less effective for older children and may even create a negative motivational climate for adolescents.

The physical and cognitive skills children acquire serve as a framework for behaviors later in life. The skills imparted to young children are to be improved upon and mastered as they mature, each in his or her own unique way. The children of today will be the teachers, educators, and leaders of a future generation. The improvement of our species depends on the availability of adults who have mastered skills and developed the competence needed to meet new challenges in unique ways.

Developmental Disabilities

Some children do not follow the same developmental progression as the majority of their peers. For reasons that may be linked to genetic disorders, environmental insults, or social impoverishment, these children lag behind in domains that are critical to skill acquisition. Some children lag behind in physical development, others in cognitive development, and still others emotional development. A *developmental disability* is defined as a pervasive disorder displayed during maturation. Some children evidence *global disabilities* that are reflected in virtually all measures of physical, cognitive, and emotional development. Individuals with severe and profound levels of *mental retardation* typically evidence global disabilities. Other children evidence *specific disabilities* that may be detectable only under very circumscribed conditions.

A long-standing debate has taken place among researchers and educators who study developmental disabilities. *Edward Zigler*, a contemporary leader in the field of education, is a central figure in what is referred to as the *developmental difference debate*. He has written extensively on the similarities and differences of two general theoretical approaches to the study of individual differences—*developmental theories* and *difference theories* (Zigler and Balla, 1982a).

Developmental theories propose that children free of genetic disorders, neurological disease, and environmental trauma develop and learn in fundamentally the same way. The differences that exist among children can be best described in terms of two indices: how fast a child learns a skill (rate of learning) and a child's terminal proficiency (level of learning). Comparisons between rates of learning indicate that children with mental retardation learn more slowly than do children without mental retardation. However, proponents of developmental theory emphasize that the mentally retarded child is not abnormal in the sense that he or she cannot learn the skill; rather, he or she requires additional training and practice in order to match the performance of his or her age-equivalent peers. It is also the case that comparisons among children's optimal performance of a skill typically show that children with mental retardation are not as proficient as children without mental retardation. Mentally retarded children typically evidence slower performance and greater variability in performance. Developmental theorists suggest that some of the differences between a mentally retarded and nonretarded child's performance can be explained in terms of cognitive factors, but that most of the performance differences can be explained in terms nonintellectual factors, particularly those that affect motivation to learn and perform.

A child's past experiences may have profound effects on the tendency to approach or avoid skill-learning tasks. Studies of children with mental retardation indicate that because of histories of failure and lack of success, the children tend to be *outerdirected*. Compared to children without mental retardation, they rely more on the guidance and direction of adults and less on their own abilities and skills (Zigler and Balla, 1982b). Because of their low expectancies of successfully solving problems on their own, children with mental retardation often display *learned helplessness*; they choose neither to act nor to attempt to meet the challenges that are part of skill learning tasks (Weisz, 1982). Equally important is the observation that the behaviors of children with retardation tend to be influenced more by external rewards than by internal rewards. When given the choice, they appear to behave more on the basis of their perceptions of how others might act or how others expect them to behave than on their own personal wishes and desires. For Zigler and other developmental theorists, alteration and modification of children's confidence and perceptions of efficiency are critical to the development of new physical and motor skills.

Difference theories propose that children with mental retardation have specific defects in information processing that lead them to perform differently from children without mental retardation. Researchers have found that children with retardation evidence deficits in virtually every component of the information-processing system. These differences exist on tests of cognitive functioning in which motivational factors have minimal influence on performance. Attempts have been made to improve the information-processing abilities of such children. In general, these training programs result in increased efficiency of information processing; however, the effects are not long lasting, nor do the children generalize what they have acquired from training to solving new tasks. It should be emphasized that proponents of difference theories do not necessarily believe that intelligence is an unchangeable capacity; rather, they posit that specific defects in information processing can have profound effects on the manner in which skills are acquired (Pellegrino and Glaser, 1979).

The issues that are central to the developmental difference-controversy are applicable to the education and training of all children. According to the developmental position, the basis for differences between mentally handicapped children's and normal children's rates of skill development and maximal performance levels is the same when comparisons are made between children with normal intelligence and those with superior intelligence. Children within the normal range of intelligence are predicted to acquire skills more slowly and display lower terminal levels of performance than children within the gifted range of intelligence.

Educators in the fields of special education and adapted physical education have benefited greatly from research on individual differences in physical, cognitive, and emotional development. Curricula have been developed to help children with global and specific disorders acquire physical and cognitive skills to maximize their potential.

CHAPTER SUMMARY

Childhood is a period of tremendous physical, mental, and emotional growth. From the moment of birth, an infant is placed in learning situations that demand dynamic interactions with the environment. Children's actions provide a way to test their limits and to learn about the larger world.

Children seek new challenges through playful actions and, in doing so, develop important physical and cognitive skills. They begin to understand how the world operates and what they must do to solve the problems that confront them. At certain times, children show a readiness to learn, a teachable moment, that lends itself to rapid and lasting learning. Considerable differences exist among children in terms of their readiness to learn, however. Although a child may appear biologically and physiologically prepared to learn, many factors affect how quickly and how well each individual learns.

SUGGESTED READINGS

Berk, L. E. (2000). *Child development* (5th ed.). Boston: Allyn & Bacon.

Brant, R. S. (2000). *Education in a new era*. Alexandria, VA: Association for Supervision and Curriculum Development.

Flavell, J. H., Miller, P. H., and Miller, S. A. (1993). *Cognitive development* (2nd ed.) Englewood Cliffs, NJ: Prentice-Hall.

Hughes, F. P. (1999). *Child, play and development* (3rd ed.). Boston: Allyn & Bacon.

Kline, P. (2000). *A psychometrics primer*. London: Free Press.

Wadsworth, B. J. (1976). *Piaget for the classroom teacher*. New York: Longman.

Zigler, E., and Balla, D. (Eds.). (1982). *Mental retardation, the developmental-difference controversy*. Hillsdale, NJ: Erlbaum.

Chapter 8

Skills of Young and Middle Adulthood

Adulthood is characterized as a period of life marked by major transitions. Adults are expected to decide for themselves how they will act and how they will live. Young adults must select a course for their lives that may include a career, marriage, children, and social activities. It is a period within which an individual decides whether he or she possesses the skills needed to fulfill dreams and realize the goals set earlier in life.

This chapter focuses on the transitions that take place as we progress from adolescence to young adulthood and then to middle age. A multitude of physical, mental, and emotional changes occur during this period of development. Adults accumulate knowledge and use their skills differently than children. The tasks that they face demand the capacities to integrate knowledge and to apply general principles to new problems. Important choices are based on general knowledge of how the world works and an understanding that appropriate choices depend on multiple frames of reference. Most tasks that adults face are vague; there are no set rules that govern how they are to be solved.

HISTORICAL VIEWS OF YOUNG ADULTHOOD

Historians and anthropologists provide ample evidence for a stage in life during which a transition is made from childhood to adulthood. The term *adolescence* is used to describe individuals between puberty (defined by the capacity to have offspring) and maturity (defined legally as the age of majority) (Cummings, 1995). The word *adolescence* is derived from the Latin verb *adoescere*, meaning "to grow up." It reflects a period of rapid physical and mental development and social change linked to emerging independence and establishing concepts of personal identity, or self.

Ancient Views of Adolescence

Historians observe that adolescence is a concept describing a period of life seen in many cultures. It can be traced as far back as the sixth century B.C. (Schlegel and Barry, 1991). The cultural roles associated with the period of adolescence probably emerged with the development of agriculture and the need for organized labor about 10,000 years ago, when specific skills were required to cultivate crops and foodstuffs.

Throughout the centuries, adolescence has been depicted in cultural artifacts, arts, and writing as a time for maturing boys and girls to acquire skills needed to be productive members of the family and social group. Drawings from the ancient Greek and Roman civilizations show young boys working in the fields beside older men and young girls working in homes with older women. Records of artisans and craftsmen during ancient times indicate that it was common for adolescents to receive specialized skill training. The notion of apprenticeship (a legal agreement to work for another for a predetermined period of time in return for instruction in a trade, art, or business) is found throughout the history of Western civilization (Bush and Simmons, 1981).

Cultural anthropologists have also been very interested in adolescence. A young person's position in society in many cultures and the likelihood that he or she will be able to lead a productive and successful life are determined, to a large extent, by the actions and skills displayed during adolescence. Childhood is reserved for learning the basics; adolescence is the period for proving oneself worthy to become a member of the adult social group. Adolescents who demonstrate superior competence and skill are seen as those who will, in time, assume full-fledged membership in the community. They prove during adolescence their worth and merit to those who make up their social world.

Some researchers suggest that the psychosocial dynamics occurring during adolescence are the most critical in life (Irwin, 1995; Sebald, 1984). For individuals who are entering their prime reproductive period, a brief window in time opens. The skills they display and the competencies they exhibit may determine not only whether they can attract and select mates, but also their place in society and the magnitude of resources available to them as they begin their own family lives. Securing a mate and a stable position in society are fundamental to the development of both the family structure and the passage of genetic material and knowledge from one generation to the next. Social and cultural expectancies guide mate selection and ensure the diversification of genetic material critical for the adaptability of the species. Thus, adolescents are under considerable pressure to excel in the areas of competence deemed important by their culture. Young adults who miss their window of opportunity may evidence profound and lasting negative psychological effects (Greene and Larson, 1991; Savin-Williams, 1987; Turnbull, 1983).

Rites of Passage

Formal *rites of passage* are found in most traditional cultures. Puberty rites abound in most traditional, non-Western, cultures. Typically, a ceremony of some type that announces the young boy or girl to the society's general membership is performed. Central themes of puberty rites often focus on fertility and the adolescent's future contributions to society (Schlegel and Barry, 1991). Most puberty rites symbolically reflect a period during which the adolescent is initially separated from the social group, goes through a period of physical and mental preparation, and is reincorporated into the social group. The bush schools of villages in sub-Saharan Africa provide an example of well-established rites of passage. Both boys and girls are sequestered from the village; they then participate in specific gender-linked tasks and are instructed in tribal beliefs and methods of behaving. The adolescents are taught to endure hardship and to achieve success through hard work and diligence. Schooling can last anywhere from a few months to a few years, and not all students succeed in their training. Those who succeed are viewed as being reborn; they are literally transformed in the eyes of the villagers from young girls and boys into adult women and men. Once viewed as adults, they are then provided the full privileges of membership in village society (Turnbull, 1983).

Rites of passage are much less formalized in modern Western civilization. Passing into adulthood is linked to the achievement of educational or job-related milestones, such as graduating from high school or entering the workforce. One reason given to explain why the transition from adolescence to adulthood in Western societies is not as clearly delineated as in traditional cultures is that many careers in technologically oriented industrialized countries require high levels of skill. Attaining job competence demands more extensive training; hence, longer periods of education are required of adolescents and young adults before they are ready to enter the adult world. As a result, people between the ages of 18 and 24 in modern cultures rely more on the continued support of parents and take more time to assume adult roles than young adults in preindustrial cultures (Csikszentmihalyi and Schneider, 2000; Irwin, 1995).

SKILL LEARNING IN ADULTS

Adulthood is a period that lasts several decades. The defining characteristics of adulthood have been the topic of considerable discussion among researchers. The modern concept of adulthood is much different from the concept in vogue even 50 years ago (Shephard, 1997). The time span associated with adulthood in the mid-twentieth century was often linked to workers' employment and work-related responsibilities. Early adulthood was signaled by entry into the workforce; middle adulthood was characterized by a gradual movement toward retirement; and late adulthood was strongly linked to retirement from the workforce. Workers tended to remain within a single business or industry throughout their careers. The economic and social structure of industrialized nations at the time lent itself to job stability and security.

Improvements in health services and medicine now mean that individuals live longer and lead more productive lives than in previous generations. Further, the demographics of modern industrialized societies have led to marked changes in the concept of adulthood. The baby boom generation, which includes those individuals born immediately following World War II through 1964, led to the emergence of a large group of people who now dominate modern society. They have, by their sheer numbers, redefined society. But the times are changing again. The baby boomers have enjoyed a level of job stability and security that is rapidly changing for their children. Fewer people today experience the lifetime job stability and security provided by major industries just a generation ago. Modern workers face the possibility of multiple careers during their lifetime.

Rapid technological advances, especially in information exchange and global economic practices, characterize the modern world. These fast-paced changes require rapid accumulation of skills and competencies in workers, regardless of their age or seniority. An adult education movement has arisen worldwide over the past few decades, driven by the need for businesses and industry to maintain the job performance of not only its young, novice workers, but also its older, middle-aged workers. Lifelong learning has become the way industry and business ensure that workers maintain the right skills for their jobs (Moody, 1986).

Research data suggest that the manner in which skills are learned and performed differs at various points in the life span. The factors that affect the learning processes of young adults differ both quantitatively and qualitatively from those of adults in middle age. Adolescence and early adulthood is a period of transition in which learning is defined in terms of the quantity of facts that can be accumulated. Developmentally, the young person is primed and ready to learn. During the decades of mature adulthood, however, learning is often defined in terms of how well an individual can integrate, manipulate, and master information needed to solve the ill-defined problems inherent in real world situations (Stanage, 1987).

Skill development at any age is a dynamic process that reflects the interactions among three domains of human behavior: the *biophysical* domain, which includes aspects of behavior that are habitual and automatic; the *thinking* domain, which includes those aspects of behavior related to goal-related problem solving; and the *emotional* domain, which includes feeling, arousal, and motivation. Understanding the interrelationships among these three domains of behavior will help to explain how young and middle-aged adults learn and maintain skills.

The Biophysical Domain

If we accept the view that speed and power are the primary agents of adaptive behavior, then humans are at the apex of their performance between the ages of 18 and 25 years. A young adult's level of physiological functioning often represents the standard to which the physiological functions of individuals in other age groups are compared.

Early adulthood is a period in which most of our bodies are as efficient as they will be at any time of our lives. Muscular strength increases during adolescence and peaks between 25 and 30 years of age. Concomitantly, the cardiorespiratory system's capacity to circulate sources of energy used by muscle tissue is at its most efficient. As a result, the young adult is at the apex of his or her ability to sustain high levels of physical work. The capacities of many vital physiology functions peak during the second decade of life.

Young adults not only are at the peak of their physical capacities, but also they are in a period of development during which they evidence their fastest rates of information processing. Researchers who have measured adults' simple reaction time (the time required to initiate a movement in response to the presentation of a stimulus) find that adults in their mid-20s respond more rapidly to stimuli than individuals in any other age group. Similarly, examinations of age-related differences in choice reaction time, which reflects speed of response to the onset of one of several stimuli, indicate that young adults are able to process information and select a response more rapidly than middle-aged adults. When adults are faced with tasks that involve complex response execution, young adults initiate their movements more rapidly than middle-aged or older adults (Light and Spirduso, 1990).

These data suggest that the memory structures of the information processing system are fully formed and transmission of information is operating at peak efficiency in young adulthood. Young adults who enter the workforce are often described as quick or sharp by their older colleagues. These attributes are justified, as young persons can encode information, store information in long-term memory, and retrieve information more rapidly than those who are just a decade older (see Rogers, 1985, and Stevens-Long, 1984, for details on changes in physiological functioning).

Although the young adult may feel (and sometimes appear to be) physically and mentally invincible, subtle signs of aging can be detected as early as the mid-20s. These become increasingly more noticeable as people reach middle age. Physical appearance changes gradually. There is a loss of muscle mass and a redistribution of fat in the trunk area of the body. Flexibility declines as the elasticity of connective tissue and the skin decreases. There are clear declines in cardiorespiratory function and increased evidence of diseases of the blood vessels by the fourth decade of life. The onset of *arteriosclerosis* (a thickening of arterial walls) and *atherosclerosis* (injuries to or lesions of the vascular system) degrade the capacity to circulate sources of energy to the muscles, glands, and brain.

It should be noted, however, that these changes occur relatively slowly over time and that most people fail to notice declines in physical function. As they age, most are able to perform physical work and information-processing tasks efficiently and to maintain the level of performance demanded by careers and families. Indeed, the transitions that occur from early adulthood to middle age appear to be so stable that little research has been conducted on individuals within this age group. Most studies have used the performance of this age group as a reference point when assessing the performance of those much younger or much older. Few researchers have focused on the dynamic physical and psychological processes that take place during early adulthood and middle age (Stevens-Long, 1984).

The Thinking Domain

Rationalism is the hallmark of adulthood. The behaviors and actions of young adults are looked upon differently than those of children. Adults are believed to act on the basis of the application of reasoning abilities and the utilization of knowledge to solve problems. At a fundamental level, adults are perceived as able to tell the difference between right and wrong. When a child disobeys authority or laws, the parents are held responsible for his or her actions. Adults, on the other hand, are accountable for their own actions. It is assumed that an adult has the capacity to control impulses and to understand the relations that exist between behaviors and consequences.

Piaget's theory of cognitive development has been used by many researchers as a guide to understand the thought processes of children and adolescents. His theory has also had a profound effect on researchers studying adult cognition. Piaget's system identifies the *formal stage* as the final stage of cognitive development (See Wadsworth, 1976). This stage, which occurs between the ages of 11 and 16, is characterized by two mental operations that differentiate the formal stage from previous stages of cognition. People who have entered the stage of formal operations are able to use hypothetico-deductive reasoning. Formal reasoning is central to the development of theories that explain events in nature and predict future events, and it plays an important function in everyday adult life. For example, adults are constantly faced with the task of sizing up people whom they meet for the first time. The hypothetico-deductive process is demonstrated when you develop a conception or theory about someone you have just met on the basis of direct observations only. For example, your theory about someone wearing a baseball cap and team jacket would probably be different from your theory about an individual wearing a black leather motorcycle jacket and pants. The theories that we generate about others lead us to make predictions about others and how they will behave. The usefulness of the theory depends upon how accurately it can predict the actions of others. The steps that are used to create and test theories about the nature of another person do not differ from the steps that

a scientist takes to develop theories that are designed to understand and predict events in nature.

The second characteristic of formal thinking in Piaget's system of cognitive
development is that individuals are the objects of their own thoughts; that is,
they engage in metacognitive thinking. This type of thinking involves introspection and self-awareness. The individual becomes aware of his or her own
knowledge and own ability to solve problems. Further, metacognitive thinking
involves the capacity to perform mental operations on other mental operations.
For instance, when faced with a mathematics problem that requires the transformation of equations, you use metacognitive processes. Solving the problem
demands knowledge of mathematical rules and selection of mathematical procedures that could be applied to the problem at hand. After selecting a general
rule, you will take certain computational steps to solve the problem. These
mental steps will be monitored introspectively by you, and you can report or
verbalize each mental step and the order of steps needed to solve the problem.

Piaget's theory of cognitive development has important implications for understanding the mental processes of children and adolescents. His theory is not
entirely adequate when it comes to understanding the thinking processes of
mature adults, however (Kramer, 1983). Many of the problems encountered by
adults are ill-defined and their solutions are not derived by pure logic. Some researchers have proposed that adults engage in *postformal reasoning*, which demands *metasystematic* thought. The real-life decisions that adults make, such
as selection of careers, mates, and lifestyles, are based on understanding of how
entire systems function. This type of reasoning goes well beyond the simple
logic employed when engaged in formal reasoning. Choices and decisions are
based on knowledge of how the world works and understanding that choices are
dependent upon multiple frames of reference. Career choices are driven by
multiple factors.

Postformal thought is characterized by the recognition that choices are made
within given social contexts in which there are multiple points of view. Those
in this stage of cognitive development are able to synthesize what appear to be
contradictory ideas and beliefs into coherent points of view. They recognize
that decisions are not made in terms of black or white, but in terms of knowledge that may be only temporarily true and is always open to modification and
change. Postformal reasoning permits one to deal with and integrate the uncer-
tainties of life into a meaningful structure.

A model of adult cognitive development proposed by Rybash, Hoyer, and
Roodin (1986) suggests that adults' postformal cognitive processes are distinctly
different from those of children and adolescents. The changes in cognition that
occur during childhood are relatively uniform and fixed by maturational and social factors. In adulthood, cognitive processes are channeled into specific domains
that become increasingly more complex. Unlike children, who are driven to acquire knowledge in multiple domains, adults become more unidimensional.
They select areas of knowledge in which they can become increasingly more

skilled. This *domain-specific mastery* comes about primarily from life experiences rather than from academic knowledge. With adulthood, knowledge comes to be associated less with textbook facts and more with the incorporation and organization of experiences.

Rybash and his colleagues (1986) describe the development of adult cognition in terms of *encapsulation*. This model assumes that adults, because they have a greater decision-making latitude than children, take active roles in selecting and constructing their knowledge domains. Young adults, who are breaking away from the constraints of their parents, are free to focus and allocate psychological resources to areas of activity of interest to them. A young woman may, for example, become totally absorbed in the study of dance. She will accumulate knowledge and skill by way of her actions and experience. As her skills develop, she may specialize in particular styles of dance. With years of training and experience she may come to be regarded as an expert in her field. The selection of one domain of knowledge means, however, that other domains of knowledge are not pursued. As the woman's knowledge of dance and art increases, other areas of knowledge are not nourished and, mentally, fall by the wayside.

The Rybashi researcher group likens the differentiation of skills to the branching of a bush. The numerous branches that emanate from its base represent the various knowledge factors that constitute general intelligence and adaptive behavior. During childhood, general intellectual growth occurs, and knowledge is accumulated in all of the branches near the base of the bush. Thus, childhood and adolescence are characterized by the accumulation of general knowledge, with relatively little differentiation among knowledge domains. In adulthood, the selection and specialization of knowledge domains and accompanying intellectual growth become differentiated, and some branches grow more rapidly than do others.

The encapsulation process is a lifelong quest to accumulate new skills within specific knowledge domains. An individual makes a transition from a state in which actions are based on large amounts of seemingly unrelated factual information toward a state in which information becomes more organized and easier to understand. This transition in knowledge, with accompanying skilled performance, is generated internally. Domain-specific knowledge is *self-organized*; that is, we determine what and how factual information will be integrated into our holistic model. Adults who continue to refine their knowledge bases become, over time, more unidimensional and specialized.

As individuals gain experience within specific knowledge domains, many become cognizant that even the most simple task can provide a hierarchy of complexity. A practitioner's integration of knowledge and skill leads him to focus his attention and resources on subtle task-performance factors that novices fail to notice or appreciate. Playing the piano, for example, appears to a novice as a task that simply involves the depression of individual keys. An experienced pianist, through experience, is aware of the differences in sound that are produced by minute changes in the pressure and timing of each finger on the key. This deeper level of understanding of the task at hand comes by way of practice and experience and leads to the gradual emergence of expertise.

An experienced, mature adult expands his or her knowledge base differently than does a young, inexperienced adult. A novice's approach to the accumulation of knowledge focuses on learning and retaining specific facts; an experienced adult grasps the relations that exist among seeming disparate sources of information. The experienced adult may actually filter out and attend less to the details provided in a given situation than might a novice. However, an experienced adult assesses task demands on the basis of general principles and relations that exist but are embedded within the context of a given situation (de Groot, 1946/1978; Simon and Chase, 1973).

The rate of cognitive development within a given knowledge domain is hypothesized to be affected by a variety of genetic, biological, psychosocial, and individual difference factors. Skill and knowledge acquisition may be accelerated when an individual possesses the physical and intellectual abilities that lend themselves to tasks encountered within a particular knowledge domain. For instance, the possession of specific physical and cognitive abilities may promote rapid acquisition of dance skills. Similarly, an individual's capacity to allocate mental resources may be restricted by environmental constraints, social background, income, or geographic location.

A person's continued cognitive development is marked by the continuous accumulation of self-organized knowledge. However, people differ in both their capacity and their motivation to assimilate information and to develop knowledge structures. Some may not be able to employ postformal reasoning processes; others, although able to use postformal reasoning, may elect not to allocate the psychological resources and effort needed to become skilled within a particular domain. The notion of a the late bloomer reinforces the view that it is difficult to predict when an individual will pursue a given area of skill development or the number and types of knowledge domains that will be sought.

Adult cognitive growth is not limited to a single domain. As an individual grows older, he or she may elect to focus psychological resources on other domains of knowledge. A fundamental difference between adult cognitive development and childhood cognitive development is that adult learning is not guided by maturational factors as much as is the learning of children. Adults can explore new domains of knowledge at virtually any point in adulthood. For instance, the young woman who pursues the art of dance may, later in life, become interested in medicine and health. Increased specialization in this new knowledge domain, blended with her area of specialization, may lead to a unique integration of knowledge across different domains. Innovators are characterized by their ability to combine skills developed in separate knowledge domains in unique ways. The woman whose competencies are in dance and medicine may envision a new way to combine these domains to develop programs for physical rehabilitation.

The encapsulation process is also marked by a transition in how skills are defined. In the early stages of learning, skill is often characterized in quantitative terms; for example, how much we know, how quickly we can retrieve information from memory, and how fast we can act. These measures of skill begin to lose their significance, however, as competency within specific knowledge domains is acquired through years of practice and performance in the context of real-world situations. Skills come to be characterized in qualitative terms; that is, they gain significance by providing an element of value and meaning to existence. Skilled adults often see what they do as an extension of themselves; what they do reflects who they believe they are. The skills a person displays are no longer simply tools used to acquire a source of income, but a matter of pride; they take on value, and the smooth execution of skills reflecting decades of study is a source of intense pleasure.

The Emotional Domain

Adolescence and early adulthood are characterized as periods of emotional upheaval. During this period people begin to wrestle with major *existential questions* that revolve around the meaning and purpose of life, individuality, and one's place in society. The developmental theory proposed by Erikson (1968) suggests that normal psychological development depends on the resolution of specific types of crises that are faced during the transition from infancy to adulthood. Erikson proposed that the major crisis faced by adolescents is the resolution of identity. The *identity crisis* drives people to pose fundamental questions about their own nature. The successful resolution of these existential questions leads to the emergence of the concept of *self*. Some are able to resolve their identity crisis during adolescence, others not until early adulthood. Some are unable to come to grips with the matter and never develop a clear vision of self.

It has been suggested more recently that the sense of identity depends on the way a person examines two aspects of life: the personal psychological world and the social world (Marcia, 1991). The views that an individual holds about his or her personal world are determined to a great extent by perceptions of personal skills, abilities, characteristics, and needs. Adolescents spend a great deal of time and effort in self-assessments about the way they look, think, and behave. They are often extremely *egocentric*, believing themselves to be of central importance and that no one has ever experienced life in quite the way they do. The views that we hold about our social world come from constant examination of social groups and networks. Parents, peers, significant others, and cultural history provide the basis for adolescents' view of their social world. Adolescents and young adults are driven to seek out an identity amid the rules that regulate the behaviors and actions of members of a community. They devote an extraordinary amount of time and energy toward gathering information about their personal values and beliefs and about the values of their families, society, and culture.

Marcia (1991) uses the term *moratorium* to describe periods in life when attempts are made to reconcile the personal world with the social world. In these periods, people experiment with and play different roles. Anxiety and low self-esteem are characteristic of those who are in the throes of formulating a sense of identity. The ultimate resolution of this existential struggle leads to *identity achievement*, or commitment to a particular view of self. It is important to note that formulation of identity is based more on *perceptions* of the personal and social worlds than on *objective reality*.

Adolescents' examination of their personal and social worlds lead some to see the importance of skills as a means of achieving life goals. The successes exhibited by role models and significant others are often explained in terms of the skills and competencies displayed. These observations lead many adolescents and young adults to seek specialized training and instruction. For some, the search for skills becomes an emotionally charged quest. Whether the desire is to become an engine repair specialist, a basketball player, a scientist, or a gang member, an adolescent is willing to throw himself or herself into any training perceived as critical to learning the desired skill. Self-identity becomes synonymous with what they know, what they can do, and how they perform.

A young person's decision to subordinate to the demands of a teacher or master plays an important step in emotional development. Once a choice is made, the student *decenters*, becoming less egocentric. She no longer sees the world from only her own perspective; she begins to accept others' perspectives of the world and how it operates. Self emerges when she is able to *reify* (make real) the beliefs held about who and what she is, through her own actions.

The young man or woman's drive for knowledge may be intense; he or she may be willing to expend considerable physical and psychological resources to accomplish goals. Some display extreme commitment to teachers and to learning the skills they have selected. Most influential artists, sports figures, academicians, business magnates, and politicians can trace, with great pride and sometimes with humility, the lineage of their instruction from a teacher and the teacher's teacher. Many will also describe the ordeals they endured as novices as part of the preparation for their profession or art.

Central to the learning experiences of these individuals is a gradual deepening of their understanding of the skills they are acquiring from the master teacher. The accumulation of knowledge derived from training leads the novice from a surface-level how-to understanding of the task to a deeper, why-this-works understanding. Those who go beyond the mechanical steps involved in performing a given task and begin to appreciate that their own actions and thoughts are part of the skill begin to derive pleasure from the execution of the skill itself. A novice may initially select a given area of training on the basis of perceptions of social gains and approval from others; however, as skills are mastered, emotional satisfaction is derived from the actions rather than the results. It is a period of deepening interests and emotional commitment to learning as the individual frees herself of personal ego and pledges wholeheartedly to master a trade or craft.

This is also a period of time when many newly trained adults test their mettle. They seek challenges to test their skills. The romanticized stories of the gunslingers of the American West are similar to the myths that surround samurai warriors and swashbuckling European swordsmen who sought competition with others. Although these stories are often exaggerations that serve primarily to strengthen the social myths of the hero, they represent an element of reality for many young men and women.

The certification of achievement awarded to a student at the completion of training is an important rite of passage into adulthood. It makes a statement about the person's drive and motivation, and is a tangible means by which others in society become aware of and acknowledge these attributes. For some, however, crossing the threshold of acceptance and gaining basic competence is only the beginning of their quest for excellence. Their commitment and motivation to reach the next level of skill develops into an *ideology* (world view) that they may retain throughout life. Regardless of the changes that they go through and the stresses that are encountered, ideologically committed people maintain a sense of stability and continuity (Rybash, Hoyer, and Roodin, 1986, chapter 7).

Until relatively recently, the emotional dilemmas facing adolescents were hypothesized to be resolved by most in early adulthood, with middle adulthood seen as a period of relative emotional stability. Today, the emotional landscape of the mature adult is recognized to be more complex than once thought. Indeed, the challenges that adults face and the emotions these challenges engender persist throughout middle and late adulthood. Ill-defined problems are the norm for adults; the processes involved in choosing a mate, electing to have children and then rearing them, and developing a career are complex; there is no "right" solution to many of life's decisions, just as there is no "right" way to perform these tasks once the decision has been reached.

People in middle adulthood continue to expend considerable physical and mental effort in maintaining their sense of *self* and *identity* in an ever-changing social world. They experience periods of turmoil in adulthood when they reevaluate their lives and consider how to redefine their sense of self. Marcia (1991) suggests that adulthood, for many, is a continuous cycling between periods of identity achievement and periods of moratorium. Mature adults are challenged by changes that accompany physical aging, personal and family dynamics, and career responsibilities. These environmental and social events precipitate periods of moratorium and accompanying existential angst, doubt, and anxiety. These emotions abate as people acquire the skills they need to restore a sense of self-identity.

Erikson (1968) characterizes adulthood in terms of a need to pass on knowledge and skills to the younger generation. The *generative* stage involves teaching, guiding, and mentoring younger people. It is emotionally fulfilling for adults in the third to fifth decades of life to share what they have created and transmit what they have learned to others. Erikson sees this period of life as essential to the evolution and continuity of humanity.

The link between the physical, mental, and emotional development of young adults and the physical, mental, and emotional development of mature adults is critical to the evolution of humans. The *intergenerational transmission* of information is of acute importance during adulthood. The failure of one generation to pass on skills to the next would have the same effect as the mutation of genetic material and the failure to pass biologically determined developmental codes to the next generation. From an evolutionary perspective, the continued progress of the human species depends on generation-dependent transmission of knowledge and skills. It is for this reason that, under optimal conditions, young adults are driven to acquire knowledge and skills, and mature adults are driven to provide that knowledge to the young.

CAREER SELECTION AND SKILLS

Striving to attain a particular occupation or vocation is an elementary component of psychosocial development. Even in childhood, the notion of becoming a doctor, fireman, or astronaut serves as a vehicle for the child to think in terms of a future self and accompanying skills and competencies. The work and careers that individuals select often reflect their self-identity.

Developmental Stages and Career Selection

Donald Super (1990; Super and Bachrac, 1957) suggests that career selection and development is an ongoing and predictable process that extends from childhood through late adulthood in a series of five stages. Childhood is seen as a *growth stage* during which perceptions of the world set conditions for children's fantasies about themselves and their abilities. By the age of about 14, adolescents' perceptions of career choices are modified by their personal likes and dislikes, and they become more aware of the skills that are required to enter specific careers. The *exploration stage*, occurring between the ages of 15 and 24, is characterized by a growing sense of an individual's personal needs and values and an increasing awareness of the requirements needed for entry into a particular career. The high school student who sees herself as a physician, for example, realizes the importance of maintaining high grades in her classes. Individuals also begin to test the reality of their goals by becoming involved in activities that are oriented toward chosen careers. A young woman with plans to become a doctor may volunteer as a hospital aide, for instance. These experiences may lead the young woman to select and attend a specific university or medical school for training. Experimentation may also lead to changes in plans and goals. Knowledge of what it is really like to assume the role and responsibilities of a physician, for example, may lead to a reevaluation of goals. Career development is a dynamic process in which many individual, social, and cultural factors play a role. A young man or woman is faced with the realities of socioeconomic status, personal abilities and skills, and social support structures; any or all of these factors can exert tremendous influence on personal choice.

The *establishment stage* of career development in Super's model is signaled by an individual's desire to focus his resources and effort on a given occupation. This choice usually occurs in the mid-20s; individuals begin to refine the skills central to performing their work and continue to do so until their mid-40s. The *maintenance stage* is marked by two decades of specialization and development of experiential expertise. Again, the manner in which people develop specialized skills, promotions, and esteem are related to many factors. The structure of career responsibilities changes with time. Established employees are expected not only to retain their work skills, but also to develop and expand social and interpersonal skills and the ability to make decisions and to lead and mentor younger workers. Retirement signals the beginning of the *decline stage*, a period in which workers distance themselves from their careers and decrease vocational activities.

Career Preparation

Vocations and careers have become increasingly specialized in virtually all modern cultures, particularly industrialized ones. The success and longevity of a culture depends greatly on its capacity to train and educate people to perform the tasks required to ensure that its social systems function smoothly and efficiently.

The educational systems that evolved worldwide over the past century are designed to meet the needs of an industrialized workforce. The goal of grade school and high school education is to teach children and adolescents general knowledge that can be adapted to specific work environments later in life. For much of the twentieth century, businesses and industries that recruited and employed high school and college graduates were expected to teach their employees the specific skills needed to become part of that particular workforce.

Unfortunately, the modern workplace is decidedly different than it was fifty years ago, when economies were based on traditional mass-production demands, and large numbers of well-paying jobs were available for semiskilled workers. The modern world economy has become increasingly more dependent on *high-performance jobs*; that is, technical jobs that require workers to be active problem solvers and to contribute new ideas and engage in new initiatives (O'Neil, 1997). Modern definitions of work skills are very different than those judged important only a few decades ago. Work skills are no longer defined simply in terms of speed of action and variability in performance; they are now described in terms of goal planning, expertise, mastery, and excellence (see Evers, Rush, and Berdrow, 1998, for an overview of modern job requirements).

Numerous business leaders, politicians, and social scientists have begun to question the methods used to prepare future generations of workers to meet the demands of a highly competitive global economy (for an example, see the U.S. Department of Labor's 1991 report). The consensus is that there will be an increasing demand for entry-level workers who have well-developed cognitive skills. Skilled workers in today's high-performance jobs must be able to operate independently and to acquire and synthesize information in ways that lead to creative solutions to ill-defined problems. Many of the time-honored traditional educational methods are ill-suited to prepare those who will be expected to perform in high-performance positions.

Some have promoted the view that training should employ educational methods that engage students in *active learning*, a process that emphasizes the development of deeper understanding of work tasks through contextual experiences. With increases in international markets, those who maintain jobs in high-performance business must adapt to an environment requiring constant modification of work skills (Sticht, 1997).

Career Development

Rapid changes in technology and job roles mean that modern workers perform within vastly different environments than they did only a few decades ago. Most who entered the workplace in the period from the 1950s through the 1970s were rewarded with stable jobs in which careers and futures were fairly predictable. Success in industry led to promotion and greater authority. Workers often developed strong emotional bonds with their jobs and their companies. Employers recognized and valued the mature employees as teachers and experienced decision-makers.

Workers entering the high-performance jobs of today encounter much less stability and face the likelihood that they will work for several different organizations during their lifetimes. Further, the job skills required for success may change markedly during a worker's life span. The newly employed man or woman may have considerable technical or university training; however, rapid shifts in technology have the potential to render even young workers obsolete within a few years. In order to keep up with market changes and technological advances, many members of the modern high-performance workforce will be faced with a lifetime of continued education. In order to remain competitive, many businesses and industries are developing in-house educational programs for their employees. It is in the financial interest of businesses to retain younger workers who are productive, even if constant retraining is required.

The movement toward adult education is a relatively recent phenomenon. Initially, teachers faced with the task of educating mature adults applied instructional methods designed for high school and college students. Few teachers were sensitive to the differences that exist between the learning styles of young and mature adults. Formal educational programs for high school and college classes are designed to develop knowledge bases and problem-solving skills in young adults. Mature adults have gone through the experiences of formal education and many have developed a preferred style of learning. Thus, the regimented educational formulas designed for adolescents and young adults may be poorly suited for mature adults (Schaie and Willis, 1996; Stanage, 1987).

Mature adults often amass years of experience during which they have significant freedom in selecting ways to solve problems. Further, they may bring with them to any classroom setting substantially more general knowledge than younger people. There is a strong connection between mature adults' learning experiences and the emotions that are derived from those experiences. The level of effort adults are willing to invest to resolve work-related problems often reflects a predilection to act in certain ways. Educators who attempt to teach mature adults in the same manner as young adults soon discover in these older students a strong degree of emotional attachment that mature adults associate with a particular problem-solving style. Perhaps the biggest challenge for teachers involved in adult education is to energize the *will to learn* of these students, an internalized drive to recognize and realize personal goals consonant with the goals of the educator and business concern.

Successful adult education is linked to continued enhancement of the concept of *self*. Traditional educational methods often limit students' choices and tend to focus on specific problem-solving techniques. Adult education should provide students the opportunity to integrate their own thoughts, experiences, ideas, and reasons for selecting a particular course of action to solve a problem. Mature adults, unlike most young adults, have a clear view of self and how the world functions.

However, an individual's self-concept is not fixed and immutable; the self undergoes continual modification throughout the life span. As a person ages, he experiences changes in physical capacities, career, and social status. How an individual responds to these changes plays an important role in determining how he will benefit from continued education programs and skill training. A person's self-concept is related more to his perception of reality than to objective reality. Mature adults who participate in continued education or retraining programs may perceive the process either negatively or positively. One may interpret the need for education as verification of becoming old, less valued, and useless; another may perceive the same program as an opportunity to expand areas of expertise. An individual's perception of his skills, abilities, and methods of problem solving is a prime determinant for maintaining a balanced self-concept. Successful adult education programs are often described in terms of how well they help participants restructure their perceptions of skill and motivate themselves to attain new skills.

WORK, CAREER, AND FAMILY SKILLS

Psychologists have been acutely interested in understanding and predicting the choices people make and the directions they take during their life span. Several theories of human motivation have been proposed that attempt to describe and explain the forces that drive humans to behave in the ways that they do. These theories, in general, focus on *action*; they describe human behavior as *goal directed* (future oriented), *intentional* (governed by conscious control), and *voluntary* (freely chosen). Human action is often explained in terms of having evolutionary value; that is, people are motivated to engage in behaviors that lead to knowledge and skills that enhance their chances of surviving long enough to find mates, produce offspring, and pass information to the next generation.

Action Theories

The world that each person encounters at birth is unique; for that reason, the goals each establishes and the direction each takes through life are also unique. The motives that push individuals to pursue particular careers and lifestyles are determined by myriad psychosocial factors. An early theory of motivation and life choices developed by *Lewin* (1935, 1936) addressed the complexities that exist between one's personal world and the environment in which he or she lives. Lewin's views are echoed in more recent psychosocial and cognitive action theories (Eckensberger and Meacham, 1984; Rybash, Hoyer, and Roodin, 1986).

Central to Lewin's theory is the proposition that each individual exists in a *psychological field* or *life space*. Levin drew the concept of a psychological field from Gestalt psychologists who envisioned motivation in terms of dynamic energy fields that are produced by the brain's activity. In much the same way that physical energy fields such as magnetism and electricity affect objects within a given spatial area, psychic energy fields are hypothesized to affect thoughts and behaviors. Lewin employed this concept to explain how the choices made and the directions pursued in ones life space are a result of the pushing and pulling of multiple psychological and social forces.

Figure 8.1 provides a simplified example of movement within a life space. In this example, a young girl plans to become a doctor. In order to attain her goal, she will face many challenges over an extended period of time. The challenges that stand between the girl and her goals comprise regions within her life space, with each region having a boundary. These regions represent psychological facts. It is a fact, for instance, that when the girl (P) becomes an adolescent, she must perform well enough on college placement examinations (ce) to be accepted by a college (c). Once she has met the challenge of making sufficiently high scores on her entrance exams, she must achieve high academic standings

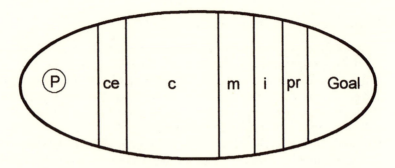

Figure 8.1.   Action Theory (Adapted from Lewin, 1936)

in order to enter medical school (m), and then complete her internship (i), and finally realize her goal of opening her own practice (pr) as a certified physician.

The direction and speed of movement through the life space is affected by multiple factors. Although the girl may fantasize about being a doctor, she may live in a social environment that limits her movements, both psychologically and physically. In order to attain a goal, a person must pass through the boundaries that surround each region and limit movement. The girl may want to go to college but lack the financial resources to do so. The motivation to attend college provides a force that pushes her toward her goal (positive movement), but financial limitations push her away from college (negative movement). Pushing and pulling forces such as these create a state of *tension* that leads to choice making. The young woman may consider the financial challenges too great and elect to take a different life path, or she may elect to take a job while attending college. Once the decision is made and she enters a new region of her life space, the psychological tension begins to dissipate, and she makes a transition toward a state of psychological *equilibrium*. She will experience less tension during the first few years of college life. Psychological tension will begin to increase, however, as she begins to realize the challenges of gaining acceptance to a medical school.

Movement through the life space is a dynamic process in which people experience cycles of tension and relief as they are pushed and pulled by psychological and environmental forces. The speed and direction of movement is determined by these attracting and repelling forces, which are the basis for *conflict* when positive and negative forces are of equal magnitude. The young woman may experience an *approach-approach conflict* if she is accepted by two equally prestigious medical schools that will place her in a desirable position for securing sought-after internships, residencies, and professional advancement. Selecting a prestigious medical school will require her to allocate all of her time and effort to medical training. The young woman may experience an *approach-avoidance conflict* if she has to choose between medical training and pursuing other goals in life, such as marriage or having children. The young woman may also experience an *avoidance-avoidance conflict* when the only offers provided are from medical schools that are not prestigious and unlikely to provide access to the type of career and specialized training she had envisioned, but she must select one in order to meet her goal of becoming a physician.

In Lewin's system, it is ultimately the *person* (P) who decides whether or not to mobilize the physical and psychological resources needed to meet and overcome challenges that constitute the boundaries of regions in the life space. Lewin conceptualized the person schematically as consisting of outer, perceptual-motor regions that permit movement through the life space and inner, personal regions that are central to making choices and decisions. Early in life, children's actions are governed primarily by perceptual-motor elements. Experience and interaction with facts within the life space, however, lead to *differentiation* of inner-personal regions. These regions become the core elements for a child's developing intelligence, traits, and personality. The differentiation process is linked to action. Individuals who are in the process of moving toward a goal will continue to learn facts and skills that are critical to meeting and overcoming the challenges of life. Those who stagnate fail to further their differentiation and become increasingly *rigid* in the choices made and the actions taken.

Action theories attempt to describe and explain the reasons why people elect different life paths and why they differ in their levels of motivation to achieve specific goals. At some point, most realize that their chance of attaining specified goals will require specific competencies that are dependent on acquiring specific domains of knowledge and skills. It is only through skill that goals can be realized. The path to achieving a goal involves the tensions and emotions that accompany success and failure.

Career Challenges

The major themes of action theory are challenge and change. The paths that lead to short-term and long-term goals are constantly modified by psychosocial factors. As a woman matures, she will encounter challenges and tasks whose resolutions are ill-defined and difficult to overcome. The high school student who sees herself as a concert violinist is probably only vaguely aware of the choices that confront maturing adults. The drives toward marriage and family and social relationships may appear trivial to an adolescent. Yet each person will have to confront these issues as he or she matures.

Existential philosophers have suggested that individual freedom brings with it the capacity for individual choice. The choices that people make at critical moments are not simply the result of objective gain-loss computations; they involve highly emotional and subjective feelings. Mature people often experience tremendously powerful emotional states when they recognize that the life goals that have motivated them since childhood will not be realized. The professional who is faced with being unable to attain lofty career goals may have to reassess what gives true meaning to life.

Job *burnout* has also been used to explain decreases in workers' motivation and disengagement from their careers. Burnout is primarily an emotional experience that includes feelings of both helplessness and hopelessness. These feelings are engendered when workers perceive that the effort they put into their work has little or no effect on the outcome. Job burnout has been explained in terms of interactions among the worker's characteristics and the demands of the job. Workers tend to seek jobs that are stimulating and challenging. Those who have mastered a given job task may find that their jobs become boring and repetitive, leading to reduced motivation to work, regardless of the level of competency exhibited. Burnout may occur not only when jobs are too predictable and routine, but also when work environments are too demanding or when job responsibilities are unclear or unrealistic. Burnout not only produces declines in motivation, it also leads workers to seek other avenues through which they can gain life satisfaction (see Schaufeli and Enzman, 1998, for an overview of job burnout).

These findings and the results of other studies provide support for the existence of a midlife transitional period in which individuals reevaluate their life goals and priorities. The phrase *midlife* crisis is often used to describe preoccupation with age, focus on past accomplishments, and feelings of turmoil and disillusionment (see Cytrynbaum, Blum, Patrick, Stein, Wadner, and Wilk, 1980, for discussion of midlife issues). Levinson (1978) suggests that this type of self-evaluation need not be viewed as a crisis, however. He characterized midlife reevaluation as a process of *deillusionment*; that is, the realization that some beliefs are no longer true and that changes must be made to accommodate the realities of life. The reordering of life goals need not be viewed as a negative situation. The process of restructuring short-term and long-term goals may lead some to seek and acquire new skills necessary to meet new challenges.

Compartmentalization of Skills

Action theorists suggest that our activities become increasingly *compartmentalized* as we mature. During adulthood, we tend to make clear distinctions among the various activities we perform. Most adults differentiate between work, hobbies, leisure pursuits, and play activities. Each of many daily activities has the capacity to attract or to repel. Choices are made, for instance, between after-work socializing or going to a gym to exercise. As choices lead to experiences, habitual actions are acquired that lead to increasingly rigid boundaries around life space regions.

Psychologists are interested in understanding the factors that compel us to select and remain engaged in specific daily activities. Csikszentmihalyi (1997) described the results of a series of studies conducted over the past 25 years that evaluated daily life activities. An experience-sampling method was employed to determine what people were doing and what they thought throughout their daily routines.

The information gathered by Csikszentmihalyi indicates that our activities tend to fall into three different categories. *Productive activities* are necessary for survival, such as performing work that makes possible the acquisition of food, shelter, and safety. Most of us expend from one-fourth to more than one-half of our physical and mental resources on productive actions. *Maintenance activities* are necessary to preserve and maintain our physical and mental resources. Sleeping, eating, and bathing help to maintain health. Similarly, structuring routines that maintain home and family environments is critical to the integrity of psychosocial family interactions. We pursue *leisure activities* during time not spent in productive or maintenance activities. Generally, our leisure activities are either *active*, involving projects designed for self-development and promoting new learning, or *passive*, centering around entertainment.

Most of us refer to productive activities as *work*, and we tend to view it in a negative fashion, as an activity that is required but not necessarily desirable. Most of us tend to see leisure pursuits as pleasurable activities. The reasons for our view of work as a necessary evil are complex. Research on the topic, however, has led some psychologists to examine the role that perceptions of productive activities have on behavior.

It is clear that our capacity to control environmental events is critical to our motivation to initiate and maintain action. Humans invest in physical and mental action that is goal-oriented. Although virtually any activity, work or play, can be goal-oriented, most work activities are perceived as pointless, boring, and routine. In the same way that children are drawn to activities that challenge their skills, adults are drawn to tasks equal to their skill levels. When activities are too simple or redundant, they take on negative attributes that cause us to push away from them. Likewise, when an activity is too difficult, it causes stress, which has negative attributes, and we push away. Only when activities present clear goals and provide us with a sense of control and challenge do they possess positive attributes that draw us toward them. Critical to the attracting or repellent force of any activity is the perception each of us holds about it.

CHAPTER SUMMARY

Childhood is reserved for learning the basics; adolescence is the period for proving ourselves worthy to become members of the adult social group; adulthood is characterized by skill mastery. An adolescent's transition to adulthood is hallmarked by rites of passage that certify that the young man or woman has the skills needed to be recognized as a member of the adult social world. The progression into adulthood is marked by meeting responsibilities such as developing a career, finding a mate, and fulfilling social demands.

The modern world has created environments that demand specialized knowledge and the ability to keep up with technological changes. The knowledge adults accumulate becomes increasingly refined, and they learn more and more about their areas of expertise. Adults spend decades learning their work, refining their skills, and assuming greater responsibilities. Successful progression during mature adulthood is defined in terms of how well we integrate, manipulate, and master information to meet the challenges we face. The life-span tasks that are confronted often require modification and refinement of goals. The paths that are taken to attain long-term goals are constantly influenced by multiple psychosocial factors.

SUGGESTED READINGS

Csikszentmihalyi, M. (1997). *Finding flow: The psychology of engagement with everyday life*. New York: Basic Books.

Csikszentmihalyi, M., and Schneider, B. (2000). *Becoming adult: How teenagers prepare for the world of work*. New York: Basic Books.

Cummings, R. (1995). *Adolescence: A developmental perspective*. New York: Harcourt Brace College Publishers.

Irwin, S. (1995). *Rights of passage: Social change and the transition to adulthood*. London: UCL Press Limited.

Levinson, D. J. (1978). *The seasons of man's life*. New York: Knopf.

O'Neil, H. F., Jr. (1997). *Workforce readiness: Competencies and assessment*. Mahwah, NJ: Erlbaum.

Rybash, J. M., Hoyer, W. J., and Roodin, P. A. (1986). *Adult cognition and aging: Developmental changes in processing, knowing and thinking*. New York: Pergamon Press.

Schlegel, A., and Barry, H., III. (1991). *Adolescence: An anthropological inquiry*. New York: Free Press.

Shephard, R. J. (1997). *Aging, physical health, and activity*. Champaign, IL: Human Kinetics.

Chapter 9

Skills of Older Adulthood

There are two very different views of what it is like to be an older adult. One view presents the older adult as a wise sage, one who has weathered the challenges of life and is comfortable with the choices made over the years. Savoring the triumphs associated with successes and learning from the lessons inherent in failures, the older adult looks forward to finding new challenges and pleasures. The second view presents the older adult as an individual who faces nothing but continual loss of physical and mental capacities and skills. No longer a valued contributor to society, the older adult withdraws and becomes increasingly isolated and depressed at the prospect of progressive loss of control over his or her world. In reality, neither of these scenarios accurately portrays the aging process.

This chapter describes the changes in physical, mental, and emotional processes that accompany the latter decades of life and how they impact both skill learning and performance.

HISTORICAL VIEWS OF AGING

The changes that take place as we grow older have been observed and speculated about for as long as modern humans have existed. As the human species evolved and developed the capacity to think and reason, humans also acquired the capacity to ponder the meaning of existence, aging, death, and the afterlife. It is clear from anthropological research that early humans attempted to comprehend and explain the passage through life and its eventual termination. They were aware that, with the passing of years, men and women changed

physically and mentally. Strength and vigor declined, as did the precision with
which skills were performed. Explanations of aging and death in preliterate societies were often couched in terms of magic and myth. Ancient tales abound
describing supernatural forces that steal away the spirit of life from leaders and
heroes.

Ancient Views of Aging

The earliest written sources of information available to gerontologists
studying historical views of older persons comes from ancient cultures of the
Near East. Examination of early writings indicates that the family unit was core
to the development of early civilizations. The most powerful figure within the
family was the oldest man. The father was responsible for establishing and en-
forcing the codes of social behavior dictated by the clan, tribe, or class in which
a family existed. Each member of the family had unique responsibilities and
duties; it was the father who ensured that these activities were carried out. The
oldest son was expected to assume the father's role someday, and considerable
efforts were made by fathers to educate and prepare sons for their place in the
immediate family and the broader society (see Larue, 1985, for an overview of
aging in the ancient world).

The father's authority was tied to his skills, strength, and vigor. The ability to
lead the family was associated with an image of power and the wisdom that can
be accumulated only through experience. There was little or no sense of retirement in these early cultures. Those who were leaders of nations were faced with
the task of demonstrating that—even as they became older—they retained
their physical strength and mental faculties. In ancient Egypt, for example, the
pharaohs of the first dynasty (about 3000 B.C.) participated in an annual festival in which they demonstrated physical strength and agility. In this ritual, the
pharaoh (wearing only a kilt and the crown and carrying the royal scepter) performed a series of prescribed runs before his people. The festival served as a
symbolic rejuvenation of the pharaoh's strength and power and a sign of his di-
vinity.

Researchers have been able to reconstruct a detailed understanding of place
of older adults in the ancient Greek and Roman civilizations (see de Luce, 1994;
Falkner and de Luce, 1992; and Slater, 1964, for overviews of this period). The
writings of both Greeks and Romans reveal that clear distinctions were made
between the manner in which men and women aged. The stages of female aging
were tied to biological development and the capacity for conceiving children.
The stages of men's lives were tied to changing social and generational roles
that were pressed on male members of the family. The responsibilities of the
oldest male of the family were dictated by the aging of the father. A natural relationship between the maturing son and the aging father enabled a smooth
shift in power and responsibilities from one generation to the next. As a father
began to reach the limits of his ability to maintain the family business (at about

60 years), his oldest son was reaching his prime productive and reproductive years. Most Athenian men married at about the age of 30, which coincided with their recently acquired authority as head of the household and business. As a son's role in the family expanded, his father's role diminished.

The Athenian city-state has been held as a model for modern democracy due to its system of government in which all adult members, young and old, had an equal voice in making state decisions. Although there were a few historically well-known Athenians who lived to an advanced age (Sophocles, 90 years; Plato, 83 years; Socrates, 70 years; and Euripides, 80 years), the number of elders who participated in government was relatively small. Only about one percent of the population lived to the age of 80. Athenian elders were respected, but their authority to lead and the extent to which their views were considered depended on their skills and demonstrated abilities to perform. Wisdom was not thought to be the result of aging; rather, it was presumed to be acquired through experience. In Plato's *Republic*, which described his view of a perfect society, philosopher-king leaders were selected at the age of 50, not because of their age but because they had decades of training designed specifically for leadership skills (Warmington and Rouse, 1956).

An examination of ancient Rome provides multiple views of the role of older men in society and politics. The ruling body of the Roman government was the *Senate*, a name derived from the word *senes* ("old man"). Romans looked favorably on the wisdom of men who had experience in life and battle. When discussions were held in the Senate, the debates were initiated by the oldest men first; discussion progressed, by age, from that point down to the youngest man. Older men, thought to be more frail and less able to maintain long debates than younger ones, were given the first opportunity to speak.

Romans defined aging in terms of performance. There were no laws regulating retirement. The older men in the elite classes gained influence and power through the accumulation of wealth. During the centuries when Rome expanded its boundaries, its citizens lived in a society in which seniority, skill, and expertise were respected and praised. The golden age of Rome, which followed a prolonged period of territorial expansion, was one in which Roman citizens, regardless of age, were active in politics, art, and business. Aging was accepted as a naturally occurring process. Although associated with negative attributes such as the loss of physical abilities and reduced interest in sexual activities, it was also linked to positive characteristics such as increased intellect and clearheaded, rational thought. The older man, freed of the passions and emotions of youth, became the perfect *sage* who could provide counsel to the younger generation. This depiction of aging was true primarily for men of wealth who were in the ruling class. To less affluent Romans, aging was probably a period of time of general anxiety and fear of impending poverty.

The decline of the Roman Empire in the fifth century A.D. resulted in fundamental changes in society and religion. Leadership was authoritarian and unchallenged. The rules of monarchs and the Christian church were followed without question by most of the population. During the violence and political chaos of the Middle Ages, the strength of the young man came to play a more important role in society than the intellectual prowess of the older man. Thus, the view of aging and the societal position of older persons changed over time. Aging was described in terms of acceptable behaviors. Specific behaviors were expected of children, adults, and the aged. Conformity was expected of everyone; those who did not follow their predetermined life path were distrusted. People expected to lose power, affluence, and value as they aged (see Troyansky, 1992, for a review of aging in the Middle Ages).

The Age of Enlightenment in the seventeenth and eighteenth centuries was marked by a shift toward an appreciation of the positive aspects of aging and long life. Older adults played significant roles in political revolutions and in the scientific revolution. The transition from monarchies to constitutional governments brought issues of social welfare and equitable treatment and the rights of all citizens to the forefront. Governments grappled with issues of support for the elderly, and established pension programs. Scientists began to examine the aging process with a view toward improving quality of life and developing treatments to remedy the maladies of old age. The shift toward the development of a rational method of dealing with aging probably occurred because increasing numbers of older adults played key roles in politics and science. Influence and power during this period was associated with intellectual rather than physical prowess. The accumulation of knowledge was a valued commodity, and older adults were seen as important sources of wisdom and guidance.

Modern Views of Aging

The industrial revolution (1750–1900) marked a period in Western civilization during which the power and influence of older adults declined. There are several reasons for this shift. The growth of cities led to a migration of people from the farms to the cities. It was typically the young who made the move. The increasing numbers of older adults and fewer numbers of young adults on farms required older adults to serve as the primary caretakers of the land for longer periods of time with less physical, financial, and emotional support from their children. As a result, the time-honored methods and traditions of passing authority from the oldest man in the family to his maturing children became less effective. The responsibility of older adults to educate younger adults and to teach them the skills necessary to farm the lands was assumed by social institutions (see Conrad, 1992; Palmore, 1990; and Sokolovsky, 1994, for overviews of aging in the twentieth century).

Older adults who did migrate to large industrial cities found themselves in a cultural milieu in which technology favored the young; the old were placed at a decided disadvantage. As young adults assumed roles in the modern workforce, older adults lost influence as teachers and as an important source of knowledge and wisdom. There was a perception for most of the first half of the twentieth century that older adults were obsolete in the developing industrial cities. Although this perception may not have been entirely accurate, it did set into motion negative views of older people and widespread belief that they lacked the abilities and skills needed in a progressive society.

During the twentieth century, social systems developed in most industrialized countries to accommodate the increasing numbers of individuals living into old age. Advances in medicine and changes in health practices have resulted in increased life expectancy, spawning a tremendous growth in the number of people who live to be over 80 years. The twentieth-century shift in the demographics of age groups was unique to humankind. The aging of modern society has imposed new challenges for older individuals and to society in general. For thousands of years the roles of older adults, the heads of a family, were well established. The roles of children, young adults, and older adults were dictated by intergenerational transmission of knowledge and the development of skills required throughout the life span. The age-dependent, time-locked pattern of skill development of previous periods of history reflected the cycle of the seasons of each year and the cycle of the human life span. The interdependence that had existed among members of families in agricultural societies of the past rapidly lost its significance in the modern industrialized world.

The profound changes in the social structure of modern society have been the basis for considerable discussion and legislation. Today's societies are faced with innumerable questions about aging and the aging process. Assumptions that were central to the early twentieth-century labor force (such as mandatory retirement) and the limits of older adults' abilities, skill, and performance, are being challenged. With the graying of the populations of industrialized nations, the pendulum is swinging once again toward an optimistic view of old age. Today, we are interested not only in living longer, but also in maintaining a high quality of life.

Healthy Aging

The tremendous increase in the number of adults who live longer has led policymakers and spokespersons for gerontology to reevaluate the concept of aging. Aging is no longer associated with disease and loss of physical and mental capacity. Modern older adults are more educated and affluent than older adults of previous generations. *Ageism*, which is a systematic stereotyping and pervasive negative view of older persons, exists in many modern cultures (Palmore, 1990). However, the notion that older persons lose their place in society is being replaced by a view that all individuals, regardless of age, can maintain an active lifestyle and can contribute meaningfully to their families and society. The World Health Organization's guideline recently described health in old age as a state of complete physical, mental, and social well-being: it is not merely the absence of disease or infirmity (Chodzko-Zajko, 1997). Central to healthy aging is the capacity to regulate behaviors so that we derive contentment from our lives. Aging is now seen as an essential and natural part of the cycle of life, a period in which people continue to learn and also pass on knowledge to others (Birren and Zarit, 1985).

SKILL LEARNING IN OLDER ADULTS

The factors that affect the learning processes of older adults differ quantitatively and qualitatively from those of children and young adults.

The Biophysical Domain

Researchers who study age-related changes in physiological functioning often employ *decremental models* of aging; that is, they assess declines in capacity. Indeed, aging is defined by Spirduso as "a process or a group of processes occurring in living organisms that with the passage of time lead to a loss of adaptability, functional impairment, and eventually death" (1995, p. 6).

Considerable research has been conducted over the past few decades that provides important information concerning physiological changes that make up the aging process. Recent advances in measurement techniques and newly invented tools provide insights into the physiological processes at virtually every level of study. Today, the aging process is examined from the level of individual molecules and cells to the most complex interactions between the systems of the body (see Spirduso, 1995, chapter 3, for an overview of the physiology of aging).

Sensory Systems

The functions of all sensory systems change with age. The visual system, because it plays such an important role in extracting environmental information, has received considerable attention by researchers. It is well established that, with age, two types of physical changes occur that degrade vision. The first of these changes, which begins between the 35th and 45th years, comes about as the lens of the eye becomes harder and less flexible. The result is that light waves traveling through the lens and projected onto the retina begin to shift. This means that it becomes difficult to focus on objects that are near the eyes. Visual acuity and depth perception are affected by subtle changes in the function of the muscles that control the action of the lens and pupil. The second change that occurs in the physiology of the visual system usually begins in the mid-50s. Circulation of blood to the cells of the retina begins to decrease, and as a result, the retinal cells degenerate and perform less effectively.

Hearing also changes in a predictable fashion as a function of age. Declines in hearing occur gradually, with those who are constantly exposed to loud sounds evidencing the greatest hearing loss. Degenerative changes of hair cells in the cochlea of the ear, which are most noticeable beginning in the seventh decade, of life contribute to loss of sensitivity to high frequency sounds.

Gradual changes in other sensory systems are also evidenced with increasing age, so that older adults become less able to extract information from the environment. Some of the loss in physiological function, however, can be compensated for by other components of the information processing system (see Kline and Scialfa, 1996, for an overview of aging and sensory processes).

Memory and Attentional Systems

Many older adults perceive a loss of memory as they age. Considerable research has been conducted over the past few decades that focuses on two aspects of older adults' memory: storage capacity and memory utilization (see Hasher and Zacks, 1988; Hultsch and Dixon, 1990; and Smith, 1996, for overviews of aging and memory). Some of the results run counter to the notion that major declines in memory capacity occur with age. It appears that age-related differences in memory cannot be explained in terms of storage characteristics. The capacity of sensory memory, which serves as the initial storage structure for the information-processing system, changes little with age. Similarly, short-term memory capacity (the amount of information that can be held in conscious awareness) declines little over the life span.

An apparent myth of age-related memory decline is that older adults can remember events that happened earlier in their lives better than events that occurred more recently. Actually, long-term memory storage abilities remain essentially the same through adulthood. The length of time information can be stored in long-term memory depends on a variety of factors. One factor that helps to explain why many older adults perceive early memories to be clearer than more recent ones is that the most enduring memories have very specific and personal significance. Memories that occur as a result of uncommon or highly emotional situations are remembered vividly over a lifetime. These vivid memories can be acquired at any time, but the frequency of such events probably decreases as individuals age and develop predictable routines. As most adult experiences are more mundane, they are not stored in long-term memory in a durable fashion. Thus, when older adults reminisce about their lives, they are more likely to remember events from the distant past than from the recent past (Schaie and Willis, 1996).

Researchers now believe that age-dependent decreases in memory performance may be better explained in terms of the manner in which information is encoded, transformed (given meaning), and retrieved than in terms of the physical structures that hold memories (Craik and Jennings, 1992; Light, 1991). One explanation for decreases in older adults' memory performance is linked to the phenomenon of *general slowing* (Cerella, 1985, 1990). The capacity to

make decisions and responses rapidly decreases with age. Measurement of reaction time demonstrates a predictable slowing across the life span. Between
the ages of 20 to 96, simple auditory reaction time slows at the rate of 0.6 milliseconds per year, and discriminated reaction time at the rate of 1.5 milliseconds
per year (Spirduso, 1995, chapter 7). The elementary nature of simple reaction
time has led some researchers to use it as an index of the general responsiveness
of the body's central nervous system. The small but reliable changes in behavioral speed have been interpreted to reflect a slowing of the rate at which information flows though the information-processing system. The systematic
slowing of mental processing and behavior has been interpreted by some
gerontologists as evidence for a general decline in the integrity of the central
nervous system. Loss of neural cells and weakening of connections and associations among cells that underlie the architecture of the brain are thought to be
the basis for less efficient processing of information and for declines in general
intelligence (Hertzog, 1989).

Another explanation for age-related changes in the performance of memory
tasks focuses on attentional processing. Numerous studies demonstrated that the
performance of both young and older adults is adversely affected as tasks are made
more complex, but the effect is greater on older adults. This *complexity effect* has
been found in tasks made more difficult by increasing the number of stimuli involved and by altering the pace at which stimuli are presented. It has been suggested that these age differences are due to the gradual decline in older adults'
ability to spread their available attentional resources to multiple task components
(Philips, Mueller, and Stelmach, 1989; Prinz, Dustman, and Emmerson, 1990).

As sensory systems decline in efficiency, older adults find it more difficult to
separate important environmental signals from less important background
noise. Consider the difficulty one has listening to a radio when the dial is not on
the proper setting. There is a mixture of music (the signal) and background
noise. The charge of the attentional system is to help the listener focus on the
signal and to inhibit the background noise. When an older adult finds it difficult
to tell the difference between signal and background noise, the ability to select
a signal can be improved only by allocating more attentional resources. Older
adults can perform simple information-processing tasks as well as young adults
when the discrimination demands are low; however, their performance is com-
promised more than the performance of younger adults when the task is made
more attentionally effortful. Older adults appear to have to expend relatively
more of their attentional capacity in order to make sense of incoming information than do young adults.

A study conducted by Backman and Molander (1991) provides a clear example of age-related differences in the ability to block out irrelevant background
noise. The putting performance of young and old golfers was assessed while a
radio program played in the background. When an informational radio program was playing, older golfers had more difficulty than younger golfers in
blocking out the radio messages and concentrating on putting performance.

The Thinking Domain

Researchers are also interested in how mental processes change with advancing age. There has been considerable interest in evaluating the metacognitive and intellectual processes of older adults.

Metacognition

Metacognition is cognition about memory, the awareness people have about their knowledge and the belief that they have the capacity to use that knowledge. Age-related differences in metacognition are influenced by an individual's perceptions of memory abilities and also by the strength of cognitive skills necessary to solve problems.

Laboratory research reveals that some aspects of metacognition change relatively little with age. When asked to report verbally how they solve specific problems, older adults proceed through the same mental steps as young adults. They evidence the same ability to evaluate task demands, recognize the memory knowledge that is needed to solve the problem and, if required, to modify the steps required to solve a problem (Hertzog, Dixon, and Hultsch, 1990).

There are, however, other aspects of metacognition that do appear to change with age. Most of these changes can be characterized in terms of an individual's *control beliefs*, a general term for several specific types of beliefs that a person holds about his or her ability to perform a given task and to achieve a specific goal. Several types of control beliefs have been found to influence the metacognitive processes of older adults. *Locus of control* beliefs represent global views held about the determinants of the world. Individuals who exhibit an external locus of control believe that world events are linked primarily to outside forces and that they have little power to institute change. Individuals with an internal locus of control believe that they can affect change in their world.

Self-efficacy beliefs differ from locus of control beliefs. These are developed about competencies to perform within specific domains of behavior. An older adult who has experienced mastery in performing crossword puzzles will generalize his self-efficacy beliefs to other types of board or table games but may have low self-efficacy when it comes to performing physical tasks or activities. *Learned-helplessness* beliefs can be generated by both general and specific control beliefs. Individuals who display learned helplessness elect to withdraw from opportunities to control the environment due to past failures and a perception that they cannot ever succeed. Older adults, because of perceptions of loss of skills and ability, may begin to depend on the direction and guidance of others and may avoid displaying their own skills and abilities (see Cornelius and Caspi, 1986, and Welch and West, 1995, for reviews of aging and self-control).

The manner in which people solve the problems they encounter has been suggested to change qualitatively and quantitatively at various stages of life (Schaie and Willis, 1996). The ways that older adults conceptualize and solve problems, both in the laboratory and in the real world, may be fundamentally different than the approaches employed by younger adults. The goals that older adults have may be quite different than those of young adults, and these differences may contribute to age-related differences in performance. Some researchers have suggested that the level of effort older adults make to perform laboratory tests of cognition may differ from the effort exerted by younger adults. The vast majority of studies of cognitive aging have contrasted the performance of college students aged 18 to 21 with adults over the age of 60. Many laboratory tests of memory and attention are designed to test specific theoretical questions and are often contrived and simplistic. Older adults, who may not have the same experience at performing laboratory tests as young college students, may view the tests as abstract exercises with little merit or significance. Because of this perception, older individuals may exert less attentional effort and employ less efficient mental strategies than young adults. Thus, older adults' problem-solving skills depend on the task at hand, their goals, and their control beliefs (Vallerand and O'Connor, 1989).

Intellectual Processes

Tests of general intelligence, because they provide multiple indices of cognitive functioning, have been used extensively to measure age-related changes in mental processes. Considerable research has been conducted to identify and measure specific factors that underlie behavior.

Recent research on age-related changes in intellectual function tends to counter the popularly held notion that there is an inevitable general decline in intelligence that parallels the declines observed in physiological capacity and function. Longitudinal studies of intelligence, which measure a group of individuals at different points across an extended period of time, reveal that subjects' performance on specific factors shows little decline until about age 60, and that the rate of decline in performance beyond 60 is relatively small until the 70s or 80s.

Many factors have an impact on older adults' mental capacities. Understanding how memory functions change with age requires evaluation of older adults' approach to learning situations. The role of noncognitive factors, such as motivation and emotion, must also be understood.

The Emotional Domain

Aging in the ancient world was viewed as a time of despair, a phase in life characterized by loss of health and productivity. The writers of the classical Athenian Greek period portrayed older men facing the horror of the mythical fates: Disease, Poverty, and Death. Men were described as selfish, overly critical, and disagreeable; women were described as feisty, argumentative, manipulative, and sexually aggressive. During the Middle Ages, a certain amount of mysticism surrounded individuals who lived to old age. Those who lived into their 60s and 70s were so rare that some thought their longevity must be due to a magical or supernatural cause. Elderly women were said to be associated with witchcraft, and many thought they made pacts with demons and devils.

The pessimism linked to aging has long been part of our cultural heritage. Although there are cases where older men and women continue to maintain power and authority and command positive views of those around them, such individuals are rare. In the main, old age in Western cultures is seen as a period of wasting in which the skills acquired in youth begin to deteriorate. Aging for many, even in modern civilization, continues to evoke negative emotions (see Kart, 1997, chapter 9).

The problems confronted by older adults are unique. As we age, we experience decreases in physical strength and endurance; issues related to health become of increasing concern to us. Older adults face changes in job roles and responsibilities, and they experience declining opportunities to use skills that were developed over decades of work; retirement is mandated for many. The deaths of friends, colleagues, and spouses have a marked affect on those who survive to old age. Even in the absence of disease states, older adults must contend with major physical, mental, and social changes that affect self-concept.

Self-concept is one of the basic elements of personality; it is a relatively consistent view about who one is and why one behaves in certain ways. Although self-concept is relatively stable, it can fluctuate in later life. It is the direction and degree of change in self-concept during aging that is of considerable interest to gerontologists. It is normal at any point in life to experience depression and sadness when faced with traumatic life events, but it is commonly believed that the incidence of depression is greater for older people. Empirical evidence challenges this perspective, however. The incidence of depression recorded in older people depends greatly on how behaviors that make up the syndrome of depression are measured and interpreted. When researchers separate *major depression*, in which the syndrome of depression is the primary source of discomfort, from *secondary depression*, which results from some other physical or mental health problem, older adults actually display fewer cases of major depression than young adults (O'Connor, Aenchbacher, and Dishman, 1993).

Further, longitudinal studies of personality, which measure characteristics of the same individual over an extended period of time, point to the inaccuracy of the common belief that depression is linked to aging (Schaie and Willis, 1996). The differences seen between the level of depression in young and older adults found in cross-sectional research studies, which compare groups of individuals who differ in age, can be explained better in terms of generational differences than in terms of aging, per se.

In summary, the picture that is emerging from gerontological research in the psychological domain is that, other than expected behavioral and mental slowing, age-related changes up to the mid-70s or so are relatively modest.

When major changes in mental processes are seen, they have more to do with an individual's life history and experiences than with simply growing older. Indeed, there are researchers who have shifted their focus away from the factors that underlie declines in health and behavior to those factors that contribute to successful aging and improvements in perceptions of mental health and general wellness. There is a growing population in developed countries of centenarians, individuals who live to be older than 100 years, who maintain their health, vigor, and mental acuity. Many older adults maintain active lifestyles and hold positive outlooks regarding what the future has in store for them. They continue to derive pleasure from meeting the challenges of life and look upon old age as a period providing unique opportunities for both learning and teaching.

The motivation to self-actualize energizes young and older persons alike. Unfortunately, most families and social agencies focus on providing and meeting only the lowest levels of an individual's needs, those that are necessary to maintain life. It is the higher levels of needs, including social and esteem needs, that enhance the experience of life. Changes in lifestyle, perceptions of aging, and ageism can thwart progress toward self-actualization. At any age, an individual's personal commitment is critical if he or she is to achieve full potential (Maslow, 1968, p. 204).

RETENTION AND MAINTENANCE OF OLDER ADULTS' SKILLS

Many gerontologists study the processes of aging to understand how to improve quality of life during late adulthood. Researchers have focused on methods that affect age-related change in both physiological and psychological function. These methods are often described in terms of *intervention treatments*, the systematic educational and training programs designed to change specific characteristics in older adults. Some intervention treatments are designed to improve physiological functioning. Exercise and physical rehabilitation programs have been used extensively to improve body functioning and to enhance older adults' quality of life. Other intervention treatments are designed to improve the function of psychological systems. Memory training and self-efficacy programs help restore mental abilities and skills that are central to quality of life.

Two relatively separate issues confront gerontologists interested in developing intervention programs for older adults. On one hand, training programs can be directed toward helping older adults regain and maintain previously learned skills that, for one reason or another, have been lost or have diminished. On the other hand, programs can also be directed toward teaching new skills to older adults. The type of task selected for the intervention treatment can have a profound effect on the learning process.

Maintaining Skills

Most treatments designed to assist older adults focus on regaining and maintaining previously learned skills. Training approaches, in general, have focused either on programs that exercise the body or the mind.

Exercise and Aging

Physical exercise interventions tend to be designed to enhance a participant's cardiovascular efficiency and muscular strength. Aerobic training programs are thought to improve quality of life by bringing about changes in somatic processes. The view that physical health is related to mental health and cognition has a long history. Further, older adults' health status has been implicated as an explanation for age-related differences in cognitive functioning. Conditions such as coronary health status and hypertension have been shown to be related to tests of cognitive function. Indeed, a large number of studies have revealed consistent relations between health status and mental functioning (Thomas, Landers, Salazar, and Etnier, 1994).

Several training studies have shown that older adults' mental abilities can be modified through aerobic exercise. Cardiovascular exercise has been implicated in improvements in problem-solving intelligence (Elsayed, Ismail, and Young, 1980), attention, and information-processing capacity (Dustman et al., 1984; Hawkins, Kramer, and Capaldi, 1992; Moul, Goldman, and Warren, 1995). Several studies, however, have failed to show a relation between older adults' cardiovascular improvement and cognitive functioning (Blumenthal et al., 1989; Blumenthal et al., 1991; Blumenthal and Madden, 1988; Madden, Blumenthal, Allen, and Emery, 1989). At this time, the general belief that aerobic exercise programs offset or reverse age-related declines in mental abilities has not garnered unequivocal research support. The results of some, but not all, studies suggest that the cognitive skills of older adults can be improved by having them participate in either aerobic or strength development programs. These mixed research results may be due to the magnitude and duration of exercise training programs or to the type of cognitive tests used to assess the effects of training. There are many methodological factors that currently make it difficult to obtain reliable measures of the effects of aerobic training (Spirduso, 1995, chapter 9).

Mental Training

Training programs developed to exercise the mind fall into two categories: those that teach the use of metacognitive reasoning and problem-solving skills, and those that augment components of the information-processing system. General metacognitive problem-solving training interventions are characterized by their emphasis on methods that help individuals make use of their available mental capacity. Older adults can be trained to compensate for declines in capacity by teaching them to channel their available capacity to fewer domains and to reorganize their problem-solving approach (Baltes, Staudinger, and Lindenberger, 1999; Willis, 1989).

The first major studies of the effects of training on older adults' mental abilities were undertaken as part of the Penn State Adult Development and Enrichment Project (ADEPT) and the Seattle Longitudinal Study (SLS) (see Tomporowski, 1997 for a review). The focus of both research projects was similar; attempts were made to determine how much cognitive training would modify specific older adults' mental abilities.

Adults in the ADEPT project were in their mid- to late 60s. They participated in five one-hour educational training sessions during which an instructor taught them a number of problem-solving strategies. The durability of training effects was assessed one week, one month, and six months after training. Training was found to enhance subjects' test performance on problem-solving questions, and these gains were maintained over a six-month period.

In the SLS project (Schaie, Willis, Hertzog and Schlenberg, 1987), subjects were categorized as "decliners" or "stable" on the basis of their performance on intelligence tests, which were administered over a number of years. All subjects then participated in five one-hour training sessions that taught them problem-solving methods. The performance of both groups of subjects improved following training. "Decliners" returned to their predecline level and subjects categorized as "stable" enhanced their level of performance. Although training would likely not return older adults to levels of performance observed in young adults, it would produce substantial gains in normally aging adults.

Central to the training methods employed in the ADEPT and SLS projects is the belief that older adults can learn metacognitive problem-solving strategies and then apply them to novel situations. Older adults are believed to benefit from relatively brief training programs because the mental exercises reinstate previously acquired knowledge. Thus, cognitive training functions much differently for experienced older adults than for young adults who have yet to learn specific problem-solving strategies.

Training programs also target specific components of the information-processing systems that are presumed to underlie optimal cognitive functioning. Declines in the performance of older adults have been explained in terms of reductions in processing speed and working memory. Training programs have been developed to isolate and remediate specific aspects of information processing. These studies show that practice can improve older adults' processing speed. The positive effects of training are thought to be due to improving stimulus encoding abilities, altering the way specific mental operations manipulate incoming information, and affecting the development of automatic attentional processing (Salthouse, 1985, 1991).

Research on memory processes indicates that although memory storage remains relatively intact, older adults have difficulty using working memory; that is, transforming and organizing information in short-term memory. These observations have led to considerable interest in memory-training interventions. Studies employing mnemonics training have consistently demonstrated improvements in the memory performance of older adults. Training programs often emphasize the *principle of encoding specificity*, which suggests that memory is improved by learning to match specific environmental cues to information as it is stored in long-term memory. Techniques that promote encoding specificity include mental retracing, use of mood states, distinctive environmental information, and hierarchical retrieval (Hill, Sheikh, and Yesavage, 1988; Yesavage and Jacob, 1984; Yesavage, Lapp, and Sheikh, 1989; Yesavage and Rose, 1984a, 1984b).

It is clear that older adults benefit mentally from their participation in psychological training programs. Training interventions provide evidence that older adults can improve their performance on a variety of mental tasks.

Learning New Skills

Intervention programs appear to promote the performance of previously learned skills in older adults. Older adults can also learn new skills, although not as quickly and perhaps not to the same level of proficiency as young adults, in most cases.

Learning occurs throughout the life span. Older adults' psychomotor performance, for example, can be improved dramatically with training. Several research studies have examined how practice affects older adults' information-processing abilities on tasks that demand rapid decision-making and response speed. In a classic study by Salthouse and Somberg (1982), a group of young adults and a group of older adults were given extended practice on four different cognitive tasks, each of which focused on a specific type of mental processing: signal detection, memory scanning, visual discrimination, and temporal prediction. The four tasks were presented to subjects as a computer-based videogame. Practice effects were assessed by measuring changes in performance on training tasks over repeated sessions and by evaluating subjects' performance on alternative versions of each task administered in lieu of practice tasks following varying numbers of repetitions of training sessions. Practice resulted in dramatic increases in performance for both young and older adults on the four tasks; response accuracy improved and reaction times declined.

Videogames have also been used to teach new skills to older adults. Subjects who played videogames evidenced significant improvements in reaction time and were less affected by task complexity than were subjects who did not practice the videogames (Dustman, Emmerson, Steinhaus, Shearer, and Dustman, 1992; Clark, Lanphear, and Riddick, 1987). The effects of the videogame interventions were hypothesized to influence brain cell assemblies that are specific to highly practiced behaviors.

Older adults' response speeds have also been shown to be affected by contingencies of reinforcement. A series of studies conducted by Baron and his colleagues (Baron and Menich, 1985a, 1985b; Baron, Menich, and Perone, 1983;

Perone and Baron, 1982, 1983) was designed to determine the extent to which behavioral slowing could be remediated through reinforcement for fast and accurate responding. In these studies, older adults were reinforced for completing response sequences within specified time periods. Older adults responded more slowly than young adults when there was unlimited time to respond; however, both young and old adults showed substantial reductions in response times when time limits were enforced. The subjects' increased response speeds were taken as evidence that age-related behavioral slowing may be attributed, at least in part, to older adults being placed in environments that do not allow the opportunity to practice rapid responding.

In summary, older adults can acquire new motor and cognitive skills via intervention treatments that stress repetition and practice. Of interest to many researchers and educators, however, are questions concerning age-related differences in rate of learning.

A general observation is that older adults tend to learn new material more slowly than do young adults; the shape of the learning curve for young adults is different than the curve for older adults. Typically, young adults improve their performance more rapidly and then top out at a higher level than older adults. Age-dependent differences in rate of learning have been obtained in a number of studies. For example, Fisk and Rogers (1991) gave young, middle-aged, and older adults extensive practice on a detection task. Practice resulted in systematic improvements in the detection speeds for all age groups; however, older adults' performance was, less affected by practice than that of young and middle-aged adults. Despite performing almost 11,000 training trials, older adults' performance was not improved to the level of adults in the other groups.

It appears that training can and does improve the processing speed of older adults on specific tasks; however, practice alone will not compensate totally for age-related changes in mental and behavioral speed. Older adults take longer to process information than do younger ones. As a result, even with extended training, older adults are placed at a disadvantage when learning virtually any task in which information is presented at a fast pace. A review of laboratory research by Cerella (1990) led him to suggest that the effects of practice contribute relatively little to the performance of many skills that require speeded decisions and movement.

However, there are many physical and mental factors that contribute to how well an individual negotiates the twists and turns of life. One approach that has been taken to understanding how people adjust to changes is to examine individual differences in the way people age.

INDIVIDUAL DIFFERENCES AND SUCCESSFUL AGING

Aging is not a single or unitary process. Every structure of the human body and every cognitive process of the human mind have been described in terms of averages. There exists for each a range of scores that reflects the degree to which individuals vary. Since aging is often defined in terms of changes in physical and mental capacities, there is a tendency to believe that the timeline for age-related changes in function and skill is similar for all individuals. In actuality, the rate of change of physical and psychological functions varies tremendously from person to person. The basis for individual differences in rate of aging lies in the interaction between physiological, psychosocial, and emotional factors.

Biological Sources of Individual Differences

People have observed for centuries that longevity tends to run in families. Modern researchers have gathered considerable information that supports these anecdotal observations. Some of the most enduring theories of individual differences in aging are based on genetic factors. Leonard Hayflick (1977) proposed that the number of times a human cell can divide and reproduce itself is limited by genetic information that is encoded in the nucleus of the cell.

Recent advances in technology have provided researchers with the ability to examine the structure of genes at a microscopic level. Important new discoveries are being made today that provide insight into the processes of aging. Laboratory observations have fostered the emergence of several theories of aging that have implications for the study of skill development and performance. What has been made clear by recent research is that it is unlikely that a single gene controls the onset and course of aging. Rather, multiple genes interact, perhaps in time-dependent ways, to initiate changes in the structures and functions of the body. Further complicating the role of genetics is the fact that the manner in which genes function is influenced by how the body responds to environmental factors.

Several theories of biological aging propose that various systems of the body are impacted from birth to death by chemical microinsults that are part of our daily lives (see Schneider, 1993, for an overview of biological theories). Chemicals in the air we breathe, in the food we eat, and released in our bodies as part of normal metabolism can alter the encoding of information in our genes. Over time, these chemical "insults" cause greater and greater demands to be placed on body and organ systems. The end result is eventual loss of function. The accumulation of malfunctioning genetic codes leads to changes that limit physical and mental performance—tissues stiffen, ligaments tighten, blood flow and the supply of oxygen to the brain decrease. As the capacities of individual systems decline, a general physiological imbalance gradually emerges. Brain and endocrine systems that are designed to regulate and maintain homeostatic balance have increasing difficulty in doing their job. These changes result in increased vulnerability to disease and viral infections. Decline in general health provides a clear marker for loss of function and decrements in the performance of physical and mental skills (Johnson, 1985).

Psychosocial Sources of Individual Differences

The manner in which we age is intimately related to the social framework in which we live. The concept of aging itself is defined by our culture. Comparisons between the views of aging held in Western cultures and ancient Asian cultures provide compelling examples of how society and the structure of the family unit play significant roles in determining the quality of life for older adults. The rules that forged the family unit in preindustrial China, Korea, and Japan emerged from a blending of religious convictions and economics.

In China and Korea, the ideals of Confucianism, which emphasize the role of the parent as teacher and the child as eager and receptive learner, led to an economic and legal system in which control was dictated by *lineage*, a ritualistic system in which the oldest male retains the material wealth of the family. The notion that all Chinese venerated older people because of their wisdom apparently is a stereotype. The respect given by the young to the old may have had more to do with potential economic gain than from a natural inclination to respect the old because of their wisdom (see Kiefer, 1992, and Thursby, 1992, for overviews of Asian perspectives on aging). Regardless of the basis of motivation for establishing relations between members of the family, the roles and duties of each member were clearly delineated and adhered to.

As members of the family aged, the roles they performed changed. A person's identity came to be associated with his or her age and how well he or she performed specific skills. Older adults contributed to the success of rural families by performing tasks that required patience and experience rather than physical strength. Older men, because of their knowledge of cultivation and farming and their understanding of weather patterns and climate, often maintained an important place in the family. Women, as they aged, organized household activities and maintained the routines of daily family life. Younger members of the family often believed that the elders were assisted in their decision making by supernatural powers reserved only for them. The lineage-based Asian family structure provided a framework for intergenerational transmission of knowledge and development of skills required for survival and success.

The social and cultural context of Asian countries provides an example of how the perceptions of a society set the stage for the perceptions of individuals within that society. Preindustrial Asian men and women perceived themselves as contributors throughout life to the success of their families. In turn, the family tended to respect older adults for the skills and knowledge they passed down to the next generation. The emphasis of Asian cultures on intergenerational transmission of information is evidenced even in today's modern industrialized societies.

Western societies are beginning to realize that the culture itself serves to limit older adults' potential for learning. When societies expect age-related learning deficits to emerge, individuals within that society will also expect to lose their abilities to learn and to teach. Instead of secluding older adults from the mainstream of society, many suggest that older adults should continue to be active and to persist in maintaining their abilities and skills. Such activities provide older adults with verification of their importance in society; they also present opportunities to experience positive emotions that are linked to the execution of skilled behavior.

Emotional Sources of Individual Differences

Positive emotional rewards are derived as skilled actions are performed. The feelings generated by executing skills and teaching those skills to others are believed to be a central factor in successful aging. In many instances, the social systems that have emerged in Western civilization have taken from older people many of the activities that have the potential to provide them the greatest psychological reward. It is a common misconception that the demands placed on older adults should be limited and that they should be placed in environments that are ordered and controlled. Removing the opportunity to continue to learn and to overcome challenges can have a profound negative emotional effect on some older adults.

Positive emotions are elicited when one chooses to take realistic risks to achieve self-actualization and mastery. Societies and families, although well-intentioned, may promote environments for older adults that are comfortable and safe but provide little opportunity to test limits and experiment with new ideas. A predictable and mundane existence can lead to physical and mental stagnation, rigidity, and withdrawal. Some intervention activities may actually impede the maintenance of the very psychological processes they were designed to promote. When activities are selected by caregivers and presented according to a rigid schedule, older adults lose the capacity to make choices. Under such conditions, outer-directed activities are often performed with little seriousness or commitment.

There are, however, hardy individuals to be found at every phase of life. These are people who continually challenge themselves and strive for the intangible rewards that accompany a job well done (Kobasa, 1979). At the center of the concept of hardiness is the view that some individuals are more intrinsically motivated than others to pit their skills against challenges they confront. Such people believe that they can exert control over their environment; they feel committed to being active players in the game of life. Indeed, the pleasures they attain from meeting these challenges are akin to the pleasures experienced during play and when participating in unstructured games. By electing to view life as a series of unpredictable challenges, the hardy individual maintains a sense of commitment, playfulness, vigorousness, and *meaningfulness* (contentment with existence and its impact on others).

The innate pleasures of total immersion in activity serve as a powerfully motivating force. Older adults have the ability to transform virtually any physical or mental task they attempt into pleasurable activity. Positive emotions emerge with the right mixture of environmental demand, perceptions of skill level, and actual skill level. Obtaining the positive emotional benefits of the experience, however, requires that the individual have an element of control over the environment. Anxiety and worry emerge when the demands of a task exceed a person's actual skill level. Monotony and boredom emerge when tasks are not sufficiently challenging. The drive to seek challenge can be thwarted when environmental conditions are predetermined and arranged by others. Older adults' playfulness and vigor can no more be engineered than can children's playfulness. People of all ages can be guided and directed to perform tasks through the use of external rewards and punishments; however, such directed actions may have relatively little meaningfulness. In order to gain positive emotions from activity, it is critical that older adults perceive themselves as initiators of action.

Aging is accompanied by changes in neuroendocrine systems that decrease the speed and magnitude of adaptive fight-or-flight responses to stressors. Loss of the integrity of neuroendocrine systems is linked to decline in physical and mental health. Older people who have the opportunity to test their skills and to overcome real and perceived challenges are more likely to maintain the integrity of their neurohormonal systems as they age. Individuals with histories of dealing successfully with stressors by applying their skills to solve problems benefit both physically and psychologically. Repeated cycles of challenge and non-challenge conditions train the neurohormonal system to conserve physical resources when environmental stress is low and to mobilize resources rapidly with the onset of a threat or challenge. The toughened older adult is more sensitive and alert to environmental information, can respond more quickly to environmental changes, and has more physical resources to meet threats than one who does not have a history of toughening experiences. Psychologically, a history of systematically and repeatedly achieving goals and overcoming stress and challenge also develops the ability to tolerate stress and to control negative emotional states such as fear and anxiety.

Learning Styles

Gerontologists agree that an important key to successful aging is learning to adapt to the physical and mental changes that accompany old age. The model of *selective optimization with compensation* developed by Baltes and his colleagues (Baltes, Staudinger, and Lindenberger, 1999) suggests that people perceive age-related declines in their physical and mental capacity and elect to compensate for these changes by channeling available resources into fewer behavioral domains (*selective optimization*). Performance within selected behavioral domains depends on the availability of two types of cognitive resources: *active reserves* and *latent reserves*. Under normal conditions, problems are solved by drawing upon active reserves; however, latent reserves are used if a specific

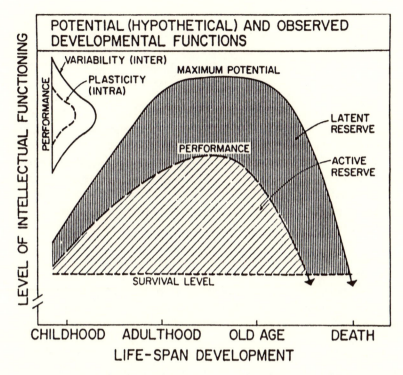

Figure 9.1.   Conceptual Relations between Potential Performance and Two Types of Reserve (Active and Latent)

From P. B. Baltes and S. L. Willis, *Aging and Cognitive Processes.* Copyright 1982. Reprinted by permission of the author and by Kluwer Academic/Plenum Publishers.

problem demands maximal performance. The availability of these two types of resources is hypothesized to change across the life span. (See figure 9.1.) Although there are age-related declines in the availability of reserves, considerable *plasticity* exists and older adults can maintain high levels of performance, given the proper motivation.

There are many people over the age of 80 who continue to perform highly complex skills at expert levels. Some artists and musicians continue to improve as they age, and some provide their best performances or works during late adulthood. There has been much interest in how people who are experts learn to compensate for changes in physical capacities and mental speed. The concept of expertise suggests that highly skilled behavior is linked to deliberate practice, which is characterized by systematic and consistent repetition. Older experts may have had many decades of deliberate practice that enables them to maintain highly automated physical and mental skills. It is also the case that decades of practice provide the older expert with an in-depth understanding of tasks that is not yet available to younger experts.

A review of the research on expertise led Spirduso (1995, chapter 7) to suggest that older adults can employ at least three strategies to compensate for loss of processing speed and reaction time. Anticipation strategies can have profound effects on the ability to respond in a given situation. The role of anticipation in the performance of psychomotor tasks was shown clearly in a classic study of young and older typists (Salthouse, 1984). The typing speed and accuracy of most professional typists change little with age. Maintenance of this skill was found to be due, at least in part, to older typists' learning to preview, or scan, the words to be typed farther ahead than younger typists. The advanced previewing provided older typists with the information required to maintain typing rates comparable to those of younger expert typists. *Simplification strategies* help us become more efficient in executing behaviors. Older adults can learn to modify their daily activities to make physically demanding tasks more manageable and less effortful. *Speed-accuracy trade-off strategies* occur when we elect to be more cautious in responding. When people are instructed in laboratory situations to emphasize either speed or accuracy in tasks, the resulting decision has a pronounced effect on performance. A portion of the slowing observed in older adults' actions may be the result of self-generated decisions concerning how to approach a given task. The manner in which older adults drive an automobile, for example, may reflect their level of caution in a given situation.

It must be recognized, however, that the process of selective optimization is a two-edged sword. Although it may be adaptive for older persons to channel their available resources to a limited number of behavioral domains, the process results in loss of performance in unselected domains. The perception of loss of physical capacities, for example, may lead older adults to shift from vigorous activities that are essential to maintaining physical health. Perceptions of loss of mental capacities may cause them to shift their resources to activities that require minimal mental effort. Since the time of the ancient Greek philosophers, the concept of *disuse*, or lack of activity or practice, has been invoked as a major cause of observed individual differences as we age (Swabb, 1991). Physical inactivity leads to atrophy, and mental inactivity leads to the loss of both declarative knowledge and procedural skills. Many of the physical and mental training interventions developed for older adults have been designed on the premise that skills lost as a result of disuse can be reestablished through educational programs.

The utilization of learned strategies is fundamental to the development of individuals' concept of self throughout the life span. At every stage of life there exists the potential for crisis and psychological tension. The resolution of or failure to resolve these crises ultimately determines the concept of self. During the transition into old age, the concept of self is critical for deriving *meaningfulness*. Learning is a continuous, transforming process and an accumulative activity. Early learning does not disappear; it simply becomes part of the learner's history.

CHAPTER SUMMARY

Aging has been viewed historically in two very different ways. There have been times when older adults were looked upon as special people who, because of their vast years of experience, possessed great knowledge, understanding, and skill. There have also been times when older adults were seen as dead weight who had little to offer because of their inability to keep up with technological and social changes.

Studying the aging process reveals that there are many age-linked changes in physical and mental functioning. However, it is clear that older adults continue to perform many skills acquired over a lifetime at high levels of proficiency. Changes in physical and mental capacities occur gradually, over decades, and most people adapt to them without constant awareness of loss of function. Successful aging involves adapting to challenges by using strategies that permit the maximization of physical and mental resources and previously learned skills.

There are some clear differences in how young adults and older adults learn new skills. Young adults have a decided advantage over older ones when new skills require rapid information processing and speeded performance. Physical and mental slowing are an unavoidable characteristic of growing older. The way that older adults interpret these age-related changes can have a profound effect on their self-concept and motivation.

The perceptions we hold of abilities and skills is as important to the older adult as to a young adult or a child. People who age successfully exhibit a spirited, continuous search for new challenges and experiences.

SUGGESTED READINGS

Kart, G. S. (1996). *The realities of aging: An introduction to gerontology* (5th ed.). New York: Allyn & Bacon.

Palmore, E. B. (1990). *Ageism: Negative and positive.* New York: Springer.

Salthouse, T. A. (1991). *Theoretical perspectives on cognitive aging.* Hillsdale, NJ: Erlbaum.

Schaie, K. W., and Willis, S. L. (1996). *Adult development and aging* (4th ed.). New York: HarperCollins.

Spirduso, W. W. (1995). *Physical dimensions of aging.* Champaign, IL: Human Kinetics.

Chapter 10

Skill Development:
Integrating Mind, Body, and Spirit

This chapter examines various philosophies regarding what it means to be human. Then it relates these philosophical views to the processes involved in becoming skilled. The goal is to provide a framework that unites and solidifies information presented in previous chapters.

It has been firmly established that skill development depends on multiple processes; some are physical; others are mental; still others are motivational. A central question asked by many educators, scientists, and philosophers, is, "How do the mind, body, and spirit work together during the process of learning?" The academic debate concerning the mind-body relation cannot be resolved here. However, it is possible to examine various attempts to understand how the mind, body, and spirit interact and impact the processes of skill learning.

THE THREE PILLARS OF HUMAN BEHAVIOR

The analysis of skilled behavior provides a unique venue from which to study three aspects of human nature: the body, mind, and spirit. As described in chapter 1, each of these aspects can be viewed as a pillar that supports the capacity to adapt and survive in a constantly changing environment.

Human behavior has been a central topic of thought and discussion since the earliest days of the existence of our species. The notion that human behavior can be conceptualized as the product of interactions between different aspects of human nature has long been part of philosophy and psychology in Western civilization (Hilgard, 1980). The history of philosophy reveals three primary points of view: the philosophy of *empiricism* stresses the mechanical aspects of human behavior; *rationalism* stresses the mental aspects; and *romanticism* stresses emotional aspects of human behavior. These three concepts of what it means to be human have provided the impetus for revolution, social change, religious, and educational movements throughout the development of Western civilization.

Empiricism

Empiricism espouses the notion that everything we know and everything we do is based on our direct experience with nature. Our sensory systems provide us with raw data that is put together in a machinelike way. Some philosophers who championed this view of human nature in the seventeenth century considered humans to be nothing more than biological machines that operated in the same way as all other bodies in the universe. A concept central to the beliefs of early empiricists and many modern scientists is *monism*, the view that everything in the universe is composed of physical matter, and there is only one type of existence—physical existence. The belief that the universe (of which humans were a part) was nothing more than a complex machine was very popular in the seventeenth and eighteenth centuries. The work of scientists such as Galileo (1564–1642) and Sir Issac Newton (1642–1727) provided compelling evidence for the machinelike functions of nature. All motions, from those of the planets to those of humans to those of individual molecules, were thought to be understandable and predictable. Consider the view of the human body held by Thomas Hobbes (1588–1679), an influential early empiricist: "For what is the heart but a spring, and the nerves but so many strings; and the joints but so many wheels, giving motion to the whole body" (Hobbes, 1651/1962, p. 19).

An empiricist philosophy of human nature deemphasizes the importance of the mind and emphasizes the role of experience as the source of all knowledge. Empiricists believe we are born into the world with our minds as empty as blank slates. In the same way that a modern computer contains no data when it comes from the factory, the human knows nothing at birth. However, both computers and humans have the potential to learn through experience. Humans possess the hardware needed to obtain information from the world into which we are born. It is through our sensory systems that we obtain the data that determine how we think and behave. Our biological hardware organizes sensory input (experiences) in much the same way that a computer manipulates bits of electrical code. Empiricists suggest that we learn by putting our experiences together via associations. Thus, knowledge is obtained only from direct contact with those aspects of the world that are physical or that can be observed and measured.

The philosophy of empiricism has had a considerable impact on the way some scientists and educators study physical and cognitive skill development. For example, the term *motor learning* has been used by biophysical researchers to define an entire area of study. The human body continues to be viewed as a machine that operates according to the principles of physics and motion. The term motor implies that human action is performed in a machinelike, programmable fashion.

Psychology, too, has been affected by the empiricist perspective on human behavior. Some psychologists contend that learning can occur only through direct experience. Behavioral psychologists suggest that learning and action are the direct result of conditioning and the associations made between actions and rewards. Likewise, some cognitive psychologists consider that the human mind operates like a computer. For them, "mind" is a concept or construct based in evolutionary biology; the brain programmed to do nothing more than perform a series of operations on sensory information. Importantly, the mind is viewed as a passive machine whose operations can be understood in terms of the principles of association.

Rationalism

Rationalism emphasizes an active mind that does more than just process and organize information. The mind may operate on incoming sensory information but it does more than simply organize and store facts; the mind has an innate, inborn capacity to generate new and unique sources of knowledge. Rationalists view humans as problem solvers who are faced with challenges that require new and unique solutions. To the rationalist, humans are driven to clarify their thoughts and bring order to them. Although we may live in a chaotic world, we can bring order to chaos through the operations of our minds. We are born with innate mental processes that provide ways to organize our thoughts and experiences. Rational thought can be attained, however, only through mental effort. Solving a problem, regardless of whether it is as mundane as threading a sewing machine or as vital as selecting a career, requires systematic mental effort. Clear thought does not come easily. Thus, rationalist philosophers emphasize freedom of choice. A person can choose to go through the chaos of life without gaining any insight into its meaning, or he can choose to apply his mind to the chaos in order to achieve an understanding of the world and his place in it.

Rationalism has also had an impact on the way some scientists and educators study physical and cognitive skill development. Motor and cognitive skills are seen as vehicles that lead students to achieve goals. Rationalists consider that much of human behavior is goal directed. Success on the playing field and in athletic competition demands that players understand the tasks they face and that they use strategies to maximize positive outcomes. Likewise, our success at overcoming developmental, social, and cultural problems is linked to our use of strategy and problem-solving skills. Our bodies may function like machines, but our minds direct our bodies' actions.

Romanticism

Romanticism emphasizes the importance of human feelings and emotions. Romanticists consider that much of human action is motivated by passion and desire. This philosophy emerged in the late eighteenth century as a reaction against the views espoused by empiricists and rationalists. Romanticists were interested in the qualities that are unique to each individual. They saw the mind as a system of structures whose processes could be understood by scientifically analyzing its components. Romanticists considered human choice and action to be primarily instinctual and irrational. For them, the best choices humans can make are those that are guided by desires of the heart rather than by the cold calculations of the mind. Thus, when it came to developing a true understanding of human action, the methods of science were thought to be irrelevant.

The views of romanticists emerged during a period of history marked by social conflict and revolution. Wars were being fought throughout Europe and North America. People found themselves continuously placed in chaotic situations that defied rational solutions. Many early romanticists participated passionately and wholeheartedly in the social and political struggles of the times, and these struggles served as the background against which they struggled with the meaning of their existence.

Jean-Jacques Rousseau (1712–1778), the father of romanticism, believed that all humans are born to be honorable and good, but that the goodness that is part of every human is subverted by political and social institutions. Humans are driven to be free and happy but become bad and are unfulfilled by the constraints of social rules and order, he thought. The best guide for our actions lies in what makes us feel honest and correct; however, choices are often made for us by others or by outside forces. Unhappiness results from choices that are driven externally rather than internally.

Romanticists such as Friedrich Nietzsche (1844–1900) considered that humans are at their best when they take chances and benefit from both success and failure. It is only through challenge that people can learn to master the world in which they live, to develop a true idea of their capabilities, and to reach their full potential. Nietzsche stressed that any experience that does not destroy us makes us stronger. Thus, a psychologically healthy person is one who is constantly testing the limits of his or her skills and abilities.

Many of the concepts central to romanticism can be seen in the modern *humanistic* movement that arose in the United States and Europe in the 1950s and 1960s. Like earlier romanticist philosophers who were influenced by the social and political revolution of their time, modern humanist philosophers linked their views to the world wars, social upheaval, and widespread economic depression that marked the first half of the twentieth century. Central to humanist philosophy is the belief that the methods of science are not designed to understand human nature. Scientists tend to isolate and measure separate components of human actions. Humanists contend that human nature has to be understood in terms of the whole person acting freely in the world. Thus, attempts to break down, reduce, and measure human action distort the essence of what it means to be human.

The Tripartite Nature of Human Behavior

The notion that normal development reflects a combination of body, mind, and spirit permeates our culture. Each of the three pillars of human action is necessary for an individual to be fully functioning; that is, to actively learn from experience and adapt to challenges. Many of the stories and tales that we read as children and as adults address the need to maintain a balance among the mind, body, and spirit. Consider the challenges of the characters in *The Wizard of Oz*—the Tin Man had no heart, the Scarecrow had no brain, and the Lion had no courage. Each lacked a quality needed to be fully functional. The point is that how we learn skills and how we put those skills to use are affected by a continual interplay between the mechanical aspects of the body, the flexibility of the mind, and the degree of motivation and desire in the spirit.

Educators, scientists, and practitioners who accept the tripartite nature of human behavior are faced with a difficult problem, however. How are the mind and the body related? Can the body influence the mind? Can the mind influence the body?

MODELS OF THE MIND

Those who are interested in understanding the mind and how it operates often develop models to help conceptualize how it functions. Models are sometimes based on physical systems; they can also be based on mathematical equations that provide abstractions of the phenomenon of interest. Typically, models are created on the basis of reasonably well-understood systems. René Descartes's seventeenth-century model of human behavior, for example, was based on principles of hydraulics. During this period in history, the rules that governed fluids and their movement and pressures within pipes and tubes were being formulated, and this new knowledge was applied with great success to complex engineering problems. Descartes applied what was known to be true of hydraulics to human movement and hypothesized that human actions were the result of the flow of fluids and resulting pressures within body segments. Thus, the principles of hydraulics, which were understood, were used to help explain human movement, which was not very well understood.

The telephone model of brain function is another historical example of a model of human behavior. The telephone was an invention of the early twentieth century that had a profound effect on millions of people. Neuroscientists of this period interested in understanding the processes of the brain sometimes described its complex neurological structures and functions in terms of the simple mechanical actions of a telephone switchboard. Today, cognitive scientists make extensive use of computer models of information processing to explain the operations of the mind. The computer, like other human inventions, has had a monumental impact on people's lives, and it, too, has been used as a model to describe and explain human thought and behavior. If history serves as a guide for our future, however, the computer model, in all likelihood, will be replaced by other, newer, models. The point is, models are devices that help explain something that researchers don't know much about (e.g., the mind) by comparing it to something that researchers know a great deal about (e.g., hydraulics, telephones, or computers). The mind is not actually a computer; rather, some of the processes of the mind operate as the processes of a computer might act.

The Emergence of Models in Psychology

The young academic discipline of psychology was at a crossroads during the early years of the twentieth century. There were, at that time, two competing views regarding the appropriate subject matter of psychology. One view was that psychology should be a rigorous, laboratory-based science that focused on the measurement and quantification of behavior; the other view was that psychology should be a naturalistic science that focused on reports of feelings, emotions, and phenomenological experiences. Both of these approaches to the study of human thought and behavior have had profound effects on the study of skill.

Those who followed a quantitative approach believed that psychology should be a science of the mind. The work of Wilhelm Wundt (1832–1920), a pioneer in the development of modern psychology, did much to set the standards for experimental research in field. Wundt was a German professor at the University of Leipzig, with experience both in physiology and in philosophy, who argued that psychology's goal was to break down complex conscious experience into the basic building blocks of the mind. He presented psychology as a type of mental chemistry in which laboratory methods revealed the basic elements of thinking and problem solving. He incorporated a method of data collection called *introspection* in which individuals were trained to describe their perceptions of stimuli and the feelings associated with the perceptions. Introspection was thought to provide a reliable and valid index of the processes of mental activity. Wundt considered psychology to be a science in the same way that physics or chemistry was a science. He was very much influenced by the Zeitgeist of the times; most educated people thought that the universe was on the verge of being totally understood via measurement and mathematical laws. Considering the advances that had occurred in the physical sciences since the time of Isaac Newton (1642–1772), it is understandable that scientists studying the mind would consider that humans would obey the laws of nature in the same way that a falling rock does.

Wundt developed the prototypical school of psychology. His voluminous writings and research studies attracted students from Europe, England, and America. For decades, Wundt's laboratory was a preparatory school for young academicians from around the world who were interested in the new field of psychology. Graduates of Wundt's program went on to develop psychological laboratories in major universities throughout Europe and America. In the United States, Edward Titchener (1867–1927), a student of Wundt, promoted psychology as a basic science of the mind. His students greatly influenced the infrastructure of the American Psychological Association, the premier organization of psychologists in the United States. One of the guiding themes of psychology in the United States today is that it should be a laboratory-based science that examines the structures of thought and mind (Titchener, 1898).

The rise of behaviorism in the early 1900s perpetuated the quantitative, scientific approach to the study of animals and humans. Academic psychologists became even more tightly bound to the belief that psychology was a field of science not unlike physics. The system of experimental psychology promoted by John Watson was modeled on the assumptions of Newtonian physics. His brand of psychology considered that a true science of behavior dealt only with those aspects of human activity that were directly observable. The mind, because it could not be measured directly, lost its central place in behavioral psychology. Research was restricted to the domain of publicly verifiable events. The complex behavior of both humans and animals was assumed to be the end result of combinations of simple reflexes. The belief was that complex behavior could be understood by breaking it down into its basic element—the stimulus-response unit. The notion was that an individual acquired all aspects of behavior through experiences that resulted in the association between environmental stimuli and the responses made to those stimuli. Behaviorism in various forms was the dominant approach used to study human activity in academic psychology through the 1960s. Questions concerning phenomenological mental states were simply not entertained as valid by behavioral psychologists; for them, the mind fell outside the boundaries of science.

The Computer Model

Many science historians consider the publication of the Miller, Galanter, and Pribram text, *Plans and the Structure of Behavior* (1960), to be a milestone in the emergence of cognitive psychology. The concepts in this text differed fundamentally from traditions that were held by the vast majority of experimental psychologists of that time. Many of the learning theories proposed during the first half of the twentieth century were tempered by the assumptions of behaviorally oriented psychology. These theories placed great emphasis on the role of reinforcement on learning. The core belief of these theories was that learning could not occur without reinforcement. Little was said of mental processes that accompany learning.

The model of learning proposed by Miller et al. (1960) stressed the roles of mental structures and their operations. The fundamental building block of their theory was the *test-operate-test-exit* (TOTE) unit, a cybernetic mental construct that functioned to analyze environmental information and to assess the degree to which one's present environment matched a desired environment. (See figure 10.1.)

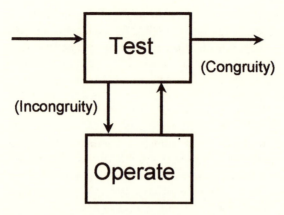

Figure 10.1.   The Test-Operate-Test-Exit (TOTE) Unit Model
Adapted from G. A. Miller, E. Galanter, K. H. Pribram. (1960). *Plans and the Structure of Behavior,*
p. 26. Holt, Rinehart and Winston, Inc.

The TOTE unit guides an individual's behavioral action plan. A plan was conceptualized as a list of tests, arranged sequentially and designed to attain a desired outcome or goal. The TOTE unit was hypothesized to underlie a broad range of human activities. A case was made for the role of the TOTE unit in skill learning, language, memory, personality, and motives.

Models of the mind developed since the introduction of the TOTE unit have become increasingly complex. The emergence of more sophisticated models is due to two factors. First, the empirical research that was conducted based on early simple models revealed that the operations of the mind are exceedingly complex. Second, models developed initially to deal with limited aspects of behavior, such as information processing, were modified to help better understand and explain how noncognitive factors such as feelings, emotions, and motivation influence behavior. The study of the psychology of skill is intimately linked to the historical progression of cognitive models of human behavior.

The introduction of the additive factors method by Saul Sternberg (1966, 1969) did much to promote the development of computer models of information processing. Sternberg's experimental methods extended those introduced by Franciscus Donders (1868/1969) and were designed to fractionate response time in order to assess how people detect, discriminate, and respond to stimuli. The additive factors method isolates stimulus encoding processes and decision processes from response production and motor movement processes. The model assumes that the flow of information travels through a series of nonoverlapping processing stages, each operating independently of the others. Analysis of the pattern of participants' reaction times under various experimental conditions provides evidence for the operations of specific stages of mental operation.

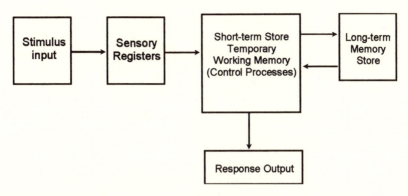

Figure 10.2.   Atkinson-Shiffrin Model of Memory Storage
From R. T. Kellogg, *Cognitive Psychology*, p. 18. Copyright 1995. Reprinted by permission of Sage Publications, Inc.

An important advance in the conceptualization of information processing and memory storage was made by Atkinson and Shiffrin (1971). They described a two-component model of memory in which information is manipulated in short-term memory and stored in long-term memory. (See figure 10.2.) Their model is based on the assumption that information flows from the environment, through sensory systems, and into short-term memory. Information in short-term memory can be manipulated via a variety of *control processes* such as rehearsal (an overt or covert repetition of information), coding (putting information into a contextual format), and imagery (translating verbal information into visual images). The model assumes that individuals have the ability to select and employ these control processes. The processes of short-term memory system underlie immediate conscious awareness; they are at the heart of each decision to remember information by transferring it to long-term memory or allowing information to decay and be lost from memory.

Inherent in Atkinson and Shiffrin's (1971) model of information processing (and other theories that followed) is a distinction between memory structures (the hardware of memory systems) and processes that control how information is organized, maintained, and used (the software of memory systems). The hardware properties of short-term memory, for example, limit the amount of information that it can hold; however, software processes can be used to manipulate information and influence short-term memory capacity limitations.

Computer models of information processing underwent marked changes when researchers began to explore how attention and effort influenced behavior. Attentional processes are critical to both the acquisition of motor and cognitive skills and their maintenance. Attention plays a role in both response preparation and response execution. The preparations that an individual makes during the time immediately preceding an action are critical to the outcome of the response. Consider the situation faced by a baseball batter preparing to hit a pitch. The initiation of the pitcher's motion serves as a warning signal that draws the batter's attention to various cues provided by the pitcher that signal the type of pitch being delivered. Before the ball reaches the hitting zone, the batter must select the swing that matches the predicted position of the ball. If a ball is pitched at 90 mph, it takes approximately 0.4 second to reach the plate. It takes 0.15 second to start a swing and make contact with the ball. This allows only about 0.25 second to decide whether to swing and what type of swing should be made. Poor batting is linked to failure to anticipate the characteristics of the pitch or failure to select the appropriate swing.

Once a response is selected and set into action, a person's attention may be directed toward the impact that the action has on the environment. The batter, for example, may attend to the swing of the bat, the impact of the bat on the ball, and the direction and distance that the ball travels after being hit. Attentional processes extract information concerning action and its consequences. As we act, the proprioceptive and sensory information generated serves as potential feedback. As discussed in previous chapters, knowledge of results and feedback play an essential role in skill development.

Skill development is linked to the quantity and quality of information stored in memory, but attentional processes determine what information will be retained. A novice batter's success depends on how well he learns from experience. Each swing of the bat provides him with information that has the *potential* to improve performance. (The word *potential* is emphasized because little learning will occur if the batter does not pay attention to the task at hand.) Allocation of attention demands *mental effort*; the extent to which our novice batter pays attention to a given task is determined by a number of factors.

It is well known that humans are not always successful at keeping their attention on task. Even the best students find that their attention sometimes wanders while reading or attending classroom lectures. And even the best baseball players occasionally have difficulty keeping their attention focused on the game. Even professional outfielders have "gone to sleep" during a game and failed to respond when a ball is hit directly to them. Attention appears to be limited and, at times, we all have to work hard to keep our minds on track.

Daniel Kahneman's (1973) text, *Attention and Effort*, is considered a classic in the field. He conceived attention as a limited-capacity resource drawn upon to perform specific tasks. As seen in figure 10.3, attentional capacity is held in reserve, much like fuel in a storage tank. These resources are expended on the basis of an allocation policy that is constantly affected by four factors: 1) the evaluation of demands that a task places on available resources, 2) momentary intentions that arise during the course of acting, 3) enduring dispositions that prepare us to attend to novel or unique events, and 4) levels of physiological arousal.

More recently, multiple capacity theories of information processing have been proposed. Sanders (1983) conceptualized attention in terms of three energy stores, each of which is controlled by a metacognitive, or executive, process. (See figure 10.4.) This model emphasizes the relations between three

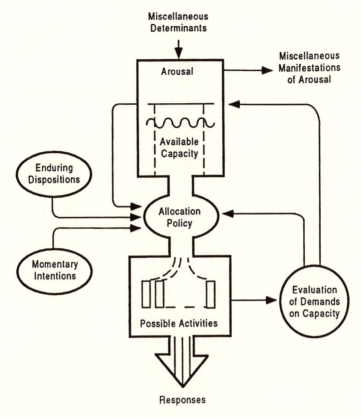

Figure 10.3.   Kahneman's Single Capacity Model of Attention
From *Attention and Effort* by Daniel Kahneman. Copyright 1973. Reprinted by permission of Pearson Education, Inc., Upper Saddle River, NJ.

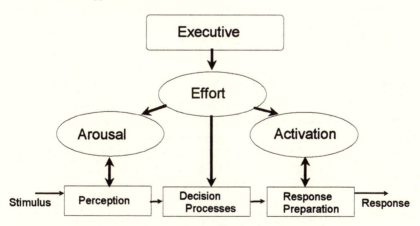

Figure 10.4.   Sanders's Multiple Capacity Model of Information Processing
From J. G. Jones & L. Hardy (1989). Stress and cognitive function in sport. *Journal of Sport Science,* 7, 41–63. Figure 4., p. 54. A simplified and modified version of Sanders's (1983) model of stress and human performance. Reprinted with permission by Taylor and Francis, Ltd.

levels of mental operations: a computational level, an executive control level, and an energy pool level. Computational processes include stimulus encoding, the storage and retrieval of information from interconnected memory structures, response selection, and response programming. The mechanistic activities of computational processes and resultant behavior are guided by processes taking place at the executive control level, where goal-directed, purposeful actions are formulated. The executive function addresses discrepancies that may exist between an organism's desired state and actual state. The executive processor evaluates discrepancies in terms of goals that can be attained via action. The role of executive processing is to plan, initiate, and monitor actions. The direction and intensity of those actions are determined by the allocation of resources that are present in three pools of energy: the effort pool, which determines the overall motivational state of the organism; the energy pool, which determines the resources that will be allocated to meet the demands encountered in the process of attaining specific goals; and the arousal pool, which is activated both by the effort pool and by stimulus input factors. The arousal pool responds in a phasic manner to variations in the quantity and quality of incoming sensory information. The allocation of energy from the arousal pool is reflected behaviorally through the speed at which an organism responds to novel stimuli or warning cues. The activation pool is affected by the allocation of effort resources and by motor movement programming and the execution of actions. The activation pool responds in a tonic manner and is reflected behaviorally in the extent to which actions are sustained over time.

Capacity theories of attention such as those developed by Kahneman (1973), Sanders (1983), and others help to explain how humans deal with (or fail to deal with) multiple tasks. The hockey goalie's performance, for example, depends on his capacity to attend to multiple sources of information and to execute precise blocks at just the right time. The goalie must attend to the sounds and actions that surround him; further, he must be able to maintain a level of physiological arousal that is optimal for executing action. The successful goalie is able to plan for a specific outcome by spreading his available attentional resources to deal with the multiple elements of playing the position. The unsuccessful goalie employs an inefficient allocation policy or lets his attentional capacity become overwhelmed by task demands.

Computer models of the mind have evolved from the simple TOTE unit to highly complex conceptualizations of the organization of mental processes. Advances in modeling have been spurred by the computational power of modern computers, the application of mathematical tools, and the detailed analysis of brain structures provided by new neural imaging techniques. Multidisciplinary groups of researchers in many universities are studying and mapping the processes of the mind. Representatives from such diverse fields as artificial intelligence, neuropsychology, philosophy, linguistics, engineering, medicine, rehabilitation, psychology, and exercise science are combining their expertise to address topics that were once thought to be beyond the boundaries of quantitative research.

COGNITIVE ENERGETICS

The models of cognition described thus far explain human behavior in terms of information and control processes. In them, relatively little emphasis is directed toward the role of physiological structures and their influence on thought and behavior. Researchers who take a *cognitive energetic* approach focus on interfaces that exist between physiological structures and psychological structures and how those systems are energized into action (Hockey, Coles, and Gaillard, 1986).

Cognitive energetics draws upon and incorporates themes that have long histories in psychological research. The models developed under the rubric of cognitive energetics are based on the assumption that people consciously attempt to optimize their performance by controlling and regulating their physical and mental states. Further, the regulation of these states can be understood in terms of cybernetic principles, which describe how an individual reduces discrepancies that exist between the psychophysiological state she expects to experience and the actual state she is experiencing.

It is relatively easy to understand how the actions of mechanical cybernetic servomechanisms are controlled. When a building becomes uncomfortably cold, the setting of a dial on a thermostat (a cybernetic servomechanism) is changed to inform the heating system that a new reference point has been selected. In response, the heater generates and distributes more warm air. The temperature increases until the thermostat's sensory mechanisms determine that the actual temperature level is higher than the reference (desired) temperature. It then shuts the heat off until its sensory mechanisms indicate that the temperature has fallen below the desired reference point, when it signals the heater to reengage. The heater vacillates between on and off, producing a constantly variable source of heat that, on average, matches the actual and desired temperatures.

Cognitive systems differ, however, in that consciousness is an internal controlling agent that directs volitional, purposeful, and goal-directed behavior; it implies the existence of free will. Cognitive energetics theorists study the mental processes and biological processes that are linked to goal-directed behaviors. As depicted in figure 10.5, state regulation is controlled via three sources of processing: computation, emotion, and mental effort. Cognitive control that is exerted via computation uses the structures and functions of the information-processing system. Information flowing from sensory systems is perceived, stored, and manipulated according to formal and logical rules. The frontal lobes of the neocortex are implicated as key neurological structures involved in the process of computation and the initiation of action. Cognitive control that is exerted via emotion does not follow formal rules of logic or reason. The limbic system, which is composed of phylogenetically older brain structures than the neocortex, initiates automatic regulatory responses by way of structures of the autonomic nervous system. Discrepant environmental conditions lead to changes

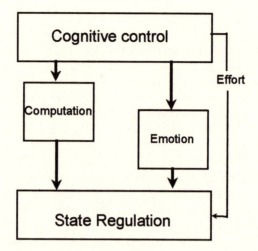

Figure 10.5.   Regulation of the Energetic State
From A. W. K. Gaillard & C. J. E. Wientjes (1998). Mental workload and work stress as two types of energy mobilization. *Work and Stress, 8,* 141–152. Figure 1, p. 142. Reprinted with permission by the author and by Taylor and Francis Ltd.

in physiological arousal (heart rate, respiration, etc.) that are linked to subjective feelings (such as anxiety and fear). Cognitive control that is exerted via mental effort reflects goal-oriented motivation that expresses itself in terms of trying harder (concentration and attentional focus) and the willingness to expend physical and mental resources. People use all three sources of processing during skill learning. The source that dominates state regulation at any moment is determined by a variety of experiential, ability, developmental, and situational factors.

Biological State Regulation

The roots of cognitive energetics can be traced to early research and theorizing about the concept of arousal and its role as a mechanism that underlies adaptive behavior (Hebb, 1955). Every activity performed, whether physical or mental, involves action and reaction to demands. Considerable neuropsychological research has been conducted during the past few decades to assess the manner in which various systems of the human body sense and respond to changes in environmental conditions. The human body has the capacity to monitor and sense discrepancies that exist between its expected state and its current state and, if necessary, to decrease the discrepancy. The body is equipped with a multitude of regulatory systems, many of which function without conscious awareness. We are, for example, unaware of the regulation of our body position as a function of gravity; nevertheless, the contractions and relaxation of muscle groups to maintain balance are ongoing.

There are biological systems, however, that, when brought into play, draw conscious awareness and influence the learning process. The sympathetic-adrenal-medullary arousal system has been implicated in the initiation of the fight-or-flight response. The neural connection between the hypothalamus (in the limbic system) and the adrenal gland (in the endocrine system) is of particular importance. When stimulated, the hypothalamus innervates a neural pathway that activates cells located in the medulla of the adrenal gland. These cells secrete adrenaline and noradrenaline into the bloodstream. The result is a brief increase in awareness, focused attention, and physical readiness to respond (Dienstbier, 1989). These neurohormonal processes are linked to optimal physical and mental performance and are associated with reports of pleasurable emotional feelings. The pituitary-adrenal-cortical arousal system links the activities of the pituitary gland and the release of hormones that travel to the cortex of the adrenal gland. The stimulation of the adrenal cortex results in a release of glucocorticoids, which function as a type of natural pain suppressor. However, high levels of circulating cortisol have been linked to reductions in performance levels and reports of negative feelings (Levinthal, 1990).

Psychobiological Arousal and Skill Learning

Arousal has been evaluated in many studies, and a number of theories of arousal have been postulated. One theme has remained constant throughout this research: arousal, depending on its level, can either facilitate or interfere with learning. Since the 1950s, much of the research in this area has focused on arousal in the context of stress, viewing it as an agent that leads to decrements in performance (McEwen and Mendelson, 1993). Researchers interested in examining the debilitating effects of high levels of arousal on performance employ the concept of stress in much the same way that mechanical engineers employed the term: stress is a force or pressure on an operator that has long-term negative consequences—breakdown or collapse. The work initiated by Hans Selye in the 1930s on the endocrinology of the stress response did much to facilitate the decremental view of arousal on performance and the notion that much of human behavior is focused on learning methods of coping with stress (Selye, 1993).

Cognitive energetic theorists differentiate a number of ways in which the concepts of stress and mental load differ (Gaillard and Wientjes, 1994). First, task-induced stress and mental load both disrupt an individual's physiological and psychological state, and both result in the mobilization of resources directed toward state regulation. The onset of a stressor, however, elicits a defensive coping response, which is directed toward reducing or avoiding a threat. The onset of a mental load elicits an active coping response, which is directed toward an analysis of the task at hand as a problem in need of solving. Second, when stressed, people report feelings of threat or being strained. When under increased mental load, however, they report positive feelings and increased energy. The distinction made between the emotional states produced by stress and mental load is similar to Selye's distinction between *distress*, which is destructive to health, and *eustress*, which is beneficial to health (Selye, 1976). Contemporary researchers similarly distinguish stress in terms of its potential for harm or for growth and challenge (Lazarus, 1993a, 1993b; Folkman and Lazarus, 1985). Third, stress results in generalized and pervasive arousal that continues to elicit coping responses even after the source of stress has terminated. The stress syndrome is characterized as a sequence of stages during which the activity of entire physiological systems heightens over time and leads to irreversible wear and tear. The arousal that is associated with mental load is more circumscribed than that produced by stress. Although physiological and psychological arousal are experienced during mental load, the arousal is maintained only until the problem is solved or terminated. Fourth, proponents of stress models suggest that the inefficient coping responses (errors) people make while attempting to reduce stress perpetuate a downward spiral of task avoidance and decreased motivation to perform the actions that are essential for success. Proponents of the workload concept suggest that people do not dwell on the errors they make; rather, they use the information as objective feedback to improve future performance. Task-relevant feedback motivates performers to engage in off-task problem analysis that, in turn, motivates them to reengage the task.

Evaluating instructional environments in terms of work load rather than stress evokes a very different picture of the impact of teaching on students. Educators who evaluate teaching in terms of stress outcomes perceive that the tasks pupils perform are taxing and capable of eliciting physical and mental defensive reactions, which gradually wear down and deplete students' resources. Instructional environments are seen as situations that may lead some students to experience distress, avoidance, and low levels of motivation. From this perspective, the teacher is also a counselor who instructs students in methods of acquiring and using coping strategies to manage the debilitating effects of stress.

The construct of mental load is inherently positive. Learning is seen as a naturally occurring process that helps students adapt to novel situations. The mental load experienced in instructional environments leads students to engage in cognitive control processes that are normal and healthy reactions to new learning situations. The central tenets of cognitive energetics theories suggest that although elements of stress in some teaching environments may have a detrimental influence on behavior, performance, and health, most learning experiences do not predispose students to poor physical and mental health.

Cognitive energetic models fill an important gap in understanding how interactions among the processes of the body, mind, and spirit influence learning and skill development. These models promote quantitative methods of measuring both physiological and psychological processes to understand the learning process.

SKILLS AS TOOLS

Skills have a function—they help us meet and overcome the demands encountered in our daily lives. There are many examples of survival benefits that are derived from learned skills. A young child who is taught the habit of stopping at a curbside and looking right and left before crossing the street decreases the chance of being struck by a vehicle. Children who have safety habits ingrained in them at an early age have a greater chance of surviving to adulthood than do children who have not been taught those basic skills.

Similar rationales are used for training novices in many sports, recreational activities, and occupations. Programs that teach people to scuba dive, hang-glide, or parachute require participants to go through considerable pretraining activities to learn safety skills. Novices are required to practice and demonstrate actions they would take if faced with various potentially dangerous scenarios. The parachutist, for example, is taught to respond in specific ways if the primary chute fails to deploy. Learning such survival skills is viewed by instructors as a critical prerequisite before trainees are allowed to engage in some sports, work, and leisure activities.

The mind helps the individual to solve problems and overcome challenges in two ways: 1) mindless thought—providing for automatic habitual actions that are executed without much thought or awareness, and 2) mindful thought—providing the means to use what has been learned and to adapt and apply it to new situations.

Mindless versus Mindful Thought

In many situations, repetitive, mindless action can be seen as advantageous to successful behavior. Consider what it would be like if you had to think about how to drive your car every time you got behind the wheel. All of the actions that we take for granted would be quite different if we could not learn to perform actions in habitual ways. Thus, there are situations in which it is adaptive to behave as if operating in a closed-loop system—a situation that is characterized by predictable relations between stimuli and responses and by actions that are performed in a mechanical fashion.

The mental automaticity that is acquired from practice is, however, a two-edged sword. There are situations in which mindless thought and action are counterproductive and even dangerous. Investigations of airplane and vehicular transportation accidents reveal that human errors often contribute to them. Mindless repetition of certain actions can lead pilots to miss vital information that is critical to flight safety.

Langer (1989) proposes that humans are shackled by mindless thought and action, and that passive, repetitive mental and behavioral activity is restrictive because it does not provide individuals with an opportunity to expand their knowledge and to be constructive. In Langer's view, people who approach problems in a mindless manner are locked into patterns of continuous reduction and regression of thought and patterns of mechanized action. Mindful thought is the preferred function of the mind because it provides humans with the potential to learn new things and control their destiny. She suggests that people who approach problems from a mindful perspective are capable of integrating new information and are open to different points of view.

Skill and Creativity

Creativity is reflected by a capacity to respond to a problem in ways that are both novel and useful (Sternberg and Lubart, 1999). The ability to develop original approaches to meet and overcome challenging situations is important not only for individuals, but also for society. Skilled behavior can be linked to the successful adaptation and evolution of the human species. Cultures that provide opportunities for individuals to develop, test, and implement new ways of dealing with societal problems gain an adaptive advantage over cultures that restrict individual originality and creativity (Csikszentmihalyi, 1999).

Academic interest in human creativity has recently become a popular area of study. Cultural anthropologists and archaeologists delve into ancient history to search for clues to the emergence of creative acts that propelled our ancestors from one level of behavioral sophistication to the next (Mithen, 1998). Psychologists suggest that creativity is a multifactorial phenomenon. Collins and Amabile (1999) propose that creative acts depend on the presence of three interactive components. The individual must possess the requisite domain-relevant skills (procedural skills acquired through training). The cognitive skills that lead to novel ways of solving domain-specific problems must also be present, as well as intrinsic motivation to persist at a challenging task until it is completed. Optimal creativity is predicted to occur when these three conditions intersect. (High levels of motivation will not overcome low levels of expertise, for example.) Creativity is not an incremental process; it occurs only when the conditions are right. Thus, it is difficult to predict when an individual will demonstrate a creative breakthrough or when to control creative processes by providing extrinsic rewards.

The component process model of creativity developed by Amabile (1983) emphasizes that skilled behavior reflects the interaction of body, mind, and spirit. Skills are tools that provide the means to use ingenuity to create breakthroughs essential to both the individual and society.

Skill and Pleasure

Many people report experiencing a feeling of pleasure when totally engrossed in performing certain activities. It is not unusual for those who engage in potentially dangerous activities (such as automobile racing, mountain climbing, or combat events) to describe moments of dissociation—a split between the rational problem-solving aspects and emotional aspects of the mind. Actions occur as if on automatic pilot; there is an accompanying feeling of complete control and invincibility. These feelings are not limited to individuals who engage in dangerous activities, however. A number of research studies have found that people sometimes experience similar feelings while performing more mundane tasks such as farming, homemaking, reading, writing, and driving (Csikszentmihalyi, 1997). Regardless of the type of task being performed, pleasurable states occur most often when people face situations that challenge their skill levels.

The pleasant experiences we derive from our actions are hypothesized to be linked to the activation of structures in the brain that modulate emotions and mood. There is considerable evidence for the existence of brain structures that control basic biological drives. There are also brain structures that provide us with pleasurable experiences when we use learned skills to overcome challenging or stressful situations. We are biologically programmed to be rewarded for learning new skills and putting them to use. It has been argued that the psychological experiences that we derive from our actions are modulated by naturally occurring biochemicals (endorphins). These substances function as both neurotransmitters and hormones, affecting sites throughout the brain and body.

Physical activity has been linked for centuries to positive changes in emotion and mood. Endurance runners, for example, describe periods during races when they stop feeling the physical discomforts of running and begin feeling exhilaration. Likewise, individuals placed in conditions of extreme physical and mental hardship sometimes describe a release from their pain and distress. A systematic scientific search for the biochemical agents responsible for these psychological changes was initiated only relatively recently. The result of this research was the isolation of what appears to be a naturally produced biochemical substance with properties that are similar to opiate drugs, such as morphine, which change our perceptions of pain.

There has been considerable discussion concerning the extent to which endorphins modulate brain functions. From an evolutionary perspective, it makes sense that humans are rewarded for learning skills in much the same way that we are rewarded for engaging in other behaviors that are critical to our personal survival and, ultimately, the survival of the human species.

The idea that skills provide the mechanism to induce a state of pleasurable enjoyment may explain, at least to some extent, what motivates people to take their skills beyond the level others have attained. Csikszentmihalyi (1975a) introduced a general theory of behavior that focuses on the positive holistic sensations experienced when a person is totally involved in an activity. He introduced the *flow* construct, a state in which an individual performs without having to actively think through the steps involved. There is action without objective thought during flow states. Csikszentmihalyi suggests that there are similarities between the flow construct and Maslow's construct of peak experience (Maslow, 1968). These terms have been used to define the uniquely exhilarating and enjoyable internal state that is sometimes experienced during intense physical and mental activity. Individuals who report experiencing the flow state consider it to be so unique and so compelling that they are sometimes willing to endure extreme hardships to experience the state again.

Csikszentmihalyi's work is directed toward assessing the subjective elements of activity, both the positive effect (*negentropic emotions*) experienced when an individual is in a flow state and the negative effect (*psychic entropy*) experienced in the absence of a flow state. In Csikszentmihalyi's general model (see figure 10.6) the type and intensity of emotion generated by a particular task or activity is determined by three factors: an individual's level of ability or skill level, the environmental demand placed on the individual, and the individual's perceptions of his or her ability to overcome the presented challenge. Boredom is experienced when environmental conditions are not sufficiently challenging; it can lead to an acute anxiety state when a highly skilled individual is not provided opportunities to use his or her abilities. A worried state is typically the outcome experienced when environmental demands begin to exceed an individual's skill level. This state may evolve into an anxiety state as environmental demands overwhelm the individual. A flow state will be experienced only when there is an even match between environmental demands and the individual's skill level.

A concept central to flow theory is that skills underlie the psychological experience that motivates people to action. With experience, an individual's skills and abilities improve; because of this skill improvement, a more challenging environment is required to attain the flow state the next time. Playing a musical instrument, for example, requires a minimum level of skill before even the simplest musical pieces can be played. The novice musician may feel a sense of exhilaration when she first masters a musical piece. With improvement in her skills, however, simple pieces begin to lose their ability to challenge her, and her mental state shifts to one of boredom. Retaining the flow experience requires a more challenging musical score or a more demanding variation of the piece. The number of hours that most concert-level musicians practice provides a straightforward example of the motivational influence of the flow experience.

Flow theory differentiates among three sources of human motivation: external motivation (behavior is linked to material rewards such as money, praise, and fame), internal motivation (behavior is linked to personal goals),

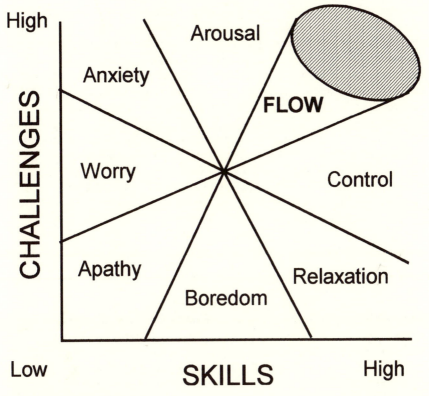

Figure 10.6.   Flow Model
From *Finding Flow: The Psychology of Engagement with Everyday Life* by Mihaly Csiksentmihalyi. Copyright 1997. Reprinted by permission of Basic Books, a member of Perseus Books, LLC.

and experiential motivation (behaviors are not linked to outcomes, but to the feeling generated by the act of performing). Experiential motivation provides the basis for the flow experience; an activity leads to joy and a heightened state of well-being (Csikszentmihalyi, 1978). Two individuals, for instance, may be equally skilled at playing a musical score; however, one may perceive that playing the piece is a chore and merely a way of acquiring fame and fortune, whereas the other might perceive playing the score as great fun and something to be enjoyed simply for its own sake. The flow experience is not related to extrinsic external rewards but, rather, to intrinsically generated emotions (Csikszentmihalyi, 1978).

Achieving a state of flow requires more than a situation in which environmental demands and skill levels are matched. The flow experience depends also on an individual's perception of his or her ability to meet the task at hand. There are situations in which one may have all the skills necessary to meet the environmental challenges presented and yet fail at the task. Csik-szentmihalyi suggests that individuals possess personality characteristics that play a role in determining the frequency and duration with which they can attain and maintain flow experiences. He sees the individual with an *autotelic* personality as one who has learned to engineer the environment to optimize opportunities to engage in activities that produce flow. It is not always the case that flow is obtained only from extreme activities such as mountain climbing, sky diving, or competitive sporting events. Flow is also experienced while performing such simple daily activities as cooking, cleaning, and painting. Any activity can be transformed into a challenging one by an individual. The person with the autotelic personality can make everyday tasks a source of flow. Individuals with autotelic personalities are seldom bored and rarely complain about monotony because they can constantly find challenges within their environment.

CHAPTER SUMMARY

Skills are more than just motor movements; they are products of the dynamic interaction of three pillars of human nature. Development of skill involves repetitive, mechanical practice that is well suited to our empirical nature. Skill also involves focusing attention on and solving problems in a rational fashion in which costs and benefits are carefully evaluated and weighed before choices are made. Finally, skills are linked to the emotions that drive the intensity and duration of physical and mental activity. These three dimensions of human behavior are interwoven. Attempts to separate these dynamic properties and to analyze them as individual components result in an incomplete understanding of skills and how they are used.

The three pillars that support human nature change as we move from birth to death. Life-span changes in physiological processes, mental processes, and motivational processes have profound effects on the skills we acquire throughout our lives and how we use those skills to adapt to the world around us.

SUGGESTED READINGS

Amabile, T. M. (1983). *The social psychology of creativity*. New York: Springer-Verlag.
Csikszentmihalyi, M. (1997). *Finding flow: The psychology of engagement with everyday life*. New York: Basic Books.
Csikszentmihalyi, M. (2000). *Beyond boredom and anxiety*. San Francisco: Jossey-Bass.
Csikszentmihalyi, M., and Csikszentmihalyi, I. S. (Eds.). (1988). *Optimal experience: Psychological studies of flow in consciousness*. Cambridge: Cambridge University Press.
Frankel, V. (1984). *Man's search for meaning* (Rev. ed.). New York: Washington Square Press.

Kahneman, D. (1973). *Attention and effort*. Englewood Cliffs, NJ: Prentice-Hall.

Langer, E. J. (1989). *Mindfulness*. Reading, MA: Addison Wesley.

van der Molen, M. W. (1996). Energetics and the reaction process: Running threads through experimental psychology. In O. Neumann and A. F. Sanders (Eds.), *Handbook of perception and action. Vol. 3: Attention* (pp. 229–276). New York: Academic Press.

Bibliography

Ackerman, P. L., and Kyllonen, P. C. (1991). Trainee characteristics. In J. E. Morrison (Ed.), *Training for performance: Principles of applied human learning* (pp. 193–229). New York: Wiley.

Adams, J. A. (1971). A closed-loop theory of motor learning. *Journal of Motor Behavior, 3,* 111–150.

Adams, J. A. (1976). Issues for a closed-loop theory of motor learning. In G. E. Stelmach (Ed.), *Motor control: Issues and trends* (pp. 87–107). New York: Academic Press.

Aiello, L. (1996). Hominine preadaptation for language and cognition. In P. Mellars and K. Gibson (Eds.), *Modeling the early human mind* (pp. 89–99). Cambridge, UK: McDonald Institute Monograph Series.

Amabile, T. M. (1983). *The social psychology of creativity.* New York: Springer-Verlag.

Ames, C. (1984). Competitive, cooperative, and individualistic goal structure: A cognitive-motivational analysis. In R. Ames and C. Ames (Eds.), *Research on motivation in education: Vol. 1. Student motivation* (pp. 177–208). New York: Academic Press.

Anastasi, A. (1982). *Psychological testing.* New York: Macmillan.

Anderson, J. R. (1982). Acquisition of cognitive skill. *Psychological Review, 89,* 369–406.

Anderson, J. R. (1983). *The architecture of cognition.* Cambridge, MA: Harvard University Press.

Anderson, J. R. (1987). Skill acquisition: Compilation of weak-method problem solutions. *Psychological Review, 94,* 192–210.

Anderson, J. R. (2000). *Learning and memory* (2nd ed.). New York: Wiley.

Atkinson, R. C., and Shiffrin, R. M. (1971). The control of short-term memory. *Scientific American, 225,* 82–90.

Baars, B. J. (1988). *A cognitive theory of consciousness.* Cambridge, UK: Cambridge University Press.

Backman, L., and Molander, B. (1991). On the generalizability of the age-related decline in coping with high arousal conditions in a precision sport: Replication and extension. *Journal of Gerontology: Psychological Sciences, 46,* P79–P81.

Baddeley, A. D. (1990). *Human memory: Theory and practice.* Needham Heights, MA: Allyn & Bacon.

Bailey, T. (1997). Changes in the nature of work: Implications for skills and assessment. In H. F. O'Neil, Jr. (Ed.), *Workforce readiness: Competencies and assessment* (pp. 27–45). Mahwah, NJ: Erlbaum.

Baltes, P. B., Staudinger, U., and Lindenberger. U. (1999). Lifespan psychology: Theory and application to intellectual functioning. In J. T. Spence, J. M. Darley, and D. J. Foss (Eds.), *Annual review of psychology, 50,* (pp. 471–507). Palo Alto, CA: Annual Reviews.

Bandura, A. (1977). *Social learning theory.* Englewood Cliffs, NJ: Prentice-Hall.

Bandura, A. (1997). *Self-efficacy: The exercise of control.* New York: W. H. Freeman.

Baron, A., and Menich, S. R. (1985a). Age-related effects of temporal contingencies on response speed and memory: An operant analysis. *Journal of Gerontology, 40,* 60–70.

Baron, A., and Menich, S. R. (1985b). Reaction times of younger and older men: Effects of compound samples and a prechoice signal on delayed matching-to-sample performances. *Journal of the Experimental Analysis of Behavior, 44,* 1–14.

Baron, A., Menich, S. R., and Perone, M. (1983). Reaction times of younger and older men and temporal contingencies of reinforcement. *Journal of the Experimental Analysis of Behavior, 40,* 275–287.

Bartlett, F. (1958). *Thinking: An experimental and social study.* New York: Basic Books.

Baumeister, A. A. (1984). Some methodological and conceptual issues in the study of cognitive processes with retarded people. In P. H. Brooks, R. Sperber, and C. Mc-Cauley (Eds.), *Learning and cognition in the mentally retarded* (pp. 1–38). Hillsdale, NJ: Erlbaum.

Berk, L. E. (2000). *Child development* (5th ed.). Boston: Allyn & Bacon.

Berlyne, D. E. (1960). *Conflict, arousal, and curiosity.* New York: McGraw-Hill.

Berryman, J. W. (1996). The rise of boys' sports in the United States. In F. L. Smoll and R. E. Smith (Eds.), *Children and youth in sport: A biopsychosocial perspective* (pp. 4–14). Madison, WI: Brown and Benchmark.

Birren, J. E., and Zarit, J. M. (1985). Concepts of health, behavior, and aging. In J. E. Birren and J. Livingston (Eds.), *Cognition, stress and aging* (pp. 1–20) Englewood Cliffs, NJ: Prentice-Hall.

Blumenthal, J. A., Emery, C. F., Madden, D. J., George, L. K., Coleman, E., Riddle, M. W., McKee, D. C., Reasoner, J., and Williams, R. S. (1989). Cardiovascular and behavioral effects of aerobic exercise training in healthy older men and women. *Journal of Gerontology: Medical Sciences, 44,* M147–M157.

Blumenthal, J. A., Emery, C. F., Madden, D. J., Schniebolk, S., Walsh-Riddle, M., George, L. K., McKee, D. C., Higginbotham, M. B., Cobb, F. R., and Coleman, R. E. (1991). Long-term effects of exercise on psychological functioning in older men and women. *Journal of Gerontology: Psychological Sciences, 46,* P352–P361.

Blumenthal, J. A., and Madden, D. J. (1988). Effects of aerobic exercise training, age, and physical fitness on memory search performance. *Psychology and Aging, 3,* 280–285.

Borstelmann, L. J. (1983). Children before psychology: Ideas about children from antiquity to the late 1800s. In P. H. Mussen (Ed.), *Handbook of child psychology* (pp. 1–40). New York: Wiley.

Brant, R. S. (2000). *Education in a new era*. Alexandria, VA: Association for Supervision and Curriculum Development.

Bronowski, J. (1973). *The ascent of man*. Boston: Little, Brown.

Brown, J. A. (1958). Some tests of the decay theory of immediate memory. *Quarterly Journal of Experimental Psychology, 10,* 12–21.

Bush, D. M., and Simmons, R. (1981). Socialization processes over the life course. In M. Rosenberg and R. H. Turner (Eds.), *Social psychology: Sociological perspective* (pp. 33–64). New York: Basic Books.

Cannon, W. B. (1929). *Bodily changes in pain, hunger, fear, and rage*. Boston: Branford.

Cannon, W. B. (1935). Stresses and strains of homeostasis. *American Journal of Medical Science, 189,* 1–14.

Carpenter, C. B. (1894). *Principles of mental physiology*. New York: Appleton.

Carver, C. S., and Scheier, M. F. (1981). *Attention and self-regulation: A control-therapy approach to human behavior*. Berlin: Springer-Verlag.

Carver, C. S., and Scheier, M. F. (1988). A control-process perspective on anxiety. *Anxiety Research, 1,* 17–22.

Cattell, R. B. (1963). Theory of fluid and crystallized intelligence: A critical experiment. *Journal of Educational Psychology, 54,* 1–22.

Cerella, J. (1985). Information processing rates in the elderly. *Psychological Bulletin, 98,* 67–83.

Cerella, J. (1990). Aging and information-processing rate. In J. E. Birren and K. W. Schaie (Eds.), *Handbook of the psychology of aging* (3rd ed.) (pp. 201–221). New York: Academic Press.

Chase, W. G., and Ericsson, K. A. (1981). Skilled memory. In J. R. Anderson (Ed.), *Cognitive skills and their acquisition* (pp. 141–189). Hillsdale, NJ: Erlbaum.

Chase, W. G., and Ericsson, K. A. (1982). Skill and working memory. In G. H. Bower (Ed.), *The psychology of learning and motivation* (pp. 1–58). New York: Academic Press.

Chi, M. T. H. (1976). Short-term memory limitations in children: Capacity or processing deficits? *Memory and Cognition, 4,* 559–572.

Chi, M. T. H. (1977). Age differences in speed of processing: A critique. *Developmental Psychology, 13,* 543–544.

Chi, M. T. H. (1978). Knowledge structures and memory development. In R. S. Siegler (Ed.), *Children's thinking: What develops?* (pp. 73–96). Hillsdale, NJ: Erlbaum.

Chodzko-Zajko, W. J. (Ed.). (1997). The World Health Organization issues guidelines for promoting physical activity among older persons. *Journal of Aging and Physical Activity, 5,* 1–8.

Clark, J. E., Lanphear, A. K., and Riddick, C. C. (1987). The effects of videogame playing on the response selection processing of elderly adults. *Journal of Gerontology, 42,* 82–85.

Clarke-Stewart, A., Perlmutter, M., and Friedman, S. (1988). *Lifelong human development*. New York: Wiley.

Cofer, C. N. (1972). *Motivation and Emotion*. Glenview, IL: Scott, Foresman.

Cohen, N., and Squire, L. R. (1980). Preserved learning and retention of pattern analyzing skill in amnesia: dissociation of knowing how and knowing that. *Science, 210,* 207–209.

Colley, A. M. (1989). Cognitive motor skills. In D. H. Holding (Ed.), *Human skills* (2nd ed.) (pp. 229–248) New York: Wiley.

Collins, A., Brown, J. S., and Newman, S. E. (1989). Cognitive apprenticeship: Teaching the crafts of reading, writing, and mathematics. In L. Resnick (Ed.), *Knowing, learning, and instruction: Essays in honor of Robert Glaser* (pp. 453–494). Hillsdale, NJ: Erlbaum.

Collins, M. A., and Amabile, T. M. (1999). Motivation and creativity. In R. J. Sternberg (Ed.), *Handbook of creativity* (pp. 297–312). New York: Cambridge University Press.

Condry, J., and Chambers, J. (1978). Intrinsic motivation and the process of learning. In M. R. Lepper and D. Greene (Eds.), *The hidden costs of rewards: New perspectives on the psychology of human motivation* (pp. 61–84). Hillsdale, NJ: Erlbaum.

Conrad, S. (1992). Old age in the modern and postmodern Western world. In T. R. Cole, D. D. Van Tassel, and R. Kastenbaum (Eds.), *Handbook of the humanities and aging* (pp. 62–95). New York: Springer.

Cornelius, S. W., and Caspi, A. (1986). Self-perceptions of intellectual control and aging. *Educational Gerontology, 12,* 345–357.

Cosmides, L., and Tooby, J. (1994). Origins of domain specificity: The evolution of functional organization. In L. A. Hirschfeld and S. A. Gelman (Eds.), *Mapping the mind: Domain specificity in cognition and culture* (pp. 85–116). Cambridge, UK: Cambridge University Press.

Craik, F. I. M., and Jennings, J. M. (1992). Human memory. In F. I. M. Craik and T. A. Salthouse (Eds.), *Handbook of aging and cognition* (pp. 51–110). Hillsdale, NJ: Erlbaum.

Craik, F. I. M., and Lockhart, R. S. (1972). Levels of processing: A framework for memory research. *Journal of Verbal Learning and Verbal Behavior, 11,* 671–684.

Crick, F. H. C. (1994). *The astonishing hypothesis: The scientific search for the soul.* New York: Scribner.

Csikszentmihalyi, M. (1975a). *Beyond boredom and anxiety.* San Francisco: Jossey-Bass.

Csikszentmihalyi, M. (1975b). Play and intrinsic rewards. *Journal of Humanistic Psychology, 15,* 41–63.

Csikszentmihalyi, M. (1978). Intrinsic rewards and emergent motivation. In M. R. Lepper and D. Greene (Eds.), *The hidden costs of rewards: New perspectives on the psychology of human motivation* (pp. 205–216). Hillsdale, NJ: Erlbaum.

Csikszentmihalyi, M. (1981). Some paradoxes in the definition of play. In A. Cheska (Ed.), *Play as context* (pp. 14–26). New York: Leisure Press.

Csikszentmihalyi, M. (1990). *Flow: The psychology of optimal experience.* New York: Harper & Row.

Csikszentmihalyi, M. (1993). *The evolving self: A psychology for the third millennium.* New York: HarperCollins.

Csikszentmihalyi, M. (1997). *Finding flow: The psychology of engagement with everyday life.* New York: Basic Books.

Csikszentmihalyi, M. (1999). Implication of a systems perspective for the study of creativity. In R. J. Sternberg (Ed.), *Handbook of creativity* (pp. 313–335). New York: Cambridge University Press.

Csikszentmihalyi, M. (2000). *Beyond boredom and anxiety.* San Francisco: Jossey-Bass.

Csikszentmihalyi, M., and Bennett, H. S. (1971). An exploratory model of play. *American Anthropologist, 73*, 45–58.

Csikszentmihalyi, M., and Csikszentmihalyi, I. S. (eds.). (1988). *Optimal experience: Psychological studies of flow in consciousness.* Cambridge, UK: Cambridge University Press.

Csikszentmihalyi, M., and Schneider, B. (2000). *Becoming adult: How teenagers prepare for the world of work.* New York: Basic Books.

Cummings, R. (1995). *Adolescence: A developmental perspective.* New York: Harcourt Brace College Publishers.

Cytrynbaum, S., Blum, L., Patrick, R., Stein, J., Wadner, D., and Wilk, C. (1980). Midlife development: A personality and social systems perspective. In L. W. Poon (ed.), *Aging in the 1980s* (463–474). Washington, DC: American Psychological Association.

Cziko, G. (1995). *Without miracles: Universal selection theory and the second Darwinian revolution.* London: MIT Press.

Darwin, C. (1859). *On the origin of species by means of natural selection.* London: Murray.

Darwin, C. (1872). *The expression of emotions in man and animals.* London: Murray.

Dawkins, R. (1976). *The selfish gene.* London: Oxford University Press.

Dawkins, R. (1986). *The blind watchmaker.* Harmondsworth, UK: Penguin Books.

Dawkins, R. (1995). *River out of Eden.* New York: Weidenfeld and Nicolson.

DeCharms, R. (1968). *Personal causation: The internal affective determinants of behavior.* New York: Academic Press.

Deci, E. L., and Porac, J. (1978). Cognitive evaluation theory and the study of human motivation. In M. R. Lepper and D. Greene (Eds.), *The hidden costs of rewards: New perspectives on the psychology of human motivation* (pp. 149–178). Hillsdale, NJ: Erlbaum.

Deci, E. L., and Ryan, R. M. (1985). *Intrinsic motivation and self determination in human behavior.* New York: Plenum Press.

Deci, E., and Ryan, R. M. (1991). A motivational approach to self: Integration in personality. In R. A. Dienstbier (Ed.), *Nebraska symposium on motivation: Perspectives on motivation* (pp. 237–288). Lincoln, NE: University of Nebraska Press.

Deci, E. L., Vallerand, R. J., Pelletier, L. G., and Ryan, R. M. (1991). Motivation and education: The self-determination perspective. *The Educational Psychologist, 26,* 325–346.

de Groot, A. ([1946] 1978). *Thought and choice in chess.* The Hague, The Netherlands: Mouton.

Delaney, R., and Ravdin, L. D. (1997). The neuropsychology of stroke. In P. D. Nussbaum (Ed.). *Handbook of neuropsychology and aging* (pp. 315–333). New York: Plenum Press.

de Luce, J. (1994). Ancient images of aging. Did ageism exist in Greco-Roman Antiquity? In D. Shenk and W. A. Achenbaum (Eds.), *Changing perceptions of aging and the aged.* (pp. 65–74). New York: Springer.

Dienstbier, R. A. (1989). Arousal and physiological toughness: Implications for mental and physical health. *Psychological Review, 96,* 84–100.

Dienstbier, R. A. (1991). Behavioral correlates of sympathoadrenal reactivity: The toughness model. *Medicine and Science in Sports and Exercise, 23,* 846–852.

Dishman, R. K. (1988). *Exercise adherence: Its impact on public health.* Champaign, IL: Human Kinetics.

Donders, F. C. (1969). On speed of mental processes. In W. G. Koster (Ed. and Trans.), *Attention and performance II* (pp. 412–431). Amsterdam: North Holland. (Original work published 1868)

Druckman, D., and Bjork, R. A. (Eds.). (1991). *In the mind's eye: Enhancing human performance*. Washington, DC: National Academy Press.

Dunbar, R. I. M. (1992). Neocortex size as a constraint on group size in primates. *Journal of Human Evolution, 20,* 469–493.

Dunbar, R. I. M. (1993). Coevolution of neocortical size, group size and language in humans. *Behavioral and Brain Sciences, 16,* 681–735.

Dustman, R. E., Emmerson, R. Y., Steinhaus, L. A., Shearer, D. E., and Dustman, T. J. (1992). The effects of videogame playing on neuropsychological performance of elderly individuals. *Journal of Gerontology: Psychological Sciences, 47,* P168–P171.

Dustman, R. E., Ruhling, R. O., Russell, E. M., Shearer, D. E., Bonekat, H. W., Shieoka, J. W., Wood, J. S., and Bradford, D. C. (1984). Aerobic exercise training and improved neuropsychological function of older individuals. *Neurobiology of Aging, 5,* 35–42.

Easterbrook, J. A. (1959). The effect of emotion on the utilization and the organization of behavior. *Psychological Review, 66,* 183–201.

Eckensberger, L. H., and Meacham, J. A. (1984). Action theory, control and motivation: A symposium. *Human Development, 27,* 163–210.

Ellis, H. C., and Hunt, R. R. (1993). *Fundamentals of cognitive psychology* (5th ed.). Madison, WI: Brown and Benchmark.

Elsayed, M., Ismail, A. H., and Young, R. J. (1980). Intellectual differences of adult men related to age and physical fitness before and after an exercise program. *Journal of Gerontology, 35,* 383–387.

Ericsson, A. A. (Ed.). (1996). *The road to excellence: The acquisition of expert performance in the arts and sciences, sports, and games.* Mahwah, NJ: Erlbaum.

Ericsson, K. A., Krampe, R. T., and Heizmann, S. (1993). Can we create gifted people? In CIBA Foundation Symposium 178, *The origin and development of high ability* (pp. 222–249). Chichester, UK: Wiley.

Ericsson, K. A., Krampe, R. T., and Tesch-Romer, C. (1993). The role of deliberate practice in the acquisition of expert performance. *Psychological Review, 100,* 363–406.

Ericsson, K. A., and Oliver, W. L. (1995). Cognitive skills. In N. J. Mackintosh and A. M. Colman (Eds.), *Learning and skills* (pp. 37–55). New York: Longman.

Erikson, E. (1950). *Childhood and society.* New York: Norton.

Erikson, E. (1963). *Childhood and society* (2nd ed.). New York: Norton.

Erikson, E. (1968). *Identity, youth, and crisis.* New York: Norton.

Evers, F. T., Rush, J. C., and Berdrow, I. (1998). *The bases of competence: Skills for lifelong learning and employability.* San Francisco: Jossey-Bass.

Evers, W. M. (Ed.). (1998). *What's wrong in America's classrooms.* Stanford, CA: Hoover Institution Press.

Ewing, M. E., and Seefeldt, V. (1996). Patterns of participation and attrition in American agency-sponsored youth sports. In F. L. Smoll and R. E. Smith (Eds.), *Children and youth in sport: A biopsychosocial perspective* (pp. 31–45). Madison, WI: Brown and Benchmark.

Falkner, T. M., and de Luce, J. (1992). A view from antiquity: Greece, Rome, and elders. In T. R. Cole, D. D. Van Tassel, and R. Kastenbaum (Eds.), *Handbook of the humanities and aging* (pp. 3–39). New York: Springer.

Feltz, D. L., and Landers, D. M. (1983). The effects of mental practice on motor skill learning and performance: A meta-analysis. *Journal of Sport Psychology, 5,* 25–57.

Feltz, D. L., Landers, D. M., and Becker, B. J. (1988). A revised meta-analysis of the mental practice literature on motor skill learning. In D. Druckman and J. A. Swets (Eds.), *Enhancing human performance: Issues, theories, and techniques, Background papers* (pp. 1–65). Washington, DC: National Academy Press.

Fisk, A. D., and Rogers, W. A. (1991). Toward an understanding of age-related memory and visual search effects. *Journal of Experimental Psychology: General, 120,* 131–149.

Fitts, P. M. (1954). The information capacity of the human motor system in controlling the amplitude of movement. *Journal of Experimental Psychology, 47,* 381–391.

Fitts, P. M. (1964). Perceptual-motor skills learning. In A. W. Melton (Ed.), *Categories of human learning* (pp. 243–285). New York: Academic Press.

Fitts, P. M., and Posner, M. I. (1967). *Human performance.* Belmont, CA: Brooks/Cole.

Flavell, J. H. (1985). *Cognitive development* (2nd ed.). Englewood Cliffs, NJ: Prentice-Hall.

Flavell, J. H., Miller, P. H., and Miller, S. A. (1993). *Cognitive development* (2nd ed.). Englewood Cliffs, NJ: Prentice-Hall.

Fleishman, E. A., and Quaintance, M. K. (1984). *Taxonomies of human performance: The description of human tasks.* Potomac, MD: Management Research Institute.

Folkman, S., and Lazarus, R. S. (1985). If it changes it must be a process: Study of emotions and coping during three stages of a college examination. *Journal of Personality and Social Psychology, 48,* 150–170.

Frankel, V. (1984). *Man's search for meaning* (Rev. ed.). New York: Washington Square Press.

Freud, S. (1910/1949). *The origins and development of psychoanalysis.* Chicago: Regnery.

Frijda, N. H. (1986). *The emotions.* Cambridge, UK: Cambridge University Press.

Gaillard, A. W. K., and Wientjes, C. J. E. (1994). Mental workload and work stress as two types of energy mobilization. *Work and Stress, 8,* 141–152.

Gallagher, J. D., French, K. E., Thomas, K. T., and Thomas, J. R. (1996). Expertise in youth sport: Relation between knowledge and skill. In F. L. Smoll and R. E. Smith (Eds.), *Children and youth in sport: A biopsychosocial perspective* (pp. 338–358). Madison, WI: Brown and Benchmark.

Gibson, E. J. (1969). *Principles of perceptual learning and development.* New York: Academic Press.

Glaser, R. (1984). Education and thinking: The role of knowledge. *American Psychologist, 39,* 93–104.

Glaser, R., and Bassok, M. (1989) Learning theory and the study of instruction. *Annual Review of Psychology, 40,* 631–666.

Greene, A. L., and Larson, R. W. (1991). Variation in stress reactivity during adolescence. In E. M. Cummings, A. L. Greene, and K. H. Karraker (Eds.), *Life-span development psychology: Perspectives on stress and coping* (pp. 195–209). Hillsdale, NJ: Erlbaum.

Guilford, J. P. (1967). *The nature of human intelligence.* New York: McGraw-Hill.

Hall, K. G., Dominques, D. A., and Cavazos, R. (1994). Contextual interference effects with skilled baseball players. *Perceptual and Motor Skills, 78,* 835–841.

Hardy, L., Jones, G., and Gould, D. (1997). *Understanding psychological preparation for sport: Theory and practice of elite performers.* New York: Wiley.

Hasher, L., and Zacks, R. T. (1979). Automatic and effortful processes in memory. *Journal of Experimental Psychology: General, 108,* 356–388.

Hasher, L., and Zacks, R. T. (1988). Working memory, comprehension, and aging: A review and a new view. In G. Bower (Ed.), *The psychology of learning and motivation* (Vol. 22) (pp. 193–225). New York: Academic Press.

Havighurst, R. J. (1972). *Developmental tasks and education* (3rd ed.). New York: David McKay.

Hawkins, H. L., Kramer, A. F., and Capaldi, D. (1992). Aging, exercise, and attention. *Psychology and Aging, 7,* 643–653.

Hayes, J. R. (1981). *The complete problem solver.* Philadelphia: The Francis Institute.

Hayes, J. R. (1989). *The complete problem solver* (2nd ed.). Hillsdale, NJ: Erlbaum.

Hayflick, L. (1977). The cellular basis for biological aging. In C. E. Firch and L. Hayflick (Eds.), *Handbook of the biology of aging* (pp. 159–186). New York: Van Nostrand Reinhold.

Haywood, K. M. (1993). *Life span motor development.* Champaign, IL: Human Kinetics.

Hebb, D. O. (1955). Drives and the C.N.S. (conceptual nervous system). *Psychological Review, 62,* 243–254.

Heckenmuller, J. (1985). Cognitive control and endorphins as mechanisms of health. In J. E. Birren and J. Livingston (Eds.), *Cognition, stress and aging* (pp. 89–110). Englewood Cliffs, NJ: Prentice-Hall.

Hergenhahn, B. R. (1992). *An introduction to the history of psychology* (2nd ed.). Belmont, CA: Wadsworth.

Hertzog, C. K. (1989). Influences of cognitive slowing on age differences in intelligence. *Developmental Psychology, 25,* 636–651.

Hertzog, C. K., Dixon, R. A., and Hultsch, D. F. (1990). Metamemory in adulthood: Differentiating knowledge, belief, and behavior. In T. M. Hess (Ed.), *Aging and cognition: Knowledge, organization and utilization* (pp. 161–212). Amsterdam: North Holland.

Hetherington, E. M., and Baltes, P. B. (1988) Child psychology and life-span development. In E. M. Hetherington, R. M. Lerner and M. Perlmutter (Eds.), *Child development in life-span perspective* (pp. 1–19). Hillsdale, NJ: Erlbaum.

Hick, W. E. (1952). On the rate of gain of information. *Quarterly Journal of Experimental Psychology, 4,* 11–26.

Hilgard, E. R. (1980). The trilogy of mind: Cognition, affection, and conation. *Journal of the History of Behavioral Sciences, 16,* 107–117.

Hill, R. D., Sheikh, J. I., and Yesavage, J. (1988). The effect of mnemonic training on perceived recall confidence in the elderly. *Experimental Aging Research, 13,* 185–188.

Hinshaw, K. E. (1991–1992). The effects of mental practice on motor skill performance: Critical evaluation and meta-analysis. *Imagination, Cognition, and Personality, 11,* 3–35.

Hobbes, T. (1962). *Leviathan.* New York: Macmillan. (Original work published 1651.)

Hockey, G. R. J., Coles, M. G. H., and Gaillard, A. W. K. (1986). Energetical issues in research on human information process. In G. R. J. Hockey, A. W. K. Gaillard, and

M. G. H. Coles (Eds.), *Energetics and human information processing* (pp. 3–40) Boston: Martinus Nijhoff.

Hole, F. (1992). Origins of agriculture. In S. Jones, R. Martin, and D. Pilbeam (Eds.), *The Cambridge encyclopedia of human evolution* (pp. 373–379). Cambridge, UK: Cambridge University Press.

Holloway, R. L. (1979). The casts of fossil hominid brains. *Readings from Scientific American: Human ancestors* (pp. 74–83). San Francisco: W. H. Freeman.

Horn, T. S., and Harris, A. (1996). Perceived competence in young athletes: Research findings and recommendations for coaches and parents. In F. L. Smoll and R. E. Smith (Eds.), *Children and youth in sport: A biopsychosocial perspective* (pp. 309–329). Madison, WI: Brown and Benchmark.

Hubel, D. (1988). *Eye, brain, and vision*. New York: Scientific American Library.

Hughes, F. P. (1999). *Child, play and development* (3rd ed.). Boston: Allyn & Bacon.

Hull, C. L. (1952). *A behavior system*. New Haven, CT: Yale University Press.

Hultsch, D., and Dixon, R. (1990). Learning and memory and aging. In J. E. Birren and K. W. Schaie (Eds.), *Handbook of the psychology of aging* (3rd ed., pp. 258–274). New York: Academic Press.

Human Evolution: Migration. (2001). *Science, 291,* 1721–1753.

Hyman, R. (1953). Stimulus information as a determinant of reaction time. *Journal of Experimental Psychology, 45,* 188–196.

Irwin, S. (1995). *Rights of passage: Social change and the transition to adulthood*. London: UCL Press.

Isaac, G. (1979). The food-sharing behavior of protohuman hominids. *Readings from Scientific American: Human ancestors* (pp. 110–123). San Francisco: W. H. Freeman.

Jacobson, E. (1929). *Progressive relaxation*. Chicago: University of Chicago Press.

James, W. (1890). *The principles of psychology* (Vols. 1 and 2). New York: Holt.

James, W. (1963). *Psychology: The briefer course*. New York: Harper. (Original work published 1892.)

Johnson, H. A. (1985). Is aging physiological or pathological? In H. A. Johnson (Ed.), *Relations between normal aging and disease* (pp. 239–247). New York: Raven.

Johnson, J. E., Christie, J. F., and Yawkey, T. D. (1987). *Play and early childhood development*. Glenview, IL: Scott, Foresman.

Kahneman, D. (1973). *Attention and effort*. Englewood Cliffs, NJ: Prentice-Hall.

Kail, R., and Bisanz, J. (1992). The information-processing perspective on cognitive development in childhood and adolescence. In R. J. Sternberg and C. A. Berg (Eds.), *Intellectual development* (pp. 229–260). Cambridge, UK: Cambridge University Press.

Kaplan, G. A., and Simon, H. A. (1990). In search of insight. *Cognitive Psychology, 22,* 374–419.

Kart, G. S. (1997). *The realities of aging: An introduction to gerontology* (5th ed.). New York: Allyn & Bacon.

Kaye, D. N., and Ruskin, E. M. (1990). The development of attentional control mechanisms. In J. T. Enns (Ed.), *The development of attention: Research and theory* (pp. 227–244). New York: North Holland.

Kazdin, A. E. (1994). *Behavior modification in applied settings* (5th ed.). Pacific Grove, CA: Brooks/Cole.

Kellogg, R. T. (1995). *Cognitive psychology*. Thousand Oaks, CA: Sage.

Kiefer, C. W. (1992). Aging in Eastern cultures: A historical overview. In T. R. Cole, D. D. Van Tassel, and R. Kastenbaum (Eds.), *Handbook of the humanities and aging* (pp. 96–135). New York: Springer.

Kline, D. W., and Scialfa, C. T. (1996). Sensory functions and aging. In J. E. Birren and K. W. Schaie (Eds.), *Handbook of the psychology of aging* (4th ed., pp. 181–203). New York: Academic Press.

Kline, P. (2000). *A psychometrics primer*. London: Free Press.

Kobasa, S. C. (1979). Stressful life events, personality, and health: An inquiry into hardiness. *Journal of Personality and Social Psychology, 37,* 1–11.

Kobasa, S., Maddi, S., and Kahn, S. (1982). Hardiness and health: A prospective study. *Journal of Personality and Social Psychology, 42,* 168–177.

Kolb, B., and Whishaw, I. Q. (1990). *Fundamentals of human neurophysiology*. New York: W. H. Freeman.

Kolers, P. A. (1975). Specificity of operations in sentence recognition. *Cognitive Psychology, 7,* 289–306.

Kramer, D. (1983). Post-formal operations? A need for further conceptualization. *Human Development, 26,* 91–105.

Kretchmar, R. S. (1994). *Practical philosophy of sport*. Champaign, IL: Human Kinetics.

Langer, E. J. (1989). *Mindfulness*. Reading, MA: Addison Wesley.

Langley, L. L., Telford, I. R., and Christensen, J. B. (1969). *Dynamic anatomy and physiology* (3rd ed.) New York: McGraw-Hill, p. 301.

Larue, G. A. (1985). Historical perspectives on the role of the elderly: The most ancient evidence. In G. Lesnoff-Caravaglia (Ed.), *Values, ethics and aging* (pp. 41–61). New York: Human Sciences Press.

Latash, M. L. (1998). *Neurophysiological basis of movement*. Champaign, IL: Human Kinetics.

Lazarus, R. S. (1993a). From psychological stress to the emotions: A history of changing outlooks. *Annual Review of Psychology, 44,* 1–24.

Lazarus, R. S. (1993b). Why we should think of stress as a subset of emotion. In L. Goldberg and S. Breznitz (Eds.), *Handbook of stress: Theoretical and clinical aspects* (2nd ed., pp. 21–39). New York: Free Press.

LeDoux, J. E. (1997). Emotion, memory and the brain. *Scientific American Mysteries of the Mind, Special Issue, 7,* 68–83.

Leonard, C. T. (1998). *The neuroscience of human movement*. New York: Mosby.

Lerner, R. M. (1986). *Concepts and theories of human development* (2nd ed.). New York: Random House.

Levinson, D. J. (1978). *The seasons of a man's life*. New York: Knopf.

Levinthal, C. F. (1990). *Introduction to physiological psychology* (3rd ed.). Englewood Cliffs, NJ: Prentice-Hall.

Lewin, K. (1935). *A dynamic theory of personality: Selected papers*. New York: McGraw-Hill.

Lewin, K. (1936). *Principles of topological psychology*. New York: McGraw-Hill.

Light, K., and Spirduso, W. (1990). Effects of adult aging on the movement complexity factor or response programming. *Journal of Gerontology: Psychological Sciences, 45,* P107–P109.

Light, L. L. (1991). Memory and aging: Four hypotheses in search of data. *Annual Review of Psychology, 42,* 333–376.

Lord, R. H., and Kozar, B. (1996). Overuse injuries in young athletes. In F. L. Smoll and R. E. Smith (Eds.), *Children and youth in sport: A biopsychosocial perspective* (pp. 281–294). Madison, WI: Brown and Benchmark.

Lundin, R. W. (1985). *Theories and systems of psychology* (3rd ed.). Lexington, MA: Heath.

Lutz, J. (1994). *Introduction to learning and memory*. Pacific Grove, CA: Brooks/Cole.

MacLean, P. D. (1970). The triune brain, emotion and scientific bias. In F. O. Schmitt (Ed.), *The neurosciences: Second study program* (pp. 336–349). New York: Rockefeller University Press.

MacLean, P. D. (1990). *The triune brain in evolution: Role in paleocerebral functions*. New York: Plenum Press.

Madden, D. J., Blumenthal, J. A., Allen, P. A., and Emergy, C. F. (1989). Improving aerobic capacity in healthy older adults does not necessarily lead to improved cognitive performance. *Psychology and Aging, 4*, 307–320.

Magill, R. A. (1993). *Motor learning: Concepts and applications* (4th ed.). Madison, WI: Brown and Benchmark.

Magill, R. A. (1998). *Motor learning: Concepts and applications* (5th ed.). Boston: McGraw-Hill.

Magill, R. A., and Anderson, D. I. (1996). Critical periods as optimal readiness for learning sport skills. In F. L. Smoll and R. E. Smith (Eds.), *Children and youth in sport: A biopsychosocial perspective* (pp. 57–72). Madison, WI: Brown and Benchmark.

Magill, R. A., and Hall, K. G. (1990). A review of the contextual interference effect in motor skill acquisition. *Human Movement Science, 9*, 241–289.

Maier, H. W. (1969). *Three theories of child development*. New York: Harper & Row.

Malina, R. M. (1996). The young athlete: Biological growth and maturation in a biocultural context. In F. L. Smoll and R. E. Smith (Eds.), *Children and youth in sport: A biopsychosocial perspective* (pp. 161–186). Madison, WI: Brown and Benchmark.

Marcia, J. E. (1991). Identity in adolescence. In R. M. Lerner, A. C. Peterson, and J. Brooks-Gunn (Eds.), *Encyclopedia of adolescence* (Vol. 1, pp. 529–533). New York: Garland.

Maslow, A. H. (1968). *Toward a psychology of being*. New York: Van Nostrand.

Maslow, A. H. (1987). *Motivation and personality* (3rd ed.). New York: Harper & Row.

McEwen, B. S., and Mendelson, S. (1993). Effects of stress on the neurochemistry and morphology of the brain: Counterregulation versus damage. In L. Goldberg and S. Breznitz (Eds.), *Handbook of stress: Theoretical and clinical aspects* (2nd ed., pp. 101–126). New York: Free Press.

McKelvie, S. J. (1985). Einstellung: Still alive and well. *Journal of General Psychology, 112*, 313–315.

Mechikoff, R., and Estes, S. (1993). *A history and philosophy of sport and physical education*. Madison, WI: Brown and Benchmark.

Miller, G. A. (1956). The magical number seven, plus or minus two: Some limits on our capacity for processing information. *Psychological Review, 63*, 81–97.

Miller, G. A., Galanter, E., and Pribram, K. H. (1960). *Plans and the structure of behavior*. New York: Holt.

Mithen, S. (1996). *The prehistory of the mind: The cognitive origins of art and science*. New York: Thames and Hudson.

Mithen, S. (1998). The archaeological study of human creativity. In S. Mithen (Ed.), *Creativity in human evolution and prehistory* (pp. 1–15). New York: Routledge.

Moody, H. R. (1986). Late life learning in the information society. In D. A. Peterson, J. E. Thornton, and J. E. Birren (Eds.), *Education and aging* (pp. 122–148). Englewood Cliffs, NJ: Prentice-Hall.

Morgan, W. P. (1989). Sport psychology in its own context: A recommendation for the future. In J. S. Skinner, C. B. Corbin, D. M. Landers, P. E. Martin, and C. L. Wells (Eds.), *Future directions in exercise and sport science* (pp. 97–110). Champaign, IL: Human Kinetics.

Morris, W. N. (1989). *Mood: The frame of mind*. New York: Springer-Verlag.

Moul, J. L., Goldman, B., and Warren, B. (1995). Physical activity and cognitive performance in the older population. *Journal of Aging and Physical Activity, 3,* 135–145.

Murphy, K. R., and Davidshofer, C. O. (1994). *Psychological testing* (3rd ed.). Englewood Cliffs, NJ: Prentice-Hall.

Murphy, S. M. (1994). Imagery interventions in sport. *Medicine and Science in Sports and Exercise, 26,* 486–494.

Mussen, P. H., Comger, J. J., Kagan, J., and Huston, A. C. (1990). *Child development and personality* (7th ed.). New York: HarperCollins.

Newell, A. (1980). Reasoning, problem solving, and decision processes: The problem space as a fundamental category. In R. S. Nickerson (Ed.), *Attention and performance VIII* (pp. 693–718). Hillsdale, NJ: Erlbaum.

Newell, A. (1990). *Unified theories of cognition*. Cambridge, MA: Harvard University Press.

Newell, A., and Rosenbloom, P. S. (1981). Mechanisms of skill acquisition and the law of practice. In J. R. Anderson (Ed.), *Cognitive skills and their acquisition.* (pp. 1–55). Hillsdale, NJ: Erlbaum.

Newell, A., and Simon, H. A. (1972). *Human problem solving*. Englewood Cliffs, NJ: Prentice-Hall.

Newell, K. M. (1991). Motor skill acquisition. *Annual Review of Psychology, 42,* 213–237.

Newell, K. M., and McDonald, P. V. (1992). Practice: A search for task solutions. In R. W. Christina and H. M. Eckert (Eds.), *Enhancing human performance in sport: New concepts and developments* (pp. 51–59). Champaign, IL: Human Kinetics.

Newton, T. (1995). *Managing stress: Emotion and power at work*. Thousand Oaks, CA: Sage.

Nicholls, J. G. (1989). The general and specific in the development and expression of achievement motivation. In G. C. Roberts (Ed.), *Motivation in sport and exercise* (pp. 31–56). Champaign, IL: Human Kinetics.

O'Connor, P. J., Aenchbacher, L. E., III., and Dishman, R. K. (1993). Physical activity and depression in the elderly. *Journal of Aging and Physical Activity, 1,* 34–58.

O'Neil, H. F., Jr. (1997). *Workforce readiness: Competencies and assessment*. Mahwah, NJ: Erlbaum.

Paillard, J. (1960). The patterning of skilled movement. In J. Field (Ed.), *Handbook of physiology: Neurophysiology* (Vol. III). Baltimore: Williams and Wilkins.

Palmore, E. B. (1990). *Ageism: Negative and positive*. New York: Springer.

Panksepp, J. (1998). The quest for long-term health and happiness: To play or not to play, that is the question. *Psychological Inquiry, 9,* 56–65.

Panksepp, J., Herman, B. H., Vilberg, T., Bishop, P., and De Eskinazi, F. G. (1980). Endogenous opioids and social behavior. *Neuroscience and Biobehavioral Reviews, 4,* 473–487.

Panksepp, J., Siviy, S., and Normansell, L. A. (1984). The psychobiology of play: Theoretical and methodological perspectives. *Neuroscience and Biobehavioral Reviews, 8,* 465–492.

Parasuraman, R., and Davies, D. R. (Eds.). (1984). *Varieties of attention.* New York: Academic Press.

Parkinson, B. (1995). Emotion. In B. Parkinson and A. M. Colman (Eds.), *Emotion and motivation* (pp. 1–21). New York: Longman.

Pavio, A. (1985). *Mental representations.* Oxford, UK: Oxford University Press.

Pellegrino, J. W., and Glaser, R. (1979). Cognitive correlates and components in the analysis of individual differences. In R. J. Sternberg and D. K. Detterman (Eds.) *Human intelligence* (pp. 61–104). Norwood, NJ: Ablex.

Perone, M., and Baron, A. (1982). Age-related effects of pacing on acquisition and performance of response sequences: An operant analysis. *Journal of Gerontology, 37,* 443–449.

Perone, M., and Baron, A. (1983). Reduced age differences in omission errors after prolonged exposure to response pacing contingencies. *Developmental Psychology, 19,* 915–923.

Peterson, L. R., and Peterson, M. J. (1959). Short-term retention of individual verbal items. *Journal of Experimental Psychology, 58,* 193–198.

Philips, J. G., Mueller, F., and Stelmach, G. E. (1989). Movement disorders and the neural basis of motor control. In S. A. Wallace (Ed.), *Perspectives on the coordination of movement* (pp. 367–417). Amsterdam: North Holland.

Poliakoff, M. B. (1987). *Combat Sports in the Ancient World: Competition, violence, and culture.* New Haven, CT: Yale University Press.

Posner, M. I. (1980). Orienting of attention. *Quarterly Journal of Experimental Psychology, 32,* 3–25.

Posner, M. I., and M. E. Raichle (1997). *Images of mind.* New York: Scientific American Library.

Posner, M. I., and Snyder, C. R. R. (1975). Facilitation and inhibition in the processing of signals. In P. M. A. Rabbit and S. Dornic (Eds.), *Attention and performance V* (pp. 669–682). London: Academic Press.

Prinz, P. N., Dustman, R. E., and Emmerson, R. (1990). Electrophysiology and aging. In J. E. Birren and K. W. Shaie (Eds.), *Handbook of psychology of aging* (3rd ed., pp. 135–149). New York: Academic Press.

Proctor, R. W., and A. Dutta (1995). *Skill acquisition and human performance.* Thousand Oaks, CA: Sage.

Proctor, R. W., Reeve, E. G., and Weeks, D. J. (1990). A triphasic approach to the acquisition of response-selection skill. In G. H. Bower (Ed.), *The psychology of learning: Advances in research and theory* (pp. 207–240). New York: Academic Press.

Puff, C. R. (Ed.) (1982). *Handbook of research methods in human memory and cognition.* New York: Academic Press.

Roberts, G. C. (1989). When motivation matters: The need to expand the conceptual model. In J. S. Skinner, C. B. Corbin, D. M. Landers, P. E. Martin, and C. L. Wells (Eds.), *Future directions in exercise and sport science research* (pp. 71–83). Champaign, IL: Human Kinetics.

Rock, I. (1984). *Perception*. New York: Scientific American Books.

Rogers, D. (1985). *Adolescents and youth* (5th ed.). Englewood Cliffs, NJ: Prentice-Hall.

Rosenbaum, D. A. (1991). *Human motor control*. New York: Academic Press.

Rumelhart, D. E., and McClelland, J. L. (Eds.). (1986). *Parallel distributed processing: Explorations in the microstructure of cognition* (Vol. 1). Cambridge, MA: MIT Press/Bradford Books.

Rybash, J. M., Hoyer, W. J., and Roodin, P. A. (1986). *Adult cognition and aging: Developmental changes in processing, knowing and thinking*. New York: Pergamon Press.

Sage, G. H. (1971). *Introduction to motor behavior: A neuropsychological approach*. Reading, MA: Addison Wesley.

Sage, G. H. (1984). *Motor learning and control: A neuropsychological approach* (2nd ed.). Dubuque, IA: Brown.

Salmoni, A. W. (1989). Motor skill learning. In D. H. Holding (Ed.), *Human skills* (2nd ed., pp. 197–227). New York: Wiley.

Salthouse, T. A. (1984). Effects of age and skill in typing. *Journal of Experimental Psychology: General, 113*, 345–371.

Salthouse, T. A. (1985). *A theory of cognitive aging*. Amsterdam: North Holland.

Salthouse, T. A. (1991). *Theoretical perspectives on cognitive aging*. Hillsdale, NJ: Erlbaum.

Salthouse, T. A., and Somberg, B. L. (1982). Skilled performance: Effects of adult age experience on elementary processes. *Journal of Experimental Psychology: General, 111*, 176–207.

Sanders, A. F. (1983). Towards a model of stress and human performance. *Acta Psychologica, 53*, 61–97.

Savin-Williams, R. C. (1987). *Adolescence: An ethological perspective*. New York: Springer-Verlag.

Scanlan, T. K., and Simons, J. P. (1992). The construct of sport enjoyment. In G. C. Roberts (Ed.), *Motivation in sport and exercise* (pp. 199–215). Champaign, IL: Human Kinetics.

Schaie, K. W. (1993). The Seattle longitudinal studies of adult intelligence. *Current Directions in Psychological Science, 2*, 171–174.

Schaie, K. W., and Willis, S. L. (1996). *Adult development and aging* (4th ed.). New York: HarperCollins.

Schaie, K. W., Willis, S. L., Hertzog, C., and Schlenberg, J. E. (1987). Effects of cognitive training on primary mental ability structure. *Psychology and Aging, 2*, 233–242.

Schaufeli, W., and Enzman, D. (1998). *The burnout companion to study and practice: A critical analysis*. Philadelphia: Taylor and Francis.

Schiffman, H. R. (2000). *Sensation and perception* (5th ed.). New York: Wiley.

Schlegel, A., and Barry, H., III (1991). *Adolescence: An anthropological inquiry*. New York: Free Press.

Schmidt, R. A. (1975). A schema theory of discrete motor skill learning. *Psychological Review, 82*, 225–260.

Schmidt, R. A. (1988). *Motor control and learning: A behavioral emphasis* (2nd ed.). Champaign, IL: Human Kinetics.

Schmidt, R. A., and Lee, T. D. (1999). *Motor control and learning: A behavioral emphasis* (3rd ed.). Champaign, IL: Human Kinetics.

Schmidt, R. C., and Fitzpatrick, P. (1996). Dynamical perspectives on motor learning. In H. N. Zelaznik (Ed.), *Advances in motor learning and control* (pp. 195–223). Champaign, IL: Human Kinetics.

Schneider, E. L. (1993). Biological theories of aging. In R. L. Sprott, R. W. Huber, and T. F. Williams (Eds.), *The biology of aging* (pp. 2–12). New York: Springer.

Schneider, W., and Fisk, A. D. (1982). Concurrent automatic and controlled visual search: Can processing occur without resource cost? *Journal of Experimental Psychology: Learning, Memory, and Cognition, 8,* 261–278.

Schneider, W., Gruber, H., Gold, A., and Opwis, K. (1993). Chess expertise and memory for chess positions in children and adults. *Journal of Experimental Child Psychology, 56,* 328–349.

Schneider, W., and Shiffrin, R. M. (1977). Controlled and automatic human information processing: I. Detection, search, and attention. *Psychological Review, 84,* 1–66.

Schonpflug, W. (1983). Coping efficiency and situational demands. In G. R. J. Hockey (Ed.), *Stress and fatigue in human performance* (pp. 299–330). New York: Wiley.

Seaward, B. L. (1997). *Managing stress: Principles and strategies for health and well-being.* Boston: Jones and Bartlett.

Sebald, H. (1984). *Adolescence: A social psychological analysis.* Englewood Cliffs, NJ: Prentice-Hall.

Seefeldt, V. (1996). The concept of readiness applied to the acquisition of motor skills. In F. L. Smoll and R. E. Smith (Eds.), *Children and youth in sport: A biopsychosocial perspective* (pp. 49–56). Madison, WI: Brown and Benchmark.

Seger, C. A., (1994). Implicit learning. *Psychological Bulletin, 155,* 163–196.

Seibel, R. (1963). Discrimination reaction time for a 1,023-alternative task. *Journal of Experimental Psychology, 66,* 215–226.

Selye, H. (1974). *Stress without distress.* Philadelphia: Lippincott.

Selye, H. (1976). *The stress of life* (Rev. ed.). New York: McGraw-Hill.

Selye, H. (1993). History of the stress concept. In L. Goldberg and S. Breznitz (Eds.), *Handbook of stress: Theoretical and clinical aspects* (2nd ed., pp. 7–17) New York: Free Press.

Shea, C. H., Shebilske, W. L., and Worchel, S. (1993). *Motor learning and control.* Englewood Cliffs, NJ: Prentice-Hall.

Shephard, R. J. (1997). *Aging, physical health, and activity.* Champaign, IL: Human Kinetics.

Shiffrin, R. M., and Schneider, W. (1977). Controlled and automatic human information processing: II. Perceptual learning, automatic attending, and a general theory. *Psychological Review, 84,* 127–190.

Simon, H. A., and Chase, W. G. (1973). *Skill in chess. American Scientist, 61,* 394–403.

Singer, R. N. (Ed.). (1972). *The psychomotor domain: Movement behaviors.* Philadelphia: Lea and Febiger.

Skinner, B. F. (1938). *The behavior of organisms.* New York: Appleton-Century-Crofts.

Slater, P. E. (1964). Cross-cultural views of the aged. In R. Kastenbaum (Ed.), *New thoughts on old age.* New York: Springer.

Smith, A. D. (1996). Memory. In J. E. Birren and K. W. Schaie (Eds.), *Handbook of the psychology of aging* (4th ed.). New York: Academic Press.

Smoll, F. L., and Smith, R. E. (1996). Competitive anxiety: sources, consequences, and intervention strategies. In F. L. Smoll and R. E. Smith (Eds.), *Children and youth in* sport: A biopsychosocial perspective (pp. 359–380). Madison, WI: Brown and Benchmark.

Sokolovsky, J. (1994). Images of aging: A cross-cultural perspective. In D. Shenk and W. A. Achenbaum (Eds.), Changing perceptions of aging and the aged (pp. 85–93). New York: Springer.

Solso, R. L. (1995). Cognitive psychology (4th ed.). Boston: Allyn & Bacon.

Sparrow, W. A., and Summers, J. J. (1992). Performance on trials without knowledge of results (KR) in reduced relative frequency presentations of KR. Journal of Motor Behavior, 24, 197–209.

Spirduso, W. W. (1995). Physical dimensions of aging. Champaign, IL: Human Kinetics.

Stanage, S. M. (1987). Adult education and phenomenological research. Malabar, FL: Krieger.

Starkes, J. L., Deakin, J. M., Allard, F., Hodges, N. J., and Hayes, A. (1996). Deliberate practice in sports: What is it anyway? In A. A. Ericsson (Ed.), The road to excellence: The acquisition of expert performance in the arts and sciences, sports, and games (pp. 81–106). Mahwah, NJ: Erlbaum.

Sternberg, R. J. (1985). Beyond IQ: A triarchic theory of human intelligence. New York: Cambridge University Press.

Sternberg, R. J. (1986). Intelligence applied: Understanding and increasing your intellectual skills. New York: Harcourt Brace Jovanovich.

Sternberg, R. J. (1988). Intelligence. In R. J. Sternberg and E. E. Smith (Eds.), The psychology of human thought (pp. 267–308). New York: Cambridge University Press.

Sternberg, R. J., and Lubart, T. I. (1999). The concept of creativity: Prospects and paradigms. In R. J. Sternberg (Ed.), Handbook of creativity (pp. 3–15). New York: Cambridge University Press.

Sternberg, S. (1966). High-speed scanning in human memory. Science, 153, 652–654.

Sternberg, S. (1969). Memory-scanning: Mental processes revealed by reaction time experiments. American Scientist, 57, 421–457.

Stevens-Long, J. (1984). Adult life: Developmental processes. Palo Alto, CA: Mayfield.

Sticht, T. G. (1997) Assessing foundation skills for work. In H. F. O'Neil, Jr. (Ed.), Workforce readiness: Competencies and assessment (pp. 255–292). Mahwah, NJ: Erlbaum.

Stoskopf, N. C. (1993). Plant breeding: Theory and practice. Boulder, CO: Westview.

Suinn, R. M. (1980). Psychology and sports performance: Principles and applications. In R. Suinn (Ed.), Psychology in sports: Methods and applications (pp. 26–36). Minneapolis, MN: Burgess.

Suinn, R. M. (1993). Imagery. In R. N. Singer, M. Murphey, and L. K. Tennant (Eds.), Handbook of research on sports psychology (pp. 492–510). New York: Macmillan.

Summer, J. J. (1989). Motor programs. In D. Holding (Ed.), Human skills (2nd ed., pp. 49–69). New York: Wiley.

Super, D. E. (1990). A life-span, life-space approach to career development. In D. Brown, L. Brooks and Associates (Eds.), Career choice and development (2nd ed., pp. 197–261). San Francisco: Jossey-Bass.

Super, D. E., and Bachrac, P. B. (1957). Scientific careers and vocational development theory. New York: Teachers College, Columbia University.

Swabb, D. F. (1991). Brain aging and Alzheimer's disease, "wear and tear" versus "use it or lose it." Neurobiology of Aging, 12, 317–324.

Swanson, R. A., and Spears, B. (1995). *History of sport and physical education in the United States* (4th ed.). Madison, WI: Brown and Benchmark.

Swets, J. A., and Bjork, R. A. (1990). Enhancing human performance: An evaluation of "new age" techniques considered by the U.S. Army. *Psychological Science, 1,* 85–96.

Swinnen, S. P., Schmidt, R. A., Nicholson, D. E., and Shapiro, D. C. (1990). Information feedback for skill acquisition: Instantaneous knowledge of results degrades learning. *Journal of Experimental Psychology: Learning, Memory, and Cognition, 16,* 706–716.

Tarr, M. J., and Pinker, S. (1989). Mental rotation and orientation-dependence in shape recognition. *Cognitive Psychology, 21,* 233–282.

Tattersall, I. (1995). *The fossil trail: How we know what we think we know about human evolution.* Oxford, UK: Oxford University Press.

Tattersall, I. (1999). *The last Neanderthal: The rise, success and mysterious extinction of our closest human relatives.* Boulder, CO: Westview.

Tattersall, I., and Matternes, J. H. (2000, January). Once we were not alone. *Scientific American, 282,* p. 56–62.

Thomas, J. R., Landers, D. M., Salazar, W., and Etnier, J. (1994). Exercise and cognitive functioning. In C. Bouchard, R. J. Shepard, and Y. Stephens (Eds.), *Physical activity, fitness, and health* (pp. 521–529). Champaign, IL: Human Kinetics.

Thursby, G. R. (1992). Islamic, Hindu, and Buddhist conceptions of aging. In T. R. Cole, D. D. Van Tassel, and R. Kastenbaum (Eds.), *Handbook of the humanities and aging* (pp. 175–196). New York: Springer.

Tomporowski, P. (1997). The effects of physical and mental training on the mental abilities of older adults. *Journal of Aging and Physical Activity.* (Vol. 5, pp. 9–26).

Treisman, A. M., and Galade, G. (1980). A feature-integration theory of attention. *Cognitive Psychology, 12,* 97–136.

Troyansky, D. G. (1992). The older person in the Western world: From the middle ages to the industrial revolution. In T. R. Cole, D. D. Van Tassel, and R. Kastenbaum (Eds.), *Handbook of the humanities and aging* (pp. 40–62). New York: Springer.

Turnbull, B. C. (1983). *The human cycle.* New York: Simon and Schuster.

U.S. Department of Labor. (1991, June). *What work requires of schools: A SCANS report for AMERICA 2000.* Washington, DC: U.S. Government Printing Office.

Vallerand, R. J., and O'Connor, B. P. (1989). Motivation in the elderly: A theoretical framework and some promising findings. *Canadian Psychology, 30,* 538–550.

van der Molen, M. W. (1996). Energetics and the reaction process: Running threads through experimental psychology. In O. Neumann and A. F. Sanders (Eds.), *Handbook of perception and action.* (Vol. 3, pp. 229–276). New York: Academic Press.

Vanderschuren, L. J., Niesink, R. J., and Van Ree, J. M. (1997). The neurobiology of social play behavior in rats. *Neuroscience and Biobehavioral Reviews, 21,* 309–326.

VanLehn, K. (1989). Problem solving and cognitive skill acquisition. In M. I. Posner (Ed.), *Foundations of cognitive science* (pp. 527–579). Cambridge, MA: MIT Press.

van Wersch, A. (1997). Individual differences and intrinsic motivations for sport participation. In J. Kremer, K. Trew, and S. Ogle (Eds.), *Young people's involvement in sport* (pp. 57–77). New York: Routledge.

Vygotsky, L. S. (1978). *Mind in society: The development of higher psychological processes* (M. Cole, V. John-Steiner, S. Scribner, and E. Souberman, Eds. and Trans.). Cambridge, MA: Harvard University Press.

Wachs, T. D. (1982). *Early experience and human development.* New York: Plenum Press.

Wadsworth, B. J. (1976). *Piaget for the classroom teacher.* New York: Longman.

Warmington, E. H., and Rouse, P. G. (1956). *Great dialogues of Plato.* New York: New American Library.

Washburn, S. L. (1979). Tools and human evolution. *Readings from Scientific American: Human ancestors* (pp. 1–21). San Francisco: W. H. Freeman.

Watson, J. B. (1926). What the nursery has to say about instincts. In C. Murchison (Ed.), *Psychologies of 1925* (pp. 1–34). Worcester, MA: Clark University Press.

Watson, J. B. (1930) *Behaviorism* (Rev. ed.). New York: Norton. (Original work published 1925.)

Weinberg, R. S. (1981). The relationship between mental preparation strategies and motor performance: A review and critique. *Quest, 33,* 195–213.

Weinberg, R. S. (1994). Goal setting and performance in sport and exercise settings: A synthesis and critique. *Medicine and Science in Sports and Exercise, 26,* 469–477.

Weisz, J. R. (1982). Learned helplessness and the retarded child. In E. Zigler and D. Balla (Eds.), *Mental retardation: The developmental-difference controversy* (pp. 27–40). Hillsdale, NJ: Erlbaum.

Welch, D. C., and West, R. L. (1995). Self efficacy and mastery: Its application to issues of environmental control, cognition, and aging. *Developmental Review, 15,* 150–171.

Welford, A. T. (1968). *Fundamentals of skill.* London: Methuen.

Wells, A., and Matthews, G. (1994). *Attention and emotion: A clinical perspective.* Hillsdale, NJ: Erlbaum.

Wickens, C. D. (1992). *Engineering psychology and human performance* (2nd ed.). New York: HarperCollins.

Wiggins, D. K. (1996). A history of highly competitive sport for children. In F. L. Smoll and R. E. Smith (Eds.), *Children and youth in sport: A biopsychosocial perspective* (pp. 15–30). Madison, WI: Brown and Benchmark.

Williams, J. L. (1973). *Operant learning: Procedures for changing behavior.* Monterey, CA: Brooks/Cole.

Willis, S. L. (1989). Improvement with cognitive training: Which old dogs learn what tricks? In L. W. Poon, D. C. Rubin, and B. A. Wilson (Eds.), *Everyday cognition in adulthood and late life* (pp. 545–569). New York: Cambridge University Press.

Wilmore, J.H., and Costill, D.L. (1999). *Physiology of Sport and Exercise* (2nd ed., p. 72). Champaign, IL: Human Kinetics.

Wilson, E. O. (1975). *Sociobiology.* Cambridge, MA: Harvard University Press.

Wilson, E. O. (2000). *Sociobiology: The new synthesis.* Cambridge, MA: Harvard University Press.

Winner, E. (1996). The rage to master: The decisive role of talent in the visual arts. In K. A. Ericsson (Ed.), *The road to excellence: The acquisition of expert performance in the arts and sciences, sports, and games* (pp. 271–301). Mahwah, NJ: Erlbaum.

Winstein, C. J., and Schmidt, R. A. (1989). Sensorimotor feedback. In D. Holding (Ed.). *Human skills* (2nd ed., pp. 17–47). New York: Wiley.

Wood, D., and Middleton. D. (1975). A study of assisted problem solving. *British Journal of Psychology, 66,* 181–191.

Woolfolk, R. L., Parrish, W., and Murphy, S. M. (1985). The effects of positive and negative imagery on motor skill performance. *Cognitive Therapy and Research, 9,* 335–341.

Wulf, G., and Weigelt, C. (1997). Instructions about physical principles in learning a complex motor skill: To tell or not to tell. *Research Quarterly for Exercise and Sport, 68,* 362–367.

Yerkes, R. M., and Dodson, J. D. (1908). The relation of strength of stimulus to rapidity of habit formation. *Journal of Comparative Neurology and Psychology, 18,* 459–482.

Yesavage, J. A., Lapp, D., and Sheikh, J. I. (1989). Mnemonics as modified for use by the elderly. In L. W. Poon, D. C. Rubin, and B. A. Wilson (Eds.), *Everyday cognition in adulthood and late life* (pp. 598–611). New York: Cambridge University Press.

Yesavage, J. A., and Rose, T. L. (1984a). The effects of a face-name mnemonic in young, middle-aged, and elderly adults. *Experimental Aging Research, 10,* 55–57.

Yesavage, J. A., and Rose, T. L. (1984b). Semantic elaboration and the method of loci: A new trip for older learners. *Experimental Aging Research, 10,* 155–159.

Zentall, S. (1975). Optimal stimulation as theoretical basis of hyperactivity. *American Journal of Orthopsychiatry, 45,* 549–563.

Zigler, E., and Balla, D. (Eds.). (1982a). *Mental retardation, the developmental-difference controversy.* Hillsdale, NJ: Erlbaum.

Zigler, E., and Balla, D. (1982b). Motivational and personality factors in the performance of the retarded. In E. Zigler and D. Balla (Eds.), *Mental retardation: The developmental-difference controversy* (pp. 9–26). Hillsdale, NJ: Erlbaum.

Zimbardo, P. G., and Gerrig, R. J. (1999). *Psychology and life* (15th ed.). New York: Longman.

Index

About the Author

PHILLIP D. TOMPOROWSKI is Associate Professor of Psychology in the Department of Exercise Science at the University of Georgia.